# Toward Inclusive Academic Librarian Hiring Practices

editors
Kathryn Houk
Jordan Nielsen
Jenny Wong-Welch

*Association of College and Research Libraries
A division of the American Library Association
Chicago, Illinois 2024*

The paper used in this publication meets the minimum requirements of American National Standard for Information Sciences–Permanence of Paper for Printed Library Materials, ANSI Z39.48-1992. ∞

Library of Congress Control Number: 2024942510

Copyright ©2024 by Association of College and Research Libraries

All rights reserved except those which may be granted by Sections 107 and 108 of the Copyright Revision Act of 1976.

Printed in the United States of America.

28  27  26  25  24   5  4  3  2  1

# Contents

vii    Acknowledgements

ix    **Foreword**
*Tarida Anantachai, Camille Chesley, Twanna Hodge, and Jamia Williams*

## PART 1: TRAINING FOR SEARCH COMMITTEES AND STAKEHOLDERS

3    **Chapter 1.** Launching for Search Success: Establishing and Training Search Committees in Academic Libraries
*Tarida Anantachai and Nicole Westerdahl*

15    **Chapter 2.** Including Voices and Mitigating Bias: Evaluative Practices for Final Interviews
*Xan Arch and José Velazco*

27    **Chapter 3.** Setting up Candidates for Success: Using a Library Community of Practice to Develop Screening Tools and Candidate Questions to Minimize Bias in Hiring
*Claressa Slaughter, Charlotte Beyer, Chelsea Eidbo, Jaena Manson, and KatieRose McEneely*

41    **Chapter 4.** Creating an Equity Advisor Program on any Scale
*Paula H. Martin*

55    **Chapter 5.** Discussing, Understanding, and Assessing: Moving Beyond the Performative to Examine the Candidate Diversity Statement
*Breanne Crumpton, Mollie Peuler, and Kelly Rhodes*

## PART 2: REMOVING BARRIERS FOR CANDIDATES

**73**    **Chapter 6.** Ensuring Empathy in Interviewing through Open Communication
*Gail Betz, Hilary Kraus, and Amy Tureen*

**83**    **Chapter 7.** I Still Don't Fit: How Academic Libraries Create Barriers in the Profession Before Hiring Even Takes Place
*Simone Williams*

**97**    **Chapter 8.** Trans and Gender Diverse Inclusion in Academic Library Hiring
*Keahi Adolpho, Stephen G. Krueger, Luke Sutherland, and Adrian Williams*

**111**    **Chapter 9.** Beyond Compliance: Accommodating Differently in The Interview Process
*Jennifer M. Jackson*

**123**    **Chapter 10.** Improving Inclusion with Universal Design in the Academic Library Hiring Process
*Katelyn Quirin Manwiller, Heather Crozier, and Samantha Peter*

**137**    **Chapter 11.** Planning for the On-Campus Interview: Creating a Descriptive Library Accessibility Guide for Job Candidates
*Kimberly A. Looby*

## PART 3: TRANSFORMING THE PROCESS FOR ALL

**161**    **Chapter 12.** Remote Interviews, Processes, and Documentation: How COVID changed Hiring at One Academic Library
*Arielle Lomness, Sajni Lacey, and Donna Langille*

**181**    **Chapter 13.** The Interview Pivot: Implementing Changes to Interview Protocols to Respond to Pandemic Restrictions and Provide Greater Inclusion
*Mary Beth Lock, Elizabeth Ellis, and Summer Krstevska*

**201**    **Chapter 14.** Reflections on a Faculty Cluster Hiring Approach at a Large PWI Academic Library
*Shawnta Smith-Cruz, April M. Hathcock, and Scott Collard*

| | |
|---|---|
| 221 | **Chapter 15.** Disrupting the Academic Librarian Hiring Process Through Transparent Communication<br>*Michelle Colquitt, Shamella Cromartie, Anne Grant, Kelsey Sheaffer, and Megan Sheffield* |
| 239 | **Chapter 16.** Walking the Walk: Searches that Demonstrate Commitment to an Inclusive, Diverse, and Equitable Library Workplace<br>*Marlowe Bogino, Ash Lierman* |
| 255 | **Chapter 17.** Approaches to Inclusive Recruitment: Practical and Hopeful<br>*Adriana Poo, Anamika Megwalu, Nick Szydlowski, Kathryn Blackmer Reyes, Peggy Cabrera, and Ann Agee* |
| 267 | **Chapter 18.** Developing Recommendations for More Inclusive Academic Librarian On-Site Interviews<br>*Christina M. Miskey, Kathryn M. Houk, and Jason Aubin* |
| 297 | **Chapter 19.** From Applicant to Employee: Developing and Evaluating an Inclusive Hiring and Onboarding Process<br>*Gary R. Maixner, Kindra Orr, and M. Sara Lowe* |
| 319 | **Afterword**<br>*Kathryn Houk, Jordan Nielsen, and Jenny Wong-Welch* |
| 323 | **About the Authors** |

# Acknowledgments

We would like to thank our colleagues, the authors of the chapters in this book. Thank you for your commitment of time, energy, and caring in both writing your chapters and working on the projects you describe within them. Thank you for your patience and good humor throughout the process as we learned what it is to be editors of an academic volume.

# Foreword

*Tarida Anantachai, Camille Chesley, Twanna Hodge, and Jamia Williams*

The topic of inclusive hiring practices has increasingly garnered notice within academic libraries over the past several years. On the one hand, like many sectors, higher education (and, by extension, the academic libraries within them) has certainly felt the effects of the Great Resignation or Reshuffling during the COVID-19 pandemic, with many employees either voluntarily leaving academia or considering doing so (Fried, 2023). On another hand, the national racial awakening of 2020 saw a spike both in equity, diversity, and inclusion (EDI)–focused positions (Maurer, 2020; Bledsoe & Frederick, 2021) and in renewed conversations around recruiting and diversifying our workforces more broadly (Frederick & Wolff-Eisenberg, 2021). As many academic libraries later resumed hiring in the midst of these intersecting crises, there also came a growing recognition of the need to revisit how they approached this process—particularly in attracting a more diverse candidate pool and in better demonstrating their own commitments to fostering EDI while doing so. While it is not a more official phrase, one could almost consider this surge as the Great Reckoning and Rehiring. In fact, one need only scan the proceedings of the most recent ACRL 2023 Conference to find additional examples of this (Mueller, 2023)—with at least a dozen presentations, papers, posters, and other discussions around some aspects of the recruitment and hiring process.

As Black, Indigenous, and people of color (BIPOC) librarians who ourselves have been active participants in these processes (on both sides of the table) during this critical time, we count ourselves among the many who can affirm the impact that inclusive hiring can have on candidates' experiences, including the simultaneous evaluations that they are making about their potential libraries. We see this as a long overdue, prime opportunity for libraries to reconceptualize what has long been a complex, bureaucratic, and institution-centered process to be instead more transparent, empathic, and person-centered. There have been some movements toward this goal, with some professional associations requiring salary transparency for those libraries intending to post vacancy announcements on their job boards (Art Libraries Society of North America, 2022; Society of American Archivists, 2021). While this is a positive step forward in empowering job seekers as they consider their potential opportunities, libraries themselves must also put measures in place to center equity within their own hiring processes in order to further attract and holistically support job seekers through this time-intensive and laborious process.

This volume further reflects the increased attention to this growing conversation. Yet rather than focus simply on how to diversify our applicant pools (and, by extension, our organizations), it also breaks down the many other stages and considerations those involved in hiring should earnestly bear in mind, including the need for intentional, thoughtful preparation and self-examination by those libraries looking to hire. As bureaucratic and historically oppressive systems have oftentimes done, academia has been slow to interrogate itself and how the structures it has adopted have excluded and prevented those who do not fit the status quo from achieving success within its ivory walls. Academic libraries are an extension of this disparity and have also long needed to put in the organizational work to reimagine their processes in order to model the inclusive environments they espouse to be.

The first part of this volume provides a few examples of how they can do so by first taking a step back from the actual recruiting and hiring process. "Part 1: Training for Search Committees and Stakeholders" explores the necessary foundational work that search committees should complete or pursue before the formal search has even begun. Many of the chapters in this section focus on better ensuring that the search committee members themselves have the adequate preparation and competencies necessary to foster an inclusive and equitable process. Some of the topics in this part discuss search committee training, including how to create an inclusive and equitable experience for search committee members themselves as they navigate their work together, and guidelines on how these search committees can gather fair and thoughtful evaluative feedback from their colleagues across the organization. Other chapters discuss other tools and tactics for mitigating bias in the search process, such as the use of screening software in conjunction with developing meaningful interview questions, the creation of equity advisor programs in order to train designated search advocates, and the examination and assessment of candidate diversity statements.

"Part 2: Removing Barriers for Candidates" identifies a number of barriers that candidates may face, and some strategies for how to remove them. This part examines inclusivity for trans and gender diverse academic library workers during the hiring process and after. In addition, it advocates accessible practices that must be incorporated into both online and physical interview spaces. Whether it is the decision to have a diversity statement, salary negotiations, or accessibility accommodations—libraries must do intentional planning that includes kindness, compassion, and empathy. Those in the library who champion EDI should also be involved; for example, including the EDI committee in the hiring process may also help identify barriers, as well as opportunities for increasing inclusivity.

"Part 3: Transforming the Process for All" further expands upon the shift from inclusive talk to the development and implementation of inclusive practices. Out of necessity, many institutions were forced to quickly pivot to hiring online during the COVID-19 pandemic, creating unprecedented changes in procedure. Several chapters address how, in this new virtual environment, libraries can create an equitable and inclusive search process that aligns with best practices. Other authors offer practical tips for creating inclusive searches and modifying established practices, such as hosting webinars for interested job seekers, sharing interview questions with candidates ahead of time, and revising interview-day agendas. Other chapters address the importance of transparent communication between the search committee, library stakeholders, and the candidate and ensuring that the process of designing an inclusive and equitable search process is iterative by interrogating the library's search procedures after the fact. Oftentimes, libraries consider their inclusive hiring efforts concluded with a signed contract. However, several chapters detail additional efforts that libraries are taking, such as hiring new librarians in clusters and developing inclusive onboarding procedures to help librarians be successful in their new positions.

While the discussions within this volume will provide valuable insights for a number of academic libraries, it is worth noting that our best efforts to create inclusive hiring practices will amount to nothing if we don't also consider retention and changing our institutional cultures. We must consider the barriers that people face in the hiring process, but also consider the climate and the environment of the library so that our future colleagues can thrive after they are hired. Inclusive hiring should not be a trend, but the norm. It is time to better advocate for those coming into academic librarianship, so library administrators, hiring managers, and everyone has to contribute to this work. We also want to emphasize that this labor cannot just be the responsibility of BIPOC and their allies within the library. It is time to lead by example and encourage those who may have been complacent within our libraries around EDI efforts, hiring, and retention by providing them the opportunity and space to have those tough conversations about policies and cultural practices (Doan & Kennedy, 2022). If you want to be part of the solution, grapple with some tough truths, and be more than a trend within your academic library, then this book is for you!

# References

Art Libraries Society of North America. (2022, June 30). *ARLIS/NA JobList adopts salary transparency requirement* [News release]. https://www.arlisna.org/news/arlisna-joblist-adopts-salary-transparency-requirement

Bledsoe, K., & Frederick, J. K. (2021, August 17). Advancing strategy through staffing: Diversity, equity, and inclusion library leadership roles [Blog post]. *Ithaka S+R*. https://sr.ithaka.org/blog/advancing-strategy-through-staffing

Doan, J. M., & Kennedy, R. B. (2002). Diversity fatigue: Acknowledging and moving beyond repetitious emotional labor. In A. Brissett and D. Moronta (Eds.), *Practicing social justice in libraries* (pp. 145–153). Routledge.

Frederick, J. K., & Wolff-Eisenberg, C. (2021, March 17). *National movements for racial justice and academic library leadership: Results from the Ithaka S+R US Library Survey 2020*. Ithaka S+R. https://doi.org/10.18665/sr.314931

Fried, M. (2023, February 7). The great resignation and higher education employees [Blog post]. *Ithaka S+R*. https://sr.ithaka.org/blog/the-great-resignation-and-higher-education-employees

Maurer, R. (2020, August 6). *New DE&I roles spike after racial justice protests*. Society for Human Resource Management. https://www.shrm.org/resourcesandtools/hr-topics/talent-acquisition/pages/new-dei-roles-spike-after-racial-justice-protests.aspx

Mueller, D. M. (Ed.). (2023). *Forging the future: The proceedings of the ACRL 2023 Conference*. March 15-18, 2023, Pittsburgh, Pennsylvania. Association of College and Research Libraries

Society of American Archivists. (2021, May 26). *SAA Council approves requirement for salary transparency* [News release]. https://www2.archivists.org/news/2021/saa-council-approves-requirement-for-salary-transparency

# Part 1
# TRAINING FOR SEARCH COMMITTEES AND STAKEHOLDERS

CHAPTER 1

# Launching for Search Success

## Establishing and Training Search Committees in Academic Libraries

*Tarida Anantachai and Nicole Westerdahl*

When those involved in academic hiring are considering inclusive hiring practices, the discussion oftentimes focuses on the different strategies they can implement to reach a diverse candidate pool and what they should individually address in their evaluation and interview procedures. While it is true that our individual actions and decisions, when combined, can help to dictate what occurs throughout a search, we cannot rely simply on our own singular activities piecemeal if we intend to support a truly inclusive and equitable search process. Instead, we must also mindfully create a strong structural foundation with all those involved at the onset—or rather, before a search actually commences.

This situation is especially pertinent in academic libraries, where the bulk of this work is typically done via a search committee—that is, a group of representatives who bring their unique perspectives and range of experiences (or perhaps lack thereof) of search processes to the table. Indeed, the search committee is a key part of the academic librarian hiring process, and its members collectively can have significant influence on the recruitment, review, interviewing, and hiring of their future colleagues. Before starting a search, it is essential to consider how to launch this process with this team to better ensure that equitable and inclusive hiring practices are in place more collectively at an organizational level rather than simply individually by those who happen to incorporate them.

In this chapter, we will examine the integral considerations that go into the launch of a search process and some strategies for creating search committee training at this stage. We will provide an overview of our institutional context and describe the steps we took to develop our training program, including generating support and buy-in across all levels of staff. We will share details about the content of our training and specific resources we shared with search committees. Finally, we will reflect on our program, identifying successes, challenges, and opportunities and suggesting strategies to strengthen future training programs.

# Background and Building Momentum

The impetus behind establishing this program came partly from two intersecting experiences and interests that had been part of our experience at Syracuse University Libraries. Over the years, we had the opportunity, between us, to actively participate in more than a dozen search committees for a range of different positions—from librarians and nonlibrarian staff, to managers, to student workers. These processes previously did not embed any intentional efforts at inclusive hiring and recruiting. At the same time, as longtime inaugural members (and chairs or cochairs) of our Libraries' Diversity and Inclusion Team, we were already driven toward identifying opportunities within our Libraries to more intentionally integrate equity, diversity, and inclusion (EDI) into various processes and policies. Having seen firsthand how our searches had typically been conducted and recognizing the great potential to improve our recruitment and hiring practices, we had already sought out resources to help us in doing so. Much of our research involved collecting information on different approaches, attending targeted workshops and conference sessions (such as at the Inclusion, Diversity, Equity, and Accessibility in Libraries & Archives Conference and the Joint Conference of Librarians of Color, among others) on inclusive hiring, taking professional development courses (such as those offered by DeEtta Jones & Associates and Library Juice Academy), and connecting with colleagues at other institutions who had already begun some of these initiatives. In doing so, we recognized that many of these practices would counter what had long been considered standard and status quo at our Libraries. While we had already begun to build our own internal momentum toward these efforts, we also recognized that we needed concrete examples to demonstrate their meaningful impacts more tangibly to others within our organization.

We soon found a prime opportunity in two searches in which we were both directly involved—including one for an internal human resources manager (who we also saw as a potential future advocate of inclusive hiring efforts) and another in which one of us was appointed as search committee chair. Observing that there was still some misunderstanding and hesitation among our colleagues regarding some of the ideas we had gathered (particularly with regard to providing questions in advance and embedding EDI-focused questions), we saw these two searches as a way to gently pilot some new approaches, which could then provide us some concrete examples of observable positive outcomes. We found that others on the search committees, as well as our candidates, were pleased with these small but impactful changes. These colleagues were then able to appreciate how providing questions in advance increased transparency and accessibility for our candidates, as well as supported them in bringing forward richer examples and responses to our questions. They also recognized that asking targeted EDI questions further communicated our commitments to EDI and allowed us to assess how candidates might apply these tenets to their work.

Now having demonstrated some successes within these two searches, we were able to build more interest among our colleagues in the possibility of exploring these efforts more broadly. As cochairs of our Diversity and Inclusion Team, we offered to advise future search committees on some of the strategies they could also implement, as well as stressing the importance of communicating and integrating EDI values into the search committee structure itself—rather than it being led by those individuals who just happened to be passionate about inclusive hiring. Of particular note, we were invited by a department head to advise a combination of forthcoming search committees they would soon be leading, including joining their initial launch meeting to provide an overview of inclusive hiring practices. This invitation then led us to being further invited to search committee meetings during their finalist candidates' interviews and continually serving as advisors when other questions arose throughout the process. Having a department head with positional power within our organization who could also promote what we had been proposing proved to be important for developing more advocacy at the management level. Additionally, now having multiple examples under our belts across a range of searches greatly allowed us to further advocate for time with our Libraries' management team, eventually being welcomed to present our work to them. It was during this meeting that we emphasized the work we had already done, the positive results, and the more structural changes to the search committee process that we felt our Libraries could still positively adopt—in other words, the search committee training we had gradually developed and were eager to offer.

Recognizing that interweaving equity and inclusion into all steps of the process also required a bit of a mindset shift for those used to the standardized approaches, we emphasized the importance of providing these trainings to all search committees at the moment they first convened. Our aim was to provide them with doable, actionable steps that they could undertake, as well as the reasoning behind the steps. Just as importantly, we wanted to communicate the significance of their work for the organization. The committee has a great deal of influence—not only in bringing in a future colleague who can impact the library for many years to come, but also in serving as the face of the library and its culture to the potential candidates who are simultaneously evaluating them. As a result, we determined that the way in which committees worked together, built their own understanding of the process, and ultimately created a committee culture would be everyone's collective responsibility to uphold. Some of the strategies we used, as well as topics discussed, are detailed in the sections that follow.

# Picking Up Speed: Developing Our Training Program

As our opportunities for providing search committee trainings expanded, we became more intentional in our work to develop the training program. One of our first steps was to seek clarification from university human resources about the Libraries' and Syracuse University's recruitment and hiring practices and policies. While we both had experience with the search process, we could often only guess at the behind-the-scenes activities of the human resources operations. Reviewing this information confirmed the existence of the gaps we perceived in inclusive practices and policies and also made it clear that there was flexibility that would enable the Libraries to require search committees to participate in inclusive hiring training.

We pooled our inclusive hiring knowledge and resources (several of which are highlighted in this chapter) and organized them according to the gaps we identified. The topics fell roughly into four categories: recruiting; reviewing candidates; interviewing; and incorporating EDI throughout every aspect of the hiring process. Our policies and procedures review also helped us identify what particular content would be best to include in our trainings for different audiences within the Libraries by clarifying the roles of human resources staff, Libraries management, and search committee members. Libraries management was generally responsible for developing job descriptions and establishing required and preferred candidate qualifications. University human resources provided input on these job descriptions and then standardized postings on its job board, adding mandated language and often eliminating language we wished to include, such as language specifically encouraging women and job seekers from historically marginalized groups to apply even if they did not feel they met all of the qualifications. Search committees convened after the opening had been posted to the university's job board, and they often were not even formed prior to that point. While we felt that search committees should be part of the job description process, this idea was not more widely accepted. We determined that writing and editing job descriptions and candidate requirements should at least be included in the training for Libraries management. Search committees, on the other hand, could benefit more from focusing on developing a shared understanding of the meaning of those requirements and how to apply them in evaluating candidate materials.

Having identified the content of our trainings, we considered how we could best deliver them. We initially rejected a training-the-trainer approach for search committee chairs because it was clear that not every chair was comfortable with conducting this training—and in particular addressing committee members' questions about it—on their own yet. Including the entire committee also helped establish EDI efforts as everybody's responsibility. We also believed training all search committee members would foster greater accountability. We both felt that a presentation and discussion format would be the best way to encourage search committee participation and engagement. One-hour trainings appeared to be the most realistic time commitment for their schedules, although we would have preferred more time (and both of us could speak on the topic for days!). We identified what would be the most impactful and actionable advice we could provide from each of our content areas within that hour. Although we had not yet produced written content, we considered it important to provide search committees with detailed materials that reinforced our messaging and that they could refer to later. These included resources that we felt were a digestible length and full of concrete examples and recommendations, to be discussed later.

# Reaching Cruising Speed: Program Implementation

As described above, our personal efforts attracted interest and individual engagement, leading to an invitation to present our work to the Libraries' management team. This opportunity was key to generating management support for our training program. Our presentation, focused on the positive, emphasized the benefits of an inclusive hiring program and highlighted the important role management plays in prioritizing and supporting it. While the Libraries' management team appreciated the broad data and studies supporting the positive impact of inclusive hiring practices, we found that offering our own examples of successful efforts within the Libraries' search committees were most persuasive. Having a champion of our work on the management team also strengthened our case, especially in the internal team discussions afterward when we were not present.

After we received approval from the management team, the Libraries' internal human resources manager began including our training sessions on the checklist of required search committee tasks. Search committee chairs were responsible for scheduling a training session with us for their committee. We asked that the full search committee meet with us for each new search, even if all members had previously completed training with us. We felt that repetition of key concepts would help participants with recall and practice and would provide validation for adopted practices, and we could also focus on concepts and recommendations not previously shared or fully explored. We tailored our trainings, introducing unique aspects for each search based on review of the job postings and preliminary discussion with the chair.

We found that directly asking committee members questions about their search plan generated more thoughtful engagement with our content and produced a sense of committee ownership of their inclusive hiring efforts. In our experience, one of the most effective ways to identify questions to ask was to review job postings and identify responsibilities, qualifications, and competencies that were ambiguous or about which committee members might disagree. For example, we asked a special collections curator search committee the following questions:

- The job description highlights the goal of achieving "a more complete record and focus on diverse voices and life experiences" in the collections. Have you considered how the position qualifications and requirements might exclude those most qualified to meet this goal?
- One of the qualifications is an "accredited MLS with a special collections focus and an advanced degree in a relevant discipline or an equivalent combination of education and experience." How are you defining that equivalency?
- How will you be weighing the job qualifications in your candidate review rubric? Which are most important? Which are least important?
- A number of the qualifications include language like "strong understanding," "proven ability," and "familiarity." Have you considered looking for potential to build ability and familiarity?

While we designed our training program with generating buy-in and engagement in mind, not all search committee chairs and members were willing participants. Regardless of their initial engagement level, we typically recommended that search committee members participate in antibias training, which the university periodically offered to employees. If these trainings were not available in the appropriate time frame, we pointed search committees to Project Implicit's Implicit Association Tests (Project Implicit, 2011). Both options helped persuade resistant committee members that implicit bias is a real thing that they experience, resulting in increased awareness of the need for inclusive hiring practices. We also asked search committees how we could help them, such as asking what aspects of hiring have been difficult or frustrating in the past. For example, a chair for a cataloger search committee reported that the required presentation during the interview caused a number of good candidates to withdraw from the search process. This led to a conversation about what purpose the presentation served in the interview. The major reasons for its inclusion were that it was a generally accepted requirement for all librarian position interviews, that a cataloger might need to train colleagues on new systems and procedures, and that giving presentations was often used as an indicator of potential to meet promotion criteria. We determined that there was no formal requirement from a human resources perspective for presentations in the interview process (which we would have opposed anyway) and worked with the chair to identify alternative methods for assessing these skills that did not require a presentation. Alternatives include reviewing previous evidence of scholarship and professional service (e.g., publications, posters, conference organizing) or asking candidates to describe their plans to meet promotion criteria. By removing this obstacle, we successfully convinced the chair that our other recommendations would also be worthwhile.

# Mission Specifications: Search Committee Setup and Launch

## Forming the Search Committee

While not formally part of the initial version of our training (this was an oversight on our part), an integral part of the search process that we thought was worth discussing here is the foundational aspects around forming and norming the search committee's work together. For one, it is extremely important to consider who will be involved in the search itself and the fact that the selection of these search committee members can greatly dictate the flow of the search. Oftentimes, the default may be to include those who would more regularly interact with the candidate after hire—for instance, the supervisor, other peers within the same department, and a colleague in another department with whom their work may frequently intersect. While on the surface this approach may make logical sense, it also has the potential to create tunnel vision and focus only on the micro rather than macro impacts of that individual across the organization. For librarian searches, focusing on peers also often means that the default is to assign only other librarians to this process; rather, it is important to consider and invite participants across all levels of staff (and possibly even student workers) and empower those in nonlibrarian roles to fully engage in serving on search committees.

Another consideration for search committees is the dynamics that may be at play based on the members involved. In particular, if there are supervisory relationships or those who hold positional leadership roles within the library on the committee, it is important to determine how that may affect the discussions and decisions within a search. This is not to say that supervisors and managers should not be involved in searches with their direct reports or others within their sphere of influence; we will discuss how such circumstances can potentially be addressed below.

Search committees may also often designate someone from a historically marginalized group to ensure diversity, a practice that had been standardized at our institution; however, this tokenizing practice upholds the problematic notion of filling a diversity quota and unfairly puts the expectation that that person will serve as the voice of EDI. This is also why it is important that all members of the search committee need to engage in such trainings on bias and cultural competence. It is especially important considering the severe underrepresentation of racialized librarians within the library profession at large (American Library Association, 2012); assigning them to committees in order to bring in racial diversity results in a disproportionate amount of unrecognized, and at many times invisible, service labor they already shoulder in continually being tapped to serve such capacities (Matthew, 2016).

## The Search Committee Culture

It is also important to consider that, any time a group is brought together, natural dynamics can also emerge—or, ideally, strategic dynamics can be set forth by those leading the group. As noted earlier, the power dynamics of a committee can dictate the level of comfort felt by other members in honestly voicing their opinions. If supervisors or others with positional power should be on a search committee, it is incumbent on them to ensure that their voice not shut down or otherwise influence others' voices (which is true for any committee and for groups more generally). Even before the committee is formally formed, this process could involve talking separately with those with less positional power to better determine their own comfort levels, rather than just arbitrarily assigning them to the committee, and learning what measures could be taken to support and help to empower them. Such an approach is especially important for the search committee chair, who holds a formal leadership position by the nature of the role and should thus strive to mindfully create an effective, inclusive committee culture.

Some early considerations in establishing the committee culture include determining the goals and expectations of the search and all those involved and documenting strategies on how those will be collectively achieved. Ensuring that all search committee members understand what their individual roles are is essential. For instance, establish expectations such as if the chair or others will help to facilitate meetings, if certain individuals might take notes (or rotate the role), which action items will be whose, and so on. It is similarly important that chairs clearly communicate what the purposes of each meeting will be so that all members have clear expectations and are able to prepare as needed; this information can be bookended with a recap at the end of each meeting of what was discussed and decided, and to determine next steps.

Search committee chairs should also consider how to conduct inclusive meetings and discussions that model the EDI principles they want to instill in the search. There are many resources on inclusive meeting culture that can and should be implemented in these discussions (Harvard University Office for Equity, Diversity, Inclusion & Belonging, n.d.; Heath & Wensil, 2019); this practice is especially important considering the natural amount of bias that each member holds and how that will influence candidate discussions (more on this below). When discussing candidates, for instance, the chair could allow others to speak before them or adopt a rotation of responses so that one person is not always driving the initial conversation. Within meetings, it is important for the chair or meeting facilitator to take note of any dominant participants and how they can invite others to the conversation; along those same lines, they could also provide additional mechanisms for members to share their opinions outside of formal meetings.

It is also important to foster a culture of search committee accountability. For example, we encouraged the use of candidate review rubrics and awareness of our implicit biases, their impacts, and how to mitigate them (University of Washington Human Resources, n.d.). One particular reading that we often recommended was Cunningham, Guss, and Stout's "Challenging the 'Good Fit' Narrative" (2019), which discusses the very coded and problematic nature in which "fit" has often been employed in hiring decisions and the fact that search committees thus need to have processes in place to actively counter it. Search committees can take that a step further by committing to being their own accountability partners. Committees that take the time to establish inclusive meeting practices can then further cultivate a culture where they can be more empowered to challenge each other's assumptions, counter biases and inequities together, and speak up. For example, if someone feels a candidate's application has been overlooked, they can bring that into the conversation, revisit the application, and explore why. Accountability also includes taking individual ownership of the recruitment process, including proactively determining any individual people to invite to apply for open positions and contacting those who could potentially provide recommendations on individuals or communities to solicit. It also includes specifically targeting those networks centered on historically underrepresented groups, such as the various National Associations of Librarians of Color (AILA, APALA, BCALA, CALA, and REFORMA), the We Here job board (https://www.wehere.space/submit-a-job), and disability groups, but also those that may be more job-specific—for instance, networks for women in STEM communities for any science and technology-related positions. At the same time, given the general lack of racial representation within the Libraries at the time, we also emphasized the importance of not continuously requiring nor putting the onus on the few racialized library workers there to circulate job advertisements to their communities—again, due to the tokenized labor aspects inherent in such requests.

# Mission Debriefing: Reflecting on Our Program

Our training program resulted in several successes. We generated more awareness of and engagement with inclusive hiring practices throughout the Libraries, reaching not just management and search committee chairs but also the librarians, supervisors, and staff who serve on search committees. This awareness helped position EDI work as everybody's responsibility, not just the Diversity and Inclusion Team's. We also established persistent, positive changes to the search process at the Libraries: providing questions to candidates in advance, not requiring all librarian candidates to give presentations, and incorporating evaluations relating to EDI as a standard and prioritized practice were three major wins that benefited both candidates and search committees.

Based on personal observation and anecdotal feedback, we saw an increase in search committees' ability to assess candidate EDI strengths and weaknesses—both in developing questions to probe these skills and in their competencies to evaluate responses and application materials. We provided a number of resources of sample questions that committees could use for inspiration, such as those created by other academic institutions (Northern Illinois University Affirmative Action and Equity Compliance, n.d.; Brown University Office of Institutional Equity and Diversity, n.d.). We also enabled committee members to more meaningfully evaluate candidate responses, recognize what types of EDI-related answers were more successful than others, and frame questions to address the intended evaluative goals. We helped committees find ways to tailor these questions to how applicants have applied or would more tangibly apply EDI to their work. This approach also allowed committees to assess their candidates' active engagement and ongoing learning in this space and whether their responses demonstrated this engagement and learning meaningfully or not. For example, committees used "What practices do you incorporate into your teaching to ensure all students are supported in their learning?" for an instruction position, and "How do you ensure your metadata records respectfully describe people and events?" for a metadata position.

Looking back, there are of course opportunities we missed that could be pursued in future iterations of such a program and that we have both been implementing in some form at our current institutions. Although committee composition and culture are discussed in this chapter, we did not provide enough guidance in this area, especially in the earliest stages of our training program. Search committees were only convened for the hiring of full-time employees, which meant we missed a significant population—including part-time and our 200-plus student employees. While this area was outside the scope of our program, inclusive hiring practices can and should be incorporated when hiring all types of employees, and we could have done more to encourage that.

While we are able to identify successes and opportunities, our neglect of formal assessment means that we were not able to robustly demonstrate the impact of those changes. Incorporating assessment throughout our program, just as we encouraged search committees to do, would have greatly strengthened our efforts and allowed us to identify high-impact practices. Ideally, we would have analyzed candidate diversity data before and after implementing the program, but we could have better incorporated assessment even without access to that data. Surveying training participants rather than relying on informal, unprompted feedback would have provided specific information regarding participant attitudes about the training session and their ability to incorporate our guidance during the search. Testing participant awareness of inclusive hiring practices before and after our training sessions could have also improved our understanding of what information participants were learning and where they needed more help. This understanding would allow us both to adjust our training in the future and to identify topics for immediate follow-up with search committees as needed. We could also solicit feedback from candidates themselves about their experience. This practice would require careful consideration of privacy and adjusting for potential positive bias with successful candidates and negative bias with unsuccessful applicants, but it could be a valuable source of information about candidate perceptions and preferences.

Sustainability was on our minds from the beginning: one of our goals when developing the program was to ease the burden of labor on ourselves by centering and prioritizing inclusive hiring work as everyone's responsibility. However, we quickly recognized that managing the program was still a substantial commitment, and, in addition to the labor of running the training program itself, we needed to continuously advocate for our work. The Libraries' hiring program was generally informal and decentralized, and responsibilities and firm requirements for searches were often unclear. The organizational culture had not generally prioritized equity and inclusion work, and the pervasive false sense of urgency meant that EDI was often jettisoned to save time. Sustainability became even more of a concern when we left to accept positions with other institutions.

To help alleviate the burden of labor and, eventually, to ensure the continued existence of the training program after our departures, we did invite all Diversity and Inclusion Team members to contribute to the training program even prior to our departures. Acknowledging that inclusive hiring was not everyone's area of expertise, we focused on helping our Diversity and Inclusion Team volunteers feel comfortable conducting trainings. We shared our training documentation and resources with interested members and discussed our thought processes when reviewing job descriptions and otherwise preparing for training sessions. Finally, volunteers observed one of the cochairs leading a training session before conducting one themselves.

Addressing the decentralized hiring process and overarching organizational culture has continually created challenges. During the time we were cochairs, one of us was part of the Libraries' management team, so we were typically aware of upcoming searches and could plan accordingly. As of this writing, current Diversity and Inclusion Team members do not have representation on that team, leading to training requests with less lead time to prepare a tailored session or requests from search committee chairs that the training be skipped entirely if it does not align with their schedules. Given how embedded this process was intended to be within search processes, some initial solutions to this problem include asking that human resources or others involved in the creation of job descriptions notify Diversity and Inclusion Team members of upcoming searches in advance. Flexibility in content delivery and level of detail can also help; while ideally all trainings would be guided by the training program we designed, an inclusive hiring conversation via e-mail is better than not having that conversation at all. We also found that word of mouth from training participants has been the most powerful tool in advocating for sustainability; previous training participants serving on search committees often emphasized the usefulness and relevance of the trainings to their search committee chairs and were then more likely to prioritize training when serving as chairs themselves.

# Conclusion

Search committees are integral to the work of our libraries in ultimately bringing new talent to an organization. It is absolutely imperative, then, that we thoughtfully consider the formation and influence of these groups, how they establish their own committee microcultures, and how they can effectively function and inclusively work together in recruiting, evaluating, and welcoming *all* candidates, including their eventual future colleague. Yet as is the case with all of the topics within academic librarian hiring, inclusive and equitable search committee composition and training are not enough. These efforts mean nothing if our institutions are not doing the work to actively cultivate inclusive and equitable organizational structures beyond hiring, including challenging the status quo, welcoming being challenged, and making the structural and institutional changes necessary to support all employees throughout their experience after hire. Our institutional cultures must intentionally welcome, support, and center the needs and experiences of our racialized and underrepresented colleagues, including examining and reimagining the standardized practices, policies, and individual behaviors embedded within them. For even within our search processes, candidates are considering not only where they might be hired, but also our institutions' ability to support and retain them afterward. It is everyone's responsibility to reimagine our many other systems and practices to better ensure we do.

# References

American Library Association. (2012). *Diversity counts*. https://www.ala.org/aboutala/offices/diversity/diversitycounts/divcounts

Brown University Office of Institutional Equity and Diversity. (n.d.). *Guide to diversifying faculty searchers: Equity-minded interview questions*. https://www.brown.edu/about/administration/institutional-diversity/sites/oidi/files/Equity-Minded_Interview_Questions.pdf

Cunningham, S., Guss, S., & Stout, J. (2019). Challenging the "good fit" narrative: Creating inclusive recruitment practices in academic libraries. In D. M. Mueller (Ed.), *Recasting the narrative: The proceedings of the ACRL 2019 conference, April 10–13, 2019, Cleveland, Ohio* (pp. 12–21). Association of College and Research Libraries. https://scholarship.richmond.edu/university-libraries-publications/42

Harvard University Office for Equity, Diversity, Inclusion & Belonging. (n.d.). *Inclusive meeting guide (small-scale meetings)*. https://edib.harvard.edu/inclusive-meeting-guide

Heath, K., & Wensil, B. F. (2019, September 6). To build an inclusive culture, start with inclusive meetings. *Harvard Business Review*. https://hbr.org/2019/09/to-build-an-inclusive-culture-start-with-inclusive-meetings

Matthew, P. (2016, November 23). The invisible labor of faculty of color on campus. *The Atlantic*. https://www.theatlantic.com/education/archive/2016/11/what-is-faculty-diversity-worth-to-a-university/508334

Northern Illinois University Affirmative Action and Equity Compliance. (n.d.). *Sample interview questions—Diversity and equity*. https://www.niu.edu/diversity/_files/equal-opportunity/sample-interview-questions-diversity-and-equity.pdf

Project Implicit. (2011). *Take a test*. https://implicit.harvard.edu/implicit/takeatest.html

University of Washington Human Resources. (n.d.). *Inclusive hiring*. https://hr.uw.edu/diversity/hiring

CHAPTER 2

# Including Voices and Mitigating Bias

## Evaluative Practices for Final Interviews

*Xan Arch and José Velazco*

Inclusive hiring practices such as implicit bias training for search committee members, advertising the position broadly, and using rubrics to evaluate candidate applications are becoming more standard in academic libraries. The latest edition of the American Library Association (ALA) *Guidelines for Recruiting Academic Librarians* includes these practices, and, in particular, tasks the search committee with the responsibility of "understanding the potential for implicit bias or artificial barriers, and acting to avoid these and to ensure equity in their decision making." (ALA, 2017, "Role of the Search Committee" section). Through the early stages of a hiring process, the search committee plays a central role in the enacting of any institutional or professional guidelines to mitigate bias and ensure an equitable search (ALA, 2017).

Less attention has been paid to the ways in which a broader range of participants beyond the search committee interact with a hiring process and the role these participants play in an inclusive search. As Cunningham, Guss, and Stout (2019) comment, "the library literature on hiring is heavily focused on the activities of the search committee, while in practice the search committee represents only one piece of the interview process" (p. 13).

Most crucially, at the final interview stage, this broader group of participants beyond the search committee takes on an evaluative role. These additional evaluators may be colleagues within the library, library student workers, or stakeholders from around the institution who attend an interview meeting, presentation, or meal. They are included in the search process to provide more perspectives on candidates as well as to foster participation and investment in the hire. At the end of the interview, this additional group of evaluators is often given an avenue for feedback on the candidates and the search committee uses the feedback to help make its decision.

However, without structure or guidance, the feedback from these additional evaluators may be at best mixed in quality and at worst a significant opportunity for bias to enter the search process. The comments received from non–search committee members may be germane to the candidates' ability to succeed in the position, or they may be about the candidate's appearance or their choice to have a glass of wine with dinner (Dennihy, 2015). With limited opportunities to interact with candidates and limited guidance on the evaluative focus of these interactions, non–search committee members may experience and evaluate candidates only in terms of their personal qualities or identity characteristics. A desire to contribute to the process and a lack of structure in candidate interactions may mean that even individuals who understand the abilities and experience needed to perform the job may center their feedback on identity and personal qualities.

On the other hand, stakeholder feedback can be a valuable source of information for a search committee and can help these additional individuals feel invested in the process of searching for their future colleague. How then can we revise our hiring processes to reduce the likelihood of feedback that is unrelated to a candidate's ability to perform the duties of the job, but still maintain the ability for individuals beyond the search committee to meet and evaluate candidates? At University of Portland's Clark Library, we recently revised our hiring procedures with the goal of creating more inclusive and equitable search processes. As part of this effort, we changed the ways in which we solicited feedback and tested these changes through a 2021 search process. The results yielded recommendations for other libraries looking to better incorporate stakeholder feedback beyond the search committee.

# Positionality

As founding members of the Clark Library's Hiring Practices Committee and co-creators, along with several other colleagues, of the practices and templates described in this chapter, we brought our own personal and professional identities to this work. The first author is a white, able-bodied cisheterosexual female who, before beginning to examine academic hiring, had often been unaware of and likely a beneficiary of the biases inherent in traditional academic hiring practices. The second author is a first-generation college student and Latino immigrant, who navigates the tension between his identity and advocacy for communities of color and his adopted country. This work has allowed him to better understand and create guidelines to reduce the biases within the hiring process as he continues to examine his own sense of belonging within a traditionally white institution.

# Institutional Context

The University of Portland is a private Catholic university in Portland, Oregon, enrolling approximately 3,700 students. The Clark Library employs librarian faculty and staff, and our traditional hiring practices were informed by university guidelines, along with documents and institutional memory from past searches. We hired using previous interview schedules, saved lists of interview questions, and many recollections and opinions about what had worked well.

In 2019, the dean of the library created a Hiring Practices Committee to review our hiring practices and create a manual for the library. Several factors came together in 2019 and 2020 to inspire and sustain this critical revision of our library's hiring practices. First, the dean of the library participated in Oregon State University's (n.d.) search advocate training. The documents from this training provided purpose and structure for many of the revisions our committee ultimately made. Additionally, in relation to gathering stakeholder feedback, this training emphasized clear job requirements for advertised positions and the creation of a common understanding for both search committee members and external stakeholders of the ways in which a candidate can demonstrate their qualifications related to these requirements.

Another major inspiration for change, particularly for the question of gathering stakeholder feedback, was a library faculty search in 2019. Although it was a successful search, the experience highlighted some significant problems with the interview and evaluation process. The search was for a technical services librarian, and our standard interview practices included a presentation. The search committee invited all library faculty and staff to the candidate presentations. In the evaluation forms from the attendees, much of the feedback related to the candidates' speaking style, slide appearance, and overall self-presentation. As we reviewed this feedback, it raised questions about how these comments related to a candidate's success in their role. For example, if a candidate is an uneven presenter, how does this impact their ability to manage technical services? How does their aesthetic sensibility when creating their presentation materials relate to their collection development experience? The experience highlighted two significant problems: our interview requirements for candidates and our methods for obtaining feedback based on these requirements.

This critical examination of the role of the presentation led to further research into these less structured elements of the traditional interview process, including presentations and candidate meals. As described in *Core Best Practices for Academic Interviews*, a structured interview "is one where the process and questions are decided in advance and the same questions are used for every candidate" (Arch et al., 2021, "Structure and Consistency" section). If structured interviewing practices allow for more equitable evaluation of candidates (McCarthy, Van Iddekinge, & Campion, 2010), unstructured elements of the interview are more likely to garner inequitable feedback as the information gained will vary between candidates and may not relate to the job qualifications. For the 2021 Association of College and Research Libraries (ACRL) conference, the dean of the library co-presented on research surveying library leaders on the unstructured elements of hiring practices. The study found that

> both informal social elements and formal public presentations ...are often valued for reasons *other* than determining the ability of a candidate to do the job; and they are frequently incorporated into evaluating candidates, often by providing non-search committee members opportunities to submit feedback on candidates. (Arch & Gilman, 2021, p. 131)

This finding that stakeholders use unstructured interview elements to evaluate candidates, but often in a way unrelated to a candidate's ability to perform the job, further bolstered our desire to critically rethink our interview practices, especially when it came to stakeholder input.

At the University of Portland, our library's four-person Hiring Practices Committee was a diverse group, encompassing different functional areas of the library, both faculty and staff, and both majoritized and minoritized identities. We started by reviewing existing literature on library and university hiring. We then created documents to guide everything from the formation of search committees and the construction of candidate interview schedules to the final search committee debriefing. Once the hiring manual was completed, we committed to regular revisions, particularly because the literature in this area progresses rapidly and best practices emerge frequently. The initial test of the new manual was the hiring of a new library faculty member in 2021. This was the first library search that included a non-library search committee member (per our new guidelines) and the first that included a non-voting search advocate who monitored the work of the committee and made suggestions to reduce bias throughout the process.

The changes we made in our search processes and tested through the 2021 faculty search provide a set of recommendations to those considering how to incorporate stakeholder feedback in ways that are clear to interview participants and fair to candidates. These fall into the categories of creating the interview schedule, preparing interview participants, creating a feedback form, and working with stakeholder feedback.

# Changes to Try: The Interview Schedule

The interview schedule is the one element of a search that most affects the stakeholder perception of a candidate because it creates the opportunities for evaluation. A typical interview schedule is made up of structured sessions, such as meetings with interviewers, and unstructured sessions where the questions and content are not predetermined. Because unstructured time with candidates has been found to increase bias in evaluations (McCarthy, Van Iddekinge, & Campion, 2010), designing a schedule that minimizes unstructured evaluative times will help reduce the likelihood that a candidate is being judged on aspects that are not related to their ability to do the job.

Two traditional interview schedule elements that involve non–search committee members and have intrinsically less structure are mealtimes and presentations. Our revision of the hiring manual strongly suggested the elimination of evaluative mealtimes from interview schedules. It is possible that a job (such as library dean or development officer) may require social dining with others and therefore it could be necessary to create job qualifications related to this type of external interaction and assess candidates accordingly. However, this is not the case for most roles in the library.

In order to begin eliminating evaluative mealtimes from our interviews, for our 2021 search, we asked library student workers to take candidates to lunch and talk about their experiences in the library. We labeled these lunches on the candidates' schedule as non-evaluative, and we told the students in advance that we would not be requesting feedback from them. It was paid work time with free lunch for the students and a chance for the candidates to connect with students at the university.

The interview dinner was more complicated as we had a long tradition of candidate dinners being a chance for librarians to have a meal out and see if they connected with candidates on a personal level. This often resulted in evaluative feedback related to how enjoyable or awkward these interactions were for the attendees. While these comments were not always fair to the candidates, we did not feel that eliminating the dinner was best since sometimes the connections among participants provided candidates with a sense of their future colleagues and allowed them to ask questions about the university and library in a less formal setting. We therefore asked dinner attendees to complete their candidate feedback form at the end of the workday so they could make a personal connection during dinner but not allow these less structured elements to contribute to their candidate evaluation. That meant the meal itself could be non-evaluative, but we could still welcome candidates over dinner and foster connections with potential future colleagues.

Presentations or job talks are another standard aspect of academic hiring processes, including in libraries. However, as mentioned, these interview elements often result in feedback not only on candidate ideas but also on their presentation style, when, unlike non-library faculty, many library jobs do not require teaching or public speaking. Galvan (2015) addresses this relationship between these presentations and the intrinsic performative aspects:

> The academic job talk is similarly concerning, as the growing tendency to record and make available such talks transforms the interview process into a mediated performance. An intellectual understanding of bias isn't

enough, it must be interrogated to dismantle the mechanisms which produce bias. (para 18)

Interrogating the job talk meant understanding the relationship between how the candidate interacted with the group and the job qualifications themselves. If we were hiring someone who would be regularly teaching or presenting, then providing an opportunity for stakeholders to evaluate their ability in this area would be important. However, if the role does not require regular public speaking, a job talk might be less appropriate and might lead to feedback on candidate performance that is unrelated to their potential for success in the position.

In our 2021 search, we piloted a different group interaction for the interview, asking candidates to lead a group discussion on a topic of their choice instead of giving a presentation. See appendix A for sample guidelines for candidates and participants. Because the role was a manager, we hoped to give non–search committee members a chance to evaluate the candidates on their ability to lead a group through a discussion topic and arrive at clear outcomes. While this interview element was still unstructured in that the participants had a different experience with each candidate, moving to a facilitated discussion instead of a job talk helped ensure that the session was more targeted toward the job requirements. In the 2021 search, these facilitated discussions were successful in that they not only gave participants a chance to evaluate candidates on their ability to lead a group through a discussion, which was germane to their potential as a manager, but the interview sessions also had the unexpected benefit of allowing the library staff to generate ideas and work together in ways that would not be possible during a job talk.

# Changes to Try: Preparing Participants

However a library decides to structure the interview schedule, it's important to prepare stakeholders beyond the library to evaluate candidates fairly and provide them with guidelines as to what kind of feedback is being requested by the search committee (Endo, 2022).

Creating a common understanding of candidate evaluation might start with implicit bias training. These trainings are increasingly ubiquitous as a way for universities to create individual awareness of potential for bias in a hiring process, but they are often reserved for the search committee. Providing resources to all search participants allows for a reminder that awareness of implicit bias is an important principle in hiring that stakeholders should keep in mind while evaluating candidates.

Finally, preparing interview participants may also include a reminder to keep all candidate materials confidential and not to research candidates outside the interview process. While these are basic hiring practices, they are often communicated exclusively to the search committee even though any participant with an evaluative role in an interview may decide to seek external information and may judge candidates based on that information rather than their interview. This investigation might be as simple as asking a trusted colleague at another institution what they know about a candidate or a quick internet search on the candidate's background. While these actions may be undertaken with the best intentions, they risk bringing information into the hiring process that is at best uneven between candidates and at worst a bias risk.

At the Clark Library, our committee created a template email to send to anyone planning to attend a meeting or presentation by a candidate. It includes a link to the job description, a package of recorded content on the topic of implicit bias, and reminders about candidate confidentiality and not researching candidates. With this information, we prepared interview participants to evaluate candidates as fairly as possible, based on the interview and the position's qualifications. See appendix B for this template email.

# Changes to Try: The Feedback Form

After the interview, the search committee solicits feedback from stakeholders, often via a form. The structure and content of this form are important guides for participants. Common elements include the ability to rate candidates, often on specific aspects of the job or of the interview session, and a section to enter any additional comments on candidates. Without clear guidance, stakeholders will provide a broad range of feedback, much of which may not relate to a candidate's chance of success in the job.

In the interest of further structuring the feedback we received and reducing the possibility of comments that do not address a candidate's qualifications for the job, we designed a form that provides the same quantitative and qualitative mix as our traditional feedback form but focuses the evaluator narrowly on the job qualifications by providing exact job requirement language at the point of evaluation as well as links to the full job description. See appendix C for a sample feedback form.

# Changes to Try: Working with Feedback

Despite the best efforts of a search committee, stakeholders may still provide feedback that is not germane to a candidate's ability to do the job. Some may not have read or understood the guidelines in providing feedback, but others may feel strongly that a candidate's "fit" is most important to create a harmonious workplace. The more feedback a search committee gathers, the more likely it is that some of it is not appropriate for evaluation. This inappropriate feedback comes with risk—once a search committee has reviewed this feedback, it can color their perceptions of a candidate, even if they do not agree with the comments.

One solution is to have the feedback reviewed by a search advocate or other non-search committee member before being provided to the search committee. The review would be specifically to look for comments that are not related to a candidate's ability to do the work of the position and comments that relate to social identity characteristics that are unrelated to the job. These comments may seem neutral or even positive in some cases, such as "it would be great to have a woman in this position," but ultimately if it is unrelated to stated job qualifications, it should not be released to the search committee. We have used the tactic of feedback review twice now, once with the previously mentioned library faculty search and again with a university-level search committee, and in both cases, there have been identity-related comments that have been removed before the search committee has been given the feedback.

# Conclusion

Moving toward more equitable and inclusive hiring processes is challenging, especially when it comes to interrogating long-held practices. The individuals working in our institutions were hired under these practices and may have successfully hired others using them, so questioning these methods can feel threatening to current employees. Increasingly though, we are realizing that these changes are needed because our hiring methods have gone unquestioned and are, at their core, often exclusionary and inequitable (Sensoy & DiAngelo, 2017).

However, even as more libraries review their traditional methods of hiring, these revisions often focus on search committee work and behaviors. Updating hiring practices must go beyond the work of the search committee to include an understanding of how we bring a broader group of stakeholders into the search process and how we help these stakeholders provide feedback that is useful to the search and equitable to the candidates. The four processes described in this chapter—structuring an interview schedule, preparing participants, creating a more structured feedback form, and working with feedback—all speak to ways we can involve our library and university colleagues in a search process that creates greater inclusivity in the search rather than introducing additional bias. At the Clark Library, we have created and tested new guidelines for these last stages of a hiring process and look forward to continuing to refine them in each search, as we are always learning more about how to bring institutional stakeholders into our hiring practices, while focusing on creating a more inclusive environment for candidates and an equitable process of evaluation.

## APPENDIX A

# Interview Discussion Parameters

## Sample Facilitated Discussion Topic

The Clark Library's Public Services department works to create policies and services that are responsive to user needs and preferences. Recently, this has included removing patron fines, shipping materials to distance education students, providing online instruction sessions, and allowing long-term laptop loans for students in need.

Please lead participants in exploring strategies for creating, promoting, and maintaining public service policies that are welcoming and inclusive of all users.

## Instructions for Candidate

Candidates should facilitate a discussion on the chosen topic that:
- frames the topic and conversation for the available time
- includes the perspectives of different stakeholders
- engages participants of varying communication styles
- provides participants with a clear idea of possible next steps

## Sample Instructions for Participants

The [Job Title] Search Committee has asked the candidate to guide a discussion on this topic. Our goal for this session is to assess the candidate's ability to facilitate an inclusive dialogue that results in a clear understanding for participants of the possible next steps from the discussion. This session will be successful only if participants are fully engaged and the candidate has an opportunity to facilitate a lively conversation. To that end, please:
- Be prepared with your own thoughts and questions on the topic.
- Be yourself! It will be good for the candidate to engage with different communication styles, so participate in the manner that is most comfortable for you.
- As you participate, please observe what you think works well (or any challenges) regarding the candidate's facilitation approach so that you can share those observations with the search committee.

## APPENDIX B

# Sample Template Email from the Clark Library Hiring Manual—Invitation to Interview for Non-Search Committee Members

Hello and thank you for agreeing to participate in the [Position Title] interview.

In accordance with our commitment to inclusive hiring, it's important that all participants are familiar with the required and preferred elements of the job description and are ready to evaluate the candidates based on these elements, rather than other factors that may invite bias.

Before attending the interview, please make sure you have reviewed the job description: [Link to Job Description]. For the candidate evaluation, we will be asking you to comment specifically on how the candidate's skills matched the qualifications we are looking for.

Please also consider reviewing the following implicit bias resources. They may be familiar to you from work on other library search committees, but we appreciate you refreshing your memory on how bias can affect hiring processes.

- Implicit Bias, https://equity.ucla.edu/know/implicit-bias/
- Project Implicit, https://implicit.harvard.edu/implicit/

Finally, as we share candidate files, it's important to keep candidate names confidential outside our library and alert the hiring manager if you know any of the candidates already. Please do not Google candidates as you may find information, even if unrelated to the particular candidate, that influences your reaction to their interview.

Thank you for your assistance in selecting our next [Position Title]. Please let me know if you have questions.

# APPENDIX C

# Sample Feedback Form from the Clark Library Hiring Manual

Please reflect on your interactions with this candidate and their application materials in responding to the following questions. Please confine your responses to how the candidate is able to meet the qualifications of the position, as listed in the job description: [Link to Job Description]

1. Based on your review of the candidate's materials and/or presentation, to what extent do you agree that they would fulfill the duties outlined in the job description?

2. To what extent did your interaction with the candidate illustrate their ability to meet the job qualification of: [specific job language]

(repeat #2 as needed)

3. Any additional comments you'd like to provide related to specific job qualifications? (Please list relevant job qualifications you are commenting on. Job description: [link to job description])

# References

American Library Association. (2017, June). *Guidelines for recruiting academic librarians.* https://www.ala.org/acrl/standards/recruitingguide

Arch, X., Birrell, L., Martin K. E., & Redd, R. (2021, November 29). *Core best practices for academic interviews.* American Library Association. https://alair.ala.org/handle/11213/17612

Arch, X. & Gilman, I. (2021). One of us: Social performance in academic library hiring. In D. M. Mueller (Ed.), *Ascending into an open future: The proceedings of the ACRL 2021 conference* (pp. 125–136). Association of College and Research Libraries.

Cunningham, S., Guss, S., & Stout, J. (2019). Challenging the "good fit" narrative: Creating inclusive recruitment practices in academic libraries. In D. M. Mueller (Ed.), *Recasting the narrative: The proceedings of the ACRL 2019 conference, April 10–13, 2019, Cleveland, Ohio* (pp. 12–21). Association of College and Research Libraries.

Dennihy, M. (2015, February 15). *When they watch you eat.* Inside Higher Ed. https://www.insidehighered.com/advice/2015/02/16/essay-meals-are-part-interview-process-academic-job

Endo, R. (2022). Beyond "good-faith" efforts: Diversifying the faculty ranks in teacher education through equity-conscious recruitment practices. *Action in Teacher Education, 44*(3), 181–195.

Galvan, A. (2015, June 3). Soliciting performance, hiding bias: Whiteness and librarianship. *In the Library with the Lead Pipe*. http://www.inthelibrarywiththeleadpipe.org/2015/soliciting-performance-hiding-bias-whiteness-and-librarianship/

McCarthy, J. M., Van Iddekinge, C. H., & Campion, M. A. (2010, Summer). Are highly structured job interviews resistant to demographic similarity effects? *Personnel Psychology, 63*(2), 325–359. https://doi.org/10.1111/j.1744-6570.2010.01172.x

Oregon State University. (n.d.). *OSU Search Advocacy Program*. Retrieved April 5, 2024 from https://searchadvocate.oregonstate.edu

Sensoy, Ö., & DiAngelo, R. (2017). "We are all for diversity, but…": How faculty hiring committees reproduce whiteness and practical suggestions for how they can change. *Harvard Educational Review, 87*(4), 557–580. https://doi.org/10.17763/1943-5045-87.4.557

CHAPTER 3

# Setting Up Candidates for Success

## Using a Library Community of Practice to Develop Screening Tools and Candidate Questions to Minimize Bias in Hiring

*Claressa Slaughter, Charlotte Beyer, Chelsea Eidbo, Jaena Manson, and KatieRose McEneely*

Over the past few years, our library has looked at our hiring process during the COVID-19 pandemic. While examining our hiring process, we developed strategies for improving communication with the candidates. Through this process our focus has been on expectations both internally for the search committee and on the side of the candidates. Our library is a smaller team with members who have little experience being on the hiring side of the table. Many have not been trained in best practices for how to hire and assess candidates, which can lead to confusion of what is important in the hiring process. This situation can lead to a breakdown in communication with team members struggling with the process, which also impacts the candidates' experience and can introduce bias.

In this chapter we will discuss our process for improving communication with candidates and how we established a hiring committee community of practice to collaborate in the creation of screening tools for different stages of candidate screening as well as in the development of the questions in the first-round interview, which was on Zoom. Communities of practice are defined as a group of people who come together with a shared set of problems or challenges with the goal of sharing knowledge and information (Iverson & McPhee, 2008). As of 2022 the library has established communities of practice (CoP) for reference, instruction, and evidence synthesis. Since this hiring process was for a position to support systematic and scoping reviews, the collaboration happened within the Evidence Synthesis CoP.

# Institution Description

Rosalind Franklin University of Medicine and Science (RFUMS), located in North Chicago, Illinois, is a private not-for-profit graduate school focused on health science education. RFUMS is divided into six colleges—the Chicago Medical School, the College of Health Professions, the College of Nursing, the College of Pharmacy, the Dr. William Scholl College of Podiatric Medicine, and the School of Graduate and Postdoctoral Studies—with around 2,100 students.

Boxer Library serves the students, faculty, and staff of the entire university. RFUMS serves exclusively graduate health sciences programs and is not affiliated with a larger university or hospital system. RFUMS does not have a designated hospital like an academic medical center, so students learn at a variety of clinical sites within various communities. The fact that we do not operate as a part of a larger institution or hospital system allows us to design and adapt policies with more freedom than other health sciences libraries may experience. At the time of this publication, the Boxer Library team consists of 19 individuals: an associate vice president (AVP), an administrative director, four professional librarians, three nonexempt library staff (library associate, library assistant, and library clerk), and ten student workers. Currently all positions within the library team including librarians are classified as nonfaculty administrative staff.

*Disclaimer: We mean for our chapter to serve as inspiration for other institutions, not as permission to make changes. Each institution follows a specific hiring process that may be dictated by policy and even laws. Please review your institution's hiring policies and discuss with your appropriate departments before you make changes.*

# Why We Changed Our Hiring Practices

## Where We Started

RFUMS's mission is to serve humanity through the interprofessional education of health and biomedical professionals and the discovery of knowledge dedicated to improving wellness. Interprofessional education is where students from different professions work together and learn from one another to support patient care (World Health Organization, 1988). To support the strong emphasis of embedding interprofessional education within the curriculum, the upper administration encourages the idea of team-based practice within every unit across the university. Effective collaboration and teamwork are central to who we are as a university. The library team minus the student workers consists of only nine individuals for 2,100 students spread across over thirty academic programs. One activity that requires effective teamwork is the process of recruiting new members to join the library team. Since everyone works together in our smaller library team, everyone's input is important in the recruiting and interview process. Therefore, all members of the library team participate in the interview process. Outside of a basic structure, our institution leaves hiring procedures up to individual departments.

The search process can be a very labor-intensive process, which has an even greater effect on a small team where the amount of time and labor needed to recruit a new member has a significant impact on our team members' workload. Too large a workload can lead to low morale and burnout, which can impact the well-being and effectiveness of the team (Kendrick, 2017). Successful recruitment is a two-way street with goals for both the search committee and the candidate. For the search committee, the main goal of recruiting is to find individuals who can do the job and make our team stronger and more impactful at our institution. This goal does not mean finding a candidate who aces the interview, but rather one who reassures the search committee that they have the potential to grow into the role and collaborate with others on shared projects. Within the recruitment process, bias can be embedded into traditional interviewing practices, which keeps those historically excluded from librarianship out of the profession. This bias sometimes prevents the search committee from identifying candidates' strengths and potential impact in the role they are interviewing for. Ideally, the hiring process should include those with different life experiences and backgrounds with the goal of assembling a strong and impactful team.

Beginning in 2021, the AVP of the library began attending presentations centered around equitable hiring practices. She knew that the best way to change hiring practices with equity in mind was to involve a team instead of only one or two people. In early 2022, the library began using a community of practice model for various library activities and initiatives. Communities of practice were first defined by the cognitive anthropologist Jean Lave and the education theorist Etienne Wenger-Trayner in 1991. Wenger-Trayner defines communities of practice as "groups of people who share a concern or a passion for something they do and learn how to do it better as they interact regularly" (Wenger-Trayner & Wenger-Trayner, 2015). It became apparent that using this model could be the venue where discussions around these changes could occur. The rest of this book chapter will highlight the hiring procedures prior to 2022, the changes made to the hiring practices within the community of practice, internal and external feedback to the changes made, and future directions for the procedures within the community of practice model. Other institutions can take information gained here to guide the development of their own practices when appropriate.

# Hiring Practices Prior to 2022

## STEP 1: CREATING A JOB DESCRIPTION AND POSTING

The first step would begin with defining and reviewing the role before publishing the position. To do this, the library AVP would write or review a job description that would typically include the job's responsibilities, required qualifications, and preferred qualifications. This job description would then be submitted to the human resources (HR) department, which would review it to ensure that the position had the appropriate salary grade. Once approved by HR, the position would be approved by the supervising vice president and the finance department before HR would create a final job requisition.. Once the requisition was active, advertisements for the job were automatically sent out to job websites such as Indeed and Monster, as well as to the university website. The AVP would then create a job ad based on the original requisition which could be sent out to library-related e-mail discussion lists.

This method of constructing and circulating our job posts was fairly successful in attracting the right candidate. However, we began to notice some repeat discrepancies. For one, not sharing the salary range would either deter potential candidates from applying or would attract candidates whose salary preferences exceeded our budget. We also noticed that we needed to alter the required and preferred qualifications if we did not get enough eligible candidates in our first round of posting.

## STEP 2: ASSEMBLING A SEARCH COMMITTEE

Before the candidate search could officially begin, a search committee would be formed. Each institution has its own rules and procedures for assembling search committees. As stated earlier, our institution and HR department allow each department the freedom to determine how search committees are assembled. Within our library, the search committee was composed of the AVP, administrative director, and librarians. Within the search committee were a search committee chair and a hiring manager. The search committee chair would coordinate the screening and interview process, and the hiring manager would make the final decision of which candidate to offer the position to, as well as instructing HR to make an offer to the chosen candidate. The selection of who served as hiring manager and search committee chair would be at the discretion of the AVP. Our search committee met a couple of times during the hiring process to identify core competencies for the role, select candidates to bring in for interviews, and select candidates after the interview to either offer the position or bring in for a presentation (depending on the position).

Our search committee discovered that each member of the committee had varying criteria for evaluating the candidates. In addition to having varying criteria, search committee members also evaluated the candidates based on how they performed in the interview, which could lead to bias.

## STEP 3: SCREENING CANDIDATES

Screening candidates was done in two stages. First, each individual in the search committee would go through the applications and look for a few basic criteria in order to select their top three. From there, the search committee would meet to select and recommend their top three candidates. If multiple people recommended the same top three, we could easily proceed to the interview stage. If the committee members' selections varied too much, the search committee chair would break the tie or make the decision to repost the position.

While the search committee was generally on the same page for what we were looking for in a candidate, we had no formal rubric to evaluate the candidates. Because we lacked standardization, we found that sometimes individual search committee members' criteria were at odds with one another, thus making the hiring process take longer.

## STEP 4: INTERVIEW

Candidate interviews would be conducted in a series of four small groups within the library team, which included the AVP, administrative director, library staff, and librarians. Each group would have a fifteen-to-forty-five-minute session to ask whatever questions they wanted, with time set aside for the candidate to ask questions. The first round of interviews would usually take two hours and, if a presentation was required for the candidate search, the search committee would select who to move to the next round. The structure of the presentation would be a thirty-to-forty-five-minute presentation on a topic related to the role. If no presentation was required, the search committee would make a recommendation to the hiring manager of which candidate would be the first one to receive an offer from HR. Prior to 2020, the interviews were held exclusively in person, but after 2020, they were held virtually via Zoom.

Our lack of standardization for interview questions created a couple of dilemmas. First, we didn't always know if we were asking our candidates relevant and thorough questions. We also had no way of knowing if each candidate was being asked the same questions in each interview group, which could invite bias into the evaluation process. Also, it was not uncommon for interviewers to be inexperienced in interviewing and the hiring process, which sometimes led our search committee to feel unprepared or nervous during the interview, possibly giving a negative impression of the library team and influencing the candidate to not accept an offer.

## Why Changes Were Needed

The hiring process outlined above met the goal of recruiting new talent to our team. However, there were elements of our procedures that needed improvement. One area of focus in the last two years has been considering equity in all areas of library practice, which includes hiring. The goal was to recruit high-quality talent in an efficient way to minimize the labor and stress on both the library team and the candidates, preventing burnout for all involved. Discussed below are the areas that we changed to improve the search process for both the candidates and us.

# Changes to Hiring Procedures Made by the Community of Practice

## Increasing Transparency: Salary Transparency

Salary transparency has become more important in the hiring process in recent years, due to the importance of pay equity in the workplace. This emphasis on ensuring that employees are paid equitably has led to state legislatures requiring salaries or salary ranges to be posted on job advertisements. While the general trend may be toward more salary transparency, there is still a lag in seeing actual salaries posted on job ads. According to the *Ithaka S+R US Library Survey 2019*, 59 percent of public institutions shared salary information or salary ranges on job listings, compared to 24 percent of private institutions (Frederick & Wolff-Eisenberg, 2020). There are a variety of reasons why library job postings may not have the salary listed. Institutional policies may dictate whether or not salary is listed on a job posting. Our institution did not have a policy for or against posting salary ranges in job postings, so the only places we posted salary ranges were sites that required them. However, when reviewing our practices, one of the main values we decided on in our community of practice was transparency. This value was reflected in a variety of the changes we made, but one of the more obvious aspects was salary transparency. Employers may choose to be transparent about salary at different parts of the interview process, but we decided to be clear about salary from the very beginning to save time and effort for both us and our potential candidates. We were unable to list the salary range in the actual job description, but we did make sure to add it to any posts advertising the job on social media or e-mail discussion lists. If potential candidates saw a job ad where the salary was not listed and e-mailed the AVP, she would tell them the salary range. By listing the salary range on a job posting, we made it clear the amount of money we had to pay for the position, which allowed job seekers to make informed decisions on whether or not they should apply for our position. We believe that posting a salary range is a low-effort but high-reward change.

## Setting Up Interviews

To increase clarity and transparency for the candidates, the search committee chair would reach out to the selected candidates identified by the committee for first-round interviews via e-mail (instead of phone, as was the practice prior to 2022). Within the e-mail would be the job title; who the position reports to; salary range; hours per week; a listing of the core duties; if the role was remote, hybrid, or in-person; number of days on site if it was hybrid; contact information for the search committee chair; and a Doodle poll to identify a potential block of time for interviews. The search committee chair would ask that the candidate let the chair know if they would like to move forward with the interview or not within a specific time period, such as a few days, as well as encouraging questions from the candidate. The benefits of using e-mail versus phone as previously done was that everything was written in a way that could be reviewed at the best time for the candidate, as some could be working during the time of the phone call.

## Using Rubrics to Standardize Evaluations and Screenings

We identified the need to find ways to more equally evaluate new candidates, which led us to develop rubrics for different stages of the screening process. Using Google Forms, we created a simple survey that each member of the search committee would fill out while screening applications. The survey questions would be based on the requirements posted in the job ad and would give us a streamlined way to effectively evaluate candidates. The second Google Forms survey we created focused on the interview portion. This survey was to be filled out by each member of the search committee immediately after each interview. This gave us a rubric to grade how successful we thought the candidate would be based on their answers to our prepared interview questions.

One of the largest challenges in the interview process was evaluating the candidates' answers to the questions. As mentioned in an earlier section, some search committee members did not have experience in interviewing candidates and might be unsure of what to ask. We decided that having a set list of interview questions before the interview process allowed the search committee to feel more prepared for the interview, while also ensuring we had a more equal measure to evaluate our candidates. This practice helped us to avoid the "right fit" narrative, in which candidates are selected for positions not because of their skills or experience, but because the search team *feels* that the candidate would do well. Inclusive hiring research discusses this narrative and how it can lead to bias and possibly discrimination in the hiring process (White-Lewis, 2020).

## Supporting the Well-Being of the Candidates

### SENDING THE APPLICANT QUESTIONS AHEAD OF TIME

We started to supply candidates with the list of questions we had prepared ahead of time. Our goal, ultimately, is not to catch our candidates off guard by asking them a difficult question. While one could argue every job requires some level of being able to think on your feet, we decided our objective is not to see how well our potential candidates could perform mental and verbal gymnastics. Our goal was to find a candidate who could succeed in the position they were interviewing for. One way to find a successful candidate is by giving them the tools they need to succeed.

### VIRTUAL INTERVIEWS

One of the easiest changes we identified in our community of practice was to continue to host interviews virtually, even as more and more people returned to campus. Holding interviews virtually could relieve the potential costs and stress of traveling to our campus for candidates. It also makes the scheduling process for all involved much easier since we could now conduct these interviews from anywhere. It was important to us for the interview to take place exclusively online, with each person of the search team calling in separately, as a way to foster meeting equity. Meeting equity "ensures that remote employees receive the same level of engagement, collaboration and access to a meeting room experience as those who are physically seated around the table" (PR Newswire, 2022). This practice ensured that every person, including the candidate, accessed the interview on the same platform rather than the candidate being online and all (or some) of the search team being together in person.

### BREAKS

As a two-hour interview can prove arduous in a virtual format, we felt the candidates needed a break. The break usually came shortly after the midpoint of the process. Gail Betz (2022) writes about the importance of breaks to recenter, make any adjustments, and prepare for the rest of the interview. This can be applied to all candidates. Being able to turn the camera off and take a few minutes to stretch, leave the room, look over their questions again, get something to eat or drink, or simply just do something less strenuous can ease tension.

# Benefits of Implementing These Changes

In the spring of 2022, the library advocated for and was awarded funding for a newly created scholarly communications librarian position. This search was the perfect opportunity to test out the new hiring practices developed by the community of practice. These hiring practice changes have been positive, both for the library and for the candidates. The changes also created a general positivity about going into interviews as candidates had multiple opportunities to confirm that this position was of interest to them. Below are some of the things we discovered when putting these changes into practice.

## Developing Better Communication with the Community of Practice

To develop better communication with both the candidate, the community of practice, and the search committee, we wanted to create a more stable and repeatable set of hiring practices that did not rely on one or two people keeping track of everything, but instead relied on the entire hiring team coming together to make the changes and create a more effective process. We saw an opportunity to change both policy and language around hiring.

With the aid of the Google Forms results, the community of practice chair had the ability to further the conversation about who to hire without anyone forgetting details. The use of a Google Form also created a more congenial atmosphere around hiring. Conversation and promotion of each other's thoughts proved positive so all the members of the team feel successful in the candidate search and hiring process.

## Salary Transparency

The transparency of salary clarifies expectations for the position. We wanted to ensure that the candidates understood what they would be paid so that those who wanted more would not be bogged down applying to a library outside of their salary range. Some people with a desired salary outside of the range still applied. The AVP contacted them individually to reiterate that our institution would not be able to match their desired salary. Most greatly appreciated this level of transparency and clarity and elected to continue in the pool with the new information.

## Hiring Information Sessions for Candidates

For the scholarly communications librarian search, the library held information sessions, which were advertised through professional association e-mail discussion lists, in which the AVP answered questions from prospective candidates and clarified parts of the position description. Feedback from those who attended those sessions said that they found the information helpful and stated that the session did encourage people to apply. The sessions were also helpful for the AVP, as it helped her gauge where candidates were reading the job ad, as well as ways to improve job descriptions.

## Prewritten Questions for Candidates

When candidates had been chosen to interview, the library sent prepped questions ahead of time. This had two ultimate results for our hiring purposes. The first was that the library had a set of questions that would be used for each candidate we would be interviewing, with only job-specific sections being altered to suit the interview.. In addition, library staff no longer had to come up with their own questions, which might not have been the right questions. From experience, not having a fixed list of questions can allow information to slip by.

The second result was that giving candidates a set of questions allows them to come into the interview more prepared and, hopefully, more confident. The candidate having no idea what they are going into can negatively impact the interview, especially for people who struggle with interviews in general, even though they might be a good fit for the role. The blog *Hiring Librarians* asked its readers if they provided questions ahead of time, and the bulk of the respondents stated that they do, while others stated they do not because their place of employment is not geared for that but that they are curious about the potential positive effects that can be created (Weak, 2022). In addition, "gotcha" and off-the-cuff questions, designed to throw off candidates, can breed animosity or unpleasant social media posts about the institution doing the hiring. Preselected questions and preparation time allow the candidate to make better rounded answers and gives them a better opportunity to learn about the library. We found that, despite the candidates having access to all of the questions, there was still a wide range of candidate preparation and interview performance. We felt that we could tell which candidates took time to prepare for the interview.

## Having Breaks

The addition of a break gave everyone in the interview process, a breather. While it did not have a major impact on the library side, candidates noted their appreciation of having a chance to relax for a few minutes in the middle before diving back into the interview. Since early 2020, the ability to go to a fellow librarian's desk and have an informal chat to plan something has evaporated. Most, if not all, plans have to be made in a scheduled Zoom meeting, so there are far more meetings. Meeting fatigue is not affecting just our staff, but also the candidates, who have possibly had many interviews before ours, and the break in the middle is a good way to combat their fatigue (Cole & Mross, 2022).

# How Other Institutions Can Change
## Salary Transparency

There are a few ways you can try to implement salary transparency in your searches. First, check with your HR department to find out if you are allowed to post salaries in job descriptions. If you are, putting the salary in the job description will ensure that the information will be available wherever candidates find the job posting. If your HR department does not allow listing salary in the job description, there are other ways to be transparent about salary that do not affect actual job postings. You can be clear about salary in any informational sessions and social media posts, and in communications with candidates (such as when you reach out to offer a first-round interview).

## Communities of Practice

Since new positions will be working and engaging with multiple types of staff, it is important to have multiple voices included in the design of the hiring process. One way to accomplish this is to use a CoP so that the hiring committee has a dedicated space to discuss their goals, values, and the skills wanted for new positions. Our institution fully switched to utilizing CoPs for each service area of the library before we made the hiring changes outlined in this chapter. However, it is not necessary to fully transition to CoPs in order to utilize them in the hiring process. If your institution is not ready to embrace CoPs for most of your teamwork, you can create a CoP for hiring in particular. This CoP would be a place to discuss the following questions:

- *What are the values of your library team?* These are values that you would seek for any position. Many specific skills of a job can be learned fairly quickly, so we find it more important that we recruit candidates who are excited by teamwork and the prospect of learning.
- *What should your hiring process look like?* Gather your team's opinions on what really matters in an interview process for each position.
- *What is helpful language to have written up for easy access?* Our team thought it important to add language to our job descriptions that makes it clear that we want people to apply even if they do not meet all of the requirements. We are happy to interview candidates from a variety of experiences because we understand that having the specific skills for a job is not the only way to be successful in a position.
- *What questions will be asked during the interview?*
- *How do you want to evaluate each candidate?* Set rubrics can help each member of your hiring team consider the same skills and values when evaluating candidates.

## Forms and Questions

Institutions can take advantage of online tools to collaborate on question creation and to create feedback forms to evaluate candidates. Since our institution utilizes a Google enterprise license, the library team used Google Forms and Google Docs. Google Forms was used for candidate evaluation in the initial screen and interview stages, and Google

Docs was used to collaborate on questions to ask each candidate. If your institution does not use Google, these forms can be adapted to other online collaboration tools your institution supports, such as Microsoft Office (Teams, Forms, Word) or even library-focused software such as Springshare LibWizard. Once these resources are created, they can easily be modified for each new position as, many times, some general questions are asked of each candidate. For example, as a medical library, we ask all of our candidates questions about health sciences librarianship.

# Conclusion

As a library that is a part of a private not-for-profit graduate school focused on health science education, we understand that our conditions for changing our hiring practices may be unique. While our changes to our hiring practices are still in their early stages, we have received positive feedback from our recent job candidates and our library team. Our library team has specifically noted that they find value in the CoP model for our search committee meetings as well as the rubrics for grading candidates, and our candidates have expressed appreciation for receiving questions ahead of time, having the opportunity to attend information sessions, participating in virtual interviews, and having interview breaks and salary transparency. We hope to continue to see success brought about in these changes as we continue to grow our library team.

# APPENDIX A

# Additional Resources

Association of College and Research Libraries. (2017, June). *Guidelines for recruiting academic librarians.* https://www.ala.org/acrl/standards/recruitingguide

Bélanger, A., Ayotte, S., & Beaubien, S. (2022). Hiring early career professionals with kindness and respect: A practical approach for library diversity residencies. In P. Gorecki & A. Petrovich (Eds.), *Residencies revisited: Reflections on library residency programs from the past and present* (pp. 93–110). Library Juice Press. https://scholarworks.gvsu.edu/library_books/33

Birrell, L., & Strong, M. A. (2021). *Core Best Practices for Academic Interviews.* University of Alberta Libraries. https://doi.org/10.18438/eblip29971

Cosgriff-Hernandez, E., Aguado, B. A., Akpa, B. S., Fleming, G. C., Moore, E., Porras, A. M., Boyle, P. M., Chan, D. D., Chesler, N., Christman, K. L., Desai, T. A., Harley, B. A. C., Killian, M. L., Maisel, K., Maitland, K. C., Peyton, S. R., Pruitt, B. L., Stabenfeldt, S. E., Stevens, K. R., & Bowden, A. (2022). *A roadmap towards equitable hiring to diversify biomedical engineering faculty.* EdArXiv. https://doi.org/10.35542/osf.io/8hcw5

Cunningham, S., Guss, S., & Stout, J. (2019). Challenging the "good fit" narrative: Creating inclusive recruitment practices in academic libraries. In D. M. Mueller (Ed.), *Recasting the narrative: The proceedings of the ACRL 2019 conference, April 10–13, 2019, Cleveland, Ohio,* (pp. 12–21). Association of College and Research Libraries. https://scholarship.richmond.edu/university-libraries-publications/42

Dadas, C. (2018, Summer). Interview practices as accessibility: The academic job market. *Composition Forum, 39.* https://compositionforum.com/issue/39/interview-practices.php

Fletcher, L., Grandy, R., Thurman, F., & Whitney, R. (2022, May 2–6). *Pandemic transitions: The impact of COVID 19 on hiring and onboarding in academic libraries* [Poster presentation]. Medical Library Association Annual Conference, New Orleans, LA. https://researchrepository.wvu.edu/faculty_publications/3113

Kraus, H., Taylor, J., Phillips, L., Clark, K., Eames, L., Rabinowitz, C., Van Gorp, B., Zabriskie, C., Schroeder, R., & Todara, J. (2022, April 29). Further questions: Do you send questions to candidates before the interview? [Blog post]. *Hiring Librarians.* https://hiringlibrarians.com/2022/04/29/further-questions-do-you-send-questions-to-interviewees-before-the-interview/

McLoughlin, C., Patel, K. D., O'Callaghan, T., & Reeves, S. (2018). The use of virtual communities of practice to improve interprofessional collaboration and education: Findings from an integrated review. *Journal of Interprofessional Care, 32*(2), 136–142. https://doi.org/10.1080/13561820.2017.1377692

Raschke, G. K. (2003, January). Hiring and recruitment practices in academic libraries: Problems and solutions. *portal: Libraries & the Academy, 3*(1), 53–67. https://doi.org/10.1353/pla.2003.0017

Schwartz, A. E., & Durkin, B. (2020). "Team is everything": Reflections on trust, logistics and methodological choices in collaborative interviewing. *British Journal of Learning Disabilities, 48*(2), 115–123. http://doi.org/10.1111/bld.12305

Willihnganz, S. C. (2006, November). Panel 3: The unintended consequences of transparency. *The American Surgeon, 72*(11), 1126–1132. https://doi.org/10.1177/000313480607201126

# References

Betz, G. (2022, April 6). Navigating the academic hiring process with disabilities. *In the Library with the Lead Pipe.* https://www.inthelibrarywiththeleadpipe.org/2022/hiring-with-disabilities/

Cole, C., & Mross, E. (2022). Ensuring more inclusive hiring processes. *Journal of the History of Philosophy, 60*(3), 507–515.

Frederick, J. K., & Wolff-Eisenberg, C. (2020, April 2). *Ithaka S+R US library survey 2019.* Ithaka S+R. https://sr.ithaka.org/publications/ithaka-sr-us-library-survey-2019/Iverson, J. O., & McPhee, R. D. (2008).

Iverson, J. O., & McPhee, R. D. (2008). Communicating knowing through communities of practice: Exploring internal communicative processes and differences among CoPs. *Journal of Applied Communication Research, 36*(2), 176-199. https://doi.org/10.1080/00909880801923738

Kendrick, K. D. (2017). The low morale experience of academic librarians: A phenomenological study. *Journal of Library Administration, 57,* https://doi.org/10.1080/01930826.2017.1368325

"Employees Feeling the Burdens of Meeting Inequality in the Hybrid Work Environment." (2022, January 25). PR Newswire. Retrieved from https://www.prnewswire.com/news-releases/employees-feeling-the-burdens-of-meeting-inequality-in-the-hybrid-work-environment-301467715.htmln

Lave, J., & Wenger, E. (1991). *Situated learning: Legitimate peripheral participation*. Cambridge: Cambridge University Press. https://doi.org/10.1017/CBO9780511815355

Wenger-Trayner, E., & Wenger-Trayner, B. (2015, June). *Introduction to communities of practice: A brief overview of the concept and its uses*. https://www.wenger-trayner.com/introduction-to-communities-of-practice/

White-Lewis, D. (2020). The facade of fit in faculty search processes. *Journal of Higher Education, 91*(6), 833–857. https://doi.org/10.1080/00221546.2020.1775058

WHO Study Group on Multiprofessional Education of Health Personnel. (1988). *Learning Together to Work Together for Health: Report of a WHO Study Group on Multiprofessional Education of Health Personnel: the Team Approach* (No. 769). World Health Organization.

CHAPTER 4

# Creating a Search Equity Advisor Program on Any Scale

*Paula H. Martin*

Procedures around academic library hiring can vary from institution to institution. Some institutions have centralized, prescribed procedures guiding filling open positions, from how the committee is formed to the process the committee goes through for recruiting, screening, interviewing, and selecting; and some institutions have a more decentralized approach, with ad hoc committees or hiring managers creating their own way of hiring. In many cases, search committees have considerable authority to conduct their recruiting, screening, and evaluation without outside intervention (Cahn et al., 2022). Hiring by committee in higher education gained popularity in the 1980s (Bromert, 1984) and evolved in unique ways at different institutions. Whether by intentional choice or by acceptance of convention, certain groups are underrepresented in academia because of barriers that exist in the hiring process and antiquated methods of recruiting, screening, and evaluating candidates (Liera, 2020). Because of all the problems inherent in the search process, universities started developing programs in which committees would be assigned a neutral advisor or advocate who would focus on ensuring the process was optimized for equity.

The exact number of such programs is unknown since universities might not share their hiring processes publicly. For the same reason, the exact processes, purpose, and assessment of these programs are also kept private. From my review of public-facing websites of various institutions, including Oregon State University, the University of

California system, the University of Florida, the University of Wyoming, and others, the role of these programs is to train individuals to facilitate, in a nonjudgmental way, the process of hiring to eliminate bias, facilitate discussion, examine assumptions, identify and advocate for equitable best practices, and advocate for diversity, equity, inclusion, and accessibility (DEIA) considerations (DeFelice, 2019; Michigan Tech Human Resources, 2023; UC Berkeley Division of Equity & Inclusion, 2023; UCI Office of Inclusive Excellence, 2023; University of Wyoming Office of Academic Affairs, 2022).

For academic libraries on campuses where these programs do not exist (and perhaps are unlikely to exist), it's still possible to take the principles of these programs and apply them on a smaller scale, utilizing the most applicable elements. This can be especially helpful for smaller libraries that do not engage in hiring at the frequency of larger libraries and might not have the support of the larger institution in implementing best practices for equitable hiring.

# What Is a Search Equity Advisor Program?

These programs can have varied names—some are called search equity advisors, equity advisors, equity advocates, or something similar. For this chapter, I will refer to these programs as search equity advisor (SEA) programs, and the individuals in these roles as equity advisors (EAs). A partial list of universities with SEA programs can be found in the tool kit (https://tinyurl.com/SEAtoolkit2023).

SEA programs train employees (often faculty, but not always) to be an outside advisor on search and screening committees and provides the trainees skills around recognizing and interrupting bias, creating materials like job postings and screening matrices, facilitating conversations and disagreements, and implementing other elements of an equitable hiring process. While the exact training included in SEA programs varies by institution, the training includes learning elements of skills to disrupt bias and developing an understanding of how hiring processes limit hiring for diversity. These programs also often provide ongoing support for EAs, formal and informal assessment of experiences of both the EAs and other committee members, and adherence to a prescribed method of recruiting, screening, and hiring new employees.

Institutions create their own objectives for SEA programs and determine the precise role that the EA will have in the hiring process. Most institutions with these programs do not publicly share their specific implementation practices or assessment, and as of 2022 there is limited research on the effectiveness of the programs as a whole, though there is evidence supporting some specific interventions supplied by these programs. One intervention provided by EAs is supported by behavioral science research that suggests that in small groups like search committees, bias can be countered by the presence of someone in the room who can provide nudges to consider other points of view when bias emerges (O'Meara, Culpepper, & Templeton, 2020). Another intervention provided by SEA programs is targeted, evidence-based training for those involved with search committees (Sekaquaptewa et al., 2019). Finally, an EA can provide counter-stereotypical exemplars, which could have at least a temporary effect on bias (Lai et al., 2014).

The SEA concept is growing, with institutions creating their own programs, including Oregon State University, the University of Illinois, the University of Michigan, the University of California system, and others. These programs are beginning to flourish in medium-to-large-size institutions with dedicated diversity, equity, and inclusion offices.

# The EA Role

The role of the EA is one of a process advisor and facilitator rather than an enforcer. The EA is present to be an expert on implicit bias, institutional policies, and legal considerations and also serves as a nonjudgmental presence to provide nudges when implicit bias arises. As with the scope of SEA programs and training implementation, the role of the EA can vary by institution and also by the needs of an individual search committee. The EA could provide any of the following:

- assisting with development of the job posting, including assessing language, considering required and desired qualifications, and identifying ways the posting could be improved to appeal to a broader applicant base
- creating a screening matrix and guidelines that encourage objective assessment of candidates
- assisting with creation of interview questions at each round
- advocating for equitable, inclusive, accessible interviewing practices
- facilitating conversations, noting where implicit bias emerges, and ensuring that each member of the committee has a voice
- anonymizing candidate application materials before distribution to the committee and conducting an equal opportunity audit of the candidate pool
- serving as a confidential conduit for candidates to request accommodations and share food preferences and sensitivities, and offering to arrange meetings with affinity groups
- serving as an expert in university practices and legal considerations, sometimes with the authority to pause the search if problematic behavior emerges

As a practical consideration, ad hoc or grassroots programs can choose what elements to include based on their own needs or institutional support and can also start with a more limited role and scale up as resources become available or outcomes are met.

# Why Consider an SEA Program?

Search committees in academia are often chosen not because of the members' commitment to equitable hiring or DEI principles, but because they are experts in specific subject matter or simply the employee who has the time to devote to the responsibility, which leads to incorporation of personal preferences instead of more objective measures (White-Lewis, 2020). Even among individuals who express a desire to diversify faculty and engage in equitable hiring practices, members at predominantly white-serving institutions have biases that favor traits and experiences associated with whiteness (White-Lewis, 2021). One study suggests that academic libraries tend to hire based on fit rather than professional criteria or other objective methods (Ozek, 2010). However, the concept of fit can be problematic, involving racial or other bias and serving as coding for not fitting in the dominant structure of the organization.

Bias easily finds its way into the deliberation process in ways that are sometimes unconscious and sometimes conscious opinions based on social norms, individual experiences, and other conditioning. In an effort to disrupt bias and discrimination in the workplace, academic institutions adopted programs that mandated antibias training for all employees, similar to what corporations have implemented. Unfortunately, there is no evidence that mandated broadly applied antibias trainings are effective in the reduction of bias (Cahn et al., 2022;) and research suggests they could indeed backfire (Dobbin & Kalev, 2018). Members of high-status groups can react particularly unfavorably to organizational training and messaging around diversity initiatives and antibias training, which can lead to a negative effect on institutional culture (Dover, Major, & Kaiser, 2016). As an alternative to mandating training for all, universities are instituting programs where they give in-depth training to a group of advisors who can sit in on search committees to eliminate implicit bias and ensure best practices are followed for equitable hiring. Their role is less to teach about bias and more to guard the process itself (Cahn et al., 2022).

While research has not yet fully emerged to make broad claims about the usefulness of these programs and more time is needed to tell if this approach affects hiring outcomes on a large scale, there is potential that it could at least address inequities in the search process itself. In a few case studies of existing programs, participants reported that the presence of an EA "awakened them to the potential for inequity" and caused them to recognize the informality and lack of consistency in prior searches. Some search committees appreciated having a presence that "kept them honest" and questioned assumptions. The EA "kept everyone's mind on the process" (Cahn et al., 2022). Another study stated that EAs' intervention and questioning of practices played a significant role in advancing racial equity (Liera, 2020). One additional analysis concluded that the SEA program was generally received well and provided useful context and information to counter bias, with most search committees appreciating the presence of the EA (DeFelice, 2019). While SEA programs do not have universal appeal and success in all cases, they can have localized impact on individual searches.

# Initial Considerations for Your SEA Program

Prior to instituting an ad hoc program, some initial assessment can help you make the decision on if this is a worthwhile investment of time and effort, or if there is a better path for equitable search strategies, demonstrated in other chapters of this publication. This work will include learning if there are faculty or staff who have time and interest to take on the EA responsibility and if there would be broad support for such a program in your library. It can also help to identify the most pressing needs, if there is financial or other reward for the extra work, and if there are partnerships that could enhance your process. The other goal to pre-assessment is to find out if there is interest and infrastructure for this program to continue—even in the event of staffing turnover and budget changes.

## Assess Effectiveness of Current Protocols

The first step in assessing your own current hiring effectiveness is to have an idea of current best practices for equitable hiring. This publication is a great resource, and there are others in the tool kit (https://tinyurl.com/SEAtoolkit2023). A literature review of recent publications on academic and other equitable hiring can also be helpful. If your campus has an office for diversity, equity, and inclusion, an Equal Employment Opportunity specialist, faculty who specialize in equitable human resources practices, or other departments that have explored these programs, those can also be resources to make sure you understand current best practices for hiring. Other resources include colleagues at other institutions, state and national library organizations, and other organizations with a mission of diversity and equity in the workplace. Academic library conferences also often include presentations and workshops on this topic.

The next step is to solicit feedback from those who have either served on search committees or been hired recently to find out what their experiences were through the process. This can help identify your successes and shortcomings. At this time, it can help to review any manuals, instruction, evaluation materials, or trainings to look for shortcomings in the process and understand how much freedom is given to search committees to work independently in your organization. Through the process of examining current protocols, attitudes, employee workloads, and campus resources, it's possible to find your greatest needs and prioritize intervention implementation.

## Assess Available Resources and Partners

There are two types of resources and partnerships to consider. The first category is within your own campus or organization. By networking with people with whom you have a positive relationship and who have similar interests, you can determine if there is already a movement on campus to create an SEA program or if there are others with whom to collaborate to distribute the work of creating and sustaining a program. This type of model could have success in assisting with each other's searches by engaging in collective brainstorming. This networking can also help to find people who have been involved in these programs at other institutions or who have connections that can be used to access training programs and best practices. During this process, it's also a good idea to find out if there is any institutional funding that could be used to offer incentives for volunteers, pay for prepackaged or external training, or hire a consultant to assess your current practices and advise how to build your own program. Other resources include campus DEI offices, human resources, and campus committees or groups that advocate for equity in the workplace.

External resources and partners could also be helpful. Some larger universities with established SEA programs will allow guests to join EA training and might be willing to share training curricula, their own best practices, or other assistance in setting up your program. If you have established partnerships with sister institutions or universities with similar characteristics and resources, it might be possible to work collaboratively and collectively to design a program that could be used by all participants—which can be especially helpful for institutions that are not continually in a hiring process. Creating an SEA curriculum and procedure could also be undertaken by a committee of a state or regional library association—this approach would help any institution with limited resources, and a standing committee would ensure a rotating group of dedicated individuals.

Finally, if funding could be attained, there are services-for-hire that can build a program, conduct the training, and help to put an assessment process in place. This funding could come from an institution's flexible funds for DEI projects, from endowments specifically earmarked for similar purposes, and through external grants.

## Determine the Scope of the Program

Prior to launching an SEA program, it's a good idea to determine long- and short-range goals and which aspects you would like the EA to be responsible for do. The scope of your program will depend on institutional conventions, your identified needs and goals, and the resources you have available to you. On large campuses, these programs might be voluntary or mandated and have separate pools of EAs for faculty or staff searches, and there might be enough EAs trained to meet an ideal of search committees always having an advocate from a different department or division. Smaller schools might have to make some allowances based on the resources they have available.

Questions to ask to determine your scope are located in the tool kit (https://tinyurl.com/SEAtoolkit2023) and are formulated to assess your library's readiness and ability to take on the work of developing an SEA program. Your institution might find additional means of self-assessment. These questions focus on the character and nature of your current hiring model, the resources in your library or external network, the institutional parameters around searches, and your financial outlook.

With the answers to those questions, you can determine the scope of the EA role. At some larger institutions, the goal of the program is to have the EA be someone from outside the department who is involved in every aspect of every search, starting with crafting the job and continuing through determining where to post it, creating a matrix to score candidates, determining interview logistics, conducting interviews, facilitating conversations around selection, and making a recommendation for hire. In these instances, the EA might also sit in on all interviews, both phone and on-campus, and serve as a resource for facilitating accessibility considerations and connecting candidates to affinity groups. Depending on your available resources and the amount of time the EA has available to devote, the EA could take a slightly different role, with any combination elements mentioned in the section titled "The EA Role."

If we consider the goal of the program to be protecting and enhancing the process, you can determine which part of the process is the greatest priority. One place to start would be training the EAs to facilitate conversations, make sure each member of the committee contributes to the analysis, and be able to identify bias as it arises.

# Scaffold the Plan

For institutions that have the resources for a campus or multicampus SEA program, it is possible to include every element of equitable hiring and all best practices into the execution and assessment of a project. For smaller institutions, or those without a dedicated campus-wide focus on DEI initiatives, it can make sense to consider a scaffolded approach that starts on a smaller scale and adds elements as staffing, budget, and other resources allow.

After you have a self-assessment of current practices and available resources, you can decide what the most pressing needs are for hiring. It could be eliminating bias, ensuring an accessible process, facilitating debate, creating objective assessment standards, or anything that is mentioned in the previous section on the role of the EA or that arises from your own assessment. The role you assign to your EAs could be as large or small as you can manage with your current staff's workload. The benefit of creating a scaffolded approach is that a pilot project could be created, implemented, and assessed on a smaller scale that would give you qualitative and quantitative data on whether to propose a larger-scale plan or request additional staffing or resources. Results from a pilot project can also be shared across campus, creating momentum to support a more far-reaching program. The tool kit (https://tinyurl.com/SEAtoolkit2023) contains a sample time line, which includes investigating local resources, identifying candidates for your program, creating an assessment group, establishing your values and goals, communicating to stakeholders, and refining the role and training protocol.

The plan can include scaffolding; for example, the first pilot could focus on interrupting bias in screening and evaluating candidates, with an emphasis on recognizing bias and facilitating discussion, and save the other EA responsibilities for when the program has more support and resources available. Subsequent versions could add in EA responsibilities as they appear on the priority list made in preplanning: for example, writing job postings, reviewing interview questions and processes, offering to connect candidates to affinity groups proactively, creating and managing an objective matrix, and so on. Awareness of what level of involvement is likely to show successful outcomes can help to ensure a successful pilot, which in turn will increase the likelihood of campus awareness and interest. If the initial project is too involved to be executed with available staffing and resources, chances are high that it will not be attempted again.

# Determine Model for Appointing EAs

The EAs should be chosen through an application process, thereby guaranteeing that each person going through training will have both an interest and an aptitude for this work. Advisors should be people who would normally be able to serve on search committees and who have time to partake in the training requirements and ongoing communication. EAs should also be people who are able to have positive communication in difficult conversations and who have confidence to speak up throughout the search committee proceedings. Some institutions limit EAs to faculty or those who have extended tenure or stature in the organization; smaller institutions will have broader guidelines.

Volunteers should be compensated or given work release to engage in this work, particularly if you determine to move forward with a program that assigns a complex and labor-intensive role for EAs. This compensation can be for the training itself and for each instance of service as an EA, or it could be a lump sum for each year served. If funding isn't available for EAs, consider a work-release option where EAs could have something removed from their responsibilities to make room for this project. Another approach could provide explicit service credit under your organization's reappointment, tenure, and promotion process, which could be particularly appealing to junior faculty. Utilizing one of these approaches not only creates equity in how work is distributed, but also indicates that this work is valued and prioritized in your organization. DEI work and other projects can fail when the institution is not willing to consider it a priority, and offering incentives can be a great way to broaden your pool of EAs to distribute the work over a greater number of people. It can also create a more competitive process for selection.

Another option would be to identify a current employee who could take on this role as part of their regular duties, serving on all search committees. This could be an employee who has human resources duties, is involved with development of DEI programs, or who has a related job description for supporting this work. If your path forward involves collaborating with other departments or institutions to pool resources, consider if the application process will be undertaken separately in each department or if you will utilize the same process and engage in collective selection. Before soliciting EA applications, make sure to have a finalized list of duties and expectations, as would be expressed in a job description, and communicate honestly about the difficulty of taking on this type of leadership role.

# Determine the Training Program Curriculum

The training curriculum will depend on what responsibilities will be in the EA job description, what time and resources are available for training, and how you decide to implement your search committee guidelines. Training could be in-person or online, synchronous or asynchronous, and should include some element of discussion and problem-solving. Discussion could include verbal exchanges or a discussion board format and could also include role-playing, experience sharing, or group problem-solving using case studies or fictional examples. Successful training for other programs has relied heavily on the inclusion of social sciences research around implicit bias and DEI considerations. Other elements routinely covered in training include employment law, accessibility considerations, expertise in institutional hiring practice, examination of implicit bias and how to intervene when it surfaces, strategies for having difficult conversations, and general best practices around initial screening, interviewing, and assessing candidates. This can happen in a values-centered framework that considers institutional mission statements and goals around equitable hiring and diversity.

Training and onboarding can vary in length based on the goals of the training. For established programs, the training can be anywhere from a few hours to several days. For a pilot program approach with limited objectives, your training will be on the shorter end of the spectrum. Training can also be shortened by assigning pretraining readings and exercises. All guidelines and training materials should be given to EAs so they can periodically review the contents, and periodic refreshers on narrow topics can be a helpful way to spread out the time commitment.

The creation of materials can involve guest speakers and discussion facilitators, modeling on training programs from institutions willing to share their materials, Creative Commons–licensed materials, utilization of video training from LinkedIn Learning or similar subscription services, or creation of original materials from existing research around antibias or employment law issues. For libraries that choose the guest speaker/expert lecturer approach, it's helpful to have funding for honoraria to compensate for expertise, even if the expertise is coming from within your organization. Training materials that include elements of discussion, pair-and-share, debate, opinion and expertise sharing, role-playing, and small group work is particularly helpful in giving EAs a lasting memory of the principles of EA work. The tool kit (https://tinyurl.com/SEAtoolkit2023) contains a sample training curriculum and additional resources to help you customize your training program.

Some institutions welcome guests to experience their EA training workshops; while this wouldn't be an opportunity to copy the exact training in the workshop, it can give an idea of the depth and breadth of training sessions. Depending on available time and resources, the training could be shorter or longer. For institutions with funding to launch an SEA program, a consultant could take over the entire initial training, providing more time to develop training materials specific to the institution.

Another element of ongoing training and support is the creation of a tool kit of centrally located resources that can assist the EA, the rest of the search committee, and anyone who might have questions about the program. This could be public-facing or private for the initial pilot program. Examples can be found on the SEA websites for the University of California, Santa Barbara; the University of California, Berkeley; Washington University; the University of California, Davis; and Oregon State University. A directory of SEA website examples can be found in the tool kit (https://tinyurl.com/SEAtoolkit2023).

# Choose a Communication Strategy

Effective communication can give SEA programs legitimacy and indicate to the organization that this is something that has great importance. Communication that solicits input from those who work in the library and external stakeholders, giving them the opportunity to provide feedback as the program progresses, can make it easier to rally support for the SEA project and the objectives and values on which it is based. Communication that is inclusive and positive and recognizes many points of view is more likely to be effective than murky, vague, cynical communication, and opaque language, judgmental statements, and lack of trust are barriers to effective communication. Communication should begin in the earliest stages of planning, with the goal of keeping this on everyone's mind and involving as many people as possible in the creation and execution of the project.

When the project officially begins, after the implementation plan is in place, consider having a kickoff party or festive town hall that gives everyone a chance to hear about why this is important work and what it aims to accomplish. Involve options for feedback and expressions of public support, and release a periodic newsletter on the progress being made. If the time line turns out to be unrealistic or there are other barriers to success, communicate those with honesty so that the communication lends transparency to the process. When the planning is complete and the project is ready to pilot, it would be a great time for a celebratory event describing how the process went and the expected outcomes.

Positive communication within your organization is essential for buy-in. There are also communication methods for those outside of your immediate staff that will create interest and further collaboration opportunities. Within your university, provide updates to administration that forms the chain of command for the library, whether that be academic affairs, student affairs or support, or another administrative unit. Consider providing updates to faculty or staff senate and the university's office for diversity, equity, and inclusion, and provide interested faculty and staff a method for opting into updates. Make this program's goals part of your published strategic plan, and highlight how it is similar to plans at your peer institutions. If your institution has a library board, library council, or friends of the library group, create communication opportunities with those groups including updates and opportunities for feedback. This broad approach will generate outside discussion of the SEA program and can identify additional funding sources and collaboration opportunities.

Outside of your organization, there are other ways to communicate the development of your program. Posting your intention of creating an SEA program on forums and e-mail discussion lists can generate interest and suggestions for success. State library associations and smaller conferences are great places to present in-progress projects that don't yet have assessment data; attendance at any conferences, meetings, or forums can create informal communication channels to discuss projects and plans.

When your SEA program has operated long enough to have assessment data and plans for future additions, consider presenting your findings at conferences or forums. Distribute your findings broadly among administrators and interested parties. Communication is equally important around successes and shortcomings, particularly if you can supply adjustments to optimize the program. Whichever communication methods are chosen, remember that regular, routine, positive communication will generate the greatest amount of support.

A final element of communication to consider is having a website publicly available, chronicling the progress of the program and outcomes. This website can explain the goals of the program, the expected outcomes, and the approach that is decided upon, and highlight the committee members and EAs who have chosen to be involved with the process. Access to this information will generate interest and inform those who find it serendipitously.

# Determine Assessment Strategies

Assessment will be an important part of this project, whether you choose a small or large scope for your SEA program and EA responsibilities. Assessment can take many forms, each with its own value. To make assessment easier, fully document each stage of the process. Keep detailed agendas and minutes of each meeting, and document all ideas and possible plans, even if they are not chosen for the final project parameters. Record the reasoning for your decisions, where specific ideas and methods originated, what conversations and outreach occurred, and any other elements of your planning process. Keep documentation of available campus resources, applicable research, materials gathered from other institutions and outside sources, and any other information discovered along the way. This documentation will be helpful if different employees cycle in and out of the committee and can help if you would like to share your process in a conference presentation or academic journal.

The effectiveness of SEA training can be assessed in a similar manner to library instruction for students. Data can be gathered by administering pre- and posttests to assess the knowledge of each participant; these can test knowledge of topics covered in training, such as employment law, university policies, estimations of statistics of the diversity of library workers, knowledge of implicit bias, and other topics. Participants can also be asked to provide feedback at various points of the training: for example, after each module or lesson. This in-the-moment assessment can gauge how useful the participants find the training and have them name specific things they have learned.

Another assessment consideration is the feedback from EAs of their experience: if they found their presence to be effective, if their training prepared them for their role, if their presence was welcome or resented. EAs could also be encouraged to keep a journal of what tactics they used to protect the process and nudge against bias and how it felt to be in their role. Finally, it is valuable to have feedback from the members of the search committee on their impression of the experience of having an EA on the committee, if it changed the course of screening and evaluation, and if they noted any problematic behaviors arise from the presence of the EA. If enough searches can be conducted, data can also be gathered about the outcomes of each search. Assessment can happen via survey, and some examples exist in literature (DeFelice, 2019; Cahn et al., 2022; Liera, 2020). Other methods of assessment could be focus groups, one-on-one interviews, and short-answer questions during the committee's last meeting. Samples of assessment questions are included in the tool kit (https://tinyurl.com/SEAtoolkit2023).

# Future Considerations

The science around the methods and practices used in equitable searching is evolving, and it is unlikely that a one-size-fits-all solution will emerge. The success of programs like SEA or other search committee interventions will depend on constant evaluation and evolution as best practices arise. Because most institutions do not want their specific programs to be public, owing to legal and intellectual property considerations, success will involve continual experimentation and research.

Other elements that will affect the outcomes of hiring include changes in legal considerations, public backlash to DEI efforts, legislative intervention, and continual budget cuts and reduction in staffing. Those wanting to implement programs without broad institutional support will need to do extra planning and analysis and take care to design a sustainable solution. Even if an SEA program is not feasible, there are many lessons learned from the literature that can be applied in other ways, and specific interventions are found in other chapters of this book. Through trial and error, and dedication, any institution can find ways to improve its processes if it prioritizes this work.

# References

Bromert, J. D. (1984, April). The role and effectiveness of search committees. *AAHE-ERIC/Higher Education Research Currents* (ED243355). [Reprinted from *AAHE Bulletin*, pp. 7–10]. ERIC. https://files.eric.ed.gov/fulltext/ED243355.pdf.

Cahn, P. S., Gona, C. M., Naidoo, K., & Truong, K. A. (2022). Disrupting bias without trainings: The effect of equity advocates on faculty search committees. *Innovative Higher Education, 47*(2), 253–272. https://doi.org/10.1007/s10755-021-09575-5

DeFelice, J. (2019). *An evaluation of the Search Advocate Program at Oregon State University: Identifying strengths and opportunities for development* [Master's thesis, Oregon State University]. ScholarsArchive@OSU. https://ir.library.oregonstate.edu/downloads/wd3762640

Dobbin, F., & Kalev, A. (2018). Why doesn't diversity training work? The challenge for industry and academia. *Anthropology Now, 10*(2), 48–55. https://doi.org/10.1080/19428200.2018.1493182

Dover, T. L., Major, B., & Kaiser, C. R. (2016, January). Members of high-status groups are threatened by pro-diversity organizational messages. *Journal of Experimental Social Psychology, 62*, 58–67. https://doi.org/10.1016/j.jesp.2015.10.006

Forscher, P. S., Lai, C. K., Axt, J. R., Ebersole, C. R., Herman, M., Devine, P. G., & Nosek, B. A. (2019). A Meta-Analysis of Procedures to Change Implicit Measures. Journal of Personality and Social Psychology, 117(3), 522–559. https://doi.org/10.1037/pspa0000160

Ifidon, E. I., & Ugwuanyi, R. N. C. (2013). Effective communication in academic libraries: An imperative for knowledge delivery. International Journal of Library and Information Science, 5(7), 203–207. https://doi.org/10.5897/IJLIS11.066

Lai, C. K., Marini, M., Lehr, S. A., Cerruti, C., Shin, J. L., Joy-Gaba, J. A., Ho, A. K., Teachman, B. A., Wojcik, S. P., Koleva, S. P., Frazier, R. S., Heiphetz, L., Chen, E. E., Turner, R. N., Haidt, J., Kesebir, S., Hawkins, C. B., Schaefer, H. S., Rubichi, S.,... Nosek, B. A. (2014). Reducing implicit racial preferences: A comparative investigation of 17 interventions. *Journal of Experimental Psychology: General, 143*(4), 1765–1785. https://doi.org/10.1037/a0036260

Liera, R. (2020, September). Equity advocates using equity-mindedness to interrupt faculty hiring's racial structure. *Teachers College Record, 122*(9), 1–42. https://doi.org/10.1177/016146812012200910

Liera, R., & Ching, C. (2020). Reconceptualizing "merit" and "fit": An equity-minded approach to hiring. In A. Kezar & J. Posselt (Eds.), Administration for social justice and equity in higher education: Critical perspectives for leadership and decision-making. Routledge.

Michigan Tech Human Resources. (2023). *Equity advisors.* https://www.mtu.edu/hr/hiring/equity-advisors/

O'Meara, K., Culpepper, D., & Templeton, L. L. (2020, June). Nudging toward diversity: Applying behavioral design to faculty hiring. *Review of Educational Research, 90*(3), 311–348. https://doi.org/10.3102/0034654320914742

Ozek, Y. H. (2010). Potential fit to the department outweighs professional criteria in the hiring process in academic libraries. *Evidence Based Library and Information Practice, 5*(4), 99–101. https://doi.org/10.18438/B8B632

Sekaquaptewa, D., Takahashi, K., Malley, J., Herzog, K., & Bliss, S. (2019). An evidence-based faculty recruitment workshop influences departmental hiring practice perceptions among university faculty. *Equality, Diversity and Inclusion, 38*(2), 188–210. https://doi.org/10.1108/EDI-11-2018-0215

UC Berkeley Division of Equity & Inclusion. (2023). *Faculty equity advisors.* University of California, Berkeley. https://diversity.berkeley.edu/faculty-equity-advisors

UCI Office of Inclusive Excellence. (2023). *Equity advisors.* University of California, Irvine. https://inclusion.uci.edu/action-plan/equity-leadership-programs/advance/equity-advisors/

University of Wyoming Office of Academic Affairs. (2022). *Search equity advisors program.* https://www.uwyo.edu/acadaffairs/academics/sea-program/

White-Lewis, D. K. (2020). The facade of fit in faculty search processes. *The Journal of Higher Education, 91*(6), 833–857. https://doi.org/10.1080/00221546.2020.1775058

White-Lewis, D. K. (2021). Before the AD: How departments generate hiring priorities that support or avert faculty diversity. *Teachers College Record, 123*(1), 1–36. https://doi.org/10.1177/016146812112300109

CHAPTER 5

# Discussing, Understanding, and Assessing

## Moving Beyond the Performative to Examine the Candidate Diversity Statement

*Breanne Crumpton, Mollie Peuler, and Kelly Rhodes*

Our University Libraries are located in the southern region of the United States and are part of a public, historically white institution with an enrollment of over 20,000 students. Like many academic libraries, ours is critically examining what it means to have a diverse, equitable, and inclusive organization. With this in mind, we turned to the hiring process to focus our efforts on evaluating applicants' materials. At Appalachian State University, librarians hold faculty status, and so this chapter might refer to librarians as such. The hiring process, however, is equivalent to other professional librarian positions at different institutions in which candidates go through a two-round interview process: a phone or Zoom interview, and then a full-day interview with a presentation component.

As with any academic library, it is important to understand the institutional context in which we find ourselves. Appalachian State University opened its doors in 1899 to white men and women. The first African American student would not live on campus until 1963 (Special Collections Research Center, n.d.). Since this time, the number of historically underrepresented faculty has been slow to grow. Appalachian State University's Office of Institutional Research, Assessment and Planning (IRAP) captures diversity only through a racial lens and does not capture other historically underrepresented groups on campus, such as transgender faculty, faculty with disabilities, or faculty from nondominant religions. As of 2021, 12.9 percent of total faculty across the institution are from underrepresented races, compared to 9.5 percent in 2013. The University Libraries have seen similar growth with 12.5 percent underrepresented faculty in 2021 compared to 8.1 percent in 2013 (Appalachian State University, 2022a). While these numbers might look promising, it is important to note that these successful hires were followed by employees leaving the university. As a result, we continue to struggle with retaining diverse faculty.

Additionally, both Appalachian State University and the University Libraries have completed their latest strategic plans which include language that addresses "advancing diversity, equity, and inclusion" with subgoals to work on successfully attracting, retaining, and supporting historically underrepresented faculty (Appalachian State University, 2022b; Appalachian State University Libraries, 2022a). Alongside this new strategic plan, the Office of Diversity was restructured, and the restructuring resulted in the hiring of a new chief diversity officer for the campus along with additional support for their position. The new strategic plans and the hiring of the new chief diversity officer indicate a move in the right direction. However, at the writing of this chapter, the metrics, benchmarks, and plans for assessment are not yet available. As a result, we have little guidance on how to measure success and progress at the library and university levels.

In this case study, three faculty librarians will share the University Libraries' ongoing, often grassroots, efforts in evaluating faculty position applications, with a focus on creating and implementing a rubric to evaluate diversity statements. We will discuss (1) the way our libraries approached creating a diversity rubric to evaluate applicant diversity statements and provide clearer instructions in the job description, (2) our experience implementing and norming the rubric for use in the search committee process, (3) lessons learned applying the rubric in the search process, and (4) the important conversations to consider in the outcomes of the work and how to sustain it moving forward. It is important to note that the University Libraries also created a rubric that addresses the job description's minimum qualifications and other areas of interest; however, this case study will focus on our experience with developing and deploying a diversity statement rubric.

# Literature Review

Colleges and universities have long recognized the importance of diversity within the academy and have employed various strategies in their attempts to create a diverse workforce including outlining diversity, equity, and inclusion (DEI) priorities at the university, college, and departmental levels. Diversity statements provide applicants with the opportunity to share their experiences in professional work, scholarship, and professional service. These statements may also assist the search committee in its processes of evaluating applicants for positions. The practice of requiring diversity statements from faculty applicants is becoming more common, but it is not without controversy, and there are arguments for and against the use of these statements in the hiring process.

While there is literature on examining the recruitment, hiring, and retention of academic librarians while also prioritizing DEI, as of the writing of this chapter, we were unable to find academic library literature focused specifically on the inclusion of diversity statement prompts or on rubrics to be used when considering applicant materials. Instead, literature from academic institutions at large can be considered and reviewed. It is widely acknowledged in the higher education literature as well as the academic community that there are benefits as well as disadvantages to requiring diversity statements within application materials. Without a basis of strong literature in academic libraries, the arguments often fall back on assumptions and best guesses. As Bombaci and Pejchar (2022) surmise, opponents often suggest that diversity statement prompts can serve as a political litmus test or a threat to free speech; proponents believe that diversity statement prompts highlight and reward a commitment to DEI efforts. Despite these debates, minimal systematic research exists on the topic.

Conversations about the challenges and opportunities provided by diversity statement prompts have taken place in a variety of spaces, including social media. An example can be seen by reading a Twitter thread started by Guilford (2022). The original tweet and respondents levied some critiques against requiring diversity statements. The biggest concern discussed was that diversity statement prompts were a way to get applicants to self-disclose information they could not be legally asked for. Other concerns include that the statements could be used as a political test, that foreign nationals might be at a disadvantage because they would not have reference points to discuss DEI issues in the United States context, and that diversity statements are merely a performative way for organizations to communicate their commitment to diversity. These responses were indicative of the wide range of conversations taking place about the use and value of diversity statements.

Some researchers have attempted to use a variety of qualitative and quantitative survey methods to determine the value of including diversity statement prompts. Examples of this type of work include that of Bombaci and Pejchar (2022), who surveyed diversity and inclusion experts to analyze the challenges and advantages of diversity statements. The data they collected focused on diversity statements as part of the hiring process. The outcome of their research supports the use of these statements as a means of bringing value to the applicants and broader institutions.

Goulden et al. (2019) applied a regressive analysis to the data from three different sources to compare the demographic composition of applicants for positions at the University of California, Berkeley, to the national pool of available applicants; they also tracked the demographics of the candidates as searches moved from one stage to the next.

Other studies critically examine the contents of submitted diversity statements written in response to application prompts. These include Sylvester et al.'s (2019) study, which analyzed diversity statements written by thirty-nine participants to develop a framework, and that of Schmaling et al. (2015), who used thematic analysis to identify how applicants were addressing the prompt and what personal diversity characteristics they were disclosing.

Several excellent resources indicate different ways that applicants can speak to their experiences and contributions to DEI. A notable aspect of the literature emphasizes the importance of clear instructions on how applicants can describe their contributions in the diversity statement in order to assist the search committee in evaluating applicants' DEI knowledge and efforts in the context of the library's goals (Sylvester et al., 2019, p. 164).

# History of Diversity Statements at Appalachian State University

The authors' experiences have been that the history of diversity statement prompts at the University Libraries is mostly institutional knowledge, and we have been unsuccessful in locating an official record of past job descriptions. This fact underlines the grassroots nature of the current work. We do know that the University Libraries have historically provided little guidance to applicants on what to include in a diversity statement or to search committees on what to consider when evaluating these statements. By reviewing the position descriptions we were able to locate, we determined that since at least 2018, work within the University Libraries in asking for a diversity statement has been inconsistent and has changed over time. For a review of how the requirement has changed, see Table 5.1.

**Table 5.1.** Examples of University Libraries' Diversity Statement Prompts from Past Job Postings

| Year | Language Used |
| --- | --- |
| 2018 | No language used. |
| 2019 | A written response to the supplied Diversity and Inclusion Commitment Question. |
| 2021 | A statement addressing commitment to diversity, equity, and inclusion. |
| 2021 | A separate document sharing how you would further diversity, equity, and inclusion efforts in the role of [position title]. |

So, what should applicants include in a diversity statement, and how can the diversity statement prompt provide guidance and clarity on what applicants should address? In creating diversity statement requirements, it is incumbent that institutions be clear about where they are in their ongoing contributions and commitment to DEI and disclose their progress, including successes and failures.

# Position Description

Prior to the creation of a new diversity statement rubric, applicants were scored on an evaluation matrix and these statements were viewed as supplemental support materials. With the new separate diversity statement rubric, search committees could then give the statement an independent score. The goal was for this new system to prioritize candidates from diverse backgrounds and candidates who were heavily involved in DEI work.

In reviewing the application process, asking for a diversity statement has become one of a number of components the University Libraries is using to evaluate the applicants' understanding and commitment to DEI. Other components include common language in our job postings. Our position descriptions have two main sections that guide our evaluations of applicants: minimum qualifications, and other areas of interest. Every posting includes the following minimum qualification language: "Demonstrated commitment to diversity, equity and inclusion." Additionally, this areas-of-interest language—"Demonstrated commitment and experience within the areas of diversity, equity, and inclusion"—is now required in every faculty job description moving forward. As a result, additional independent rubrics were created for both the minimum qualification around DEI as well as this new area of interest. Again, these rubrics are outside the scope of this current chapter but can be viewed in Appendix A.

# Starting the Process Toward a Diversity Statement Rubric

Prior to 2019, the University Libraries did not have a strategic way to evaluate the applicant statements and to consider the impact the evaluation should have on the entire application packet review. In 2021, a search was underway to hire a tenure-track position, and the search committee made the decision to prioritize creating a rubric to direct the evaluation of applicants' diversity statements. While we did not know it at the time, our initial foray into developing a rubric would serve as a road map for creating a library-wide diversity statement rubric.

We began the work by researching and reviewing diversity rubrics in use at other institutions and considering what might work best for the University Libraries' needs.

As stated previously, the literature on using diversity statements rubrics for library-level hiring is scarce, but there are many examples available of university-level diversity statement rubrics. Brandeis University Diversity, Equity, and Inclusion (n.d.), Brown Office of Institutional Equity and Diversity (n.d.), Cornell University Office of Faculty Development and Diversity (n.d.), and University of Michigan Center for Research on Teaching and Learning (2017) all served as foundational rubrics for the search committee to learn from and build upon. While these rubrics varied in specific details, they all provided direction on what to consider when evaluating diversity statements. The search committee reviewed the sample diversity statement rubrics and considered the important elements, including rating system, rubric categories, language used, and organization and format. The goal was to customize and learn from these examples to create a diversity statement rubric that could best contribute to the University Libraries' diversity goals and initiatives.

The search committee used these examples and research to develop a rubric to evaluate applicant diversity statements (see Appendix B). This new rubric used a 3-point scale and had one category. Previous evaluations of the statements did not include a rubric and often depended upon an assumed shared understanding of what a specific applicant wrote in their statement. The rubric provided specific language that would guide the committee as they read and considered a statement. For example, one criterion that might lead to assigning a diversity statement a score of one was this: It was "unclear what unique efforts the [applicant] would undertake at Appalachian [State University and] merely [stated that] …they would do what [was] asked, if hired." In contrast, a criterion that might lead to assigning a diversity statement a score of three was this: The diversity statement "details [applicant's] plans to promote diversity, equity and inclusion through research, service and teaching at Appalachian [State University,] within their department, and/or campus-wide." Once the search committee finalized the rubric, library administration was consulted to confirm that they could move forward with using it to formally evaluate applicants. The goal of the developed rubric was to evaluate one piece of the application packet, the diversity statement, and to road test a process and expand upon the work from there.

# Creating a Library-wide Diversity Statement Rubric

At the conclusion of the previous tenure-track search, there were many conversations about the role of diversity statements, including within the Inclusion, Diversity, Equity, and Accessibility Committee, current and past search committee members, and general conversations among faculty and staff. These conversations generated additional grassroots efforts within the library. Eventually, library colleagues added a discussion of the challenges and benefits of diversity statements to the agenda of the University Libraries' Departmental Personnel Committee (DPC). The DPC, a governing body within the library composed of pre-tenure and tenured faculty, is responsible for maintaining the *Library Faculty Guidelines* (Appalachian State University, 2022b).

On the recommendation of the DPC, a subgroup was formed to create a diversity statement rubric for faculty searches and formulate more explicit language for the job description around what was expected of applicants in providing a diversity statement. In addition to three volunteer members from the DPC (including one who was on the aforementioned faculty search committee), the subgroup also included the associate dean, representing library administration, as well as one of the co-chairs for the library's Inclusion, Diversity, Equity, and Accessibility Committee to help provide a DEI perspective. The rubric from the previous search would be used as a base model.

The subgroup met three times across a one-month period. At this time, the University Libraries were preparing to engage in numerous faculty searches with one search already actively developing its job description. These searches presented an opportunity for the subgroup to not only revise the diversity statement rubric for wider implementation, but also actively work it into the search process.

The subgroup built on the prior search's diversity statement rubric in several ways. First, the rubric was expanded to review the statement through three lenses: understanding of DEI, commitment to DEI, and furthering Appalachian State University's commitment to DEI. The prior rubric primarily focused on the third lens, what efforts or ideas applicants had for promoting or engaging in DEI efforts. We wanted to expand it to help capture different levels applicants might be at in terms of DEI understanding and commitment in more nuanced ways. For example, a new graduate in the field might have an expansive understanding of DEI and ideas for promoting it but might not have had the time or opportunities to engage in much DEI work. They could still score relatively high even while bringing minimal experience.

Second, the focus on new graduates also informed other conversations around the rubric, particularly in the language used. References to "research, service, and teaching" are usually associated with faculty-level positions and expectations. This language was rewritten to include "work, service, research, and/or coursework" to capture examples a new graduate as well as someone coming from a nonfaculty position might bring to their statement. Furthermore, the group incorporated additional language around evidence involved in educating oneself on DEI issues, while softening areas that were asking for evidence of experience. We read through the rubric with a new graduate in mind, considering what their diversity statement might look like.

Finally, the subgroup developed language for the prompt for the job description. Prior job descriptions required applicants to submit a "statement on diversity" as part of their application package. Under this vague prompt, statements ranged in length, content, and consideration, making them difficult to evaluate and relying more on search committee members' subjective analysis. As mentioned above, these statements were also more or less supplemental in nature to the overall evaluation. Now that our processes were evolving to consider the diversity statements as a separate part of the job application, we wanted to be clearer in our expectations of applicants. The new prompt for the Statement of Diversity Values in Librarianship includes specific instructions for applicants, including page length, asking for details addressing how their "coursework, professional work, service, and/or scholarship" supports DEI and offering an opportunity to new graduates and those without much experience. Here is the prompt the subgroup created:

> Statement of Diversity Values in Librarianship: Please provide a written statement (no more than one page) detailing how your coursework, professional work, service, and/or scholarship has supported the fundamental values of diversity, equity, and inclusion. Applicants who have not yet had the opportunity for such experience should note how their work will further the Appalachian State University's commitment to diversity, equity, and inclusion. Learn more at http://diversity.appstate.edu.

The subgroup hoped that this new in-depth prompt would result in stronger diversity statements that didn't vary as widely as those statements the library received previously. For a look at the full rubric, see Appendix C.

# Lessons Learned

Through our conversations, we were able to identify specific steps we can take to continue to improve the diversity statement prompt, the diversity statement rubric, and their implementation. One important lesson learned is the need for clearer language in the diversity statement prompt. For example, consider this sentence: "Applicants who have not yet had the opportunity for such experience should note how their work will further the Appalachian State University's commitment to diversity, equity, and inclusion." This language seems to imply that only those applicants with no opportunities or experience need to speak about how they would further Appalachian State University's commitment to DEI. As a result, with inconsistencies in how the prompt was interpreted, there was difficulty in evaluating statements in which applicants did not address any future plans or ideas.

Another critical lesson is the necessity to bring the entire library on board with the intended goals of the diversity statement rubric as well as clearly communicate the specific desired outcomes of using the rubric. Given the conflicting opinions on the use of diversity statement prompts and rubrics in the literature as well as the general professional librarian community, it makes sense to be transparent about the University Libraries' work and explain the literature and case studies that have shaped decision-making.

# Moving Forward

In retrospect, it would have been helpful to pilot the library-wide rubric on a number of sample diversity statements before implementation in order to test for efficacy. The University Libraries' goal was to have the diversity statement rubric highlight applicants who articulated and provided evidence of their demonstrated commitment to and experience within the areas of DEI. In addition, the use of the diversity statement rubric would be a valuable tool that search committees could use to identify the skills, interests, and expertise applicants might bring to the organization. With consideration of our shared experience developing and implementing a rubric as well as what is currently known from an examination of the literature, the authors recommend the following for anyone who wants to move this type of work forward.

One step forward is to consider the training and documentation that must be developed to outline and guide the use of a rubric. Some of the literature consulted identified the issue that statement assessment is most likely to fail when evaluators are not given clear instructions on how the statements are to be evaluated. Providing clear instructions and guidance could help decrease the likelihood of this happening. Another step forward is to work with library administration to prioritize and support the work with both resources and formally communicated commitment. The University Libraries' grassroots work with the prompt and rubric began to shift to a more administrative level of support, and there were clear benefits. Administrative support has a certain weight, and without it, library employees may not collectively prioritize this work or may see it as optional. The hope is that this type of support could make the important work part of the library's system of priorities and not dependent only upon the interest of select individuals. The authors of this chapter realize the importance of describing how, specifically, the library defines diversity and commitment to DEI. Without specific definitions, the work is limited in how it can move forward, and a library should develop a system of definitions that can be used to support and evaluate progress. An important question is, "What does success look like?"

# Conclusion

We are committed to continuing our efforts to review and revise this process with the goal of developing a rubric that can move us forward by allowing applicants to share their contributions in the areas of DEI. We will continue to build consensus on when and how the diversity statement prompt and rubric will be used. This process takes time, and in hindsight, we should have been more thoughtful about this process, gathered wider input from faculty, and taken more time to discuss these tools and get agreement about how it would contribute to moving the libraries DEI efforts forward in the hiring process. We also need to develop clarity on how the rubric will be used in evaluating applicants, specifically how to implement a process for norming the rubric (i.e., to facilitate understanding of its use) and scoring of applicants (i.e., to facilitate consistency within the search committees). The work of Sylvester et al. (2019) on creating a diversity statement framework provides an excellent pathway for thinking about how applicants can share their contributions in specific and meaningful ways:

> (a) conceptualize diversity/DEI commitments as part of the intellectual work of faculty, entailing the DEI-relevant knowledge, skills, competencies that individuals would use in their faculty roles, rather than simply identity membership or ideological beliefs; (b) explicitly articulate this definition to prospective applicants; and (c) provide prospective applicants with guidance around this definition, including examples that reflect the diverse ways that faculty might demonstrate their commitments to DEI.

This experience has helped us realize the importance of examining what we have done in the past as a way to inform our work in the future. The authors feel we have learned so much in the process of creating and implementing a diversity statement rubric. This experience, although not perfect, has been an instrumental step in moving our University Libraries' DEI efforts forward. Our continuing goal is to support applicants' ability to demonstrate their commitment to DEI throughout the search process.

# Addendum

Since the writing of this chapter, the political landscape has shifted in North Carolina. In February 2023, the University of North Carolina System Board of Governors approved the addition of a "Prohibition on Compelling Speech" section under "Political Activities of Employees" to the policy manual. The "Prohibition on Compelling Speech" states

> To mitigate the risk of compelled speech that undermines the intellectual freedom and fostering of free expression … the University shall neither solicit nor require an employee or applicant for academic admission or employment to affirmatively ascribe to or opine about beliefs, affiliations, ideals, or principles regarding matters of contemporary political debate or social action as a condition to admission, employment, or professional advancement. (University of North Carolina System, 2023, II.5)

Therefore, as employees of the University of North Carolina System, the authors are no longer able to legally move forward with this work at this time. However, the authors believe that people at other institutions will still find value in the work we have been able to accomplish.

# APPENDIX A

# Rubrics for Minimum Qualifications and Other Areas of Interest

## Instructions for Evaluating the Minimum Qualifications and Other Areas of Interest Using the Rubric Below

The following rubric is designed to evaluate applicants' minimum qualifications based on demonstrated commitment to diversity, equity, and inclusion **and** other areas of interest based on demonstrated commitment and experience within the areas of diversity, equity, and inclusion.

- Evaluate minimum qualifications using the rubric below.
- Add the total rating to the **minimum qualifications** portion of the rubric provided by Library Human Resources.

| | **Demonstrated Commitment to Diversity, Equity, and Inclusion** |
|---|---|
| 1 | • Uses vague terms to describe diversity without indicating an awareness or understanding of challenges underrepresented individuals in higher education face and the factors influencing underrepresentation of particular groups in academia, or<br>• No indication of efforts to educate self about diversity topics in higher education, or<br>• Discounts the importance of diversity and/or seems to be unaware of the challenges that underrepresented individuals face in academia. |
| 2 | • Uses terms to describe diversity <u>with some</u> awareness or understanding of challenges underrepresented individuals in higher education face and the factors influencing underrepresentation of particular groups in academia, or<br>• Some evidence of efforts to educate self about diversity topics in higher education, such as attending workshops, webinars, classes, etc., or<br>• Demonstrates some knowledge of the importance of diversity, equity, and inclusion and/or some awareness of the challenges that underrepresented individuals face in academia. |

| **Demonstrated Commitment to Diversity, Equity, and Inclusion** ||
|---|---|
| 3 | • Understands and is knowledgeable of diversity, equity, and inclusion within the social, cultural, and historical contexts of higher education and recognizes the obstacles people from these backgrounds face from systemic barriers, or<br>• Evidence of continuous efforts and initiative to educate self about diversity topics in higher education, or<br>• Addresses why it's important for faculty to contribute to meeting the above challenges. |

- Evaluate other areas of interest using the rubric below.
- Add the total rating to the **other areas of interest** portion of the rubric provided by Sujata Paudel.

| **Demonstrated Commitment and Experience within the Areas of Diversity, Equity, and Inclusion** ||
|---|---|
| 1 | • No acknowledgment of the need to engage in diversity, equity, and inclusion initiatives, or<br>• Descriptions of diversity, equity, and inclusion efforts are brief or vague. |
| 2 | • Some acknowledgment of the need to engage in diversity, equity, and inclusion initiatives but has vague ideas on how to engage, or<br>• Demonstrates some experience, and if none, demonstrates some understanding of addressing diversity, equity, and inclusion through work, service, research, and/or coursework, or<br>• May have participated peripherally in efforts promoting diversity, equity, and inclusion. |
| 3 | • Clear acknowledgment of the need to engage and ideas on how to engage in diversity, equity, and inclusion initiatives, or<br>• Significant direct experience advancing diversity, equity and inclusion through teaching, service, research, and/or coursework, or<br>• Commitment over time and consistently working toward advancing diversity, equity, and inclusion, or<br>• Led an effort around diversity, equity, and inclusion. |

## APPENDIX B

# Diversity Statement Rubric from 2021 Tenure-Track Faculty Librarian Search

| | **Diversity Statement** |
|---|---|
| 1 | • Unclear what unique efforts the candidate would undertake at Appalachian. Merely says they would do what is asked, if hired.<br>• May have participated peripherally in efforts promoting diversity, equity, and inclusion. |
| 2 | • Plans are vague without mentioning objectives, expected outcomes, specific tasks. |
| 3 | • Details plans to promote diversity, equity and inclusion through research, service, and teaching at Appalachian and within their department and/or campus-wide.<br>• References ongoing efforts at Appalachian and ways to improve and modify them to advance diversity, equity and inclusion.<br>• Describes participation in initiatives that promote diversity, equity, and inclusion. |

## APPENDIX C

# Library-wide Diversity Statement Rubric

## The Diversity Statement for Inclusion in the Job Ad as a Supplemental Document

Statement of Diversity Values in Librarianship: Please provide a written statement (no more than one page) detailing how your coursework, professional work, service, and/or scholarship has supported the fundamental values of diversity, equity, and inclusion. Applicants who have not yet had the opportunity for such experience should note how their work will further Appalachian State University's commitment to diversity, equity, and inclusion. Learn more at http://diversity.appstate.edu.

## Instructions for Evaluating the Diversity Statement, Using the Rubric Below

The following rubric is designed to evaluate applicants' diversity statements based on understanding and commitment to diversity, equity, and inclusion and how they would further Appalachian State University's commitment.

Read the diversity statement.

Evaluate the diversity statement by giving points for where the statement falls within each category. A strong diversity statement need not include contributions in every area, but must demonstrate a substantive commitment to diversity, equity, and inclusion in one or more of these areas.

Add the total rating to the **required qualification** portion of the rubric provided by Library Human Resources.

| Understanding of Diversity, Equity, and Inclusion | |
|---|---|
| 1 | • Uses vague terms to describe diversity without indicating an awareness or understanding of challenges underrepresented individuals in higher education face and the factors influencing underrepresentation of particular groups in academia, or<br>• No indication of efforts to educate self about diversity topics in higher education, or<br>• Discounts the importance of diversity and/or seems to be unaware of the challenges that underrepresented individuals face in academia. |

Discussing, Understanding, and Assessing    69

| 2 | • Uses terms to describe diversity <u>with some</u> awareness or understanding of challenges underrepresented individuals in higher education face and the factors influencing underrepresentation of particular groups in academia, or<br>• Some evidence of efforts to educate self about diversity topics in higher education, such as attending workshops, webinars, classes, etc., or<br>• Demonstrates some knowledge of the importance of diversity, equity, and inclusion and/or some awareness of the challenges that underrepresented individuals face in academia. |
|---|---|
| 3 | • Understands and is knowledgeable of diversity, equity, and inclusion within the social, cultural, and historical contexts of higher education and recognizes the obstacles people from these backgrounds face from systemic barriers, or<br>• Evidence of continuous efforts and initiative to educate self about diversity topics in higher education, or<br>• Addresses why it's important for faculty to contribute to meeting the above challenges. |

| **Commitment to Advancing Diversity, Equity, and Inclusion** ||
|---|---|
| 1 | • No acknowledgment of the need to engage in diversity, equity, and inclusion initiatives, or<br>• Descriptions of diversity, equity, and inclusion efforts are brief or vague. |
| 2 | • Some acknowledgment of the need to engage in diversity, equity, and inclusion initiatives but has vague ideas on how to engage, or<br>• Demonstrates some experience, and if none, demonstrates some understanding of addressing diversity, equity, and inclusion through work, service, research, and/or coursework, or<br>• May have participated peripherally in efforts promoting diversity, equity, and inclusion. |
| 3 | • Clear acknowledgment of the need to engage and ideas on how to engage in diversity, equity, and inclusion initiatives, or<br>• Significant direct experience advancing diversity, equity and inclusion through teaching, service, research, and/or coursework, or<br>• Commitment over time and consistently working toward advancing diversity, equity, and inclusion, or<br>• Led an effort around diversity, equity, and inclusion. |

| **Furthering Appalachian State University's Commitment to Diversity, Equity, and Inclusion** ||
|---|---|
| 1 | • Unclear what unique efforts the candidate would undertake at Appalachian. Merely says they would do what is asked, if hired, or<br>• Provides no plan on how they would further Appalachian State University's commitment to diversity, equity, and inclusion. |

| | Furthering Appalachian State University's Commitment to Diversity, Equity, and Inclusion |
|---|---|
| 2 | • Plans are vague and general without addressing specifics or concrete details, or<br>• Indicates interest in participating in efforts already underway but no ideas how to add to the effort. |
| 3 | • Provides multiple ideas on how to further diversity, equity and inclusion at Appalachian, or<br>• References ongoing efforts at Appalachian and ways to improve and modify them to advance diversity, equity and inclusion. |

# References

Appalachian State University. (2022a). *Faculty profile* [Statistical dashboard]. Office of Institutional Research, Assessment and Planning. https://analytics.appstate.edu/dash_fac_prof_public

Appalachian State University. (2022b). *Appalachian State University strategic plan 2022–2027: Empowering human potential through the Appalachian experience.* https://www.appstate.edu/about/strategic-plan/

Appalachian State University Libraries. (2022a). *University libraries' strategic plan, 2022–2027.* https://library.appstate.edu/sites/default/files/strategic_plan_2022-27.pdf

Appalachian State University Libraries. (2022b). *Library faculty guidelines.* https://library.appstate.edu/sites/default/files/library_faculty_guidelines_2022_09_30.pdf

Bombaci, S. P., & Pejchar, L. (2022). Advancing equity in faculty hiring with diversity statements. *BioScience, 72*(4), 365–371.

Brandeis University Diversity, Equity, and Inclusion. (n.d.). *Rubric for evaluating diversity statements.* https://www.brandeis.edu/diversity/dei-recruitment-hiring/rubric-for-evaluating-diversity-statements.html

Brown Office of Institutional Equity and Diversity (n.d.). *Diversity statements and evaluation rubrics.* Brown University. https://www.brown.edu/about/administration/institutional-diversity/sites/oidi/files/Diversity%20Statement%20and%20Evaluation%20Rubrics.pdf

Cornell University Office of Faculty Development and Diversity. (n.d.). *Rubric assessing candidate on diversity, equity and inclusion.* https://web.archive.org/web/20220813231755/https://facultydevelopment.cornell.edu/rubric-assessing-candidate-on-diversity-equity-and-inclusion/

Goulden, M., Stacy, A., Frasch, K., & Broughton, J. (2019). Searching for a diverse faculty: What really works. *Peer Review, 21*(4), 28–34.

Guilford, Meg. K [@mkguliford]. (2022, Feb. 6). I'm just gonna step out on this ledge and argue that DEI/ diversity statements are nothing more than mechanisms for [Tweet]. Twitter. https://twitter.com/mkguliford/status/1490427724116152324?s=11

Schmaling, K. B., Trevino, A. Y., Lind, J. R., Blume, A. W., & Baker, D. L. (2015). Diversity statements: How faculty applicants address diversity. *Journal of Diversity in Higher Education, 8*(4), 213–224.

Special Collections Research Center. (n.d.). *Timelines.* Appalachian State University. https://collections.library.appstate.edu/collections/university-archives-records-management-services/timelines

Sylvester, C-Y. C, Sánchez-Parkinson, L., Yettaw, M., & Chavous, T. (2019). The promise of diversity statements: Insights and an initial framework developed from a faculty search process. *NCID Currents, 1*(1). https://doi.org/10.3998/currents.17387731.0001.112

University of Michigan Center for Research on Learning and Teaching. (2017). *Diversity statement evaluation rubric.* https://sites.lsa.umich.edu/nextprof-science/wp-content/uploads/sites/130/2020/04/Diversity-Statement-Rubric.pdf

University of North Carolina System. (2023, February). Political activity of employees. In *The UNC Policy Manual,* 300.5.1. https://www.northcarolina.edu/apps/policy/doc.php?id=125

# Part 2
# REMOVING BARRIERS FOR CANDIDATES

CHAPTER 6

# Ensuring Empathy in Interviewing through Open Communication

*Gail Betz, Hilary Kraus, and Amy Tureen*

The academic interview process can leave a lot of room for candidate uncertainty, resulting in hiring experiences that are neither compassionate nor humane. Applicants are often left asking themselves a multitude of questions: What will the search committee want to know about my work? Where will the interview be held? What will meals look like and who will they be with? How are applicants evaluated? What does "professional dress" mean in this organization? Is this a city, state, or country I can thrive in? These questions are both important and common, but the answers tend to be in short supply.

In some instances, organizations have simply not taken the time to review and reflect on their processes. In others, they may be actively committed to providing limited information, believing that this allows candidates to demonstrate their research, deduction, and extemporaneous speaking skills. Both approaches, however, risk creating less equitable experiences for applicants from marginalized and historically decentered groups (Liera & Hernandez, 2021; White-Lewis, 2019). This is due to both the hidden privileges obscured by the invisible knapsack effect (McIntosh, 1989) and a tendency to avoid interrogating which individuals and identities benefit from so-called "professional norms" while simultaneously failing to compare said norms against identified best practices (Liera & Hernandez, 2021; White-Lewis, 2019).

By centering transparency, communication, caring, and empathy in their interview processes, organizations can avoid unnecessary distress for candidates. This approach may allow candidates who are not selected to exit the interview process with positive feelings for the organization, potentially prompting them to apply for additional opportunities in the future or recommend the organization to friends and colleagues. Successful candidates are provided with early insights into organizational values and expectations, enabling easier and more effective integration into the culture and organization during and beyond onboarding.

# External Communication in the Empathetic Interview Process

The academic library hiring process follows a fairly traditional structure: post job → receive applications → review applications → interview by phone → interview in person → hire. Generally speaking, this structure provides candidates with very little insight into the organization beyond an abbreviated job description, a federally mandated diversity statement, and a first review date. This bureaucratic approach can be challenging for libraries to combat, primarily because many of the requirements and limitations of a job ad are set by campus-level human resources departments. As a result, libraries sometimes have limited flexibility in crafting more informative and welcoming job ad templates or establishing a more person-focused early-stage hiring process. However, all is not lost! Once library hiring committees complete their paper review and begin inviting candidates to first-round interviews, they have the opportunity to engage in a number of strategies to make the candidate experience more humane, all of which are rooted in a central theme of proactively engaging in a high level of communication between the candidate and the hiring library. Despite working at very different institutions in very different parts of the United States, we have collectively found that taking a proactive approach to communication when hiring is essential. Doing so both reduces the perception of bureaucratic indifference and directly seeks to challenge the inherent power differential that is a hallmark of a place wherein all information and decision-making power are held exclusively by the hiring institution. By providing clear, ready, and substantial information to candidates, hiring committees can make the process a more balanced relationship in which both the institution and the candidate are mutually assessing one another for compatibility.

# The Screening Stage

After reviewing all submitted application documents, search committees generally reach out to a relatively small subset of highly qualified candidates for screening interviews, which typically take place by phone or in video meetings. The screening interview itself is the first time most candidates are introduced to the human element of a hiring organization, rather than the bureaucracy they encountered when submitting their application packet. This can be disorienting and tends to throw the power imbalance of the traditional interview process into relief. However, organizations can use proactive communication processes to make it less overwhelming. For example, sharing the names, pronunciation of said names, pronouns, short bios, professional roles, and even photos of search committee members ensures candidates are aware of who they will be meeting and provides some insight into perspectives the interviewers may bring to the table. Similarly, providing detailed logistics for the interview, such as the exact time and time zone from which the committee will be calling, how long the interview will last, and how much time is set aside for candidate questions helps them know what to expect. If the screening interview has a video component, providing candidates with explicit instructions regarding having their camera on or off allows candidates to consider their surroundings and attire and make intentional choices. Even something as simple as sharing the phone number that will be used by the search committee so candidates can be sure their phone doesn't block it as an unknown number will help to make the process smoother and reduce unnecessary stress on the candidate.

Perhaps the most contentious issue regarding transparency in the interview process is the decision to provide or not provide interview questions in advance. Institutional policies differ widely, and anecdotal preferences, sometimes reframed as supposed best practices, run the gamut of perspectives on this topic. Some individuals feel that it's important to see how candidates think on their feet when answering unexpected questions. Others worry that providing questions may cause candidates to overprepare, potentially even writing out responses in advance and simply reading them aloud. (There is yet another robust and contentious argument about the validity of written answers versus memorized or extemporaneous ones, which we will not assess in this chapter.) Given these disagreements, it seems unlikely that a profession-wide consensus will be reached anytime soon.

The authors, as both candidates and hiring committee members, have experienced far more positive than negative outcomes from sharing questions prior to the interview. When candidates don't have to prepare for any of dozens of potential questions, they can focus on planning more substantive, informative, and detailed answers to the questions they do expect. Providing questions in advance also improves the experience for candidates who need more time for cognitive processing or who process written information more quickly and effectively than verbal. All of the authors have had candidates explicitly state that they felt a significant reduction in anxiety when they knew the questions prior to the interview. While candidates who have documented disabilities and know how to self-advocate effectively may feel empowered to ask for this as an individualized accommodation, many candidates don't feel comfortable disclosing or don't know what they can ask for. Providing questions in advance to all candidates improves transparency for everyone and moves us closer to a truly equitable search process.

When facing resistance to providing interview questions in advance, either in a specific hiring committee or across an entire organization more broadly, encourage colleagues who oppose to consider their motivations for *not* providing the questions in advance. Oftentimes the desire to require exclusively extemporaneous answers is rooted in deficit thinking, with the hiring committee shifting from a role in which they seek to determine how a given candidate might meet the needs of the organization to a role where they are actively seeking weaknesses, testing for limitations, and attempting to identify reasons they should not hire the candidate. This orientation is not beneficial to either the candidate or the organization and communicates an unspoken belief that people cannot grow and learn. Avoid disingenuous claims that extemporaneous interviews indicate a capacity for teaching or, in one rather memorable search committee discussion, giving ad hoc elevator speeches to faculty members. This correlation is simply not true, and not only because both lesson plans and elevator speeches are created in advance and then refined over time and repeated use. If it is important to your organization for candidates to think on their feet, consider asking a single extemporaneous question at a later interview stage and always adjust the assessment rubric to accommodate an answer that will not be thought out and will necessarily be largely context-free.

# The On-Campus Interview

Prior to the COVID-19 pandemic, the vast majority of second-round academic library interviews took place in person at the hiring institution's campus. During much of 2020 and 2021, many interviews shifted 100 percent online, an approach that reduced interview-related expenses and made the hiring process more equitable in a number of ways. Frustratingly, only a few organizations continue to offer fully virtual interviews now that widespread travel restrictions have been replaced with recommendation-only policy. Instead, universities appear to be retrenching in traditional models and requiring in-person second-round interviews now that city, state, and federal policy permits it. As a result, this section assumes an in-person interview, although some of the concepts are equally applicable to virtual interviews.

Scheduling an on-campus interview means making a greater commitment to candidates, and therefore requires a greater commitment to information sharing and transparency. Consider what details are not in your job posting but would benefit applicants who are deciding whether to accept an interview invitation. Following are some suggestions of information to consider providing to on-campus candidates.

Did you include the salary range in your job posting? If not, now is the time to share it, as well as information about benefits so candidates for whom those are insufficient can gracefully exit the process without further waste of time or ultimately unnecessary travel expenditures. The institution gains nothing by playing coy and dedicating financial and personnel resources to interview a candidate who will ultimately decline the position based on information that could easily have been provided in advance. Candidates who decline employment based on benefits or salaries that do not meet their needs will appreciate and may recommend an institution that is mindful about not wasting their time, money, or other resources. Candidates who face a nasty last-minute shock, on the other hand, are far less likely to speak well of the organization or recommend it to others.

Beyond just salary and benefits, consider what candidates may want to know about your library, institution, and region as they're debating accepting an interview invitation. Do you have a union? If so, share the contract. Would the candidate be relocating? Provide information about housing options, local communities, schools, and other things related to living in the area. This is also a good opportunity to provide information about campus-wide affinity spaces or communities so that candidates coming from marginalized backgrounds get a sense of the culture they could be a part of. Sharing links to websites about formal or informal identity-based groups allows candidates to self-select if they are a member of any marginalized groups without disclosing to the search committee or forcing the search committee to guess if that information is useful. Candidates can then use that information to learn more about resources or events, as well as reaching out to folks on campus who might have similar lived experiences.

While seasoned candidates can typically guess at and prepare for industry standard aspects of an on-campus interview, there are often unspoken cultural or institutional norms that they cannot be expected to guess. Do you have expectations for appropriate standards of dress or other conduct during the interview or associated meals? If so, be explicit ahead of time. This could be as simple as noting that casual dress (including jeans and athletic shoes) is fine for the interview dinner, but business attire is preferred for the day of the interview. That said, this is another opportunity to consider the value and relevance of the information you'll be sharing in advance. Are these expectations necessary? Do they unfairly impact certain groups? For example, candidates with mobility or sensory disabilities may need to dress in a specific way to be comfortable in a day-long interview. Other candidates may have limited funds to procure formal business attire, particularly if you aren't able to cover travel expenses for them in advance. Is your organization truly willing to pass over a qualified candidate who elects to present themselves in a way not common at your workplace? Consider what these newly articulated but previously unspoken expectations contribute to your decision-making process when selecting a future employee. If they aren't necessary, don't judge candidates on these factors at all. If some of them are, share those expectations in advance so the candidate is aware of the organizational values and can adapt to meet them.

Think proactively about logistics for on-campus interviews. Candidates may be traveling long distances to participate, taking time off work, and potentially incurring up-front costs. If your institution can cover any travel expenses in advance, make candidates aware of the degree to which this is possible; if any costs must be paid by the candidate, make sure they know the procedure for requesting reimbursement and how long they can expect it to take. Seriously consider providing funds to support costs associated with the interview that are not immediately evident, such as providing reimbursement of pet boarding or childcare costs. As a rule, candidates should also have the mobile numbers of members of the search committee who will be providing local transportation and travel support, such as picking them up at the airport or driving them to dinner. Whenever possible, adjust the interview schedule for time differences. This may mean starting or ending an interview slightly earlier or later to accommodate a candidate's home time zone or offering a candidate an additional optional night's accommodation to enable them to adapt to the local time zone.

# Dietary and Accessibility Considerations during the On-Campus Interview

Any on-campus interview involves several meals or snacks, sometimes including a dinner with library employees. Since candidates may not feel comfortable disclosing food allergies, sensitivities, and preferences, the person arranging these should reach out and ask the candidate about their needs. Consider offering menus and websites from a few local restaurants and letting the candidate choose. Menus allow candidates to make informed decisions on food preferences and requirements; providing restaurant websites allows candidates to look for pictures of the space and accessibility information without disclosing that need to their dining companions. If your campus is in a historic part of town, it is common that local businesses in charming buildings are not fully accessible for candidates with disabilities.

The more detailed the information provided, the better candidates can prepare for the upcoming interview. An itinerary for the entire interview should be created and shared well in advance. This should include the stakeholders attending each segment, their roles, and what the purpose of the meeting or event will be. Breaks should be included throughout the day where the candidate is given the opportunity to be alone, and a dedicated space should be provided for that purpose. The number of breaks, when they are scheduled, and how long they are should be communicated to candidates in advance so they can plan appropriately. Many candidates need breaks to tend to personal needs that they may not feel comfortable disclosing, such as taking medications, stretching, meditating, or checking in with family members they care for.

It's also important to consider if there is flexibility within the schedule to allow candidates to meet with select campus constituencies. Offer them those options by identifying potential groups while also asking them whether there are others you haven't considered. Provide the same opportunities to all candidates, regardless of which you think might be of interest. Meeting with different groups on campus, whether affinity groups, committees, or other departments the candidate will work with, can present specific issues for physical accessibility. Many academic campuses are spread out, often with architectural components that are not conducive to seamless accessibility for candidates with mobility issues, and some are located in regions with weather extremes that may have negative effects on candidate health. Even if the on-campus interview does not include moving from one building to another, there is typically a tour component to show the library space itself to the candidate. While it's important that the candidate understand the space they will be working within, it's also critical that information about the accessibility of the space be provided to the candidate in advance so they can make informed decisions about how they want to move through the building. Including information about stairs and elevators, accessible restrooms, office spaces, and any other unique features in the building before beginning the tour and asking the candidate how they would like to proceed provides both autonomy and safety for candidates without forcing anyone to disclose personal information.

# The Presentation

One element of many academic library interviews is the presentation. Before you assign one, consider why. Is it essential to your evaluation of candidates? What is the presentation intended to reveal, and is this an efficient way to surface that information? If the answer to either of these questions is no, is there a better alternative? In some cases, such as hiring an instruction librarian, search committees and other stakeholders may feel that a presentation, often taking the form of a sample class, is important to the decision-making process. Applicants for department heads, division heads, and dean roles may be asked to present their vision for their unit or the library. In all cases, provide the prompt well in advance of the interview and give the candidate all the information they need to perform well. For example, in a sample class, share the syllabus and assignment details, as well as the likely characteristics of the hypothetical student participants. In a vision presentation, provide candidates with resources they can use to create a vision that is applicable to your organization. This may mean providing access to statistics, current and past strategic goal information, or survey results that are applicable to the division, department, or service under consideration.

Remember to give candidates any resources they may need, such as logins to your library databases and information about the physical layout of the space. Ask if there are materials they would like to use that you can provide, such as a rolling whiteboard or document camera. Most of all, be explicit about what you hope to learn from their presentation. Do you want to know if they can clearly communicate at a level appropriate to a particular group of students? Are you looking for a demonstration of active learning? Are you hoping to see they know how to identify service gaps or ideate new solutions to a persistent problem unique to your organization? Ask candidates to focus on whatever is essential to your decision-making process. Failing to tell a candidate what you are looking for and then penalizing them for not meeting your unspoken expectations is unethical. Similarly, if you know that certain answers won't be acceptable to the organization, such as closing a service desk or reducing hours, share this information with the candidate so they can avoid stepping into an unseen bear trap. Consider asking candidates to reflect on their process during the planning and execution of the presentation; this may provide as much, if not more, insight into the candidate than the presentation itself.

A number of accessibility issues can arise during presentations for both the candidates and the audience. From the candidate's perspective, having prior knowledge of the physical space and equipment they will have access to gives them the opportunity to prepare accordingly or ask for modifications to the space. Clarity in the prompt, as well as the rationale behind the presentation, reduces anxiety and allows candidates to focus on the most important aspects of the content, rather than worrying about slide design or other extraneous aspects that can be distracting. Ensuring that the candidates have access to microphones so the audience can hear clearly, and that microphones are passed around during questions so the candidates can hear clearly, is helpful. If there are folks in the audience who need accommodations to actively participate in assessing the presentation, ensure that candidates are aware of what those accommodations are without disclosing who needs them or why. When assessing a presentation, disregard commentary around a candidate's tone, how much they moved around the physical space, or any other social behaviors that have no bearing on a candidate's ability to teach, collaborate, lead, plan, and so on.

# Internal Communication and Candidate Evaluations in the Empathetic Interview Process

Hiring committees are responsible for both internal and external communication regarding candidates under consideration. This includes communication to and within the search committee itself as well as to other internal stakeholders who may play a role in candidate assessment and selection. Search committees should clearly identify what skill sets and abilities they are seeking, as well as, if necessary, the rank order priority of those traits. This approach both functions as a form of nominal norming and encourages candidate assessors to focus on specifics, rather than form a general opinion that may be far more subjective than objective. It is critical to be explicit about the importance of objectivity during all searches, even searches that occur back-to-back or overlap.

For example, if a candidate is giving a sample instruction session for their presentation, tell attendees in advance what you're looking for (e.g., the ability to communicate clearly, identifying learning objectives, managing a question-and-answer session). Avoid nebulous qualities like professionalism or presentation style, and never include qualities that invite reviewers to assess a candidate's accent, speaking style, dress sense, or other personal details. Remind stakeholders in assessment roles of these priorities both the day each candidate arrives and at the time that formal assessment feedback is requested. Seriously consider providing stakeholders with a structured note-taking document for presentations and for both small and large group meetings. These documents should prompt stakeholders to assess candidates on specific points and include examples of the ways the prioritized qualifications may manifest. It is not necessary to collect these documents after each candidate session; instead, they should be used as reference materials for stakeholders to provide reflective feedback after the conclusion of the candidate interview. Consider requiring all feedback providers to disclose their name upon submission of their feedback, particularly at organizations that struggle with anonymity being used as cover to make inappropriate or unprofessional remarks.

Rubrics should be used by the search committee at all phases of candidate assessment and should exclusively assess either qualifications named in the initial job ad or responses to the preestablished questions. Assessing traits and skills not identified in the job ad both is acting in bad faith and vastly expands the risk of personal bias. This does not mean the candidates cannot be asked questions extemporaneously, but their responses should either not be assessed via rubric or be assessed in the context of a stated job requirement. Before using a rubric, the hiring committee should assess the rubric itself and work together to identify what a low-scoring, midrange-scoring, and high-scoring answer or evidence of skill might be. Where committees are unable to do this, the question or qualification should be either rethought or scrapped.

Candidate assessment should also take into account traits and skill sets that are changeable or correctable. For example, downgrading a candidate for mispronouncing a word is inappropriate, as this can be corrected in the future with a brief conversation. Noting the differences in the amount of training two candidates will need to meet expectations in a specific example is reasonable, although candidate assessors should be encouraged to avoid editorializing these observations with their predictions regarding the amounts of time, effort, or resources required. Attempting to predict what aspects of a job a candidate will or will not enjoy based on their previous job experience, without explicitly asking the candidate, is also inappropriate. When early-career candidates are in the pool, assessors should be reminded that these individuals may have had fewer opportunities to perfect their answers, learn library jargon, or gain skills not traditionally taught in library and information science graduate programs, and, as a result, assessors should extend a measure of grace. If stakeholders provide feedback you feel is irrelevant or not helpful for your evaluation of the candidate, be prepared to disregard it.

Remind stakeholders that interview communication can and should go in both directions. Opportunities for the candidate to ask questions should be numerous and actively cultivated throughout the interview day. Candidates should be allowed to ask the same questions of several people; objecting to repeating an answer or otherwise indicating the candidate should have remembered a previous answer is wholly inappropriate. Additionally, remind stakeholders that they are expected to focus on what skills identified in the job ad the candidate can bring to the organization, not what they would personally like the incumbent to be able to do. Be sure to gather feedback promptly to avoid misremembering and creeping bias. The search committee should also be reminded to assess candidates based on the interviews themselves, rather than interactions extraneous to the search itself. Everyone likes to get a thank-you letter, but a candidate's decision to send one or not should not be a criterion upon which a new colleague is selected.

# Conclusions

Establishing interview processes that center candidates' experiences and prioritize individuals' humanity is highly reliant on expanding our communication practices both with candidates themselves and among those tasked with identifying and assessing skilled candidates. Those interested in creating more humane interview processes must come to the challenge willing to interrogate the unspoken assumptions of their organizational and industrial cultures, to differentiate between norms and best practices, and to commit far more time, energy, and resources to the hiring process than they likely historically have done. The process is inherently iterative, meaning individuals and organizations committed to this work must remain constantly vigilant to identify places and situations where more communication can make the interview process even more humane, compassionate, equitable, and just. Creating humane search workflows and experiences is not a goal that can be achieved in any final way but, rather, the ongoing practice of refinement as we collectively learn more about the vast diversity of needs, experiences, and available resources that impact the experience of academic library job searches for candidates, search committees, and hiring organizations. Ongoing communication is central to this endeavor and, in many ways, the very touchstone of iterative improvement.

# References

Liera, R., & Hernandez, T. E. (2021). Color-evasive racism in the final stage of faculty searches: Examining search committee hiring practices that jeopardize racial equity policy. *The Review of Higher Education*, 45(2), 181–209. https://doi.org/10.1353/rhe.2021.0020

McIntosh, P. (1989, July/August). White privilege: Unpacking the invisible knapsack. *Peace and Freedom Magazine*, 10–12.

White-Lewis, D. K. (2019). The facade of fit in faculty search processes. *The Journal of Higher Education*, 91(6), 833–857, https://doi.org/10.1080/00221546.2020.1775058

CHAPTER 7

# I Still Don't Fit

## How Academic Libraries Create Barriers in the Profession Before Hiring Even Takes Place

*Simone Williams*

# Introduction

While academic libraries have increasingly supported initiatives to make the hiring process more inclusive, they have failed to completely cultivate equitable workplaces. According to the US Bureau of Labor Statistics (2019), the library profession is largely homogeneous (white and female), and there has not been a significant demographic shift in the profession despite various initiatives to diversify the profession. This sobering data requires a more thorough examination of the structural processes that make hiring for diversity difficult rather than the current focus on recruiting for diversity as a solution to a perceived lack of diversity in the pipeline.

In this chapter, I will discuss how US academic libraries create barriers to equity and inclusion before recruitment takes place. This discussion will be strongly based on my own perspective as a Black woman working as an academic librarian and a combination of researched observations and ideas from personal and community experience. It must also be mentioned that this chapter aims to serve as a disruption in the discourse on more inclusive hiring practices, which is dominated by non-POC voices. Therefore, this chapter will focus heavily on increasing Black, Indigenous, and POC (BIPOC) representation in academic libraries. I argue that the library profession is inherently isolationist and rigidly hierarchical. Librarians and other library staff tend to network only within the profession and tend to hire those with advanced degrees or years of experience. These tendencies contribute to a lack of diversity in candidate pools. Academic libraries are even more entrenched in this rigidity since they are embedded in cultural institutions that represent the dominant culture and typically reinforce systemic inequalities (Evatt-Young & Bryson, 2021; Crist & Clark Keefe, 2022). This rigidity leads to a cycle of the profession remaining mostly white and female. Additionally, hiring based on having an advanced degree, or having experience, does not allow for early-stage recruitment (recruiting students as early as high school or promoting student workers and paraprofessionals to higher ranked positions). Libraries will continue to struggle with proactive and intentional recruitment if this career pipeline problem is not addressed. In this chapter, I will help identify pre-recruitment biases and recommend practical next steps to close the recruitment gap to make hiring practices more equitable.

# Current Hiring Advice and Trends

Over the past few years, the library profession has sought ways to make hiring practices more equitable and to keep pace with the rapid changes in libraries. The literature around hiring in academic libraries either critiques, analyzes, and advances discussions of hiring practices or focuses primarily on procedural best practices (Cunningham, Guss, & Stout, 2019). Both categories are important to study to better understand hiring practices related to diversity and equity in addition to understanding the current and future landscape of academic libraries. While employment for librarians and other library professionals is expected to grow, in recent years, hiring practices in library and information services (LIS), especially at the academic level, have remained practically unchanged (Eckard, Rosener, & Scripps-Hoekstra, 2014).

## More Competition

Not only are academic library positions highly competitive, but many of these positions require a master of library science (MLIS) degree and years of work experience (Tewell, 2012). Successful job candidates for these roles also typically have significant experience working in academic libraries, performing committee work, writing in scholarly publications, and attending professional conferences (Eckard, Rosener, & Scripps-Hoekstra, 2014). This competitiveness does not even take into account the extremely taxing interview process, which includes submitting extensive applications, undergoing interview prescreening, and undergoing multiple rounds of interviews.

## Globalized Profession

Additionally, the profession is becoming increasingly globalized and requires more specialized skills. There are too few librarians and library staff to meet the complex needs of a globalized community, especially in academic libraries (Luckhert & Carpenter, 2019; Burton, 2019). The library field is siloed not only between who it serves—public, academic, corporate—but also across cities, states, territories, and countries. Libraries across different countries and different systems are disconnected despite the perceived idea of interconnectedness of shared knowledge and culture due to globalization. To close this knowledge gap and create more interconnected libraries, libraries need a more diverse workforce to build and sustain a global network and to meet the growing demands of their respective communities. Ayinde and Kirkwood (2020) argue that jobs across sectors, including libraries, have to have workforces that are socially intelligent, transdisciplinary, and cross-culturally competent to compete in a globalized and technological world. Developing such a workforce would require libraries to be more cognizant of their hiring practices and aim to hire more BIPOC individuals since they represent the global majority. Therefore, more equitable hiring practices are needed to help build this globalized workforce, and barriers to entry in the profession need to be removed. Little of the literature in LIS, however, examines how to create more equitable hiring practices to increase the number of BlPOC employees.

## Equitable Hiring Practices of BIPOC Employees

In examining the LlS literature, one finds only a few key studies that emphasize diversity and equitable hiring practices related to BIPOC employees. Galvan (2015) argues that BIPOC employees have a barrier to entry into the profession because hiring practices in LIS are mostly performative and hiring for diversity when done in the context of whiteness is antithetical to equitable hiring practices and diversity. Whiteness in this sense is defined as "a set of relations that are historically, socially, politically, and culturally produced and intrinsically linked to dynamic relations of White racial domination" (Özlem & DiAngelo, 2017, pp. 560. These white or white-oriented institutions such as colleges, universities, and academic libraries reproduce white racial domination through their curriculum, policies, culture, and traditions (Özlem & DiAngelo, 2017). This white reproducibility extends to who these institutions hire. Galvan (2015) demonstrates that libraries hire for whiteness or aim to hire those who perform whiteness even if they identify as BIPOC since libraries serve to protect the status quo and attempt to be neutral (including race neutral). Therefore, by hiring for whiteness, a library decreases the likelihood of disrupting white power structures and can deflect claims of racialization.

Additionally, academic libraries hire for diversity not because they should, but only to increase or replace the number of BIPOC employees, which fails to address the systemic issues regarding the lack of diversity in LIS (Garnar, 2021). Libraries must also recognize that promotion of whiteness serves as a barrier to entry into the profession. The monoculturalism of academic libraries and academic institutions (mostly all white culturally or demographically) can serve as impediments for Black employees who have to deal with discrimination, racism, and acculturation (Brook et al., 2015). Therefore, even if libraries hire people who identify as BIPOC, those people can be subject to marginalization and isolation if they do not fit in with the organizational culture or model of whiteness (Cunningham, Guss, & Stout, 2019). BIPOC faculty often face questions by students, fellow faculty members, and the larger campus community about their legitimacy, especially their authority and credibility (Riley-Reid, 2017). This questioning can lead to BIPOC faculty feeling isolated and can ultimately contribute to lower job satisfaction and potentially greater attrition.

Cunningham, Guss, and Stout (2019) argue that too little literature focuses on how to recruit and retain BIPOC library professionals and that there has not been a thorough examination of this topic. What most library professionals know about recruiting or retaining BIPOC employees comes from a 2017 Association of Research Libraries SPEC kit survey (Anaya and Maxey-Harris, 2017), which is anecdotal and does not prove that libraries were devoted to equitable library practices since all survey respondents were library directors in the United States. Additionally, most of the respondents stated that they were simply working on strategies to create a more diverse workforce instead of implementing these strategies, again lending veracity to the idea that equitable hiring practices are performative. Cunningham, Guss, and Stout (2019) also demonstrate that when BIPOC employees are hired, they often express dissatisfaction with their positions due to racism, racialized microaggressions, and isolation. BIPOC employees also have the additional onus of dealing with cultural taxation after getting hired. Cultural taxation refers to the additional work that BIPOC employees often perform that is not remunerative but often expected of BIPOC university employees especially if they are the only BIPOC person or among only a few BIPOC individuals in their department or unit. This work includes being experts in diversity-related areas even if they are not and being asked to perform service work related to diversity or to mentor BIPOC students (Garnar, 2021).

Boddie et al. (2020) provide one of the most comprehensive recommendations for making academic library hiring practices more equitable and diverse. They propose some of the following: creating consistent and standardized hiring practices for diverse recruitment, minimizing the burden candidates carry, conducting ongoing and transparent assessments, and developing an inclusive culture and supporting the profession. While these suggestions are helpful, they are not exhaustive enough to address the widespread problems with increasing diversity and equitable hiring practices and, again, do not address the systemic issues impacting equitable hiring practices.

Thielen and Neeser (2020) demonstrate that academic libraries are attempting to create more equitable hiring practices by recruiting from outside of LIS by eliminating the use of the word *librarian* and accepting a degree equivalent to the MLIS. However, most job postings required an MLIS or even required an additional master's degree despite these efforts. Additionally, these postings required that applicants have skills related to tasks that academic librarians traditionally perform, so an actual outsider could not successfully apply for a position in an academic library. What this study illustrates is that attempts at inclusive hiring are marred by traditionalism and that academic libraries have not fully embraced candidate-centric hiring practices. Thielen and Neeser argue that by taking these steps LIS is opening the profession to more diverse talent and making it easier to incorporate elements of diversity, equity, inclusion, and accessibility principles into the hiring process. However, Thielen and Neeser's (2020) study is not representative of all library job postings because their research specifically focused on data professionals whose skills and experience are often outside the norm of the traditional library profession. Overall, many academic libraries use a formulaic approach when hiring, requiring the MLIS degree since it is the terminal degree for most academic librarians. Simpson (2013) argues that the "MLS has been the primary means through which the profession creates a unifying identity with a shared set of values and knowledge/skills." Therefore, hiring those without an MLS or MLIS remains controversial since many academic librarians believe there is this idea that non-MLIS or -MLS librarians demean or threaten the integrity of the profession or that librarians, especially at the academic level, do not require the same credentials as their colleagues in different departments or units.

Garnar (2021) provides some best practices for hiring BIPOC employees. Garnar argues one way to make academic hiring more appealing to prospective BIPOC employees is to create a pipeline to the profession that includes scholarships, paid internship opportunities, fellowships, and staff positions. This recruitment process should also provide transparency about the institutional culture, job expectations, and demographics of the library, institution, and surrounding community. Again, Garnar's work, while important, focuses mainly on retention and what employers can do retroactively after BIPOC employees are already hired. Although this is not explicitly stated in Garnar's work, creating or a fixing the pipeline to careers in LIS can be contextualized as treating BIPOC employees as a problem. The term *pipeline problem* has often been used as a duplicitous tactic to keep pools as nondiverse as possible because it puts the blame on the candidates for not having the requisite skills for a position rather than on hiring processes (Shufran, 2020).

# Practical Solutions

To make hiring practices more inclusive in LIS, especially of BIPOC academic librarians and staff, organizations can use several practical solutions to lessen the barriers before hiring and increase inclusivity. The first involves identifying the problem conditions that limit equitable hiring practices and a diverse workforce and filling in some of the gaps or advancing discussions of previous literature. As Ossom-Williamson et al. (2021) argue, libraries have espoused diversity and equity, but have failed to make any meaningful progress in these areas; libraries remain hostile environments for Black patrons and workers and have remained exclusive instead of inclusive. Ossom-Williamson et al. attribute this exclusivity to the continued "interplay of policy, cultural fit, and consolidation of power [that] allow simultaneous racist action and inaction" (p. 141). Shearer and Chiewphasa (2022) take their assessment of the lack of diversity further by arguing that incremental change in libraries cannot move the profession forward and examine what the profession would look like by reimagining inclusive hiring practices where libraries met their goals of recruiting BIPOC faculty and staff.

## Increasing the Hiring Pool

One of the primary causes for the lack of inclusivity and diversity in academic libraries is the limited hiring pool. Raschke (2003) demonstrates that searches for academic libraries are costly and require significant resources (costs for travel and advertising, time served on search committees) and estimates that hiring a candidate can cost up to $13,000, the equivalent of $22,000 today. Additionally, Raschke demonstrates that the hiring pool in academic libraries is restricted by traditional academic search processes that aim to make it as small as possible, and the hiring pool is further diminished by unqualified candidates, by highly qualified candidates who decline job offers, and other factors that constrict hiring in academic libraries, including an aging population and a highly competitive job market in academic libraries. Because this situation is a problem, the hiring pool must be broadened to include not only persons within the library who are non-degreed or non-degreed in LIS but also persons outside of traditional library networks. Library networks tend to be insular, comprised mostly of library professionals. This fact often only increases insularity and homogeneity as these networks tend to be mostly white (Vinopal, 2016). Libraries can use strategies implemented by other organizations to make themselves more viable employers or places that candidates would like to come and work, especially if these libraries can demonstrate they are committed to hiring BIPOC employees (Alburo et al., 2020).

## Ending Recruitment Silos

Academic library positions also tend to be posted in only a limited number of spaces (university websites, general library e-mail discussion lists, websites for those seeking jobs in higher education, and domain-specific websites), which serves as another barrier to employment if individuals outside of these networks do not know where to look (Cunningham, Guss, & Stout, 2019). Therefore, when positions are open, academic LIS professionals tend to inform only those within the field of job openings, even if they know people who have transferable or compatible skills that make them qualified for the position. The emphasis on transferable skills is already taking place outside of libraries and has helped other organizations build more diverse workforces. Alburo et al. (2020) argue that libraries can learn from these other organizations to look for employees who may have transferable skills although they may not have experience in an academic library. They use the example of public library employees (public libraries have the highest number of non-white library staff) as having skills needed to work in an academic library. At our institution, for example, we hired a public librarian for a faculty position in which the candidate had no previous experience. However, the faculty recognized that the candidate had many transferable skills from their previous position, and the candidate expressed a willingness to learn about the position and the new skills they needed. The person hired also was a member of an underrepresented group. The insularity of libraries is even worse in academic libraries because we operate as a silo within a silo. Not only are academic libraries normally smaller than other academic units or departments on campus, but library workers are also concerned only with operations within the libraries and are further siloed by operations within their own LIS departments or units. Again, this insularity often leads to workers within LIS being uninformed or misinformed about the tasks their coworkers perform and unaware of the skills they may have.

## Internal Recruitment

Libraries need to evaluate talent from within their organizations to determine their employees' aptitude for certain tasks and provide support to those individuals to secure higher ranking positions. This method requires that libraries build leaders from within instead of seeking employees who may appear more credentialed on paper. While impressive résumés and curricula vitae may indicate that an academic library has attracted the best and brightest talent in the field, they may also conceal inequities in promoting talented staff within an organization, many of whom may be BIPOC. The best staff is often waiting to advance within an organization, and academic libraries can invest in helping these individuals to complete their MLIS degrees if a position requires it. Not only will this approach mitigate attrition, but it is also good practice and helps the library in future recruitment efforts. Academic libraries must also practice early recruitment.

## Early Recruitment

Early recruitment can take on many forms and requires that libraries provide employment opportunities to new LIS graduates or offer employment contingent upon completion of an LIS degree. Some academic libraries have created positions where the MLIS is not even needed given the comparative return of interest for the cost of said degree (Espinal, Sutherland, & Roh, 2018). These positions are mostly non-tenure track or support staff positions. Academic libraries have helped to keep their environments inequitable by promoting either precarious temporary positions or long-term, low-to-no-advancement positions to BIPOC employees. Essentially, academic libraries show they are not truly serious about diversifying their staff when they create these positions and market them to

BIPOC employees (Hathcock, 2019). This approach, in turn, contributes to a culture where BIPOC employees cannot advance and continues the cycle of higher rates of attrition or little to no recruitment of BIPOC employees.

A primary source of contention about hiring non-LIS-degreed staff in academic libraries is concerns that the profession will be delegitimized or that salaries will degrade (Kirschner, 2021). LIS degrees are becoming more expensive, and most patrons are not even aware that many frontline staff may or may not have an LIS degree or be librarians (Kirschner, 2021). Academic librarians and library staff already exist in a liminal and marginalized space in relation to other faculty due to the perception that library faculty do not contribute to student success and learning as teaching faculty. Additionally, in higher education the master's degree is often devalued in relation to the PhD, and those with fewer credentials are considered less expert or perceived as contributing less to the campus. Therefore, the attempt to maintain the status quo is regressive and limits our potential growth and diversity initiatives. The need for LIS professionals cannot keep pace with a competitive job market. LIS must contend with competition for better paid professional positions, low to stagnant wages, and problems with recruitment and retention (Cooke & Jacobs, 2018). At my institution, other academic units and departments often allow faculty and staff to work on a contingent basis without having a terminal degree, and these hires are given up to two years to complete their degree programs. While some academic libraries may follow this model, I am unsure of how widespread or accepted hiring entry-level professional staff, especially librarians, is without a terminal degree. While some academic librarians may have been hired without their MLIS, the question remains: Are there enough academic libraries that are willing to hire those who do not have a terminal degree? This also becomes an equity issue if there is no uniformity in hiring faculty across the academy. We should allow workers to grow into the profession. Academic libraries can follow the lead of some public library systems that are not requiring the MLIS degree for most, if not all, library positions (Kirschner, 2021).

Academic libraries can recruit earlier by visualizing their ideal candidate before a vacancy exists or needs to be filled and how hiring this person can help diversify the organization. Academic libraries already have the burden of dealing with an aging workforce in addition to requiring many skilled and educated candidates, and they can decrease the barrier to entering the profession by meticulously crafting job postings. It is not enough to create selection criteria based on a particular skill set or educational level; potential candidates should be considered due to their association with the populations they serve, their emotional intelligence, and their adaptability. These considerations are important since being familiar with the region allows candidates to effectively assess the communities' needs and proactively engage in the community. Being able to adapt and having high emotional intelligence are important not only for helping candidates to customize services and programs to address community problems, but also for equipping them with the tools to meet the communities where they are or shift to meet them. Libraries should emphasize experiential learning and depart from the traditional LIS curriculum and career pathways. Additionally, academic libraries can perform more effective outreach to underrepresented communities.

## Outreach

Although data shows that US universities are becoming more racially and ethnically diverse, and despite various initiatives to diversify the profession, academic library staff is still largely white (US Bureau of Labor Statistics, 2019). Additionally, there has been less than a 1 percent increase of BIPOC library professionals overall since 1986, although enrollment of BIPOC students in graduate library programs has increased from 6.7 percent in 1986 to 17.4 percent in 2018 (Yoon & McCook, 2021). This sobering statistic indicates that, while BIPOC students are interested in LIS and are being accepted into LIS programs at higher rates, they either are not completing the programs or are not being hired in proportion to the number of those enrolled in the programs. These numbers also indicate that BIPOC library professionals are leaving the profession at higher rates than their white counterparts (Ndumu, 2021). Therefore, academic libraries must perform more effective outreach to underrepresented communities, focusing on hiring employees who not only are representative of the communities they serve, but who also are culturally aware of these communities and their needs. When developing outreach, we must consider if the cost of the MLIS is worth it when BIPOC individuals are hired at so much lower rates as librarians. Instead, we should be asking what competencies these students already have that will make them employable instead of performing outreach once they have entered the profession. We need to consider developing assessment tools to understand why BIPOC employees are leaving the profession and perform outreach to allow them reentry to the profession.

Outreach, especially to persons who identify as BIPOC, must also take place beyond predominately white institutions. Currently, only one institution among historically Black colleges and universities (HBCUs) has a library and information science program, and the number of Black students entering LIS programs has decreased since one of the best-known LIS programs at an HBCU closed in 2003. Moreover, there are only a few library schools at minority-serving institutions (Garnar, 2021). This situation not only means that LIS programs at HBCUs provide value by graduating Black students, but also indicates that academic libraries must do considerable outreach to students attending HBCUs or minority-serving colleges and universities to encourage them to apply for academic library positions and must post more consistently on minority-centered e-mail discussion lists. Additionally, academic libraries can recruit at professional conferences and job fairs hosted by BIPOC organizations or hosted within their potential BIPOC employees' respective communities. Again, this approach broadens the hiring pool because it allows academic libraries to hire BIPOC faculty and staff in greater numbers. Meeting at conferences or at job fairs also allows academic librarians representing their organizations to create informal networks with potential employees.

## Fit

Libraries also must challenge the concept of fit. The concept of fit permeates the profession and is compounded in academic libraries, where employees must fit within the organizational culture of the library and the university. LIS literature discusses fit, but only in relation to fulfilling requirements for the position instead of critically assessing the concept of fit. Fit is about much more than getting the job and is related more to likability and assimilation than actual skill, previous work experience, or ability to perform the job (Cunningham, Guss, & Stout 2019). Therefore, fit must be examined through a lens of professional and institutional bias. BIPOC applicants may have their applications rejected or might not be hired due to the intrinsic bias of librarianship, and they might face the same barriers if there is intrinsic institutional bias at the university level.

## Mentorship

Additionally, academic librarians can make hiring practices more inclusive by allowing equal access to mentoring and support and formalizing the mentoring process before BIPOC employees are hired. While mentoring and support are often considered part of the onboarding process at some academic libraries, these should be considered before hiring takes place. Mentorship is critical to the hiring process since several measures must be considered before establishing a mentor-mentee relationship, especially if that relationship is to be successful. While mentorship has many benefits, such as acclimating the mentee to their new organization and providing support, mentoring relationships can also be challenging. Mentoring requires time, understanding, training, and competency. There might also be personality clashes between mentor and mentee (Johnson, Smith, & Haythornthwaite, 2020). These challenges can lead to untenable mentorship goals that threaten mentorship programs. Some of the challenges include mentors and mentees becoming disengaged with the program or a disconnect between mentor and mentee if they are not properly matched or if neither is interested in forming a relationship, which can lead to miscommunication or negative feelings (Goodsett & Walsh, 2015).

More importantly, organizations need to consider a multilayered approach to mentorship that examines many factors, such as age, race and ethnicity, gender, sexual orientation, and so on, when pairing mentors with mentees. This multilayered approach is vital when recruiting for race or ethnicity especially since there are so few BIPOC librarians and staff. Anantachai et al. (2016) argue that BIPOC employees are better equipped to advance or feel less marginalized when they have access to a supportive group of coworkers and work in a collegial environment, and this environment often includes colleagues who have shared interests or experiences. In other words, BIPOC employees perform better if they have a community at work. Part of this work begins through being intentional about mentoring opportunities within the organization.

However, it is also important that BIPOC mentees do not have a false sense of belonging, especially if the person in question is considered a diversity hire (Anantachai et al. 2016). BIPOC employees should also be allowed to create career communities within their organizations to be able to openly explore their career options and professional challenges. It is also important that faculty and staff support mentees, either by devoting time to the mentee themselves or, if the organization is too homogenous and siloed to help underrepresented mentees thrive, by helping to build mentorship networks externally.

## Serving on Search Committees

It is also imperative that BIPOC employees be involved in the search process for new employees. Often BIPOC employees are removed from the search process, either because there are not enough of them to serve or because they are intentionally left out. This imperative does not mean that BIPOC employees should serve on committees due to their perceived expertise on diversity or to meet a diversity quota, but that they be actively involved in the hiring process, whether that be helping write job descriptions, developing rubrics, or serving on search committees. Search committees can reinforce whiteness, and qualified minority candidates can easily be weeded from the hiring pool, especially if no person from a minority background is present. Normally, having a minority present can help the interviewee advance further in the interview process and can serve as a check on sometimes all-white hiring committees. There should also be some level of antibias training and other equitable hiring supports embedded in the hiring process to ensure that BIPOC faculty and staff are not overburdened from serving on search committees and that non-BIPOC faculty and staff have a more equitable hiring model.

At academic libraries, if BIPOC library staff do not want to serve on search committees, search committees should enlist the help of nonlibrary BIPOC faculty and staff to serve as equity advisors to ensure that the hiring process retains its integrity and that BIPOC candidates are considered as viable prospective employees. For example, our university has equity advisors, many of whom are BIPOC faculty members, on all hiring committees. If an institution does not have equity advisors, faculty and staff can advocate for a similar program to increase representation on search committees.

## Demystifying Library Work

Lastly, academic libraries can make hiring practices more inclusive by demystifying library work. This might not seem like a practical way to increase inclusive hiring practices on its surface; however, the demystification process requires us to challenge what librarians or what library workers do and what librarians look like. Demystifying what librarians do also feeds into librarians' own biases of vocational awe and neutrality and can often mask issues related to diversity, equity, and inclusion (Ettarh, 2018). The profession has been unable to debunk many stereotypes associated with library workers, such as that librarians tend to be book-loving, cardigan-wearing nerds who love to tell people to be quiet and mostly are middle-aged white women (Schlesselman-Tarango, 2016). While the perception that the profession is mostly white and female is rooted in truth (demographic data proves this, as mentioned earlier), the profession is much more diverse in terms of what librarians do and what they look like.

This situation calls for library professionals to become more acutely aware of how we are represented and counter these stereotypes with more accurate representations of what librarians look like to reflect what little diversity the field does have. For example, the *Guardian* newspaper featured an article (Bramley, 2017) titled "Tattoos and Baseball Caps: This Is What a Librarian Looks Like—in Pictures," which helps to challenge the stereotypes of what librarians look like and features BIPOC librarians. While campaigns like this may be effective at increasing BIPOC representation by showing that BIPOC librarians or library staff do exist, it is just as important to capture their stories and personal experiences because merely being present does not mean that they have a presence or are reflected in the culture of the library. As Galvan (2015) states, we can have these images, but policy language and organizational structures continue to codify whiteness or the white perspective. How involved are BIPOC individuals in creating policies, or how many of them occupy positions of power to challenge the status quo? If we aim to attract more candidates to the field, especially those from more diverse backgrounds, we need to work harder to demystify the profession.

# Conclusion

In this chapter I have demonstrated that academic libraries have a long way to go in creating more equitable and diverse workplaces, addressing gaps in the body of LIS literature concerning equitable hiring and diversity in academic libraries. While the recommendations offered in this chapter are practical, that does not necessarily mean that they will be practiced, especially if those who identify as BIPOC are removed by the hiring process either intentionally, by default, or by proxy. If the culture of academic libraries does not change, then equitable hiring practices and achieving true diversity will not be possible. The fact that this chapter even focuses on practical solutions or best practices helps to uphold the status quo of hiring practices within LIS because the solutions offered do not dismantle the current structures of whiteness in academic libraries.

# Acknowledgments

I would like to acknowledge my research assistant, Lamonta Swarn, for her hard work in compiling the literature review.

# References

Alburo, J., Bradshaw, A. K., Santiago, A. E., Smith, B., & Vinopal, J. (2020). Looking beyond libraries for inclusive recruitment and retention practices: Four successful approaches. *Critical Librarianship, 41*, 85–109.

Anantachai, T., Booker, L., Lazzaro, A., & Parker, M. (2016). Establishing a communal network for professional advancement among librarians of color. In R. Hankins & M. Juárez (Eds.), *Where are all the librarians of color? The experiences of people of color in academia* (pp. 31–53). Library Juice Press.

Anaya, T., & Maxey-Harris, C. (2017, September). *SPEC Kit 356: Diversity and inclusion*. Association of Research Libraries. https://digitalcommons.unl.edu/cgi/viewcontent.cgi?article=1415&context=libraryscience

Ayinde, L., & Kirkwood, H. (2020). Rethinking the roles and skills of information professionals in the 4th Industrial Revolution. *Business Information Review, 37*(4), 142–153. https://doi.org/10.1177/0266382120968057

Boddie, A., Fiedler, B. P., Haslam, M., Luna, E., Martinez-Flores, E., Padilla, T., Wainscott, S. B., White, C., Day, A., Cheng, J., George, K., Green, H., Melilli, A., Mazmanyan, K., & Brombosz, C. (2020, February). *Inclusion and equity committee: Recommendations for diverse recruitment report*. University of Nevada, Las Vegas. https://digitalscholarship.unlv.edu/lib_iec_reports/4

Bramley, E. V. (2017, May 29). Tattoos and baseball caps: This is what a librarian looks like—in pictures. *The Guardian*. https://www.theguardian.com/fashion/gallery/2017/may/29/tattoos-and-baseball-caps-this-is-what-a-librarian-looks-like-in-pictures

Brook, F., Ellenwood, D. and Lazzaro, A.E. (2015), "In pursuit of antiracist social justice: denaturalizing whiteness in the academic library", Library Trends, 64 (2), 246-284.

Burton, S. (2019). Future skills for the LIS profession. *Online Searcher, 43*(2), 42–45.

Cooke, N. A., & Jacobs, J. A. (2018). Diversity and cultural competence in the LIS classroom: A curriculum audit. *Urban Library Journal 24*(1), Article 2. https://academicworks.cuny.edu/ulj/vol24/iss1/2/

Crist. E. A., & Clark Keefe, K. (2022, July). A critical phenomenology of whiteness in academic libraries, *The Journal of Academic Librarianship 48*(4), Article 102557. https://doi.org/10.1016/j.acalib.2022.102557

Cunningham, S., Guss, S. & Stout, J. (2019). Challenging the "good fit" narrative: Creating recruitment practices in academic libraries. In D. M. Mueller (Ed.), *Recasting the narrative: The proceedings of the ACRL 2019, April 10–13, 2019, Cleveland, Ohio* (pp. 12–21). Association of College and Research Libraries.

Eckard, M., Rosener, A., & Scripps-Hoekstra, L. (2014, March). Factors that increase the probability of a successful academic library job search. *The Journal of Academic Librarianship, 40*(2), 107–115. https://doi.org/10.1016/j.acalib.2014.02.001

Espinal, I., Sutherland, T., & Roh, C. (2018, Summer). A holistic approach for inclusive librarianship: Decentering whiteness in our profession. *Library Trends, 67*(1), 147–162. https://doi.org/10.1353/lib.2018.0030

Ettarh, F. (2018. January 10). Vocational awe and librarianship: The lies we tell ourselves. *In the Library with the Lead Pipe*. https://www.inthelibrarywiththeleadpipe.org/2018/vocational-awe/

Evatt-Young, D., & Bryson, B. S. (2021). White higher education leaders on the complexities of whiteness and anti-racist leadership. *Journal Committed to Social Change on Race and Ethnicity (JCSCORE), 7*(1), 47–82. https://www.jstor.org/stable/48645361

Galvan, A. (2015, June 3). Soliciting performance, hiding bias: Whiteness and librarianship. *In the Library with the Lead Pipe*. http://www.inthelibrarywiththeleadpipe.org/2015/soliciting-performance-hiding-bias-whiteness-and-librarianship/

Garnar, M. L. (2021). *Understanding the experiences of academic librarians of color* (Publication No. 2618560641) [Doctoral dissertation, University of Colorado Colorado Springs]. ProQuest Dissertations & Theses Global.

Goodsett, M., & Walsh, A. (2015). Building a strong foundation: Mentoring programs for novice tenure-track librarians in academic librarians. *College and Research Libraries, 76*(7), 914–933. https://doi.org/10.5860/crl.76.7.914

Hathcock, A. (2019, January 18). Why don't you want to keep us? [Blog post]. *At the Intersection*. https://aprilhathcock.wordpress.com/2019/01/18/why-dont-you-want-to-keep-us/

Johnson, W. B., Smith, D. G., & Haythornthwaite, J. (2020, July 17). Why your mentorship program isn't working. *Harvard Business Review*. https://hbr.org/2020/07/why-your-mentorship-program-isnt-working

Kirschner, T. (2021, November/December). We all win—Training and advancement for non-MLIS library workers. *Public Libraries*. https://publiclibrariesonline.org/2022/01/we-all-win-training-and-advancement-for-non-mls-library-workers/

Luckhert, Y., & Carpenter, L. I. (Eds.). (2019). *The globalized library: American academic libraries and international students, collections, and practices*. Association of College and Research Libraries.

Ndumu, A. (2021). Shifts: How changes in the US black population impact racial inclusion and representation in LIS education. *Journal of Education for Library and Information Science, 60*(2), 137–161.

Ossom-Williamson, P., Williams, J., Goodman, X., Minter, C., & Logan, A. (2020). Starting with I: Combating anti-Blackness in libraries. *Medical Reference Services Quarterly, 40*(2), 139–150.

Özlem, S., & DiAngelo, R. (2017). "We are all for diversity, but…": How faculty hiring committees reproduce whiteness and practical suggestions for how they can change. *Harvard Educational Review, 87*(4), 557–580.

Raschke, G. K. (2003). Hiring and recruitment practices in academic libraries: Problems and solutions. *portal: Libraries and the Academy, 3*(1), 53–67.

Riley-Reid, T. (2017). Breaking down barriers: Making it easier for academic librarians of color to stay. *The Journal of Academic Librarianship, 43*(5), 392–396.

Schlesselman-Tarango, G. (2016). The legacy of lady bountiful: White women in the library. *Library Trends, 64*(4), 667–686.

Shearer, J. J., & Chiewphasa, B. B. (2022). Radical re-imagination: Centering a BIPOC library workforce in an asset-based autoethnography. *Reference Services Review, 50*(1), 113–126. https://doi.org/10.1108/RSR-07-2021-0029

Shufran, L. (2020, October 1). Think diversity is a "pipeline problem"? Look at your processes instead [Blog post]. *Gem.* https://www.gem.com/blog/diversity-hiring-pipeline-problem

Simpson, B. (2013). Hiring non-MLS librarians: Trends and training implications. *Library and Leadership Management, 28*(1). https://llm.corejournals.org/llm/article/view/7019

Tewell, E. C. (2012, October). Employment opportunities for new academic librarians: Assessing the availability of entry level jobs. *portal: Libraries and the Academy, 12*(4), 407–423. https://doi.org/10.1353/pla.2012.0040

Thielen, J., & Neeser, A. (2020). Making job postings more equitable: Evidence based recommendations from an analysis of data professionals job postings between 2013–2018. *Evidence Based Library and Information Practice, 15*(3), 103–156. https://doi.org/10.18438/eblip29674

US Bureau of Labor Statistics. (2019). *Labor force statistics from the current population survey.* https://www.bls.gov/cps/

Vinopal, J. (2016, January 13). The quest for diversity in library staffing: From awareness to action. *In the Library with the Lead Pipe.* https://www.inthelibrarywiththeleadpipe.org/2016/quest-for-diversity/

Yoon, J. W., & McCook, K. D. (2021, April). Diversity on LIS school students: Trends over the past 30 years. *Journal of Education for Library and Information Science, 62*(2), 109–118. https://doi.org/10.3138/jelis.2020-0031

CHAPTER 8

# Trans and Gender Diverse Inclusion in Academic Library Hiring

*Keahi Adolpho, Stephen G. Krueger, Luke Sutherland, and Adrian Williams*

We do not know how many trans and gender diverse people work in libraries in the United States. Like the US Census, the American Library Association's demographic survey of its members (which is by no means a complete or accurate representation of the profession) asks if respondents are male or female (Rosa & Henke, 2017). In addition to erasing anybody who is not one of these two things, this question does not provide information on whether respondents are trans or gender diverse. And yet, we are here: all four of the authors of this chapter are trans people who work in academic libraries, and any accurate survey of the field would show that we are far from the only ones. What this means is that we and all other trans and gender diverse academic librarians have gone through at least one hiring process. While there is variation between and within institutions, we are confident in assuring you that all of these processes need a great deal of work to be trans-inclusive; indeed, many of them actively harm trans and gender diverse candidates. In this chapter, we provide practical guidance for institutions on how to make their hiring processes supportive of candidates of all genders; in addition, we offer advice for trans and gender diverse job seekers in the academic library realm.

# Scope

The scope of this book is limited to the inclusive hiring of academic librarians, and so the scope of this chapter is limited to the hiring of trans and gender diverse academic librarians. However, much of the guidance around job postings, interviewing, and interacting with candidates can be useful for hiring library employees of all levels.

Working toward trans and gender diverse inclusion in academic libraries starts before the hiring process begins. Search committees and library administration can do everything right while hiring, and yet still fail to support trans and gender diverse workers once they have been hired. In fact, addressing inclusion only in the hiring process, rather than understanding it as a holistic undertaking, can mislead candidates into accepting jobs that will ultimately harm them. While this chapter focuses on hiring, that limitation is not meant to indicate that this is the only (or most important) issue.

Additionally, while we are writing for two audiences, we encourage people of all genders to read the whole chapter. Trans and gender diverse people do not automatically know how to incorporate gender inclusion into our work; we end up on search committees just like anybody else and need to learn accordingly. Perhaps more importantly, the authors want cis people to read and think about the section of guidance for trans and gender diverse job seekers. The realities highlighted there will complement the general practices described in the rest of the chapter. Lastly, this chapter is not intended to be a first step in learning about trans and gender diverse inclusion in the workplace; not everything can be a Trans 101. Readers are assumed to possess foundational knowledge about trans and gender diverse people and basic practices of inclusive behavior. If you do not have this, start by doing that learning rather than trying to apply the ideas in this chapter without it.

# A Note for Trans and Gender Diverse Job Seekers

None of this is fair. It is a failing of society and of our profession that trans and gender diverse candidates need to think about issues that cisgender candidates generally do not. This chapter is not intended to indicate that it is right or OK that we need to worry about the things discussed here; it should be the responsibility of everyone in the profession to make it inclusive, not that of trans and gender diverse candidates to protect themselves from ignorance and bigotry. But as of now, academic librarianship cannot be trusted to treat people of all genders equitably, and so we need to navigate that reality until it changes.

# A Note on Positionality

The authors of this chapter are all trans or gender diverse and work in academic libraries. We have been on both sides of the academic librarian hiring process, and our perspectives and proposals are informed by our personal experiences and what we have learned from other trans and gender diverse library workers.

Trans and gender diverse people are not a monolith. The way we understand and express our genders, the way society interprets and treats us based on our (in)visibility, and our intersectionalities (along the lines of race, ethnicity, disability, etc.) further shape our experiences. We can speak from our own research and experiences, but we do not represent all trans and gender diverse people; do not discount the perspectives of others in favor of what we say in this chapter.

Equally important to naming our positionality as authors, we must name the positionality of the profession. The institution of academia is founded on—and continues to pursue—settler colonialism, its classrooms constructed on seized and violently stolen land, and built off the labor of enslaved and exploited peoples. This colonialist structure is purposeful and, in spite of more widespread trends toward diversity, equity, inclusion, and accessibility (DEIA) in recent years, ultimately pervasive. Academic libraries exist within these structures. Transantagonism and cisnormativity are part of everyday library systems and policies, including cataloging and classification, public service interactions, building security, and more. Hiring practices are not an exception, but rather a reflection of who the academy as an institution is seeking to uphold the existing structure. Therefore, there is no neutral starting point from which we can provide advice on mitigating the present situation. The methods that academic libraries use to hire are inherently harmful and exclusionary. Though the proposals we make in this chapter will hopefully improve things for trans and gender diverse library workers, they cannot solve the massive problem in how academia genders and surveils bodies. By default, there is no such thing as a trans and gender diverse inclusive hiring process in a country that requires the knowledge and use of legal names and legal genders. The practical measures outlined in this chapter also need to be paired with much broader changes.

# Literature Review

As far as we can ascertain, nothing has been published on trans and gender diverse inclusive hiring practices in academic libraries. Therefore, this literature review will touch on some adjacent topics, with the understanding that the lack of directly applicable material on this topic says a great deal on its own.

The vast majority of the limited materials about trans and gender diverse people in libraries focus on information-seeking behavior (Beiriger & Jackson, 2007; Drake &

Bielefield, 2017; Huttunen, Hirvonen, & Kähkönen, 2020; Jardine, 2013; Pohjanen & Kortelainen, 2016; Taylor, 2002), patron-focused services and spaces (Jennings, 2017; Krueger & Matteson, 2017; Marquez, 2014; Rawson, 2009; Sancho-Brú, McIntyre, & Bermúdez Raventós, 2019; Schwartz, 2018; Smith-Borne, 2019; Thompson, 2012), and cataloging/metadata (Adler, 2009; Adolpho, 2019; Angell & Roberto, 2014; Billey, Drabinski, & Roberto, 2014; Billey & Drabinski, 2019; Cohen, 2019; Johnson, 2010; Polebaum-Freeman, 2019; Roberto, 2011a; Shiraishi, 2019; Thompson, 2016; Wagner, 2019). A few publications cover youth services (Austin, 2019; Sokoll, 2013). Others address broader initiatives and practices (Byrne, 2020; Doherty & Coghill, 2020; Krueger, 2019). Outside of personal blog posts and brief news items, only a handful of people have written about the existence of trans and gender diverse librarians at all, and these pieces primarily center personal experiences rather than professional practices (Fisher et al., 2019; Jones et al., 2019; Roberto, 2011b).

Direct references to the hiring process for trans and gender diverse librarians are rare, but not nonexistent, in published professional literature. In an article interviewing several library workers in Canada, Hazel Jane Plante points out that

> Trans folks working in libraries will likely encounter barriers that cis folks won't, such as when providing credentials and references to hiring committees (e.g., we often have degrees granted under previous names or have to give references who knew us by different names and pronouns). (Jones et al., 2019)

One chapter of the book *Supporting Trans People in Libraries* about gender-inclusive job postings and interviews emphasizes that, if a work environment is supportive to begin with, then facilitating an inclusive hiring process should come naturally (Krueger, 2019). Krueger urges employers to "Do the labor first, or people will leave as soon as they can after finding out the truth" (Krueger, 2019, p. 67).

Since academic librarian hiring processes often map to that of teaching faculty (whether the librarians at a particular institution are considered faculty themselves), it is useful to look at publications on trans inclusion in academic hiring more broadly. Even this, however, is limited: "While there is a growing body of literature that discusses trans* and gender non-conforming students' experiences on college campuses, little has been written on how faculty and staff experience higher education" (Jaekel & Nicolazzo, 2022, p. 634). An Inside Higher Ed piece points out that "transgender people on the market have to negotiate a host of additional difficulties, even before getting a campus visit and interview"; the author recounts withdrawing from a search partway through the campus visit due to the transphobic and ignorant behavior of the search chair (Hanna, 2016). Participants in a study on the experiences of trans and gender diverse faculty and staff cite some of these difficulties, including struggling to get references to use their correct pronouns and having to engage with transphobic search committee members (Jaekel & Nicolazzo, 2022, p. 650).

In academic libraries and academia more broadly, there is a dearth of literature addressing gender-inclusive hiring practices. Trans and gender diverse employees are rarely considered, let alone centered. Meaningful studies on the existence and experiences of trans and gender diverse library workers are needed, as well as practical guidance on gender inclusion for current and prospective employees of academic libraries.

# Guidance for Employers

Before forming a search committee, employers should make a holistic review of how search committees are constructed and what qualifies an individual to serve. Committee members need to be carefully considered because of the direct role they play in candidate selection. Employees who are not actively engaged in learning or implementing DEIA, and those who do not understand the need for a diverse staff, should not be selected for search committee work (Jones & Murphy, 2019, p. 79).

Candidates will interact with many people beyond the search committee. A truly gender-inclusive hiring process requires a workplace where all employees put the knowledge of how to appropriately treat trans and gender diverse people into practice; however, very few libraries do the work necessary to counter transantagonism in their staff (all libraries should do this, of course, but that is a topic outside the scope of this chapter). That said, there are specific points of contact that must be preemptively addressed to support and protect trans and gender diverse candidates. The person who makes background checks or arranges travel will likely need the candidate's legal name, and they must be explicitly instructed never to share this if the name of use differs. Whoever is responsible for scheduling interviews needs to be trained on how to talk to candidates without assuming gender (for example, do not call a candidate "Mr." or "Ms." based on their name). These are a few examples; the specifics will vary, so the best solution is to go over the whole process with attention to gender inclusion and implement policies and training as needed.

## Job Listings and Applications

When creating a job listing, start with the basics:
- Remove all gendered language. When describing the potential candidate, "he or she" erases the possibility that the person may use other pronouns. Use they/them pronouns throughout the job posting.
- Include the salary range for the position. This is best practice anyway, and it is especially relevant to trans and gender diverse people considering the

percentage of trans Americans living in poverty (29%) is more than twice that of the general US adult population (James et al., 2016).

- Supply information on benefits, or an easy way to find that out without asking directly (which can force someone to out themself). For many trans and gender diverse job seekers, transition-related health care coverage is a deciding factor in whether a particular role is even a viable option.
- Review application forms to ensure that you are asking for only the information you need at each step. For example, you do not need to know candidates' legal names until the background check, so hold off on asking until then.
- Be specific about what information you need. "Name" is ambiguous—legal name, or name of use? Similarly, "legal gender" has a different answer for many people from "gender identity" (and both answers can be complicated). In addition to not asking for any information you do not need, let candidates know precisely what they need to supply.
- If application forms include fields for pronouns or salutations, these need to be both open-ended and optional.
- Clearly and accurately identify who sees what information. Many employers are legally required to collect demographic data. State explicitly that answering these questions is optional and that responses will not be viewed by the hiring committee (as long as this is actually true), but rather anonymized and reported to the Equal Employment Opportunity Commission (Krueger, 2019, pp. 60–61).
- If gender identity and gender expression are included in your institution's nondiscrimination policy, include that in the job posting. (If not, that is another thing to address.)

Requiring candidates to supply a diversity statement may sound nice, but in practice it often ends up perpetuating assumptions that all candidates are cishet, white, and abled and focusing on personal feelings of self-identified allyship rather than actual work (Sumerau et al., 2021). If you do request a diversity statement, think carefully about what you are trying to learn about the candidate and frame the question accordingly. If a candidate is actually incorporating DEIA into their work in a meaningful way, that should show up in their general application materials and answers to interview questions. Build those issues into your interview process rather than asking for a separate diversity statement just to check a box.

Since elements of the academic hiring process are often outside the control of the library, you may not be able to implement gender-inclusive practices if your institution's human resources does not follow them. There is no reason to require an applicant's legal name during the application process, but your library might be forced to use a form that asks for this. In such cases, do two things. First, create whatever work-arounds you can.

Add a note to the application instructions letting applicants know that they should put their name of use on the CV and cover letter, not their legal name if that differs. Add a step to the process where someone not on the search committee organizes application materials and removes legal names before they are passed on for review (and of course train this person not to share the information with anyone). Second, push back! If the library is unable to make changes to the application software to remove terminology around legal names, it should advocate for change with those who have the power to do so. If rejected, continue to push, making it clear that the systems harm trans and gender diverse applicants and will therefore result in a less diverse applicant pool as people opt for more inclusive institutions.

## The Interview Process

Most academic librarian interviews include a phone or video screening as well as a more extended on-campus visit (or all-day virtual interview) for finalists. Making these gender inclusive has some overlap, as well as particular elements in each portion to be aware of.

First-round interviews generally mark the first time the whole search committee will hear and/or see a candidate. For many trans and gender diverse job seekers, this stage creates additional sources of justifiable concern: how the search committee might react to our voice and/or appearance, including whether anyone will misgender or mispronoun us or react badly based on their own biases and assumptions. While first interviews can be nerve-wracking for all candidates, it is important to be aware of this added stressor for trans and gender diverse workers.

For plenty of people—especially a lot of nonbinary people—being out is not a choice, or at least it is a pretty awful one. Since so many people have the harmful habit of assigning gendered language based on how someone looks or sounds, a candidate may be forced to choose between outing themself or being misgendered or mispronouned throughout the interview process. If a library has only men's and women's restrooms prominently visible, someone who is not one of those genders will either have to use one of those options regardless or take the risk of asking for other options (which may not exist).

## Search Committee Action Items

- Search committee members who are comfortable doing so should share their own pronouns. This could be done verbally during introductions, in display names on videoconferencing platforms, or both. Do this with all candidates regardless of whether the search committee knows or thinks that they are trans or gender diverse.
- Refrain from guessing which pronouns a candidate uses. If there is a need to discuss the candidate in the third person before you learn their pronouns, refer to them by their name, or use they/them pronouns. This means not defaulting

to she/her or he/him pronouns based on assumptions about an applicant's name during the initial review process or their voice and appearance during interviews. Do this regardless of whether the candidate is present. If you later learn that the candidate goes by different pronouns, switch to those.

- Avoid assuming a candidate's gender. You cannot know anybody's gender unless they tell you, and you should never ask this in an interview, as it is none of your business and illegal to factor into the hiring process (US Equal Employment Opportunity Commission, n.d.). In practice, this means not referring to any candidate using gendered language that the candidate has not used for themselves and also not assuming that they would use a certain restroom or join particular employee affinity groups.
- Make sure everyone who interacts with the candidate has been told the correct name and pronouns (if the candidate has shared these). Correct anyone who mispronouns or misgenders the candidate. Do not leave it to the candidate to correct people; the power dynamics inherent to the hiring process can make this a particularly difficult and stressful conversation to have. This correction should happen briefly in the moment and be simply about what pronouns the candidate uses. If the person who made the error reacts badly or over-apologizes, move on quickly to minimize discomfort for the candidate. Speak to the person who made the mistake after, if necessary.

The search committee should also keep in mind that candidates may have overlapping marginalized identities. Trans and gender diverse inclusion includes issues around disability and accessibility, race and ethnicity, and more. When reflecting on or answering questions about DEIA in the library and university more broadly, consider trans and gender diverse inclusion as it intersects with other forms of inclusion and marginalization. For example, are your all-gender restrooms accessible? Are your only affinity groups for people of color separated by gender?

# Candidate Questions

Many marginalized people use the allotted time for candidate questions during interviews to ask questions that will help us better understand workplace culture and attitudes around DEIA. As a search committee, be prepared to answer questions about trans and gender diverse issues, experiences, and inclusion at the library, at the institution, and in the surrounding area. What specific steps have been taken to protect and support trans and gender diverse employees (especially if your location has anti-trans laws)? Do provided health insurance options cover transition-related care? Are there employee affinity groups that support trans and gender diverse workers? While it can be tempting to point to things like putting pronouns in e-mail signatures, this does not meaningfully demonstrate trans and gender diverse inclusion. If you cannot identify any other support, then your institution has a lot of work to do. Do not pretend to be more welcoming or safe than you are; supply candidates with a realistic picture and let them decide accordingly. Your goal is not to convince trans and gender diverse people to work for you—it is to become a place where we want to work.

## Contacting References

When contacting references, employers should be conscious of the possibility that references may have outdated knowledge of a candidate's name and pronouns. They may be ignorant of the fact that their current or former employee is trans or gender diverse, or even actively transantagonistic. When gathering references, employers should ask all candidates how they would like to be referred to while conducting the reference checks. Search committee members should make sure to remain diligent in sticking to how the candidate wants to be referred to with references.

## After Hiring

Trans and gender diverse inclusion in hiring does not end when a candidate has signed their written offer. Recruitment and retention reinforce one another. Structural changes to onboarding practices, workplace culture, and accountability for any misgendering, mispronouning, microaggressions, or other mistreatment need to be implemented in order to retain trans and gender diverse library workers.

# Guidance for Trans and Gender Diverse Job Seekers

For trans and gender diverse people, questions to consider before starting a job search largely revolve around two areas: how you want to present yourself, and what your needs and deal-breakers are in an employer. There is no right or wrong approach; everyone has different answers to both questions. These answers may also change as you gather information about what you can realistically expect. We are not trying to recommend a particular approach to anyone; that said, there are some common issues to reflect on so you can determine what works best for you.

## Outness and Presentation

How you present yourself includes everything from what name, salutation, and/or pronouns (if any) you put on your application materials, to how you dress during in-person and video interviews, to whether you come out as trans or gender diverse to potential employers. These decisions depend on any number of individual factors. Can you risk losing a job opportunity because someone reacted badly, or are you in a position to filter out any employers where that is an issue? Some candidates ask in every interview about the protections we can expect there as trans and gender diverse employees, but plenty of people will not want to or cannot risk doing that—sometimes you really just need a job or do not feel like coming out.

Whatever you decide to do, it is a good idea to let your references know what name and/or pronouns you would like them to use for you when talking to potential employers. If you do not feel safe disclosing this information to references, make a plan for communicating any discrepancies to prospective employers when they reach the reference check stage. You can ask them to refer to you a certain way to specific references or make a note on your reference list like "(knows candidate as [name])." This is not a perfect system by any means; even if you find an effective way to convey this information, it may require implicitly outing yourself to the potential employer. And even then, you cannot trust the person calling your references not to out you, intentionally or otherwise. Also bear in mind that they might not limit calls to the people you list as references; they can call previous employers off your CV as well.

If you want to, you can try to mitigate potential mispronouning by sharing your pronouns from the beginning of the job search process. It is fine to put them on application materials—though often search committee members ignore or forget pronouns—but remember that those of us who use they/them or neopronouns are essentially outing ourselves by doing so because of the common misconception that pronouns always reflect gender. You may be completely fine with that, and it is also one way to screen employers by seeing how they respond: it can be valuable information to see whether anyone on the search committee actually uses the pronouns you have supplied them with.

## Interviewing

For some trans or gender diverse people, video and phone interviews add layers of complication. Maybe you frequently get misgendered or mispronouned on the phone, but the way others react to your physical presentation tends to change that. Maybe the opposite is true. After reflecting on how these different platforms impact others' perception of your identity, make a plan for if misgendering or mispronouning happens. If you want to share your pronouns, video calls lend you the option of placing them in your display name, while a phone screen requires you to verbally state them. Because of the prevalence of ignorance and bigotry around how to respectfully talk to and about trans and gender diverse people, neither method is a reliable protection against members of the search committee mispronouning you anyway. Are you going to correct someone if they get it wrong, and if so, how many times are you willing to do that? Walking through these scenarios beforehand will help you stay focused in the moment.

Interview anxiety can be brutal for anyone and is only heightened by the experience of being a trans or gender diverse candidate whose job security is significantly more tenuous than that of cisgender counterparts. It is therefore also worth asking how you will take care of yourself before and after the interview. Consider planning a soothing activity or asking a friend to debrief with you. The Trans and Gender Diverse LIS Network (*Trans and Gender Diverse LIS Network*, n.d.) is a closed community for trans and gender diverse LIS workers and students where you can find support.

The questions discussed above may be worth revisiting before second-round interviews, as your answers might have changed now that you have made it this far. If you did not already decide to do so earlier, are you interested in coming out as trans or gender diverse to the search committee and potential future coworkers? How do you want to be introduced to each new group or person you meet, how can you increase the chances of that being respected, and how will you respond if it is not? How will you handle any misgendering or mispronouning that might occur? Are you interested in asking direct questions about trans and gender diverse inclusion at the library, or would that risk outing yourself when you don't want that?

## Strategically Applying to Institutions

Many trans, gender diverse, and other marginalized library workers screen institutions before applying (Betz, 2022). One method is looking at library and university diversity statements, demographic statistics, staff directories, and climate surveys. University HR pages often have publicly available resources for new employees about benefits, so you may be able to review health insurance information as well. Lastly, community word of mouth can be really helpful in determining if a particular institution might be a good environment for you. If you do not already know someone who works at the institution where you are applying, you can ask your professional networks if anyone has experiences they would be willing to share or if they know of someone else you could reach out to.

Since academic librarian roles so often involve relocating, it is important to think about where you would feel safe and comfortable living, as well as to what extent that can be a deciding factor for you. If there are states or cities whose anti-trans or other legislation means you cannot envision living there, plan accordingly when you are looking for jobs. Other factors to consider might be the type of institution and its policies (some religious institutions are not places where you can be out and keep your job), or whether the health insurance covers trans-related medical needs, if you have any or plan to in future. You can also apply for jobs where you are not sure about these issues rather than ruling them out preemptively. You can ask the search committee (or, better, the queer and/or trans and gender diverse employees that already work there) about all of this if you are comfortable doing so.

Please note that we as the authors do not say any of this with resignation for how things are, but rather to help inoculate early-career or recently out trans and gender diverse candidates to some of the concerns found in the typical academic hiring process. It is not fair that a lot of trans and gender diverse people need to plan for these things, but it is currently how the system works, so prepare yourself and take steps to minimize harm to you as much as possible.

# Conclusion

There is no such thing as truly trans and gender diverse inclusive hiring practices in a society that is cisnormative and transantagonistic. Our recommendations should thus be understood as methods to decrease the harm that academic hiring practices so often enact on trans and gender diverse candidates, since real inclusion is currently a structural impossibility. Considering that trans and gender diverse people have different needs depending on our particular contexts (such as the intersections of our identities, how we are perceived by others, and our legal documentation), it is impossible to have a single set of practices that meets the needs of every trans or gender diverse person. Further research on the workplace experiences of trans and gender diverse library workers is needed.

Hiring is just one area of work, and it should not be undertaken in isolation from other efforts around gender inclusion. Improving workplace culture and increasing retention will strengthen recruitment efforts, whereas focusing only on recruitment results in falsely signaling safety to trans and gender diverse library workers when it does not actually exist. DEIA efforts must invest in structural changes rather than the mere appearance of inclusion. While our chapter begins with recruitment and goes through the hiring process chronologically, we do not believe trans and gender diverse inclusion in libraries starts or stops here or that steps should necessarily be completed in the order laid out here. Our profession exists within (and contributes to) a complicated matrix of oppression. Working to improve the inclusion of trans and gender diverse library workers in academic hiring processes is only one necessary feature in moving toward a professional environment that equally values people of all genders.

# References

Adler, M. (2009). Transcending library catalogs: A comparative study of controlled terms in Library of Congress subject headings and user-generated tags in LibraryThing for transgender books. *Journal of Web Librarianship*, *3*(4), 309–331. https://doi.org/10.1080/19322900903341099

Adolpho, K. (2019). Who asked you? Consent, self-determination, and the report of the PCC Ad Hoc Task Group on Gender in Name Authority Records. In J. Sandberg (Ed.), *Ethical questions in name authority control* (pp. 111–131). Library Juice Press.

Angell, K., & Roberto, K. R. (2014). Cataloging. *TSQ: Transgender Studies Quarterly*, *1*(1–2), 53–56. https://doi.org/10.1215/23289252-2399587

Austin, J. (2019). Lines of sight and knowledge: Possibilities and actualities of transgender and gender-nonconforming youth in the library. In B. Mehra (Ed.), *LGBTQ+ librarianship in the 21st century* (pp. 167–196). Emerald Publishing Limited.

Beiriger, A., & Jackson, R. M. (2007). An assessment of the information needs of transgender communities in Portland, Oregon. *Public Library Quarterly*, *26*(1–2), 45–60. https://doi.org/10.1300/J118v26n01_03

Betz, G. (2022, April 6). Navigating the academic hiring process with disabilities. *In the Library with the Lead Pipe*. https://www.inthelibrarywiththeleadpipe.org/2022/hiring-with-disabilities/

Billey, A., & Drabinski, E. (2019). Questioning authority: Changing library cataloging standards to be more inclusive to a gender identity spectrum. *TSQ: Transgender Studies Quarterly, 6*(1), 117–123. https://doi.org/10.1215/23289252-7253538

Billey, A., Drabinski, E., & Roberto, K. R. (2014). What's gender got to do with it? A critique of RDA rule 9.7. *Cataloging and Classification Quarterly, 52*(4), 412–421. https://doi.org/10.1080/01639374.2014.882465

Byrne, A. (2020). Organizational change and gender identity: When good intentions fall short. In H. L. Seibert, A. Vinogradov, & A. H. McClellan (Eds.), *The library workplace idea Book: Proactive steps for positive change* (pp. 91.-94). ALA Editions.

Cohen, A. (2019). Free to be … only he or she: Overcoming obstacles to accurately recording gender identity in a highly-gendered language. In J. Sandberg (Ed.), *Ethical questions in name authority control* (pp. 133–154). Library Juice Press.

Doherty, M. T., & Coghill, D. E. (2020). Virginia Commonwealth University Libraries' gender-inclusive work group experience. In H. L. Seibert, A. Vinogradov, & A. H. McClellan (Eds.), *The library workplace idea book: Proactive steps for positive change* (pp. 95-100). ALA Editions.

Drake, A. A., & Bielefield, A. (2017, July). Equitable access: Information seeking behavior, information needs, and necessary library accommodations for transgender patrons. *Library and Information Science Research, 39*(3), 160–168. https://doi.org/10.1016/j.lisr.2017.06.002

Fisher, Z., Krueger, S., Malamud, R. G., & Patillo, E. (2019). What it means to be out: Queer, trans, and gender nonconforming identities in library work. In A. Baer, E. S. Cahoy, & R. Schroeder (Eds.), *Libraries promoting reflective dialogue in a time of political polarization* (pp. 71–90). ACRL Publications. https://libres.uncg.edu/ir/asu/f/Patillo_Ericka_2019_What%20it%20Means%20to%20Be%20Out.pdf

Hanna, A. (2016, July 15). *Being transgender on the job market.* Inside Higher Ed. https://www.insidehighered.com/advice/2016/07/15/challenge-being-transgender-academic-job-market-essay

Huttunen, A., Hirvonen, N., & Kähkönen, L. (2020). Uncomfortable in my own skin—Emerging, early-stage identity-related information needs of transgender people. *Journal of Documentation, 76*(3), 709–729. https://doi.org/10.1108/JD-09-2019-0193

Jaekel, K. S., & Nicolazzo, Z. (2022). Institutional commitments to unknowing gender: Trans* and gender non-conforming educators' experiences in higher education. *Journal of Homosexuality, 69*(4), 632–654. https://doi.org/10.1080/00918369.2020.1848146

James, S. E., Herman, J. L., Rankin, S., Keisling, M., Mottet, L., & Anafi, M. (2016). *The report of the 2015 U.S. Transgender Survey*. National Center for Transgender Equality.

Jardine, F. M. (2013). Inclusive information for trans* persons. *Public Library Quarterly, 32*(3), 240–262. https://doi.org/10.1080/01616846.2013.818856

Jennings, B. M. (2017, July/August). Serving trans* patrons in public law libraries. *AALL Spectrum, 21*(6), 33–35. https://aallspectrum.aallnet.org/html5/reader/production/default.aspx?pubname=&edid=47ba3e77-e495-4f66-9601-de8a36d5c8d9

Johnson, M. (2010). Transgender subject access: History and current practice. *Cataloging and Classification Quarterly, 48*(8), 661–683. https://doi.org/10.1080/01639370903534398

Jones, A., Plante, H. J., Tottenham, L., Shelby, & syr. (2019). Not cis in LIS: A roundtable discussion about being trans in libraries. *BCLA Perspectives, 11*(3). https://bclaconnect.ca/perspectives/2019/09/05/not-cis-in-lis-a-roundtable-discussion-about-being-trans-in-libraries/

Jones, S. D., & Murphy, B. (2019). Recruiting and retaining and diverse workforce. In S. D. Jones & B. Murphy, *Diversity and inclusion in libraries: A call to action and strategies for success* (pp. 75–88). Rowman & Littlefield

Krueger, S. G. (2019). *Supporting trans people in libraries*. Libraries Unlimited.

Krueger, S., & Matteson, M. (2017). Serving transgender patrons in academic libraries. *Public Services Quarterly, 13*(3), 207–216. https://doi.org/10.1080/15228959.2017.1338543

Marquez, A. (2014, June 19). Supporting transgender individuals in libraries: Developing responsive policies. *The Journal of Creative Library Practice*. https://creativelibrarypractice.org/2014/06/19/supporting-transgender-individuals-in-libraries/

Pohjanen, A. M., & Kortelainen, T. A. M. (2016). Transgender information behaviour. *Journal of Documentation, 72*(1), 172–190. https://doi.org/10.1108/JD-04-2015-0043

Polebaum-Freeman, H. (2019). Violent cis-tems: Identifying transphobia in Library of Congress name authority records. In J. Sandberg (Ed.), *Ethical questions in name authority control* (pp. 155–179). Library Juice Press.

Rawson, K. J. (2009). Accessing transgender // Desiring queer(er?) archival logics. *Archivaria, 68*, 123–140.

Roberto, K. R. (2011a, Fall). Inflexible bodies: Metadata for transgender identities. *Journal of Information Ethics, 20*(2), 56–164.

Roberto, K. R. (2011b). Passing tips and pronoun police: A guide to transitioning at your local library. In T. Nectoux (Ed.), *Out behind the desk: Workplace issues for LGBTQ librarians* (pp. 121–127). Library Juice Press. https://litwinbooks.com/books/out-behind-the-desk/

Rosa, K., & Henke, K. (2017). 2017 ALA demographic survey. ALA Office for Research and Statistics. https://alair.ala.org/handle/11213/19804

Sancho-Brú, E., McIntyre, P., & Bermúdez Raventós, I. (2019). Bringing the trans and local community together: The "Trans Identities and Gender" project. In B. Mehra (Ed.), *LGBTQ+ librarianship in the 21st century* (pp. 243-270). Emerald Publishing Limited.

Schwartz, M. (2018, May 2). Inclusive restroom design. *Library Journal*. https://www.libraryjournal.com/?detailStory=inclusive-restroom-design-library-design

Shiraishi, N. (2019). Accuracy of identity information and name authority records. In J. Sandberg (Ed.), *Ethical questions in name authority control* (pp. 181-194). Library Juice Press.

Smith-Borne, H. (2019). Creating a welcoming and inclusive environment for transgender and gender fluid music library users. *Music Reference Services Quarterly, 22*(1-2), 18-29. https://doi.org/10.1080/10588167.2018.1536691

Sokoll, T. (2013). Representations of trans* youth in young adult literature. *Young Adult Library Services, 11*(4), 23-26.

Sumerau, J. E., Forbes, T. D., Denise, E. J., & Mathers, L. A. B. (2021, May). Constructing allyship and the persistence of inequality. *Social Problems, 68*(2), 358-373. https://doi.org/10.1093/socpro/spaa003.

Taylor, J. K. (2002). Targeting the information needs of transgender individuals. *Current Studies in Librarianship, 26*(1/2), 85-109.

Thompson, K. J. (2012). Where's the "T"? Improving library service to community members who are transgender-identified. *B Sides, 2012*(1), Article 22. https://pubs.lib.uiowa.edu/bsides/article/id/27908/

Thompson, K. J. (2016). More than a name: A content analysis of name authority records for authors who self-identify as trans. *Library Resources and Technical Services, 60*(3). https://doi.org/10.5860/lrts.60n3.140

*Trans and Gender Diverse LIS Network*. (n.d.). Retrieved November 7, 2022, from https://translisnetwork.wordpress.com/

US Equal Employment Opportunity Commission. (n.d.) *Prohibited employment policies/practices*. Retrieved November 1, 2022, from https://www.eeoc.gov/prohibited-employment-policiespractices

Wagner, T. L. (2019). Finding "Miss Betty" Joe Carstairs: The ethics of unpacking misnaming in cataloging and biographical practices. In J. Sandberg (Ed.), *Ethical questions in name authority control* (pp. 195-211). Library Juice Press.

CHAPTER 9

# Beyond Compliance
## Accommodating Differently in the Interview Process

*Jennifer M. Jackson*

## Introduction

For people with disabilities, the range of the disability is varied. Some disabilities may be visible while others are invisible (or even a combination of both). This chapter will discuss recommendations that can be implemented in the interview and the candidate evaluation process, to create a more inclusive and accessible interview process. However, it is important to acknowledge that this chapter is a culmination of historical and contemporary literature as well as hiring best practices examined through a disability studies lens. This chapter does not address all the possibilities for inclusive practices given the wide range of disability but encourages the reader to explore inclusive practices to promote further conversations and scholarship around disability and library hiring practices.

In examining inclusive hiring practices for people with disabilities, it is important to understand the current employment landscape for this identity group. As of 2021, 19.1 percent of persons with a disability were employed according to the US Bureau of Labor Statistics (2022). Based on this recent data across all age groups, persons with disabilities were much less likely to be employed than those without a disability, and across all educational attainment groups, unemployment rates for persons with a disability were higher than for persons without a disability (US Bureau of Labor Statistics, 2022). To illustrate the current landscape for people with disabilities within the library profession based on the last published *Diversity Counts* report, 3.5 percent of ALA members reported having a disability (Davis & Hall, 2007). Though more statistics are certainly needed within librarianship, in general disability is often not recorded in the same way as other identity markers such as race, ethnicity, gender, and geographic region. The reasons for this difference are likely multifaceted and reflect limited discussion around disability as an identity marker and underreporting of those with a disability because of the stigma and concerns associated with self-disclosure.

Additionally, to understand why employment statistics for disabled people are often drastically different from those of their able-bodied counterparts, one must realize that barriers often exist for people with disabilities that make employment and life itself a more challenging process. These barriers can range from the physical, such as buildings without ramps or doors without push buttons, to attitudinal barriers from others such as stereotyping, negative biases, or ableist language and practices. It is the aim of this chapter to address the barriers that can often exist in the interview process to establish and promote more inclusive hiring practices.

# The Americans with Disabilities Act and Academic Libraries

Prior to discussing what steps are needed to be inclusive of library candidates with disabilities during the interview process, it is important to briefly summarize the Americans with Disabilities Act (ADA) and its relationship to academic libraries. As a federal law, the ADA aligns with how most academic libraries have articulated employment opportunities for people with disabilities. The ADA was passed by Congress in 1990 and "prohibits discrimination against people with disabilities in everyday activities," guaranteeing "that people with disabilities have the same opportunities as everyone else to enjoy employment opportunities, purchase goods and services, and participate in state and local government programs" (US Department of Justice, Civil Rights Division, 2022). For the purposes of this chapter, there is not one universally accepted definition for disability. Disability literature has helped establish various models for disability, including identity, cultural, economic, charity, limits (Retief & Letšosa, 2018). Relevant to this chapter is the medical and social model. A medical model "positions disability as a medical problem, as something to be rehabilitated or treated at the individual level" (Kumbier & Starkey, 2016, pp. 472. A social model describes "a framework in which the focus shifts from individual persons' medical diagnoses and impairments toward the material, physical, and social environments that impose limitations or create barriers for people with impairments" (Kumbier & Starkey, 2016, pp. 473). It is from the social model that this chapter examines the interview and evaluation process.

As this chapter later highlights, scholars have been critical of the ADA as it takes a medical model approach when defining disability. According to the ADA,

A person with a disability is someone who:

- has a physical or mental impairment that substantially limits one or more major life activities,
- has a history or record of such an impairment (such as cancer that is in remission), or
- is perceived by others as having such an impairment (such as a person who has scars from a severe burn). (US Department of Justice, Civil Rights Division, 2022)

In 1993 the American Library Association (ALA) articulated the impact the law would have on the profession with one of the first publications from the Association of Specialized and Cooperative Library Agencies (later known as the Association of Specialized Government and Cooperative Library Agencies [ASGCLA] and dissolved September 1, 2020) entitled *The Americans with Disability Act: Its Impact on Libraries: The Library's Responses in "Doable" Steps* (Crispen, 1993). This publication was created in collaboration with a preconference on the ADA held before the 1992 ALA Annual Conference. It included commentary from preconference committee members, as well as a series of supplemental materials: "Self-Evaluation Survey for Public Libraries (Title I and Title II)," "Adaptative Technology Exhibitors," "Etiquette" for communicating with persons with disabilities, programs and services for people with disabilities, and a list of contacts from the National Institute on Disability and Rehabilitation Research of the US Department of Education highlighting technical assistance initiatives.

Though these texts were comprehensive from an administrative and library user standpoint, the material was addressed to public libraries and reflected only limited discussion of library employment. For a publication of its time, it was a useful primer for informing professionals to ensure that the ADA was reflected in various aspects of the public library environment. However, this text in many ways is out of date and does not reflect current issues and concerns of various library stakeholders or the present varied experiences or issues of people with disabilities.

# Literature Review Past and Present

When examining contemporary publications or documentation by the ALA, one finds that much of the literature is centered on the library user, with titles such as *Library Services for Youth with Autism Spectrum Disorders* (Farmer, 2013), *Creating Inclusive Library Environments: A Planning Guide for Serving Patrons with Disabilities* (Kowalsky & Woodruff, 2017), or *Serving Patrons with Disabilities: Perspectives and Insights from People with Disabilities* (Laskin, 2023). To date, there does not appear to be an updated or revised publication of *The Americans with Disability Act: Its Impact on Libraries* (Crispen, 1993) or a similar publication.

Information about hiring practices for people with disabilities in libraries is often limited to federally available resources or incorporated into a brief list of best practices for library employees with disabilities. One example is *Library Staff with Disabilities: What You Need to Know*, a compilation of best practices from ASGCLA (n.d.). These best practices, though useful in some ways, show their age and could be seen as inappropriate without the necessary situational context.

To date there is no general disability policy for the library profession, although it was advocated for by ALA stakeholders in December 2000 (ASGCLA, 2000). Had a policy been developed, it could have provided guidance for the profession to address all individuals with disabilities, including patrons and library employees. The lack of practical guidelines and policies within the profession likely contribute to the continued accounts and difficulties that people with disabilities face when seeking library employment (Anderson 2021; Betz, 2022). The lack of a policy also puts the profession creates a conflict. The organization articulates the importance of inclusivity while not examining the full range of identities that make up the profession.

The evident gap in practical knowledge is mirrored within academic literature, which highlights why topics of disability and employment within librarianship continue to be an emerging topic of discussion. As Moeller's (2019) article points out,

> Library literature, in general, looks outward at disability and accessibility, framing the conversation in terms of how to best serve users' needs. These articles often take a "retrofitting" approach that frames disability and accessibility as problems that need to be solved, and they rarely look inward at the structural inequities in the profession itself. (pp. 455–456)

Through an examination of conversations within "academic librarianship around resilience and professionalism," Moeller (2019, p. 456) articulates how these conversations promote an ableist perspective that excludes the lived experiences of those with disabilities by creating barriers to inclusion. Barriers to inclusion are also critiqued within the ADA and reasonable accommodations as a "deficit-model approach to disability" (Moeller, 2019, p. 463). Barriers are also seen in the need to request accommodations and the risks associated with self-disclosure to multiple parties during employment. These systemic barriers create vulnerability for people with disabilities.

Oud (2019) takes a qualitative approach to identifying the barriers by conducting interviews with ten academic librarians with disabilities. This research emphasizes the lack of awareness and understanding of others regarding disability-related workplace issues. "Misunderstanding of disability, especially of invisible disabilities as not 'legitimate' disabilities, also led to negative judgments and stereotypes of being lazy or not wanting to work" (Oud, 2019, p. 178). Also of note were the assumptions of high productivity and a quick pace of work.

> Interviewees frequently discussed concerns about productivity and workload. Doing more with less creates potential difficulties for all workers but can cause particular difficulties for people with disabilities who need to use different strategies or take more time to complete their work. (Oud, 2019, p. 179)

An implication of these barriers was that participants frequently mentioned that "colleagues, supervisors, and library patrons had uncomfortable reactions to their disability. Other peoples' discomfort was commonly mentioned, and many participants discussed incidents where other people were uncomfortable when confronted with their disability" (Oud, 2019, p. 181). Issues of others' discomfort, along with the discussed barriers, again prevented librarians from discussing or disclosing their disabilities to others at work. "As a result, the majority of participants reported disclosing a disability selectively, to only a few coworkers they trusted" (Oud, 2019, p. 182).

Other scholarly publications of note reflected the personal experiences of library workers with disabilities, such as the autoethnographic work of Hollich (2020), which examines what it means to pass as person with a disability. Hollich juxtaposes theoretical research with their own experience as a person with a hidden disability.

Lastly within the realm of scholarship is the recent publication *Disabilities and the Library: Fostering Equity for Patrons and Staff with Differing Abilities* (Copeland, 2023). This title begins to narrow the gap in monograph publications, being inclusive of the needs of library employees and library users with disabilities. Part V of the book, "Leadership: Inclusive Policies, Practices and Environments for Library Staff with Differing Abilities and Needs," has three chapters, each of which examines a different aspect of library employees, presenting practical information, considerations, questions, and suggestions for further reading to create mindful practices for an inclusive culture.

# Steps to Shifting the Culture

To shift the culture to be more inclusive of candidates with disabilities, it is important to articulate the practical changes that should be made within the interview and evaluation process. Below are recommendations to consider for the library profession in organizations that use search committees to recruit, interview, or recommend candidates for hire.

## Preparing for the Interview

- If the organization's ADA coordinator (or related position) is not part of search committee training, have a discussion with this individual regarding self-disclosure and disability. This conversation will help search committee members understand the context of self-disclosure. It is important that the committee understand that some candidates may disclose their disability during the hiring process, some may wait until an offer is extended, or some will wait until after beginning their employment.

- Have the search committee chairs confirm with the human resources department that standard accommodation software, hardware, and resources are available and up-to-date. The types of disability a candidate may have can vary so required accommodations may include making sure interview materials are available in a variety of formats or that Communication Access Realtime Translation (CART) or American Sign Language (ASL) interpreters are available.

- If hosting in-person interviews, be sure that interviews are in accessible locations and that directions and maps are available for physical locations.

- To ensure that the directions and maps are clear and succinct, have library employees, review the provided materials.

- When providing maps for in-person interviews, make sure accessible areas, such as parking or transportation, locations of library elevators, entrances, exits, and areas of rescue, are clearly marked.

- Provide interview materials such as the schedule of events or interview questions in advance of the interview and provide the names of the individuals with whom the candidate may be speaking or interacting. This practice can help relieve a candidate's anxiety and help them best prepare for the interview.

- Make sure that any provided documentation is available in an electronic format and is accessible for a screen reader. If any visual documentation is provided, it may also be necessary to prepare image descriptions. Image descriptions should be short, succinct statements that describe any images.

- Inform the candidate prior to the interview that accommodations are available upon request.

- Be sure to review the interview questions with the search committee prior to conducting any interview to ensure that they do not include bias or ableist language. When possible, have someone outside of your library organization review the interview questions, particularly someone familiar with employee accommodations, such as an ADA coordinator.

## For the Interview

- For online interviews hosted via Zoom or other remote meeting applications, ensure that live captioning or third-party captioning is enabled.

- Prior to asking the prepared interview questions, check in with the candidate to see if their access needs are being met. This check-in can be posed as a question: "Before we begin, is there anything you need to support your access needs?" Or identifying access needs can be modeled during introductions. After providing one's name, pronouns, and title, one could say, "My access needs are being met," or "If I turn off my camera, it is so that I may stand."
- Be aware that not all interview candidates will disclose their disability (whether visible or invisible). Regardless of the type of disability, interviewers should not ask questions in relation to a candidate's disability. Questions should be limited to expectations and requirements of the job description and assigned tasks.
- Ask similar questions of all selected candidates for the position. Questions should be centered around the specific tasks and responsibilities of the job and allow the candidate to demonstrate their expertise. Questions should not be modified to reflect a person's disability.
- Allow space and time for a copy of the questions to be provided at the interview or to allow for questions to be repeated.
- When conducting in-person interviews, be mindful of the various interview environments. Conduct interviews in spaces that have appropriate lighting and are free of barriers, such as stairs, cords in primary pathways, or excessive or distracting sounds or noises.
- Confirm that in-person interview spaces are spatially adequate and allow individuals of all abilities the space needed to move, sit, or stand with ease. This issue is extremely important for in-person job talks or presentations (Dali, 2019).
- When possible, promote fragrance-free environments. Fragrance-free environments will prevent candidates from having reactions to chemical-based scents or fragrances.
- If the candidate is required to give a presentation, the library organization should consider investing in appropriate audio equipment such as microphones and speakers. If the organization already has the equipment, make sure the equipment is functional for the interview. It is important that the candidate and the audience be able to clearly communicate with one another.
- Diversity, equity, inclusion, accessibility and anti-racism (DEIAA) should be naturally reflected in processes, procedures, and policies across academic library environments. Depending on the area or department that candidate is interviewing for, the library should highlight current DEIAA efforts at the library and campus level. It should be noted that contributions to DEIAA should not be presented as a performative measure but should be shared as sustainable or measurable practices.

- Be prepared to create alternate interview schedules. If a candidate does disclose a disability and requests an accommodation, be flexible with what the interviews may look like. This flexibility may mean including additional breaks or longer breaks.
- Anticipate that interviewees may need to take breaks in spaces that are low distraction or flexible for physical needs (for example, rooms where candidates can lie down or stretch).
- When providing tours, make sure that you are highlighting accessible pathways, such as location of elevators.
- Create the opportunity for candidates to opt out of attending meals. Participants may want to skip meals because of dietary restrictions, exhaustion, pain, or social anxiety (Anderson, 2021; Betz, 2022).
- Provide links to a campus map or information about the terrain, the route, and any suggestions on appropriate shoes that can be provided ahead of time. Having this kind of information allows disabled candidates to ask for specific accommodations or make their own informed decisions about self-accommodations (Betz, 2022).

## Candidate Evaluation

- When evaluating the candidate, be sure that the evaluation rubric or questions focus on the required skills or tasks of the job and not the social interactions during the interview process. Depending on a candidate's disability, social interactions may be challenging and create increased anxiety during the interview.
- Have someone outside of your library organization review the evaluation metric or tool to ensure it includes varying abilities and candidates' shared work experiences.
- It is important to review evaluation materials with the search committee prior to submitting candidate evaluations to again ensure that bias or ableist language is not present.

# What We Have Learned Interviewing during the COVID-19 Pandemic

The COVID-19 pandemic required libraries to pivot regarding how services and resources were provided, but it also highlighted the ways in which libraries can support accommodations for patrons, employees, and candidates with disabilities. Because of the pandemic, organizations now have access to telecommuting applications, closed captioning and recorded meetings, and increased use of electronic documents and resources. As libraries continue to think about the impact of the COVID-19 pandemic, this presents opportunities for library employees to think more creatively about the hiring processes for people with disabilities and possibilities for remote work or telecommuting opportunities associated with specific responsibilities or tasks.

The pandemic also caused individuals to think about their own relationship to disability identity in ways they may have not have previously. That may have meant caring for someone whose health was greatly impacted or who was at greater risk due to the pandemic; losing loved ones and the mental health issues associated with loss, grief, and surviving a pandemic; or, for people who considered themselves to be disabled prior to the pandemic, now being forced to self-advocate in ways they had not previously navigated. In addition, it may have included individuals who had seemingly recovered from the virus but became part of the ever-growing population of long-haulers with continuing effects on mental or physical abilities.

As university and college libraries continue to adapt to the changes created by the pandemic, those involved in the hiring process should consider how to support candidates with visible and invisible, as well as temporary and permanent, disabilities due to the pandemic.

# Outcomes for Change

As libraries implement the recommendations discussed within this chapter, the author hopes that hiring managers and those closely involved in hiring practices think more critically about possibilities for inclusion. Though this chapter examines the interview and candidate evaluation process, there are opportunities to critically examine all aspects of the hiring process, from job announcement to onboarding. The changes discussed within this chapter are nuanced, simple, and often inexpensive and can make a huge difference for those with and without a disability.

One benefit of putting these practices in place is that all employees will see these changes and should feel encouraged that their place of employment is making sustainable steps toward inclusion. These changes should naturally impact other areas and services not tied to hiring practices, such as increased scholarship and collection development regarding working, living with, and celebrating disability and increased programs and accessibility services for patrons with disabilities. It should also be noted that these recommendations for interviewing and candidate evaluation can and should extend beyond a staff or faculty lens and should be implemented across all hiring levels—student employees, staff, faculty, and administration.

In creating a culture of inclusion, academic libraries must take an active role in destigmatizing disability and dismantle the systemic barriers that force many to carry the unnecessary burden that comes with existing in spaces historically not designed for them. Rather, academic libraries should create and support a culture and community of care where people regardless of their abilities or identities feel empowered to show up and exist as they are and want to be seen.

For inclusive practices to be sustainable, academic libraries must recognize that the practice of inclusivity is not a one-and-done process. Implementing inclusive practices should be thoughtful and measured and should be assessed on a regular cycle. As academic libraries implement these recommendations, it is important to be strategic about how implementation happens. Do not try to overhaul every aspect of the interview process if the organization and its members do not have the capacity to do so. Think about starting small.

- Make a plan. Determine what aspects or efforts make sense for the organization's capacity, and decide on a flexible timeline for implementation.
- Meet with library and campus members with an interest or stake in disability culture, disability studies, or accessibility and accommodations. This practice brings a wide array of views to changing interview and evaluation practices. Depending on the outcome of these meetings, those involved may identify actionable steps for hiring practices. An added strategy is to determine the possibility of an ad hoc committee around a particular issue, such as interview questions, an evaluation rubric, or the development an accessible library tour.
- Once proposed changes have been made to the interview process, be sure to review those changes with the human resources department as it may have expertise or knowledge to be aware of prior to formal implementation.
- When possible, share the finalized changes with the entire library organization. All the details do not need to be distributed, but an acknowledgment and a summary of the changes signal transparency to the library organization and show the steps being taken to be include people with disabilities.

# Conclusion

Creating a culture beyond compliance means not only incorporating procedures and policies that support federal mandates for accommodations, but also being reflective of disability culture and experiences, creating a culture universally accessible to all. For an inclusive and equitable library culture to thrive and demonstrate DEIAA, there must be a critical examination of all aspects of the library environments—online spaces, physical spaces, and organizational structures as well as individual and community behavior. Library stakeholders across departments must come together to address what has worked well, what issues have been challenging, and what problematic behaviors, harms, or systemic structures have been failures and must be abolished.

# Acknowledgments

Many thanks to everyone who helped prepare this chapter for publication. Special thanks to my University of Illinois Chicago colleagues Linda Naru and Cathy Lantz. Your insights and feedback helped shape and form this chapter to make it a more impactful work. I also must take a moment to recognize all the people with and without disabilities that work every day to make sustainable changes in a world that was not designed with disability in mind. Continue your efforts, and, though there are days that seem as if your work is in vain, remember that you are seen, heard, and valued.

# References

Anderson, A. (2021). Job seeking and daily workforce experiences of autistic librarians. *The International Journal of Information, Diversity, and Inclusion (IJIDI), 5*(3). https://doi.org/10.33137/ijidi.v5i3.36196

Association of Specialized Government and Cooperative Library Agencies. (n.d.). *Library staff with disabilities: What you need to know.* https://www.ala.org/asgcla/resources/tipsheets/staff

Association of Specialized Government and Cooperative Library Agencies. (2000, December 14). *Facts: Why an ALA disability policy? Why now?* https://www.ala.org/asgcla/asclaissues/factsheetabout

Betz, G. (2022, April 6). Navigating the academic hiring process with disabilities. *In the Library with the Lead Pipe.* https://www.inthelibrarywiththeleadpipe.org/2022/hiring-with-disabilities/

Copeland, C. A. (Ed.). (2023). *Disabilities and the library: Fostering equity for patrons and staff with differing abilities.* Libraries Unlimited.

Crispen, J. L. (Ed.). (1993). *The Americans with Disabilities Act: Its impact on libraries: The library's responses in "doable" steps.* Association of Specialized and Cooperative Library Agencies.

Dali, K. (2019). Avoiding a senseless endurance test: Hidden disabilities and interviewing in LIS [Editorial]. *The International Journal of Information, Diversity, and Inclusion (IJIDI), 3*(1). https://doi.org/10.33137/ijidi.v3i1.32265

Davis, D. M., & Hall, T. D. (2007, January). *Diversity counts.* American Library Association. https://www.ala.org/aboutala/sites/ala.org.aboutala/files/content/diversity/diversitycounts/diversitycounts_rev0.pdf

Farmer, L. S. J. (2013). *Library services for youth with autism spectrum disorders.* ALA Editions.

Hollich, S. (2020). What it means for a disabled librarian to "pass": An autoethnographic exploration of inclusion, identity, and information work. *The International Journal of Information, Diversity, and Inclusion (IJIDI), 4*(1). https://doi.org/10.33137/ijidi.v4i1.32440

Kowalsky, M., & Woodruff, J. (2017). *Creating inclusive library environments: A planning guide for serving patrons with disabilities.* ALA Editions.

Kumbier, A., & Starkey, J. (2016). Access is not problem solving: Disability justice and libraries. *Library Trends, 64*(3), 468–491.

Laskin, Kodi (Ed.). (2023). *Serving patrons with disabilities: Perspectives and insights from people with disabilities.* ALA Editions.

Moeller, C. M. (2019). Disability, identity, and professionalism: Precarity in librarianship. *Library Trends, 67*(3), 455–470. https://doi.org/10.1353/lib.2019.0006

Oud, J. (2019). Systemic workplace barriers for academic librarians with disabilities. *College and Research Libraries, 80*(2), 169–193. https://doi.org/10.5860/crl.80.2.169

Retief, M., & Letšosa, R. (2018). Models of disability: A brief overview. *HTS Teologiese Studies/Theological Studies, 74*(1).

US Bureau of Labor Statistics. (2022, February 24). *Persons with a disability: Labor force characteristics—2021* (USDL-22-0317) [News release]. US Department of Labor. https://www.bls.gov/news.release/archives/disabl_02242022.htm

US Department of Justice, Civil Rights Division. *Introduction to the Americans with Disabilities Act.* Retrieved October 10, 2022 from https://www.ada.gov/topics/intro-to-ada/

CHAPTER 10

# Improving Inclusion with Universal Design in the Academic Library Hiring Process

*Katelyn Quirin Manwiller, Heather Crozier, and Samantha Peter*

To improve inclusion in academic library hiring practices, we must evaluate and prioritize addressing the barriers that currently exist in the process for LIS workers with marginalized identities. Despite efforts to improve the diversity of the profession over the last twenty years, our demographics remain largely the same. These efforts have also primarily excluded one of the largest marginalized groups in the country: disabled people. Approximately 26 percent of American adults live with at least one disability, and that number is likely growing due to the COVID-19 pandemic (National Center on Birth Defects and Developmental Disabilities [NCBDDD], n.d.; Roberts, Ives-Rublee, & Khattar, 2022). Disability is also more prevalent among people experiencing other forms of marginalization. Two in five Native Americans and Alaskans live with disability, as do one in four women (NCBDDD, n.d.). Moreover, oppression experienced by people of color and LGBTQIA+ individuals in America intersects with disability and systemic ableism due to the long-standing health disparities in our country (Kates et al., 2018; Ndugga & Artiga, 2023).

Unfortunately, employment is often out of reach for disabled folks. Only 19.1 percent of Americans with disabilities were employed in 2021, and ALA reports only 2.9 percent of members self-identifying as disabled in its demographic study (US Bureau of Labor Statistics, 2022; Rosa & Henke, 2017). ALA does not provide any intersectional data that would shed light on how many disabled librarians experience multi-marginalization. With the prevalence of disability in America, lack of representation in librarianship, and inherently intersectional nature of disability inclusion, it is essential that academic librarianship work to recruit and retain disabled librarians. Disability affects people in a variety of ways. Therefore, there is no one-size-fits-all solution. As a result, broader disability inclusion techniques based on the principles of Universal Design are needed to remove barriers for disabled librarians during the hiring process.

# Literature Review
## Librarianship

Disability inclusion and hiring practices is an underrepresented conversation within academic libraries. Largely the conversation around disability centers on federally mandated accessibility standards in terms of collection development and management, public spaces, library instruction, and other patron-focused topics. LIS literature has begun to address disability and the workplace, but so far has primarily focused on the job and not the hiring process (Brown & Scheidlower, 2019; George, 2020; Moeller, 2019; Oud, 2019; Pionke, 2019; Schlesselman-Tarango, 2019). Only three articles (Leonard, 2019; Anderson, 2021; Betz, 2022) discuss academic library hiring and disability despite the critical need to revise our hiring practices to make them more inclusive for every person. These three studies, like most LIS scholarship on disability, come from a predominantly white perspective. This fact is concerning as the experience of people of color from the disabled library community is missing, which echoes the lack of diversity within the library profession as a whole.

In 2019, Leonard discussed disability, hiring, and academic libraries in a short call-to-action column noting that while librarians work to make our spaces accessible for patrons, we rarely provide that model for our librarians. Leonard advocated for increased policies and training noting that "a true path to diversity starts in the hiring process" (p. 203). Anderson (2021) conducted interviews with autistic librarians related to workforce experiences. The respondents highlighted a few ways interview accessibility could be improved, including having hiring managers who are knowledgeable about autism to foster honest conversation and providing advance preparation options for interviews, such as sending questions ahead of time.

Betz (2022) is the first piece in LIS literature to center entirely on disabled librarians and the academic hiring process. Betz, who self-identifies as disabled, focuses on providing recommendations to assist librarians with disabilities in navigating the hiring process based on coping mechanisms described in interviews with disabled academic librarians. Those recommendations include adjustments to interview structure, intrapersonal coping skills, and interpersonal coping skills. Betz also highlights the importance of educating managers on the accommodations process when working to create an inclusive environment for retaining and recruiting librarians.

Beyond these three studies, accessibility in hiring is discussed in a few professional documents and research from the archival profession, one adjacent to academic libraries. The ALA Core Leadership group established best practices for academic interviews that focus on the candidates and reduce bias. Accessibility is mentioned twice in the recommendations: first to ask candidates if they need anything, such as an accommodation, to participate in the interview, and second to provide interview questions in advance (Arch et al., 2021). An article by Abney et al. (2022) addresses archivists with invisible disabilities, including disclosure in the hiring process, accommodations, and suggestions for the profession. The authors suggest that archivists should work to be allies for disabled archivists including advocating for workplaces to incorporate Universal Design (Abney et al., 2022) Additionally, the Society for American Archivists Accessibility and Disability Section published best practices for hiring people with disabilities. It outlined guidelines for crafting a job posting, evaluating candidates, conducting initial and in-person interviews, dining with candidates, making an offer, and inclusion beyond hiring (Tang et al., 2020).

Discussion about disability inclusion in librarianship has reached LIS literature only in the last few years, with very little evidence or documentation about the hiring process. As a result, we have to look to literature and concepts outside of librarianship for ideas to improve our profession.

## Universal Design

Universal Design (UD) is "the design and composition of an environment so that it can be accessed, understood and used to the greatest extent possible by all people regardless of their age, size, ability or disability" (Centre for Excellence in Universal Design, n.d.). From UD the idea of Universal Design for Learning (UDL) was created to improve inclusivity and accessibility in instruction and other nonphysical spaces through the principles of multiple means of engagement, multiple means of representation, and multiple means of action and expression (CAST, n.d.). Like UD for physical spaces, these principles work to make education more accessible for all by designing materials to be inclusive from the beginning rather than retroactively adapting and making accommodations to spaces or learning. These same principles can easily be applied to hiring and workplace environments to make them more accessible and inclusive to all from the start.

When considering how UD or UDL fits within academic libraries, the majority of the literature focuses on UD in library spaces (Spina, 2017; Staines, 2012), UDL within library instruction (Chodock & Dolinger, 2009; Hoover, Nall, & Willis, 2013; McMullin, 2022; Peter & Clement, 2020; Zhong, 2012), or UD in online learning (Lewitzky & Weaver, 2022; Linsinbigler et al., 2021; Lund, 2020). None of the literature addresses how UD or UDL can fit within hiring or workplace culture.

Applying UD in physical spaces is also discussed in the higher education literature, but there has been little discussion of UD in the academic workplace outside of Bessette (2021). This article examines how the COVID-19 pandemic helped to create a more inclusive work environment in higher education and the need to continue incorporating UD into our culture to produce an environment where everyone can thrive. It also provides us with a guiding question for inclusive hiring and workplace practices: "What are the conditions that we can create so that the most people are equipped to succeed?" (Bessette, 2021, p. 9).

Outside of scholarly literature, there has been some disability and labor-based documentation related to incorporating UD in hiring and workplace culture. Various organizations identify strategies for applying UD, such as improvements to the physical environment and employee workstations, communication practices that incorporate multiple formats, the use of technologies and tools to improve accessibility, and reconceptualizing policies to be more inclusive (Northwest ADA Center, n.d.; Office of Disability Employment Policy, n.d.). The Disability Resource Center (n.d.) at the University of Arizona provides the most direct application of UD to the workplace through its web page dedicated to inclusive workplace practices. Its framework centers on flexibility, specifically in how, when, and where work can be done.

Flexibility in how work is performed includes options to sit or stand, adjustable workstations, and choice in the order in which tasks are performed. This is also an area where UDL principles can be applied through multiple modalities of training materials and meeting attendance for employees. Flexibility in when work is performed centers around scheduling by allowing an employee to determine a schedule that best meets their needs while meeting the needs of their employer. This includes options to have more frequent breaks, later start times, or a condensed workweek. Flexibility in where work is performed applies to allowing remote work options and options in the in-person work environment. Flexible work options have demonstrated an increase in employee satisfaction and engagement (Carlson, Grzywacz, & Kacmar, 2010; Shifrin & Michel, 2022; Weideman & Hofmeyr, 2020). Since the onset of the COVID-19 pandemic, remote work has been a preferable option for many Americans, demonstrating how a practice specifically beneficial to disabled workers can help nondisabled employees also (Casselman, 2022; Schur, Ameri, & Kruse, 2020). This shift has also benefited Black employees, who had lower stress levels and a greater sense of belonging while working remotely, possibly due to fewer microaggressions and less need for code-switching (Miller, 2021; Subramanian & Gilbert,

2021). For hybrid positions or ones that cannot be done remotely, flexibility can be applied through seating and desk options that allow for easy modifications, the opportunity to sit or stand, additional monitors, adaptive software, and control over the environment where possible, including lighting, temperature, and access to private spaces.

Workplace policies are another critical element of incorporating UD into workplace culture. Creating an inclusive culture in the workplace means anticipating potential needs and proactively addressing them through policies and procedures that minimize potential obstacles for all involved (Falcone & McCartin, 2022). Employees should feel comfortable using sick time as necessary, for both physical and mental health, without penalization. Flexible dress codes allow better function, comfort, and self-expression for both disabled and nondisabled employees (Taganova, 2022; Monash University, n.d.). While some policies are dictated at the institutional level and beyond the control of the library, adopting policies and procedures consistent with UD principles in the library benefits everyone.

Flexible work arrangements are not a new phenomenon, but the early stages of the COVID-19 pandemic provided proof that many jobs are more flexible than previously believed. As academic libraries work to provide more inclusive environments, they can utilize the flexibility inherent to UD to better support disabled and nondisabled librarians alike. For our purposes, we will examine how these principles of UD in the workplace and UDL can improve the hiring practices in academic libraries.

# Recommendations for Hiring

This section will break down our recommendations for applying UD principles to the typical academic time line: creating the position description and posting, preparing the search committee for the process, and interviewing candidates. This is not meant to be a checklist with each item met before hiring is fully inclusive of disabled librarians. Instead, we present areas for flexibility, built-in accessibility, and considerations to guide analysis of hiring within academic libraries.

## Preparing for a Search

Essential to understanding inclusive hiring practices and employee retention is examining potential barriers within the library's culture. When preparing for a search, libraries need to look inward to see how their current culture may influence hiring decisions or be inhospitable to potential candidates. In preparing a hiring process where a disabled candidate can succeed, search committees need to consider what sort of disability inclusion efforts already exist in their library. Is disability integrated into the library's diversity, equity, and inclusion efforts? This means going beyond standard library accessibility efforts, which often are limited to ADA compliance, to achieving actual inclusion for disabled students and employees. For example, has the library or university provided training on topics like the diversity of disability, UD or UDL, or the accommodations process on campus? These factors help establish an environment where employees can feel comfortable disclosing disability without fear of retaliation or discrimination. Hiring should not be the first place an academic library approaches disability inclusion, as an established culture of inclusion provides the best environment for the long-term success of disabled workers and promotes retention.

## Developing the Position Description and Posting

To start the process of hiring, academic libraries should utilize UD principles in their development of position descriptions. It is essential that the positions we fill be inherently inclusive and achievable. Often library positions are subjected to budget cuts, and libraries are left with fewer people to do the same duties. While it is necessary to make the most of any open position, libraries must consider what is a realistic amount of responsibilities that one person can handle. If two positions have been condensed into one, what is being removed or reallocated to other librarians? How much time will this person be expected to spend on each of the listed job duties? Will they be asked to take on more workload than the rest of the library staff? Balancing workload to prevent burnout is an essential first step to creating a job that is manageable for a disabled (or nondisabled) library worker.

Once the expectations for the position have been evaluated, libraries should examine how flexibility in how, when, and where work is performed can be built into the position. UD's guiding principle is to plan for accessibility from the very beginning to provide the most inclusive environment. When hiring, this means holistically examining the day-to-day experience of positions when describing them to plan for accessibility beyond basic job duties. Remote work is beneficial to both disabled and nondisabled employees, so consider if it is an option for the position and how much would be reasonable. Also consider whether or not this position needs to have set hours. This may be dictated by the university, but if it isn't, can the library make space for flexible start and end times outside of dedicated hours like reference desk shifts? Lastly, consider where this new person will be located in the library. Does the space provide flexibility in terms of noise, light, and temperature control? Do the furniture and computer system need to be updated prior to bringing in a new person? Would reorganizing offices provide more flexible space for all library staff? Including an environmental description in the job posting provides candidates with a more complete understanding of the job's scope and associated responsibilities.

After the position responsibilities and work environment have been evaluated, it is time to write the job posting. Many of the recommendations presented elsewhere for inclusive job postings are applicable to ensuring it is attractive to librarians with disabilities. This includes limiting required experience to what is absolutely necessary, including the salary range on the posting, providing an equity statement, and ensuring the posting is shared on job lists that will reach a diverse pool of candidates. However, we can take these recommendations even further by anticipating the needs of disabled librarians and adjusting for the barriers they may face. Leaving out unnecessary responsibilities or requirements means not including tasks that present physical challenges, like requiring someone to lift twenty pounds. Extremely lengthy postings can be overwhelming to read and human resource–generated position descriptions can have confusing layouts. By tailoring the posting to what is absolutely necessary for the position, libraries also make the posting itself more accessible to navigate.

In addition to providing salary information, a posting should include links to available human resource (HR) documents or web pages explaining the health care plan options and any required wellness initiatives tied to health care costs. Libraries do not have control over what HR makes publicly available, but library administration can encourage their campus to be as transparent as possible for potential applicants. Health insurance plans and physical distance to health care are critical aspects of a position for disabled workers because not every city or employer provides comparable options. As a result, librarians often need to consider these factors when deciding to apply to or accept a position Including it in the posting allows applicants to get a complete sense of working for the institution. The posting should also link to other areas of the library and university website that clearly outline the institution's equity goals and commitment. This includes an accessibility page for the library that details both the physical accessibility of the building and accessible library resources. A boilerplate equity statement is fairly common, but linking to pages like these will demonstrate the actual inclusion work being undertaken—or not—by the institution. If these pages do not yet exist within the library's website, the library may need to prioritize putting that infrastructure in place before beginning the hiring process.

Overall, the search committee wants to ensure that the posting provides enough information for the applicants to determine if the position will be accessible to them. Provide any details available about the flexibility of how, when, and where work is performed for this position. If hybrid or flexible schedules are the norm at the organization, make sure that is included as an option in the position description. Likewise, if work location and hours are very rigid for that position, make sure that is clearly stated. Realistic expectations of the position sets up the applicants for greater success through both the hiring and onboarding process.

## Search Committee Training

Between posting the position description and starting the interview process, academic libraries should ensure that the members of the search committee are trained on providing an inclusive hiring process. Since institutional guidelines may restrict what the search committee can require, the chair of the committee or library administration can create a collection of current literature on inclusive hiring practices for the committee to reference. That may include sources like this book, but should also include multiple means of representation, a principle of UDL. Not all members of the committee will engage best with reading material, so also consider sharing webinars or holding discussions among the committee to familiarize everyone with these topics.

Beyond general inclusion in the hiring process, the search committee should also be trained on what is legally required under the Americans with Disabilities Act (ADA). Job applicants are protected from disability discrimination under the ADA and are afforded the right to accommodations during the hiring process (US Equal Employment Opportunity Commission, n.d.). Options to submit accommodation requests may be included in the online application system and sent directly to HR. However, a candidate would not know the interview structure when submitting an application, and therefore may not know what accommodation to request. Outside the initial application, a candidate may request an accommodation through their primary contact in the hiring process, whether HR or the search committee. Search committee members need to be aware of the process at their institution so they can correctly direct candidates if they receive requests. To best inform candidates, search coordinators can include information about the accommodations process at their institution in communication offering interviews. These federal protections are part of the efforts to ensure all candidates are treated fairly, but the ADA is not the pinnacle of accessibility. It should be treated as the bare minimum.

## Interviews

The lengthy academic interview process tends to be the most inaccessible for disabled librarians. In the initial round of interviews, prioritize flexibility and accessibility in the interview format. If possible, give candidates the option of either phone or video interviews. Phone interviews were the norm prior to COVID-19, and candidates may find them easier to navigate compared to video. For example, phone interviews allow candidates to focus on the questions instead of making eye contact, how they are dressed, their backgrounds, and other potential barriers inherent to video interviews. If the search committee is doing video interviews, what steps have they taken to ensure all candidates can equally contribute? This is another instance where the UDL principle of multiple means of representation can improve the accessibility of the hiring process. Consider if captions are available and if interview questions are shared ahead of time or live in the chat during the interview. In addition, make sure candidates have all relevant information they need about the position prior to the interview. Ideally, the job posting will have resources linked as discussed above, but sometimes postings are dictated by HR. If that is the case, share this material with the candidates in the confirmation for their interview. It is also helpful to list the members of the search committee who will be interviewing them.

While minor adjustments can improve the accessibility of initial interviews, there is much work to be done to increase inclusion during the final interview. To start, it is far past time to reconsider the length of these interviews. At minimum, they are usually a full workday and often go beyond that to include meals. That extensive period of interviewing is tiring even for healthy, neurotypical, and able-bodied librarians. It is utterly exhausting for disabled librarians, particularly for those with energy-limiting disabilities. As the authors can attest from personal experience, these interviews often require disabled candidates to use paid leave after interviews to recover from the physical and mental exertion. When creating the schedule for the interview, it is essential that search committees strive for a manageable day that includes only what is absolutely necessary for the library to evaluate the candidate and vice versa. Outside of meeting with the search committee and the director or dean, who does the candidate need to meet with to understand the responsibilities of this position? This may be cataloging staff for a technical services position, teaching faculty for an instruction position, or staff that work the circulation desk for an access services position. If a small library is hiring a person to do a bit of all those duties, it is up to the search committee to identify what is the most essential piece of the job and focus on that in the interview. Librarian candidates do not need to be interviewed by every department they will interact with inside and outside the library. Presentations are typical in academic library interviews, but consider what purpose the presentation serves in demonstrating the skills needed for the position. If instruction or other presenting is not a primary function of the position, consider an alternative option that will better reflect the work the candidate will do in the position.

In addition to reducing the length of the interviews, search committees should also reconsider including group lunches and campus tours on their interview schedule. The lunch hour is complicated for disabled candidates for a few reasons. First, it is difficult for those with complex dietary needs to be sure they will have access to safe foods at the chosen place. Even if they chose to disclose their disability and request specific meal options, the candidates will still add unnecessary stress to their day worrying about potential reactions. Second, the lunch hour is an opportunity to allow candidates to rest during a very taxing day. The search committee could provide options for lunch, including giving the candidate some time for rest or lunch with different employees. When lunch is scheduled with a specific group of people, it becomes just another interview with the additional hurdle of eating. Candidates will feel obligated to attend even if it would be safer for them to opt out.

Along similar lines, including a campus tour in the interview schedule presents additional barriers to librarians with disabilities. Historic campuses may have inaccessible buildings that have not been brought up to ADA standards. Sprawling campuses require a lot of energy for candidates to traverse. Even smaller campuses can be challenging because of hills or a large number of steps. Scheduling walking tours of campus requires the candidate to either disclose their disability to opt out or risk injury or exhaustion because they do not want to be judged harshly for not participating. If the position requires working outside of the library in some capacity, prioritize places the candidates need to know about, like a student success librarian working with academic support offices. If they will be working only in the library, skip a walking tour of campus in favor of sharing a virtual tour. Tours of the library itself are usually necessary for candidates, and the search committee can build in ways to improve flexibility during library tours. The library needs to first evaluate its building for accessibility concerns if that is not already part of its inclusion efforts. There are a number of online resources to assist with this work, including ADA checklists and guides for UD in libraries (Burgstahler, 2018; Project ENABLE, 2011). Identify these potential barriers prior to the interview, and then provide options to the candidates during the tour, like asking if they would prefer to take the stairs or the elevator instead of assuming either. Search committees should be sure to highlight any flexibility built into the design of their library and show the candidate the workspace for this position. These considerations or their absences during the tour will help the candidate evaluate if the library will be an accessible workplace for them.

In addition to removing unnecessary or potentially inaccessible aspects of the interview day, library search committees can add time in the schedule to make the day more inclusive of disabled librarians. This primarily takes the form of frequent, scheduled breaks throughout the day, particularly between taxing events like the presentation or the search committee interview. These breaks should be outlined in the schedule and be more than just time for the candidate to stop in the bathroom. The breaks should provide the candidate with access to a private area with comfortable seating, preferably where they could control the lights. For most academic libraries, these could be a conference room, classroom, or student study room. As part of these breaks, make sure candidates know where they can access a bathroom, water fountains, and places to get snacks. Providing breaks in such an area allows the candidate to rest and manage any symptoms they have privately. A candidate will likely not feel comfortable taking medication in front of the search committee or asking to turn off the lights to decrease their sensory overload. It is the best practice for the search committee to assume their candidates have access needs because the vast majority who do will not disclose during interviews out of fear it may be held against them.

After the search committee has created a schedule with disabled librarians in mind, they then need to share as much information as possible with the candidates ahead of time. Many disabled librarians will need to factor in potential accessibility barriers when planning for their interviews. Search committees can provide detailed maps to make this easier. This should be more than just the university's online campus map. Disabled librarians need to know where parking is in relation to the library or interview space, accessibility options at the hotel they will be in, how they can expect to get from the hotel to campus with estimated travel time, and information on transportation from major airports and driving. These issues often require additional planning for disabled librarians, and having it laid out for them means they can spend more energy on the actual interviews.

Lastly, search committees should provide their interview questions in advance for both rounds of the interview process. This may be controversial for some libraries as they do not want candidates to read from a script during the process. While that concern is understandable, the benefits of sharing questions in advance outweigh the potential drawbacks. Receiving the questions only during the interview itself is difficult for librarians with a number of disabilities, including those with fatigue and brain fog, who are hard of hearing, and who struggle with auditory processing. It also presents challenges to English language learners or people who are not fluent in a local dialect. Search committees should provide written questions at least twenty-four hours before the interview and let the candidate know when to expect the questions amid the communication about their interview. Advance access allows the candidates to have the written questions to refer to in the interview in addition to auditory questions. Providing the questions in advance ensures that the candidates will fully comprehend the questions and be able to provide complete answers.

# Conclusion

Disability is a commonplace, yet marginalized experience in academic libraries and American society, but it is largely ignored in efforts to create a more inclusive profession. In order to recruit and retain more disabled academic librarians, we need to remove the barriers to accessibility that are inherent to the current academic hiring process. We can do so by incorporating UD principles like flexibility into the creation of the position and posting, training of the search committee, and interview structure. Within that flexibility, we highly recommend all academic libraries provide interview questions in advance and evaluate the demands of their in-person interview schedules. Creating an accessible profession for disabled librarians starts with ensuring they can successfully navigate the challenges of the academic hiring process. By implementing these steps based on UD, academic libraries can remove the unrealistic burdens on disabled and nondisabled candidates alike as we create more inclusive hiring practices and workplaces for all.

# References

Abney, A., Denison, V., Tanguay, C., & Ganz, M. (2022). Understanding the unseen: Invisible disabilities in the workplace. *The American Archivist, 85*(1), 88–103. https://doi.org/10.17723/2327-9702-85.1.88

Anderson, A. M. (2021). Exploring the workforce experiences of autistic librarians through accessible and participatory approaches. *Library and Information Science Research, 43*(2), Article 101088. https://doi.org/10.1016/j.lisr.2021.101088

Arch, X., Birrell, L., Martin, K. E., & Redd, R. (2021). *Core best practices for academic interviews.* American Library Association. http://hdl.handle.net/11213/17612

Bessette, L. S. (2021, September). Applying Universal Design to our workplaces. *Women in Higher Education, 30*(9), 9–14. https://doi.org/10.1002/whe.21038

Betz, G. (2022, April 6). Navigating the academic hiring process with disabilities. *In the Library with the Lead Pipe.* https://www.inthelibrarywiththeleadpipe.org/2022/hiring-with-disabilities/

Brown, R., & Sheidlower, S. (2019). Claiming our space: A quantitative and qualitative picture of disabled librarians. *Library Trends, 67*(3), 471–486. https://doi.org/10.1353/lib.2019.0007

Burgstahler, S. (2018). *Equal access: Universal Design of libraries.* DO-IT, University of Washington. https://www.washington.edu/doit/equal-access-universal-design-libraries

Carlson, D. S., Grzywacz, J. G., & Kacmar, K. M. (2010). The relationship of schedule flexibility and outcomes via the work-family interface. *Journal of Managerial Psychology, 25*(4), 330–355. https://doi.org/10.1108/02683941011035278

Casselman, B. (2022, October 25). For disabled workers, a tight labor market opens new doors. *The New York Times*. https://www.nytimes.com/2022/10/25/business/economy/labor-disabilities.html

CAST. (n.d.). *CAST: About Universal Design for Learning*. Retrieved November 12, 2018, from http://www.cast.org/our-work/about-udl.html

Centre for Excellence in Universal Design. (n.d.). *What is Universal Design*. https://universaldesign.ie/about-universal-design

Chodock, T., & Dolinger, E. (2009). Applying Universal Design to information literacy: Teaching students who learn differently at Landmark College. *Reference and User Services Quarterly, 49*(1), 24–32. https://www.jstor.org/stable/20865172

Disability Resource Center. (n.d.). *Inclusive workplace practices*. University of Arizona. https://drc.arizona.edu/ud/inclusive-workplace-practices

Falcone, A., & McCartin, L. F. (2022). Strategies for retaining and sustaining the academic librarian workforce in times of crises. *Journal of Library Administration, 62*(4), 557–563. https://doi.org/10.1080/01930826.2022.2057132

George, K. (2020). DisService: Disabled library staff and service expectations. In V. A. Douglas and J. Gadsby (Eds.), *Deconstructing service in libraries: Intersections of identities and expectations* (pp. 96–123). Litwin. https://digitalscholarship.unlv.edu/lib_articles/681

Hoover, J., Nall, C., & Willis, C. (2013). Designing library instruction for students with learning disabilities. *North Carolina Libraries, 71*(2), 6. http://hdl.handle.net/10342/4358

Kates, J., Ranji, U., Beamesderfer, A., Salganicoff, A., & Dawson, L. (2018). *Health and access to care and coverage for lesbian, gay, bisexual, and transgender (LGBT) individuals in the U.S.* Kaiser Family Foundation. https://www.kff.org/racial-equity-and-health-policy/issue-brief/health-and-access-to-care-and-coverage-for-lesbian-gay-bisexual-and-transgender-individuals-in-the-u-s/

Leonard, E. (2019). Career conversations: Disability and hiring. *Reference and User Services Quarterly, 58*(4), 202–204. https://doi.org/10.5860/rusq.58.4.7144

Lewitzky, R., & Weaver, K. (2022). Developing Universal Design for Learning asynchronous training in an academic library. *Partnership: The Canadian Journal of Library and Information Practice and Research, 16*(2). https://journal.lib.uoguelph.ca/index.php/perj/article/view/6635

Linsinbigler, V., Lowder, C., Mattson, J., Murphy-Lang, A., & LoPresto, S. (2021). User-centered design of a library tutorials page: A solution to digital hoarding. *Journal of Library and Information Services in Distance Learning, 15*(2), 142–156. https://doi.org/10.1080/1533290X.2021.1938787

Lund, B. (2020). *Creating accessible online instruction using universal design principles: A LITA guide*. Rowen & Littlefield.

McMullin, R. M. (2022). Universal Design and library one-shot instruction. *Public Services Quarterly, 18*(3), 177–189. https://doi.org/10.1080/15228959.2021.2009406

Miller, K. L. (2021, May 13). Microaggressions at the office can make remote work even more appealing. *Washington Post*. https://www.washingtonpost.com/business/2021/05/13/workplace-microaggressions-remote-workers/

Moeller, C. M. (2019). Disability, identity, and professionalism: Precarity in librarianship. *Library Trends, 67*(3), 455–470. https://doi.org/10.1353/lib.2019.0006

Monash University. (n.d.). *Inclusive uniform and dress code*. https://www.monash.edu/about/who/a-culture-of-integrity-and-respect/equity-diversity-inclusion/staff/lgbtiqa/resources/inclusive-dress

National Center on Birth Defects and Developmental Disabilities. (n.d.). *Disability impacts all of us infographic*. Centers for Disease Control and Prevention. https://www.cdc.gov/ncbddd/disabilityandhealth/infographic-disability-impacts-all.html

Ndugga, N., & Artiga, S. (2023, April 23). *Disparities in health and health care: 5 key questions and answers*. Kaiser Family Foundation. https://www.kff.org/racial-equity-and-health-policy/issue-brief/disparities-in-health-and-health-care-5-key-question-and-answers/

Northwest ADA Center. (n.d.). *Universal Design in the workplace* [Fact sheet]. https://nwadacenter.org/factsheet/universal-design-workplace

Office of Disability Employment Policy. (n.d.). *Universal Design*. US Department of Labor. https://www.dol.gov/agencies/odep/program-areas/employment-supports/universal-design

Oud, J. (2019, March). Systemic workplace barriers for academic librarians with disabilities. *College and Research Libraries, 80*(2), 169–194. https://doi.org/10.5860/crl.80.2.169

Peter, S. H., & Clement, K. A. (2020, Fall). One step at a time: A case study of incorporating Universal Design for Learning in library instruction. *Scholarship of Teaching and Learning, Innovative Pedagogy, 2*(3), 28–38. https://digitalcommons.humboldt.edu/sotl_ip/vol2/iss1/3

Pionke, J. J. (2019). The impact of disbelief: On being a library employee with a disability. *Library Trends, 67*(3), 423–435. https://doi.org/10.1353/lib.2019.0004

Project ENABLE. (2011, August). *ADA library accessibility checklist*. Syracuse University. https://projectenable.syr.edu/data/ADA_Accessibility_Checklist4.pdf

Roberts, L., Ives-Rublee, M., & Khattar, R. (2022, February 9). *COVID-19 likely resulted in 1.2 million more disabled people by the end of 2021—Workplaces and policy will need to adapt*. Center for American Progress. https://www.americanprogress.org/article/covid-19-likely-resulted-in-1-2-million-more-disabled-people-by-the-end-of-2021-workplaces-and-policy-will-need-to-adapt/

Rosa, K., & Henke, K. (2017). *2017 ALA demographic study*. American Library Association. https://alair.ala.org/server/api/core/bitstreams/4d524ee4-a0ed-49d0-8162-741ca5a834b2/content

Schlesselman-Tarango, G. (2019, Winter). Reproductive failure and information work: An autoethnography. *Library Trends, 67*(3), 436–454. https://doi.org/10.1353/lib.2019.0005

Schur, L. A., Ameri, M., & Kruse, D. (2020). Telework after COVID: A "silver lining" for workers with disabilities? *Journal of Occupational Rehabilitation, 30*(4), 521–536. https://doi.org/10.1007/s10926-020-09936-5

Shifrin, N. V., & Michel, J. S. (2022). Flexible work arrangements and employee health: A meta-analytic review. *Work and Stress, 36*(1), 60–85. https://doi.org/10.1080/02678373.2021.1936287

Spina, C. (2017). Libraries and Universal Design. *Theological Librarianship, 10*(1), 5–7. https://doi.org/10.31046/tl.v10i1.464

Staines, G. M. (2012). *Universal Design: A practical guide to creating and recreating interiors of academic libraries for teaching, learning and research*. Chandos Publishing. https://www.sciencedirect.com/book/9781843346333/universal-design

Subramanian, S., & Gilbert, T. (2021, March 11). A new era of workplace inclusion: Moving from retrofit to redesign [Blog post]. *Future Forum*. https://futureforum.com/2021/03/11/dismantling-the-office-moving-from-retrofit-to-redesign/

Taganova, J. (2022, June 19). *In a post-COVID workplace, is a "professional" dress code still relevant?* The Bridge, Global Voices. https://globalvoices.org/2022/06/19/in-a-post-covid-workplace-is-a-professional-dress-code-still-relevant/

Tang, L., Malley, B., Tanguay, C., & Tumlin, Z. (2020, July/August). Toward inclusion: Hiring for people with disabilities. *Archival Outlook,* pp. 4 & 17. https://mydigitalpublication.com/july-august-2020?i=667849&p=6&view=issueViewer&pp=1

US Bureau of Labor Statistics. (2022). *Persons with a disability: Labor force characteristics—2021 (USDL-22-0317)* [News release]. US Department of Labor. https://www.bls.gov/news.release/archives/disabl_02242022.htm

US Equal Opportunity Commission. (n.d.). *Job applicants and the ADA*. https://www.eeoc.gov/laws/guidance/job-applicants-and-ada

Weideman, M., & Hofmeyr, K. B. (2020). The influence of flexible work arrangements on employee engagement: An exploratory study. *South African Journal of Human Resource Management, 18*(1), Article a1209. https://doi.org/10.4102/sajhrm.v18i0.1209

Zhong, Y. (2012). Universal Design for Learning (UDL) in library instruction. *College and Undergraduate Libraries, 19*(1), 33–45. https://doi.org/10.1080/10691316.2012.652549

CHAPTER 11

# Planning for the On-Campus Interview
## Creating a Descriptive Library Accessibility Guide for Job Candidates

*Kimberly A. Looby*

## Introduction

On-campus interviews can be some of the most stressful parts of the hiring process. You have to prepare a presentation, be ready to meet with multiple groups and answer many questions, and have questions of your own to ask your potential new employer. You also have the stress of traveling to the place of interview and meeting complete strangers. This can be draining on the most able-bodied people, not to mention people with physical disabilities or chronic illnesses or who may have other personal information about themselves that they would like to keep private during an interview. To remedy these challenges, librarians at the J. Murrey Atkins Library (Atkins Library) at the University of North Carolina at Charlotte (UNC Charlotte) proposed making an accessibility guide focused on navigating the campus and library to support applicants who may have chronic illnesses or hidden disabilities. To review the full guide as of the writing of this chapter, please see appendix A at the end of this chapter.

## University Context

For context, the library is part of an urban regional institution in Charlotte, North Carolina, and housed underneath Academic Affairs within the university. The people who work at Atkins Library are categorized as twelve-month special library faculty, staff, nonstudent temporary employees, and student employees. There are around one hundred individuals currently employed at Atkins Library. Faculty librarians are hired on contracts and must complete a process to renew their contracts every three to five years. While librarians do not go through the tenure process, they are still able to apply for promotion from assistant professor to full professor through internal committees governed by the library faculty.

All of the hiring in the library is done in tandem with the university HR. Atkins Library creates job descriptions with HR and Academic Affairs and then posts positions widely across many message boards, e-mail discussion lists, and newsletters. Within the library, hiring is completed by a committee with a chair and a variety of staff and faculty. Occasionally for higher up leadership positions, such as associate deans, there will be a faculty member from outside the library on the committee. The hiring process begins with forming a hiring committee of representatives of different library departments, reviewing applications, conducting phone interviews, and then conducting on-campus interviews. The campus interview consists of a presentation to the whole library, meeting with the search committee, meeting with the committee for reappointment and promotion, meeting with the dean, and meeting with the department that is hiring.

## Creation and Reason for the Guide

Between 2018 and 2020, Atkins Library formed a committee to assess the internal hiring practices of the library to look for areas that could be built upon or improved, such as diversity training, committee communication, how information is shared, and a wider net to post job openings. This review spawned a temporary climate committee to look at the library climate as a whole through surveys and listening sessions where anyone could talk about ideas they had for continuing to make the library a collegial, communicative, and welcoming place. The climate committee created a list of achievable goals, both long-term and short-term, that would expand practices the library already had in place in terms of accessibility, sharing internal information, increasing social and collaborative opportunities, and more. In terms of accessibility, a committee member suggested making an accessibility guide that would give future faculty candidates information about the library building to allow them to better plan their on-campus interview. While detailed maps are available on the library website, there are no pictures or descriptions of the inside of the library. The author volunteered to take on the creation of this guide because they have a personal interest in information about accessibility. At the time of creation, the guide uses Springshare's LibGuide platform and incorporates Springshare's accessibility recommendations as well as templates set by the university for uniform web pages.

When discussing the creation of this guide, the intent was to acknowledge the stress candidates experience when they prepare for an on-campus interview. While reviewing the library's hiring practices, library employees noticed that information about the physical library building was often left out. Employees agreed that this was an area where a tangible source could be created to describe the physical experience of the building in a way that would support candidates who are visiting for their on-campus interview who may have visible or invisible, hidden, or nonapparent disabilities. The working assumption was that these candidates may not want to share personal information about their health but may need to ask questions that could hint at or indicate that they have a health condition. The assumption came from librarians, such as the author, who have firsthand knowledge and experience of working in the library field with health conditions.

The internal review committee, the diversity and inclusion committee, and the accessibility committee were all in full support of the guide. Before the author got started, they wanted to make sure they had data, examples, and explanations that would advocate for each section of the guide being included and who specifically would benefit from that section. The author used firsthand knowledge of their own experience and activity in the chronic illness community, but did not do any formative assessments outside of communicating with various committees and colleagues in the library. This approach could mean experiences may be left out of the guide, so summative assessment should be done in the future, but has not been completed at the time of publishing. The main goal was to increase empathy, awareness, and privacy for hidden disabilities or chronic illnesses. During these conversations and near the end of the creation of the guide, reviewers pointed out that people who identify as being on the LGBT+ spectrum may also benefit from information in the guide.

# Intentionality and Inclusivity

## Intentionality

The goal of this chapter is twofold. First, the author wishes for readers to understand why and how they created the accessibility guide. Since this guide is about the physical experience of a particular academic library building, the author will include brief historical information about why academic libraries are built the way they are. Second, the author wants readers to understand the necessity of including an accessibility guide in their own hiring practices and how such a guide would benefit job candidates, as well as the library.

Since many people with invisible disabilities can pass as abled, it is important to provide information on accessibility. Those who may not wish to disclose themselves as disabled may prefer to avoid having to ask personal, intrusive, or other questions that may indicate they have a disability, illness, or something else that impacts their experience of a physical space. Since each individual experience with disability is unique, the author will rely on generalizations for this chapter. Readers will also begin to understand why people with invisible disabilities or may not choose to self-identify as disabled during a job interview. There will also be a brief discussion of those who identify as lesbian, gay, bisexual, queer, transx, two spirit, intersex, asexual, aromantic, nonbinary, or agender and everyone else on the LGBT+ spectrum. For readability, the author is going to use the shortened form of this acronym of LGBT+. There are many other forms of this acronym, and the author does not intend to leave anyone out while using the shortened acronym.

## Inclusivity

Throughout this chapter, the author aimed to use current trends, preferences, and thinking about word choice for describing people. Language surrounding identity is always in flux. At the time of writing this chapter, in the early 2020s, there is an online debate about how to identify yourself or someone else as being disabled. For disabilities, the author varied between person-first and disability-first terminology. There are scholarly articles, book chapters, blogs, videos, and think pieces about which should be used, and the author chose to accommodate both (Dunn & Burcaw, 2013). The identity of disability has a long history, and people of different ages and life stages reading this chapter may have strong feelings toward their identity preferences. Some people prefer to say "I am disabled," others prefer "I have a disability." As a person with a disability, the author had no inclination for either. They use the self-descriptions interchangeably in their everyday language, usually depending on which sounds better grammatically or if the author is trying to emphasize talking about people broadly or specifically. The author puts no value or moral judgment on how anyone wants to identify and views all identities as valid.

In addition to being inclusive with disabled language, the author attempted to be inclusive with gendered language as well. Multiple identities related to gender and sexuality can experience health issues with reproductive organs, fertility, carrying a fetus, and giving birth. There are multiple ways of referring to these experiences, and many people have different preferences. To be inclusive, the author varied how they referred to genders.

When writing about and describing disabilities and gender, the author wanted to include as many different disabled experiences as they could. If you, the reader, feel that your experience was not included in this narrative, especially if your experience is left out of a lot of disability narratives or discussions, please feel free to e-mail the author Kimberly Looby (Kim) at klooby@uncc.edu or klooby2@gmail.com. Kim enjoys speaking with others with disabilities and learning about their experiences.

I, the author, identify as a disabled person, a person with disabilities or both. I have rheumatoid arthritis, a connective tissue disorder; chronic pain; and hypokalemic periodic paralysis. I am choosing to disclose here to show my background and experience with disability and as a member of the disabled community. My disabilities are mostly invisible, and I can easily pass as abled. I also identify as LGBT+, though my identity is not one that is affected by bathrooms or privacy, so I reached out to multiple individuals to be sensitivity readers for those sections.

# Identity and Disclosure
## Disability Identity

Identifying as disabled is a deeply personal choice. Many people may have a condition that the general public would consider to be a disability, but the person with the condition may not identify as disabled. Some people are so used to their chronic illness, conditions, or other bodily differences that it is just normal to them. Others may think that identifying as disabled is too strong of a term because they are not disabled enough. Kohli and Atencio (2023) explore disability identity in their research on how university students self-identify as disabled, which can be applied to many others who are considering their disabled identity. One factor that may impact a person's decision to identify or not identify as disabled is whether or not their disability is visible. People with invisible disabilities often (but not always) have the privilege of passing as abled without stares, questions, comments, or other invasions of their personal space. On the downside, though, they often face more barriers with access to treatment and workplace accommodations since their disabilities are not visible (Betz, 2022).

For a more formal definition, the Americans with Disabilities Act (ADA) provides the definition that legal, professional, and other entities use when making considerations for what is a disability in the United States. If you are outside of the United States, please refer to your country's laws, if available, surrounding people with disabilities. The U.S. State Department provides the following definition:

> A person with a disability is someone who:
> 
> - has a physical or mental impairment that substantially limits one or more major life activities,
> - has a history or record of such an impairment (such as cancer that is in remission), or
> - is perceived by others as having such an impairment (such as a person who has scars from a severe burn).
> 
> If a person falls into any of these categories, the ADA protects them. Because the ADA is a law, and not a benefit program, you do not need to apply for coverage (US Department of Justice, Civil Rights Division, n.d.)

# Disability Disclosure

Disclosure is a highly personal and potentially fraught process that is specific to the individual and their need to disclose, especially on an interview day with the high stakes of being considered for a new position. Some people are very comfortable with talking about their bodies and are open about their disabilities. Some have disabilities that are obvious and visible to a sighted person. Others have disabilities that can be hidden or masked while around people. And yet others have disabilities that are episodic, meaning they can remain hidden until the disability is suddenly visible. The ability or desire to disclose a disability is often related to what the disability entails. Illnesses or disabilities that are related to reproductive organs, waste-eliminating organs, or other aspects of the body that people consider uncomfortable to discuss make it difficult for people to get the support they need (Betz, 2022).

It is important to discuss episodic and invisible disabilities in relation to this guide because the condition or disability may or may not be active on the interview day. The interviewee may be less likely to bring up or ask for an accommodation if they are able to hide the disease, condition, or disability. It is possible that the interview day could be a day when the interviewee experiences an episode, which is out of their control, and must ask for an accommodation on that day. Since disabilities can be stable, intermittent, or episodic, interviewees may have many different challenges in managing the disability on an interview day (Betz, 2022). Someone with a stable disability is more likely to be practiced at asking for what they need. Someone with an episodic disease, such as migraines, may not need anything on their interview day or may need to take medication. But a person with epilepsy may suddenly need a space to lie down. Betz (2022) and Jans, Kaye & Jones (2012) provide extensive information about risks and benefits of disclosing, which are summarized below in list form.

Benefits of disclosing disability:
- increased empathy and understanding of one's lived experience
- honest conversations about accessibility of the library
- ability to get accommodations throughout the interview process
- connection with other disabled librarians at the hiring library

Risks of disclosing disability:
- assumptions about abilities
- possibility of not being hired
- knowledge of personal health information or status
- possibility of being interacted with less—for example, asked fewer questions, people won't look at you, awkwardness
- being unable to make connections

## LGBT+ Identity and Disclosure

While most of this guide is focused on disabilities, having a guide that describes bathrooms supports another group of people who have been discriminated against and may want to keep their identities private. Self-identifying as LGBT+ is a deeply personal process with a wide variety of experience. Some people may be out to everyone, and some may be out in different areas of their lives (for example, friends, but not coworkers). To protect these identities, having descriptions of bathrooms on accessibility guides helps interviewees and speaks to the expectation that people who identify as or consider themselves to be LGBT+ or on the LGBT+ spectrum (or another current and more modern term) will be applying for positions at the library.

# University Built Environment

College campuses are notoriously confusing for finding parking and buildings. Parking is often scattered and variable in terms of who can use each lot. Parking usually fills up quickly, and folks on campus often have to park fairly far from their primary building. It is very rare to be able to park in front of the building you are going to. This situation adds an extra barrier of figuring out how to travel between the parking spot and the library building, with additional barriers of weather, geography, and path surface.

Weather is a factor no matter where the university is located; there are going to be heat, cold, snow, ice, rain, wind, storms, and so on. In terms of geography, college campuses that are flat will have fewer stairs and ramps than college campuses that are hilly or mountainous. On a flat campus, mobility devices may be able to go in most directions at any time and use the majority of paths. On a hilly campus, there may be designated pathways with ramps that are not always the shortest path to the destination. The farther one has to travel, the more time they will be exposed to the elements. As an aside, the author frequently uses the ADA paths on their campus to avoid stairs, and if you're the first person out on the pathways in the morning, you may come face-to-face with giant spiders in their webs across the paths. As someone with arachnophobia, the author would argue these paths are not accessible if covered with spiders. These factors were all included when creating the guide, (except the spiders, for now).

# Academic Libraries Physical Buildings

Since the guide focuses on the experience of the academic library, it would be remiss to not include a little bit of background information about academic libraries and why they are built the way they are. Academic libraries are often some of the oldest buildings on campus since they are usually built when the campus is established. Because they are some of the first buildings, they are often expanded and renovated over time to meet the needs of the often-growing university. This growth can create a lot of variation in accessibility in buildings depending on the building codes and other laws enforced at the time of construction.

In the United States, when academic libraries were first being built two hundred years ago, the focus of the building was to house collections of physical material, usually books. In the last few decades, libraries have moved much of their print collections to off-site storage facilities and placed more favor on innovative technology spaces and space for student study, which is reflected in newly built libraries such as North Carolina State University's Hunt library (NC State University Libraries, n.d.).

Academic libraries grew as the public university systems grew in keeping with advances in education, publishing, research, and expansions in science, social science, engineering, and other disciplines (Stewart, 2010). As for the building itself, many are built to be aesthetically pleasing and impressive (Schlipf & Moorman, 2018). Buildings' construction and updates are based upon materials available; architectural design; engineering developments; creation of and continual updates to building codes for safety, accessibility, and regulation; and the Americans with Disabilities Act (Ching & Winkel, 2012).

Someone may wonder, why not just renovate, build a new library, or fix any accessibility issues? Structures are expensive to change and renovate, and capital projects do not always come easy. Many universities are tax-funded or receive gifts from donors, grants, or fundraising campaigns (Schlipf & Moorman, 2018; Stewart, 2010). For new library buildings built between 2003 and 2009, the most expensive was $177 million, and the least expensive was $1 million in 2010 dollars (Stewart, 2010).

The first thing job candidates will encounter at the library are the doors to the building. Entrances to libraries, especially historic or old library buildings, have many features that prevent people with any kind of mobility need from easily entering the building. With the passing of the Americans with Disabilities Act in 1990, many libraries have had to make updates to their entrances to meet accessibility requirements. Since entrances are difficult and expensive to fix or rebuild, many entrances have retro features such as ramps added later, elevators on the outside of buildings, one updated door with an actuator near the ramp, and more (Schlipf & Moorman, 2018). Many doors to buildings become heavy and difficult to open; for example, the doors at the former Undergraduate Library at the University of Illinois Urbana-Champaign were notoriously difficult to open due to heaviness, placement of hinges, and lack of clarity about if one is to push or pull to open the door (*Daily Illini* Editorial Board, 2016).

Once inside the building, there is a new set of challenges involving moving between floors, such as elevators, lifts, and staircases. Building codes at time of construction will determine placement and size of elevators in libraries. If the library was built before the ADA or other codes requiring elevators, then elevators may have been added in unusual places, such as at the edges of buildings or only in new additions and may be inaccessible sizes. If there is space, platform lifts can be added near half floors or short staircases. These lifts, though, pose some other problems. Users have to manually open and close the doors and often must ride alone due to lack of space. If users have limitations with opening or closing doors, a library staff member may need to assist them, which is one more barrier to moving between floors. Stairs also pose more problems for safety and accessibility. Schlipf and Moorman (2018) provide a list of issues with staircases including floating staircases where people can hit their heads underneath, curved staircases with unevenly shaped steps, and handrails that are not easy to grip. There are also open or transparent risers or extra-long staircases that can make users feel dizzy or unwell. Staircases can also be noisy and may be hidden or far from elevators.

# Describing the Guide

The author started the guide with a very brief introduction to the building, giving the year it was built and any additions that could impact accessibility of the building. This section also serves as an introduction to the guide and how to use it, as well as a link to a PDF that can be downloaded. At the time of publication, the downloadable PDF is not screen-reader-accessible, but this problem will be fixed as soon as possible. The author built the guide in a way that would follow the candidates' path from arriving at the campus, to entering the library, to moving throughout the building, and then other information about disability on campus.

## Parking and Pathways

The first section relates to parking and pathways. UNC Charlotte is a hilly campus, and the library sits at the very top of a hill. It's visible from most places on campus but requires navigating many stairs, steep inclines, and wandering routes for mobility devices. For parking, the author described in very simple terms that there is no parking at the library but that lots are available all around the library and that accessible routes from parking to the library depend on where you park. Because describing every single pathway would be an impossible task, the author linked directly to the campus parking and routes map because it has a setting for showing accessible routes. Linking directly to the campus map also reduces the need to keep updating the guide as paths change—the college or university will always have the most up-to-date information. To make sure the candidate had necessary information, the author considered things like weather, types of walkways, gradients, and buildings to pass through. Then the author considered the person who may need this information: someone with an injury in their legs or feet, someone using a mobility device, someone who has pain or fatigue while walking. The author listed out specific diseases and illnesses to give names to conditions that people may have rather than just symptoms. Below is an example from the guide describing parking lots near the library.

> **Parking near the library**
>
> The nearest parking lots and decks have varying degrees of distance, steepness, and ramp access. Depending on where you park, the most accessible route to the library may involve a mixture of indoor movement using stairs/elevators and outdoor travel on walkways and paths. See our Directions & Parking page (https://library.charlotte.edu/visit-study/directions-parking) for information about paths to the library.

## Entrances and Doors

The next section of the guide describes doors. The author focused on entrances to the library and if they are covered, have ramps, or have actuator buttons. Doors impact mobility with their size, if they're covered or exposed to the elements, and if there are stairs or ramps leading to the doors. When describing doors, the author looked for the following things: width, actuator buttons, how many doors or how heavily trafficked the doors are, and anything else that made the doors unique. Since candidates apply for positions throughout the whole library, the author tried to be as encompassing as possible when describing the different doors throughout the building and the doors that interviewees would be most likely to use. Recovering from a knee injury, an illness, having a high symptom day or a regular symptom day of a chronic illness, using a mobility device, or having an arm in a cast may all impact someone's ability to open a door successfully. For internal doors, the author walked around the building and found that there were too many types of doors to describe. Doors that lead to bathrooms, offices, stairs, classrooms, meeting rooms, and other specialty rooms were all too different. Because of this multitude of door types, the author, with the support of other reviewers, chose to leave internal door descriptions out of the guide for brevity.

## Different Floors of the Library

Once inside the library, the candidate will now be faced with the general floors of the library, which include flooring, furniture, lighting, noise, and other features. During many rounds of review, one librarian suggested adding brief descriptions of the library floors since libraries have a wide range of ages, designs, additions, and subtractions. The author added descriptions of each floor of the library with descriptions of light, flooring, noise level, traffic level, and general use. Remember that each reader's library will likely have a map available to candidates, so be sure to include information that is not already on the map. Describing flooring and noise levels is essential for people who are hard of hearing, use mobility devices, and may be at risk for a fall from something like epilepsy or multiple sclerosis.

## Elevators and Stairs

Elevators and stairs were the most difficult part of the building to describe. Atkins Library has a lot of elevators, and the author even required the help of their building managers to identify a secret elevator that no one knew about! It turned out to be an elevator that is used only by facilities. Because the library building has undergone multiple renovations and additions, one elevator goes to four floors, another goes to five, one goes to all twelve (the library has a tower portion). Not all elevators or floors are open to everyone. Stairs were equally difficult to describe because there are many staircases throughout the building. Some are open to everyone, some are alarmed, and since the library building is two buildings in one, many staircases go to only a few floors. Describing stairs and elevators would help people with balance issues, pain, mobility devices, dizziness, or vertigo. Below is an example from the guide describing elevators in the library.

> Atkins Library has five elevators. Three elevators are open to the public, and two are employee only. The library has undergone multiple additions since it was built which affects elevator design and placement. These elevators are close to the following unit offices:

Bathrooms have many features that the author looked for when creating the guide. This included the door into the bathroom, whether or not it has an actuator button (the button that makes the door open automatically), whether there is one door or two, the path into the bathroom (is there an incline or step?), and number and location of stalls. Guide creators can also describe how heavily trafficked the bathrooms are and if they are used primarily by students or library employees. Describing the location and type of bathroom has many uses. It tells someone with mobility challenges which bathrooms have actuators and are accessible. It tells someone with bowel disorders or heavy menstrual cycles where the nearest bathroom is. And finally, it offers privacy to those on the LGBT+ spectrum who may prefer a safe, gender-neutral bathroom if the candidate would rather not use a gender-binary bathroom. Below is an example from the guide on describing bathrooms.

> **Atkins Library has a variety of bathrooms.**
>
> Our building has a variety of bathrooms to meet different needs. Please see the library's floor maps (https://library.charlotte.edu/visit-study/floor-maps) for their specific location within the library. All of the bathrooms have automatic flush toilets, automatic sinks and automatic paper towel dispensers.

The final section of the guide is simply to include the most important campus information about disability and accessibility including disability transit, accommodations, or other services. While it may not be useful for the day of the interview, it shows that the campus expects people with disabilities to apply and work for the university.

## Integration and Assessment

After writing the guide, the author sent it through multiple rounds of review. They shared it with their supervisor, their department head, library HR, the accessibility committee, the diversity and inclusion committee, the associate deans, and finally the steering committee for final approval. Everyone was in support and offered suggestions for additions to the guide. When it was completed, the author handed it off to the library HR folks since they are in charge of organizing searches and maintaining information for candidates. Currently, the guide is linked with all job postings and advertisements. Once faculty candidates are scheduled to travel, the library HR folks remind them about the guide and that they can request accommodations through the person who sets up the travel as that person has no impact or say in the candidate's final evaluation for the position.

Assessing a guide like this one poses some interesting challenges. Since one goal of the accessibility hiring guide is to prevent people from needing to self-identify, people may not feel comfortable answering questions about their personal experience. If you want to assess a guide such as this one, the author would suggest sending it to academic library e-mail discussion lists as an official survey and ask survey respondents if they would find the information in it useful during an on-campus interview. While UNC Charlotte does not have a formalized post-interview assessment process, the library could send out a survey to candidates asking if they found this kind of information useful.

## Conclusion

Having simple and detailed descriptions of your building benefits anyone who visits the building, not just folks with disabilities. Having the guide readily available and part of candidate material packets shows that the library is aware of its surroundings and sets the expectation that it be both welcoming and cognizant of people who have a wide variety of needs and abilities. It also sets the tone that the library cannot expect or assume that everyone navigates the physical world the same way and expects that people with illnesses or invisible or visible disabilities and people who identify on the LGBT+ spectrum will apply.

When creating a guide like this one, having information ahead of time should make advocating for the guide much easier in case of any pushback. While this author did not receive any pushback or challenges to creating the guide, they were ready in case people were unsure of its necessity. Having concrete examples of illnesses, diseases, or disorders and their symptoms makes clear the need of a guide like this one. If you have never had painful periods or inflammatory bowel disease, you've never experienced the need to know exactly where the closest bathroom is. If you've never had a broken arm or extreme fatigue, you've never known how heavy a door can be. If you've never had balance issues, you've never known how daunting stairs suddenly become. And since you may never see any of these needs from looking at a person, it's important to have an accessibility guide like this one ready to make candidates feel welcome and that people with disabilities, and with illnesses whether temporary or permanent, are expected to be part of the library faculty.

# Acknowledgments

I would like to thank Christin Lampkowsi and Olivia Patterson for being sensitivity readers. I would like to thank my mom, Judy Looby, for raising me to be a librarian. And I would like to thank my cat Luna for being my constant companion during my illnesses.

## APPENDIX A

# Accessibility for Job Candidates and Visitors at J. Murrey Atkins Library

This guide will provide information about accessibility at UNCC and Atkins Library. This will cover things such as elevators, bathrooms, general campus accessibility resources, parking and more.

## What is this guide?

### ATKINS LIBRARY BUILDING

This guide provides information about accessibility at Atkins Library and UNC Charlotte, covering elevators, bathrooms, parking, and more.

Atkins Library was originally built in 1964 and has undergone multiple construction additions which affect its accessibility. We hope this guide will help you navigate the library for maximum accessibility.

Use the links on the left to navigate to different sections of the guide.

### LIBRARY ACCESSIBILITY

In addition to this guide, we maintain a broader library accessibility page (https://library.charlotte.edu/visit-study/accessibility) for patrons and visitors. It contains similar information to this guide but does not focus specifically on job candidates.

For information about accessibility beyond the library and at the campus-level, visit

- Campus accessibility (https://accessibility.charlotte.edu)
- Reasonable accommodations (https://hr.charlotte.edu/pims/reasonable-accommodation)
- Disability paratransit (https://pats.charlotte.edu/transportation/disability-paratransit)
- All-gender restrooms (https://legal.charlotte.edu/legal-topics/nondiscrimination/restrooms)

# Accessible Parking at Atkins

## PARKING NEAR THE LIBRARY

Unfortunately, there is no parking near library entrances. The library is located in a central part of campus, about one-quarter mile from the nearest parking lot.

The nearest parking lots and decks have varying degrees of distance, steepness, and ramp access. Depending on where you park, the most accessible route to the library may involve a mixture of indoor movement using stairs/elevators and outdoor travel on walkways and paths. See our **Directions & Parking** page (https://library.charlotte.edu/visit-study/directions-parking) for information about paths to the library.

To use an interactive map of campus with parking and accessible pathways, visit the **Interactive Campus Map** (https://facilities.charlotte.edu/our-services/maps/interactive-campus-map) site. Under layers, open "parking" then select the boxes for "disability" and "ADA spaces" for accessible parking. Then open the layer "accessibility" then select the boxes of "ADA Pathways". You can also select "ADA Entrances" if you would like to see accessible entrances on campus.

Find general parking information including campus maps at the **Parking Overview** (https://pats.charlotte.edu/parking/parking-overview) site.

## DISABILITY PARKING

If employees use a permit to park in handicap accessible spaces, the university will ask for this information when employees register for their campus parking permit.

The university provides a **disability paratransit service** (https://pats.charlotte.edu/transportation/disability-paratransit) for people with mobility needs.

The service can pick you up at a scheduled time and bring you closer to the North Entrance of Atkins Library.

# Entrances and Doors

## PUBLIC ENTRANCES

### NORTH AND SOUTH ENTRANCES

Both of these public entryways are flat and covered. They are accessible by ramps and stairs. Both entrances have two sets of single doors with actuators and a vestibule in between.

- From the outside, buttons on your right activate the actuators
- When exiting, the buttons are on your left
- You must press a button for each set of doors on either side of the vestibule

The South Entrance enters on the **first floor** (https://library.charlotte.edu/visit-study/floor-maps/main-floor) and is also known as the "Main Entrance."

The North Entrance enters on the **ground floor** (https://library.charlotte.edu/visit-study/floor-maps/ground-floor) and is also known as the "Back Entrance."

**PEET'S ENTRANCE**

In addition to the North Entrance, you may also enter the ground floor through the Library Café, also known as Peet's.

This entrance is only available during the hours in which Peet's is open. See **Peet's hours** (https://library.charlotte.edu/visit-study/hours/library-cafe).

These doors have no actuators, but the outside area leading to this entrance is reachable by stairs with walkways that are accessible to wheelchairs and mobility aids.

## EMPLOYEE ONLY ENTRANCES

We have multiple entryways which are accessible only to those with an employee identification card.

**EAST ENTRANCE (FIRST FLOOR)**

This entryway leads to the Administration offices on the second floor.

Stairs and a ramp lead up to these doors from the outside. A keycard is required. This door has an actuator.

- From the outside, buttons on the right to activate the actuators
- When exiting, the buttons are on the left

To reach the Admin offices from this entrance, there are stairs to climb up one floor, then another door which requires a keycard.

**NORTH ENTRANCE (LOWER LEVEL)**

Another single door on the North side of the building enters into offices on the Lower Level. There is a mild slope outside leading up to this door.

From this entrance, there is access to the employee-only elevators which travel between the Lower Level and floor 3.

**WEST ENTRANCE (LOWER LEVEL)**

A single door on the West side of the building also enters into offices on the Lower Level. There is a steep slope leading up to this door.

## DOORS INSIDE ATKINS LIBRARY

Although we can't list each of the doors in the library individually, it's important to note that no internal doors have actuators except for those at ADA accessible bathrooms. There are many internal doors which require card-swipe access and automatically lock themselves to the outside. Doors with this access method include entrances to some office suites, meeting rooms, classrooms, and other specialized rooms.

Most individual offices require a physical key, and these doors can be configured to remain either locked or unlocked by default.

# Floors

The building has a total of 12 floors. From bottom to top, the floors are labeled "lower level," "ground," and floors 1–10. See the **floor maps for each floor** (https://library.charlotte.edu/visit-study/floor-maps) for more information.

## LOWER LEVEL

The lower level is not accessible to patrons. Some employee offices are located on the basement floor. The flooring is carpeted.

## FLOORS GROUND TO 3

We consider these the "main" floors of the library. They are open to patrons. Except in designated areas, these floors welcome collaboration, so we expect them to be "loud." The flooring is carpeted. These floors receive natural light.

## FLOOR 4

Floor 4 is not accessible to patrons. No employee offices are located on the fourth floor. The flooring is tiled. This floor receives natural light.

## FLOORS 5 TO 10

We refer to floors 5–10 as the "tower" floors. They are open to patrons. All areas of these floors are designated for silent study. The flooring is tiled. These floors receive natural light.

# Stairs and Elevators

## STAIRS

All stairs have contrast striping except for those in the Special Collections Reading Room (Dalton Reading Room) on the tenth floor.

## ELEVATORS IN ATKINS

Please ask an Atkins employee for assistance if you would like to use the staff elevator to move between floors.

Atkins Library has five elevators. Three elevators are open to the public, and two are employee only. The library has undergone multiple additions since it was built which

affects elevator design and placement. These elevators are close to the following unit offices:
- Research and Instructional Services (First floor)
- Area 49 (Second floor)
- Collection Services (Second floor)
- Special Collections and University Archives (Lower level, ninth and tenth floor)

*There are no elevators directly by the administrative offices, but there are multiple clear pathways between the elevators and the administrative offices.

## PUBLIC ELEVATORS
### Tower Elevators (Center of Building)

There are two, side by side elevators in the tower that provide access to the ground level through the 10th floor of the building. These elevators do not meet ADA accessible guidelines for wheelchairs and mobility aids. These elevators are close to the offices for:
- Research and Instructional Services
- Area 49
- Collection Services
- Special Collections and University Archives*

*Some offices for Special Collections and University Archives are located on the Lower Level. They can be accessed with the staff elevator.

**Note:** These elevators will undergo construction to become ADA accessible within the next few years after budget approval in 2021–2022. Please see the library home page: https://library.charlotte.edu/ for the most up to date information on the status of these elevators.

### Ground Through Third Floor Elevator (Center of Building)

The public and ADA-compliant elevator is also in the center of the building but only provides access to the ground, first, second, and third floors. This elevator is close to the following offices:
- Research and Instructional Services
- Area 49
- Collection Services

## EMPLOYEE ONLY ELEVATORS
### Staff Elevator (North Side)

The employee elevator, referred to as the staff elevator, is card swipe access only and is the closest elevator to the north entrance. This elevator accesses the lower level, ground,

first, second and third floors. It is ADA compliant and accessible to wheelchairs and other mobility devices. This elevator is close to the following offices:
- Research and Instructional Services
- Area 49
- Collection Services
- Special Collections and University Archives (lower level only)

### *Facilities Elevator (East Side)*

This elevator is reserved for use by personnel in Facilities Management and Atkins Building Operations. It provides access to the ground floor, first floor, and second floor

## Bathrooms and Lactation Room

### ATKINS LIBRARY HAS A VARIETY OF BATHROOMS.

Our building has a variety of bathrooms to meet different needs. Please **see the library's floor maps** (https://library.charlotte.edu/visit-study/floor-maps) for their specific location within the library. All of the bathrooms have automatic flush toilets, automatic sinks and automatic paper towel dispensers.

### SINGLE OCCUPANCY ALL-GENDER BATHROOMS

Find these bathrooms near the elevators on fifth–eighth floor and tenth floor. They are open to the public.

The doors to these bathrooms don't have actuators; they must be opened manually. The doors can be locked from the inside.

### DOORS WITH ACTUATORS

There are bathrooms on the ground, first, second, and third floors with actuators that open two single doors into the bathroom. The bathrooms are located in the middle of the building near the tower floors and are close to the following offices:
- Research and Instructional Services
- Area 49
- Collection Services

They are in high traffic areas and are used by students, library employees, and the public. There is one ADA/handicapped stall in each bathroom.

### DOORS WITHOUT ACTUATORS

There are bathrooms without actuators on the lower level, ground, first, second, and third floors. They are located near the following offices:
- Research and Instructional Services

- Area 49
- Collection Services offices
- Administrative offices
- Special Collections and University Archives (lower level)

These are in lower traffic areas and most often used by library staff and faculty. These bathrooms have single doors which must be manually opened. There is one ADA/handicapped stall in each bathroom.

## LACTATION ROOM

Atkins Library has a single occupancy room to provide privacy for lactation. Atkins Library does not maintain this room, and users must register and sign up with Human Resources. For more information about lactation rooms on campus, please visit **Human Resources Lactation Room** ([URL removed for chapter longevity]). This room is on the ground floor.

# Links to Information for UNC Charlotte Campus Accessibility

## ALL GENDER RESTROOMS

**Clickable Link All Gender Restrooms**
URL: [URL removed for chapter longevity]
From the website: UNC Charlotte is committed to building unisex accessible restrooms across campus to make selecting a restroom easier for all our students, faculty, and staff.

## DISABILITY PARATRANSIT

**Clickable Link: Disability Paratransit**
URL: [URL removed for chapter longevity]
From the website: Niner Paratransit provides disability transport for those with mobility impairments who are registered for the service.

## REASONABLE ACCOMMODATIONS

**Clickable Link: Reasonable Accommodations**
URL: [URL removed for chapter longevity]
From the website: The University of North Carolina at Charlotte (UNC Charlotte) provides reasonable accommodation to employees and/or applicants who are disabled or become disabled and need assistance to perform the essential functions of their positions.

# References

Betz, G. (2022, April 6). Navigating the academic hiring process with disabilities. *In the Library with the Lead Pipe*. https://www.inthelibrarywiththeleadpipe.org/2022/hiring-with-disabilities/

Ching, F., & Winkel, S. R. (2012). *Building codes illustrated: A guide to understanding the 2012 international building code* (4th ed.). Wiley.

*Daily Illini* Editorial Board. (2016, August 30). Editorial: In loving (or horrifying) memory of the UGL doors. *The Daily Illini.* https://dailyillini.com/opinions-stories/2016/08/30/in-loving-or-horrifying-memory-of-the-ugl-doors/

Dunn, D. S., & Burcaw, S. (2013). Disability identity: Exploring narrative accounts of disability. *Rehabilitation Psychology, 58*(2), 148–157. https://doi.org/10.1037/a0031691

Jans, L. H., Kaye, H. S., & Jones, E. C. (2012). Getting hired: Successfully employed people with disabilities offer advice on disclosure, interviewing, and job search. *Journal of Occupational Rehabilitation, 22*(2), 155–165. https://doi.org/10.1007/s10926-011-9336-y

Kohli, J., & Atencio, M. (2023). "The person with a disability gets to define their disability": Exploring identity formation through the voices of university students. *Disability and Society, 38*(5), 819–841. https://doi.org/10.1080/09687599.2021.1965545

NC State University Libraries. (n.d.) *Our library of the future: The James B. Hunt Jr. Library captures the innovative, forward-looking spirit of NC State University.* https://www.lib.ncsu.edu/hunt-library

Schlipf, F. A., & Moorman, J. A. (2018). *The practical handbook of library architecture: Creating building spaces that work.* ALA Editions.

Stewart, C. (2010). *The academic library building in the digital age : a study of construction, planning, and design of new library space.* Association of College and Research Libraries.

US Department of Justice, Civil Rights Division. (n.d.). *Introduction to the Americans with Disabilities Act.* https://beta.ada.gov/topics/intro-to-ada/

# Part 3
# TRANSFORMING THE PROCESS FOR ALL

CHAPTER 12

# Remote Interviews, Process, and Documentation

## How COVID Changed Hiring at One Academic Library

*Arielle Lomness, Sajni Lacey, and Donna Langille*

The University of British Columbia's (UBC) Okanagan campus is situated on the unceded, ancestral, and occupied territory of the Syilx people in what is currently known as the city of Kelowna. The Okanagan Library serves the entire campus's 12,000-plus student population and has a direct reporting line to the university librarian on the Vancouver campus. There are currently twelve librarians, archivists, and records managers who work at the Okanagan campus, with most librarians taking on a portfolio responsibility, as well as a number of subject areas. Librarians, archivists, and records managers are members of the Faculty Association and are governed by a collective agreement; however, the Okanagan Library also relies on the university's central HR and the Okanagan Library's administration team to support hiring.

In response to the COVID-19 pandemic in 2020, the UBC Okanagan campus shifted its service and instruction to primarily remote delivery and slowly transitioned students and employees back to campus in fall 2021. As of September 2022, the campus returned to offering the majority of classes and services in person, so librarians are expected to be available through hybrid modes for both teaching and reference, bringing services to a new normal. While in-person work has returned to the campus, hiring still takes place primarily online. As this practice may also be the case for other institutions, the chapter discusses our experiences serving on seven remote selection committees since 2020 and how moving to remote interviewing led to a strengthening of equity, diversity, inclusion, and accessibility (EDIA) values in our hiring practices. In doing this work, we encountered challenges and discovered practical solutions. By mapping out what worked for us, what still needs improvement, and next steps, the chapter provides templates to illuminate concrete takeaways that may also work for other libraries.

# Equity, Diversity, Inclusion, and Accessibility (EDIA)

Five years ago, the Okanagan Library's EDI Committee investigated and made recommendations on how to best integrate EDIA into our local hiring and interviewing practices, as well as how to better align internal practices with institutional EDIA frameworks (e.g., Indigenous Strategic Plan and Inclusion Action Plan). The move to online interviewing during the pandemic provided another opportunity to further these conversations and to reconsider additional EDIA needs unique to the online environment. We discussed the following: creating time during the interview day to facilitate the well-being of the candidate and the committee and what we consider to be important when making an informed decision.

# Literature Review

Reviewing the existing literature around hiring practices was essential to the Okanagan Library's efforts to improve its recruitment and selection process. The library was already acutely aware that the concept of fit in hiring is typically not aligned with fair and equitable hiring practices that promote diversity and inclusion. Indeed, Cunningham, Guss, and Stout (2019) argue that hiring for fit is typically problematic as it is often functions as a code for desirable personality traits that have not been defined by the committee as being important to perform a role; this lack of definition and clarity can result in hiring candidates who can fit better into white, ableist, and heteronormative spaces due to the unstated biases of the committee. As a potential remedy to these biases, O'Meara, Culpepper, and Templeton (2020) and Orupabo and Mangset (2021) emphasize the importance of considering a wide range of experiences and criteria for diversity outside of formal years of experience in a library, such as community or volunteer work, when reviewing applicants.

In implementing our new hiring process, we were also guided by the insights of Betz (2022), who highlighted the need for transparency and clear communication throughout the hiring process and especially about what each component of the interview day includes, particularly for candidates with disabilities. Finally, we followed the recommendations of Michalak and Rysavy (2022), who offer practical tips for conducting effective online interviews in academic libraries, such as minimizing technological demands and providing candidates with clear breaks and schedules. By integrating these perspectives into our hiring practices, we promote a more equitable and inclusive process that attracts a diverse pool of qualified candidates.

# Previous Interview and Hiring Challenges

We identified several challenges to the library's pre-pandemic hiring practices and the information provided to candidates as part of the interview process. The following section outlines the significant challenges we identified when beginning to revise the process for remote hiring.

## Job Postings

From 2013 to 2020, the leadership team drafted nearly all of the library's job postings and descriptions, with minimal input from the librarian team before posting. Leadership typically formed the selection committees after the advertisements had been finalized and sometimes posted. The absence of librarian involvement in developing job ads caused problems for librarians on the selection committees, as they often lacked understanding of how the positions fit within the library as a whole, complemented other librarians' portfolios, or contributed to achieving the library's and university's goals and strategic initiatives for EDIA. Overall, this process did not allow for collegial conversations regarding what success in a position would look like.

## Interview Day

The format of in-person interviews had changed little for many years, with generic topics and questions repeated from past committees and only minor customization for portfolio specializations and EDIA considerations. Presentation topics were provided in advance, but interview questions were not, creating a lack of consideration for accessibility and candidate support. The in-person days were long and demanding for the candidate and committee and consisted of a presentation, a formal interview, lunch with non-committee-member colleagues, a campus tour, a meet and greet with campus staff, meetings with relevant campus partners, and a dinner with colleagues. Committee members gathered informal feedback about a candidate through the nonformal interview interactions (e.g., dinner). In pursuit of greater inclusiveness and needing to remove any in-person requirements, librarians reevaluated how best to showcase the Okanagan campus from afar to interviewees.

## Procedural Checklist and Records Management

In 2018, Lomness was elected as chair of a selection committee for the first time with little direction as to the steps in the process, nor the means to seek mentorship on running a committee. She knew future librarians may face a similar challenge, so she developed a checklist to guide the hiring process from the posting phase to closing the committee post-hire. The checklist allowed all committee members and the administrative team to check on the status of the hire and provide documentation of the process. It also provided an opportunity for transparency in the hiring process and ensured consistency across selection committees. The draft checklist was created in late 2018 and further piloted and revised by Lacey throughout 2019. The library's administration team provided final feedback and approval before making it part of a new standard package to all chairs in early 2020. Through the process of creating the checklist, the librarians involved in hiring recognized the need to improve the overall organization and records management of the hiring process.

# Changes to the Interview and Hiring Process

## Documentation and Records Management

The adoption of the procedural checklist led to a decision to use the university's instance of Microsoft OneDrive to improve records management, transparency, and collaboration throughout the hiring process. Library administration loads the documentation outlined in table 12.1 to OneDrive at the start of each hiring process. The chair and committee members then determine the organization of the folders and which materials are used.

**Table 12.1.** Sample folder and documentation organization

| Folder Label | Documents in Folder |
| --- | --- |
| Procedural | • Checklist |
| HR Guidelines | • Library's Selection Committee Rules of Conduct<br>• University's Memorandum and Privacy Fact Sheet for selection committees<br>• HR's What May I Ask chart<br>• Faculty Association's Collective Agreement excerpts |

**Table 12.1.** Sample folder and documentation organization

| Folder Label | Documents in Folder |
|---|---|
| Job Description and Posting | • Draft job description<br>• Draft posting<br>• Posting Locations Tracker Template |
| Application Review Materials | • Applicant Evaluation Rubric Template<br>• Applicant Rubric Roll Up Template |
| Interview Day Materials | • Interview Scheduling Template<br>• Presentation Topic Brainstorming Template<br>• Interview Questions and Rubric Template<br>• Candidate Interview Day Package Template |
| Candidate Deliberation Materials | • Deliberation Notes and Ranking Template |

Our goal in changing the documentation procedures was to ensure that all committee members felt that they had more equitable access to and insight into the hiring process. The procedure also provided solutions to multiple challenges, including the following: supports the committee in case the chair is suddenly unable to lead on the interview day, provides guidance to librarians sitting on a selection committee for the first time, and aligns practices with colleagues from the Vancouver campus.

The documentation has continued to evolve locally with each committee and has been shared with our Vancouver campus colleagues. The checklist and organizational structure make it easier to integrate colleagues from the other campus onto our selection committees and vice versa. This structure has also increased a shared understanding of the hiring process and enabled more investment and participation among committee members.

## Job Descriptions and Committee Formation

Prior to 2020, job descriptions and their postings were primarily created by the leadership team; however, during the pandemic librarians and the Okanagan Library's EDI Committee requested greater transparency and accountability for the creation of these postings and to have an opportunity to contribute to their development. Hiring now starts with the formation of a selection committee, the election of a chair, and the chair facilitating a discussion of which templates to use, the job posting and the Hiring Equity training module provided by the Equity and Inclusion Office. The Hiring Equity module, delivered in the learning management system, complements discussions about monitoring and reporting bias from the committee, as well as how to best reflect the institution's EDIA values and goals in job descriptions. Through this process change, our goal is to equip librarians to review and provide input as to how to better integrate positions within the organization, encourage fewer work silos, and facilitate partnerships between new hires and established employees.

These changes led to Lacey drafting three EDI statements, included in table 12.2, for inclusion in all future job descriptions and postings. Selection committees have come to use these in a variety of ways, from listing them as a section, to incorporating them throughout or interweaving the principles with the duties and standards for the positions. The librarian team sees these changes as a stepping stone to creating deeper self-reflection and conversation. We hope that it continues to foster more intentional integration of EDIA into all positions at the university.

**Table 12.2.** EDI statements for inclusion in job descriptions and postings

| Statement Number | Statement Text |
| --- | --- |
| 1 | Contributes to the continued development of a library environment and culture that supports and celebrates equity, diversity, and inclusion (EDI). |
| 2 | Supports EDI by pursuing appropriate professional development opportunities and maintains an awareness of EDI initiatives at the departmental, campus, institutional and provincial level such as but not limited to UBC's Inclusive Action Plan, Indigenous Strategic Plan, and BC's Human Rights Code. |
| 3 | Works to integrate EDI into collection development, instruction, public services, and overall professional practice by working to eliminate institutional and structural systems of oppression and power (such as colonialism, racism, sexism, classism, heterosexism, ableism, and white supremacy). |

Our examination of equity and inclusion also resulted in changes to where selection committees post job opportunities for the library. Prior to 2020, the online job-posting locations did not reflect the full range of places that librarians look when seeking employment opportunities. In order to collectively identify a broader scope of locations to post positions and share work among committee members, we began utilizing a Posting Locations Tracker Template (see appendix A). The tracker has increased cross-posting on e-mail discussion lists and job boards dedicated to equitable hiring, which has allowed the library to better reach racialized and other marginalized groups.

## Reviewing Applications

A wealth of hiring literature already discusses topics such as the use of anonymized applications and rubrics, asking for personal diversity statements, and the consideration of other related degrees (Bombaci & Pejchar, 2022; Carroll, Walker, & Croft, 2022; Davis, n.d.; Johnson & Kirk, 2020; O'Meara, Culpepper, & Templeton, 2020; Paul & Maranto, 2021) in order to increase hiring of equity deserving groups. After discussions around what worked best for our library and trialing a few tactics (e.g., diversity statements), we ultimately created an Applicant Evaluation Rubric Template (see appendix B). Although the library administration team could not feasibly take on anonymization for all library searches, we were committed to a process that would minimize bias while committee members review each application for alignment with the job description and the organization's values.

The process of reviewing applications begins with the committee determining the appropriate evaluation criteria and rubric before reviewing any applications. These criteria may include specific areas related to the role (e.g., vendor relationship experience or service and role in EDIA programs), but may be more general for first-time librarian positions (e.g., budgeting experience). Each area of ranking is then given a point value (e.g., 0–3), and a corresponding description for each point value is assigned. The chair of the committee then populates the template with the basic data for each candidate, which is meant to act as a quick point of reference during discussion to ensure there are no errors around salary caps, collective agreement parameters, and so on. Finally, each committee member reviews all of the applications using their own copy of the rubric to ensure no coercion is taking place. Each member is also encouraged to use a separate rubric for each candidate to avoid comparing candidates. Once evaluations are completed, each member sends their rubric evaluations to the committee chair to create a roll-up total, which displays only the final score given to each candidate by the committee members and creates an automatic tally. The scores facilitate discussion around short-listing, or determining if moving to a final interview is immediately possible. Many of our hiring processes do not involve short-list interviewing as the pool of candidates is often small, but this process lends itself to being able to be used in either scenario.

## Communicating with Candidates

How we reach out to, update, and inform our candidates in preparation for the interview day is just as important as the interview day itself. This part of the process is still a work in progress and an area of growth for the Okanagan Library in the future. A candidate's accessibility needs and their feeling of preparedness to visit our campus or interview with us virtually should not be taken lightly. Something that has remained unchanged throughout the pandemic is library administration's role in contacting candidates to schedule interviews. All accessibility requests go through them, and currently the process of informing candidates of what we can do to support them, or to ask what else they might need, is not transparent. The chair is informed only if something is requested, but it is unclear whether all modifications and supports are outlined for all candidates. In order to improve this process from the committee side, we put together the Candidate Interview Day Package Template (see appendix C) to allow the chair to share as much information as possible in advance of the interview day. This process creates an avenue of communication between the candidate and the chair before the day of the interview and ensures the candidate has access to Zoom links and any support with Zoom before the interview day itself. We feel strongly that not solely relying on library administration as the route to contacting candidates humanizes the committee, fosters transparency in the process, and increases opportunities for questions. This is acutely important for online interviewing when campus visits are not possible and a candidate's experience with the committee, the library, and the institution needs to be developed through alternative means. We hope that this package will evolve to support the resumption of on-campus interviewing and can better reflect the supports for accessibility we can offer to the candidates in person (e.g., campus maps, quiet spaces, washrooms).

# Interview Day

## PRE-PRESENTATION

The composition of an interview day will be different for each candidate due to the needs of the position and the candidate, whether multiple units are involved in the hiring, and whether it is a contract or ongoing position. The following outlines specific improvements and new additions to our workflows for a remote interview day. As was described above, candidates are provided with an interview day package that includes all the Zoom links for each component of the day as needed, as well as contact information for who to contact should there be any issues (typically the chair and an administrative support person). In addition, we distinguish which components of the day are part of the formal evaluation for hiring versus those where they will not be evaluated (e.g., meetings to learn more about the library and university). Additionally, the chair meets virtually with candidates prior to the presentation so candidates can test technology, ask any logistical questions for the day, and share any further needs or questions around accessibility. This meeting also allows the chair to share how the selection committee and library can further support them before and during the interview day. Facilitating this through Zoom has also offered the opportunity for the selection committee to meet the candidate before the other attendees arrive, something that was not easily done while in person. We are considering how to make space for this pre-presentation time when resuming in-person interviews to ensure the candidates are given adequate private setup time.

## PRESENTATION

The candidate presentation has always allowed for us to engage additional library employees, other members of our two campuses, and the community in the interview process. We want to foster participation and ensure everyone feels welcomed. Over the last three years, we have not changed this philosophy, and Zoom has enabled us to further improve our approach to inclusivity. Many of our employees have integrated the use of their pronouns into their Zoom name, and we encourage candidates to provide theirs in the same way if they feel comfortable. Similarly, candidates are asked to provide the pronunciation of their name and to introduce themselves at the start of the presentation.

Presentations start with an introduction and land acknowledgement by the selection committee chair, which is also an essential opportunity to foster inclusion for attendees and to connect the work of the position with the traditional territories and UBC's Indigenous Strategic Plan. Over the years, this acknowledgement has been adapted depending on the position and the chair, but our current practice is to emphasize that we as library workers are working to learn and unlearn in our relationship to the land and recognizing that this work requires us to constantly reflect on the ways that UBC Library's work aligns with supporting Indigenous communities and the work of the position we are hiring for.

Finally, throughout the interview day, we have added digital practices that foster accessibility, including turning on closed captioning for all presentations and meetings, allowing attendees of the presentations to submit questions in a way that suits them (e.g., direct to the chair or moderator, turning on their microphones, writing in the chat), keeping the chat open to encourage thank-you messages and personal land acknowledgements, and encouraging attendees to use a camera when comfortable.

## FORMAL INTERVIEW

In preparation for the formal interview, the committee members have always created the interview questions in advance. As an extension of the applicant evaluation rubric, the Interview Questions and Rubric Template (see appendix D) was introduced for evaluating the responses to interview questions. The committee can detail a point value associated with each question, as well as ideas for what an answer may look like. The rubric and answer examples are meant to be broad and flexible to interpretation should candidates provide answers outside of expectations. Candidates are not penalized for stepping beyond the desired response, but instead such responses are often found to exceed expectations and show the breadth of a candidate's knowledge. While a few selection committees have used the rubric to assign point values to responses, the majority have continued to evaluate them without such an approach. Further conversations around point-value integration for interview question evaluation will evolve with future committees.

Similar to the presentation, we have also implemented many logistical and technical changes to increase accessibility. Figure 12.1 outlines example accessibility considerations that have been routinely introduced but does not demonstrate an exhaustive list. Many of these considerations arose from conversations early in the pandemic when all of our librarians were getting used to Zoom and pondering how the Okanagan Library could better create accessible interviewing environments. Unlike the virtual presentation, many of these strategies will transition well to in-person interviewing, if and when that occurs, and we will continue to use them to ensure our candidates feel comfortable and supported throughout the process.

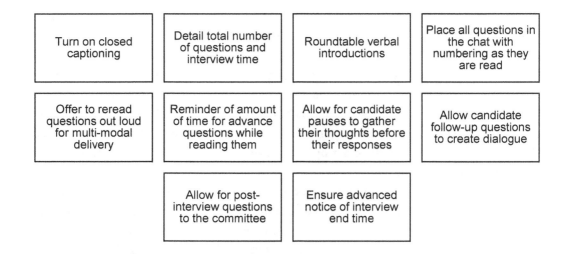

**Figure 12.1. Accessibility considerations for virtual interviews.** *Note.* This figure shows a variety of considerations that can be introduced together or independently of one another.

# Employee Participation

Selection committees at the Okanagan Library continue to prioritize the participation from all library employees in the hiring of candidates. In the past, we typically offered presentation participation and smaller meet and greets during interview days, but feedback from those events was often low and lacking detail. Introducing the use of Qualtrics, a survey software, allowed library employees to provide named or anonymous feedback to ensure our colleagues and attendees felt comfortable sharing their candidate assessments. After receiving previous personal assessments from lunches and dinners that were deemed inappropriate for the purpose of candidate selection, the library has begun requesting that all feedback align with the related duties of the position and the candidate's experience. While still unavoidable in some cases, committee members work to ensure that any personal feelings about the candidate shared through the feedback form, such as personality or behaviors during an interview, are not carried over into the deliberation. Additionally, we have worked to create intentional spaces for employees who are not on the hiring committee to engage with candidates. We want to make it clear to candidates who will be attending each portion of the day and the purpose of each event

## Deliberations

A final change in our process has been around how we conduct our deliberations. As previously mentioned, some selection committees choose to use the interview question rubric with or without scoring. Our Deliberation Notes and Ranking Template (see appendix E) can be used regardless of the way a selection committee structures the interview review process. The rubric facilitates a general ranking of candidates by each member of the committee and an overall ranking. This approach can be specifically helpful in situations where committee members do not all agree on the ranking of candidates interviewed. The notes from each committee member can be included to support their ranking of the candidate and the similarities and the differences between the members' conclusions can be seen by all. This is also important for the purposes of writing the recommendation letter for hiring, for conducting reference interviews, and for the documentation required to be retained by library administration.

# Impact of Current Processes and Looking Ahead

Library administration has been very supportive of implementing the changes we've discussed in this chapter. Anecdotally, we have received positive feedback from candidates about our hiring practices compared to other universities. However, we have no conclusive evidence that our hiring packages make the hiring process more inclusive in the absence of formal assessment. Nevertheless, we have consciously chosen to rely on self-reflection through committee debriefs and discussions with our peers from other universities and colleges so as to not burden candidates with additional labor.

The change process we have implemented is iterative and requires consistent dedication to check in with multiple units on campus, including HR, management, librarians, archivists, and records managers. We do this to ensure that we are staying flexible, responding to the needs of potential applicants, and continuing to evolve our hiring practices toward inclusivity and accessibility. In the long term, we hope that our inclusive hiring practices will support increased diversity of library staff and help to recruit and retain Indigenous, people of color, 2SLGBTQIA+, disabled, and neurodivergent folks.

Moving forward, we will continue to advocate for online interviews for most positions in order to decrease the financial and emotional stress of travel for applicants, which also supports our institution's goals for environmental sustainability. In place of continuing the practice of in-person interviewing for the candidates, we want to create positive opportunities for candidate visits, such as on-campus visits if a candidate is successful and wishes to visit before accepting the position. When online interviewing is not an option, we will ask library administration to provide as much information as possible when inviting the candidates to make sure we are meeting their needs. We hope to streamline this communication by providing an e-mail template for chairs to use that provides explicit accessibility offerings. This information includes the locations of the gender-neutral washrooms, designated space and dedicated time for them to have to themselves, wheelchair-accessible spaces, and maps of the campus and meeting locations.

We are also committed to making the selection committee process more accessible for the librarians and archivists who are serving on the committee by extending deadlines for hiring (so as to not rush the process), making expectations clear and consistent, and improving the transparency among colleagues who serve on selection committees. Furthermore, we want to ensure that there is diversity on the selection committees, but we also want to make it clear to marginalized colleagues that they are not required to accept opportunities when offered.

We encourage other organizations and colleagues to critically consider what each component of the interview day is meant to achieve when undertaking their own review and development of remote interviews. Does it add value to the evaluation of the candidate? Does it add value for the candidate to help them understand the organization? We also recommend identifying pain or tension points in the hiring process with past members of selection committees. Are these pain points a mandated part of the process, or could they improve through transparency and communication? Lastly, consider how the hiring process can set up every candidate for success. The hiring process should be about them as much as it is for the library.

# Conclusion

Throughout the pandemic, remote interviewing has pushed our library to better incorporate EDIA values into hiring and has resulted in a multitude of adjustments and new approaches to past practices. Through our reflections on working to change our practices, we have learned that success can be found through collaboration and a process of trial and error and that advocating for the best approaches for our library and our candidates should remain at the forefront of every new search. Our biggest takeaway from the process of transferring to remote interviewing is the importance of continual learning and iterative modifications to hiring processes. Academic libraries have unique and local contexts, but our hope is that this reflection and sharing of our work can support other libraries in their inclusive hiring endeavors.

## APPENDIX A

# Posting Locations Tracker Template with Examples

|  | URL or e-mail | Cost | Responsibility | Submission process notes | Final link to posting | Completion (date/initials) |
|---|---|---|---|---|---|---|
| Job Boards | | | | | | |
| Library Jobs | www.example.com | $55 | Administrative Assistant | Reviewed before approval | www.example.com/job123posting | TBD |
| E-mail Discussion Lists | | | | | | |
| Association X Jobs | example@email.com | N | Chair | website | n/a—e-mail | Y (Dec 1/AB) |
| Social Media | | | | | | |
| Library Twitter | @example | N | Communications | Chair sends to Communications Manager | n/a | TBD |

## APPENDIX B

# Applicant Evaluation Rubric Template and Examples

|  | Required |  |  |  | Experience Evaluation |  |  |  |  |
|---|---|---|---|---|---|---|---|---|---|
|  | MLIS or equivalent | Year graduated | Citizenship or permanent residency | Years of X experience (for salary caps or minimums) | Area A (e.g., budgeting) | Area B (e.g., licensing) | Area C (e.g., EDIA leadership) |  |  |
| *Candidate* | Y/N | # | Y/N | # | 0-3 | 0-3 | 0-5 | Notes | Total |
| *Kit Example* | Y | 2014 | Y | 8 | 2 | 3 | 4 | Strong experience, excellent EDIA examples | 9 |
| *Lana Sample* | Y | 2021 | Y | 1 | 2 | 0 | 5 | New grad, but related experience to support training | 7 |

## APPENDIX C

# Candidate Interview Day Package Template

## [Position Title] Interview Day Preparation Package

Candidate: [insert name]

Interview Date: [insert date]

The following document is meant to prepare you for and accompany your interview day. It includes

- Presentation topic you'll be asked to prepare for
- A few advance questions that will be asked during the interview
- A full schedule of the day and location details
- Selection Committee membership

If you have questions, concerns, or need clarification on anything below—please contact [INSERT NAME], Selection Committee Chair. If it is something urgent, please feel free to reach out to [CHAIR NAME] at [CONTACT DETAILS].

[Insert relevant logos of the library or other partnered units]

[insert page break]

### PRESENTATION TOPIC

[Insert presentation topic as decided by the committee, referencing outside sources with links and any time requirements]

### ADVANCE INTERVIEW QUESTIONS

*The following questions are being provided for you to prepare in advance of the interview. They are part of a longer list of questions totaling [include total number of interview questions], including the provided questions, that will be asked during the interview portion of the day. While notes are welcome, please do not prepare any presentation materials (e.g., PowerPoint). We would like you to prepare no more than [insert time per question] responses for each question. Also, these questions will appear throughout the interview and will not appear back-to-back, or be the first [insert number of advanced questions] questions as it appears below!*

*[If applicable] We will also be posting each interview question as they are asked in the Zoom chat so you can refer to them.*

[List advance questions]

## INTERVIEW DAY SCHEDULE

| Time [include time zone] | Activity title | Attendees/ invited guests | Purpose of this part of the day | [Zoom link or room details] + host's name of that portion |
|---|---|---|---|---|
|  |  |  |  |  |
|  |  |  |  |  |
| [Insert time]—BREAK—[# of] minutes ||||| 
|  |  |  |  |  |
| [Insert time]—BREAK—[# of] minutes ||||| 
|  |  |  |  |  |
|  |  |  |  |  |

[insert page break]

## SELECTION COMMITTEE MEMBERSHIP

The following are the members of the Selection Committee for the [title of position] position:

[List all members (voting and non-voting), including job/position titles]

## APPENDIX D

# Interview Questions and Rubric Template

## [Position Title] Librarian Interview Rubric

**Candidate:** [insert name]
**Date of Interview:** [insert name]
**Committee Member:** [insert committee member who is responding]

| Question [insert #]: [insert topic of question] [indicate Advance Question if applicable] | Asking: [insert name of committee member] |
|---|---|
| [Insert question] ||
| [Insert maximum time if advance question and time was given in advance] ||
| Prompts/follow-up questions: ||
| [insert any follow-ups to clarify responses] ||
| Notes: ||
| [insert committee member notes to candidate response here] ||
| Possible Key: [insert possible expected responses, but ensure broad consideration of a topic] ||
| Score: _____ / [insert total score possible] ||

[copy the above table as needed for the total number of questions]

| Candidate Questions | Asking: [insert name of committee member or chair] |
|---|---|
| You have finished answering our questions. Now, do you have any questions for us? List questions asked by the candidate: [insert questions as they are asked] | |

| Candidate References | Asking: [insert name of chair] |
|---|---|
| Do we have permission to contact your references? Yes/No ||

# APPENDIX E

# Deliberation Notes and Ranking Template

|  | **Candidate 1 [insert name]** | **Candidate 2 [insert name]** | **Candidate 3 [insert name]** |
|---|---|---|---|
| *Final Ranking (e.g., 1, 2)* | [insert final overall ranking decided on by committee members following deliberation] | [insert final overall ranking decided on by committee members following deliberation] | [insert final overall ranking decided on by committee members following deliberation] |
| *Viable Candidate (Y/N)* | [insert whether candidate is viable for the position following the interview] | [insert whether candidate is viable for the position following the interview] | [insert whether candidate is viable for the position following the interview] |
| *Reference Check (Y/N)* | [insert whether reference check will be completed] | [insert whether reference check will be completed] | [insert whether reference check will be completed] |
| *Committee Member 1* | [insert notes regarding viability and any quotes to be used in the recommendation letter] | [insert notes regarding viability and any quotes to be used in the recommendation letter] | [insert notes regarding viability and any quotes to be used in the recommendation letter] |
| *Committee Member 2* | [insert notes regarding viability and any quotes to be used in the recommendation letter] | [insert notes regarding viability and any quotes to be used in the recommendation letter] | [insert notes regarding viability and any quotes to be used in the recommendation letter] |

*Note.* This table can be extended with additional rows for more committee members and columns for more candidates. A preliminary ranking from each committee member by candidate is often used to facilitate the final ranking in this table, especially if ranking is not agreed upon between committee members.

# References

Betz, G. (2022, April 6). Navigating the academic hiring process with disabilities. *In the Library with the Lead Pipe*. https://www.inthelibrarywiththeleadpipe.org/2022/hiring-with-disabilities/

Bombaci, S. P., & Pejchar, L. (2022). Advancing equity in faculty hiring with diversity statements. *BioScience*, *72*(4), 365–371. https://doi.org/10.1093/biosci/biab136

Carroll, E. M., Walker, T. D., & Croft, A. (2022). White Americans report more positive than negative affect after writing a personal diversity statement. *Journal of Diversity in Higher Education*. Advance online publication. https://doi.org/10.1037/dhe0000437

Cunningham, S. J., Guss, S., & Stout, J. (2019). Challenging the "good fit" narrative: Creating inclusive recruitment practices in academic libraries. In D. M. Mueller (Ed.), *Recasting the narrative: The proceedings of the ACRL 2019 conference, April 10–13, 2019, Cleveland, Ohio* (pp. 12–21). Association of College and Research Libraries. https://scholarship.richmond.edu/university-libraries-publications/42/

Davis, J. (n.d.). Breaking the stereotype: How hiring managers can help to increase diversity and battle hiring bias in libraries. *Intersections*, American Library Association. https://www.ala.org/advocacy/diversity/odlos-blog/breaking-stereotypes-hiring

Johnson, S. K., & Kirk, J. F. (2020, March 5). Research: To reduce gender bias, anonymize job applications. *Harvard Business Review*. https://hbr.org/2020/03/research-to-reduce-gender-bias-anonymize-job-applications

Michalak, R., & Rysavy, M. D. T. (2022). Conducting effective online interviews in an academic library. *Journal of Library Administration*, *62*(1), 101–109. https://doi.org/10.1080/01930826.2021.2006988

O'Meara, K., Culpepper, D., & Templeton, L. L. (2020). Nudging toward diversity: Applying behavioral design to faculty hiring. *Review of Educational Research*, *90*(3), 311–348. https://doi.org/10.3102/0034654320914742

Orupabo, J., & Mangset, M. (2021). Promoting diversity but striving for excellence: Opening the "black box" of academic hiring. *Sociology*, *56*(2): 316–332. https://doi.org/10.1177/00380385211028064

Paul, J. D., & Maranto, R. (2021, November). *Other than merit: The prevalence of diversity, equity, and inclusion statements in university hiring*. American Enterprise Institute. https://www.aei.org/wp-content/uploads/2021/11/Other-than-merit-The-prevalence-of-diversity-equity-and-inclusion-statements-in-university-hiring.pdf?x91208

CHAPTER 13

# The Interview Pivot

## Implementing Changes to Interview Protocols to Respond to Pandemic Restrictions and Provide Greater Inclusion

*Mary Beth Lock, Elizabeth Ellis, and Summer Krstevska*

# Introduction

When COVID-19 brought with it the upending of most of our work practices in early 2020, it forced us to reckon with procedures that would allow us to continue operations. We, like many institutions, created new service protocols to allow for remote instruction and touch-free item delivery. Online meetings replaced face-to-face gatherings. Whenever possible, we simulated pre-pandemic norms in a virtual environment. Then, during the social unrest of the summer of 2020, as the Black Lives Matter movement gained momentum, we were further invigorated to evaluate all practices, including hiring practices, through a lens of greater inclusion. We were motivated to implement changes because of COVID-19 while intentionally maximizing inclusivity and minimizing barriers to our services.

Focusing attention on interviewing practices was crucial as we recognized that hiring strategies had not been thoroughly overhauled with an eye to equity, diversity, and inclusion (EDI) since before EDI was a part of the lexicon. After we had implemented changes to our interviewing practices due to COVID-19 restrictions, a further assessment was necessary to go beyond just preserving our previous practices in a virtual modality. We determined we would ensure a viable search process that allowed for opportunities to increase inclusion, equity, and comfort for our candidates. To do so, we evaluated our practices to reduce ambiguity, increase structure, seek input from candidates, and increase trust in the process.

Further, we wanted to situate our revised interview practices within broader changes in academic librarian hiring and, more specifically, find out how these abrupt changes were actually impacting the people who interview for positions in academic libraries. We conducted a survey of recent interviewees to find out if remote interviews had been practiced in searches candidates were involved in and the impact of interview changes on candidates. With this additional data, we hope to create even more inclusive interview practices that will ultimately provide for more diverse hiring.

# Background

Our library supports the faculty and students in the Undergraduate College and graduate programs in the School of Divinity, School of Business, and School of Professional Studies in our midsize, private university. The student population of these combined programs is above 8,700. The school employs 932 faculty on the main campus (as of fall 2021), and the library employs sixty-three librarians and library staff. The librarians have faculty status and are contract employees without tenure. While this report of changes implemented in our hiring practices for both faculty and staff reflects the library's ongoing strategies to increase inclusion, it's worth noting that changes implemented in the library's hiring process do not necessarily reflect trends across all departments at our parent institution.

In 2020, while largely locked down due to COVID-19, the library needed to adjust interviewing practices to fill one critical vacancy for an instruction librarian. During the late spring and summer of 2020, the university was strictly enforcing a rule to prevent all but essential employees on campus. Those who could report to campus had to maintain strict social distancing protocols. As a result, we were minimizing the number of people allowed in the building at one time. Additionally, lockdown protocols were in place and people had a general reluctance to travel. It was under these circumstances that we needed to find an alternative way to interview and hire. Our long-standing practices of inviting candidates to campus, providing them hotel and travel accommodations, and having them endure a daylong (sometimes day-and-a-half-long) interview, required significant reengineering.

A new hiring protocol was developed to conduct the prehire process entirely online. This was our first foray into remote interviewing. After the search committee's review yielded a short list of candidates to pursue, the interview process began. The initial candidate screening was done through Spark Hire (https://go.sparkhire.com/video-interview-platform), a video interview platform in which candidates receive a link to answer predetermined questions developed by the search committee. The Spark Hire videos served as the initial interview and allowed the search committee to review applicants and determine who would be continuing their candidacy beyond the first round. The second round of interviews for the successful candidates were followed up with a round of Zoom (https://zoom.us/) meetings with the search committee and the finalists. The final interview included not just the search committee, but also the dean, associate dean, peer review committee of the librarian's assembly, a representative of the provost's office, and the entire research and instruction team that this particular position would be hired into. The interview itinerary included a forty-five-minute presentation to the entire library. In other words, the process mimicked the in-person interview experience exactly. No change to the hiring process was implemented except for replacing an in-person meeting with a remote one. At this stage in our development, we did not consider changes such as allowing interviewees to have cameras off or providing final interview questions in advance. It simply continued with our existing interview strategy in a way that protected the health of the interviewers and the interviewees. While the institution did recognize that interviewing this way was certainly less expensive than an in-person interview that included airline tickets and hotel stays, the decision to interview remotely was practical rather than intentional. The underlying hope was that one day soon, we would return to a traditional, in-person interview experience (and that would be preferred!).

Following our initial remote interview experience, the university implemented a soft freeze on positions, and the library could not do any additional hiring for about a year. As a result, the library did not do any further review of how we might make our hiring practices more inclusive. We had a relatively stable workforce, and our attentions were directed at how best to continue to meet our constituents' needs throughout the early stages of the pandemic. Then, in the summer of 2020, the university announced an early retirement package to the campus. From June 2020 to January 2021, six employees, (five staff members and one faculty librarian) took advantage of early retirement, necessitating us to evaluate our hiring protocols as we sought to backfill these positions while still in the grips of a pandemic. With the sudden large number of vacancies to fill and realizing that remote interviews were not an interim solution but would be the norm for the near term, we recognized that existing practices overlaid in an online environment wasn't the answer we needed to make our hiring practices more accessible and inclusive. We were determined to do a thorough review of hiring practices to ensure we were utilizing the best practices in our changing environment.

Our library was not alone in this reckoning. Through fall 2020 and winter 2020–2021, attention to hiring practices across academic libraries was proliferating. With the rise of social justice issues and a greater clarity on how hiring practices affect equity, we realized that this was an opportunity for our library to evaluate what else we might do to refresh our hiring practices. Around this time, several librarians from our institution also attended the American Library Association's (ALA) Midwinter meeting in January 2021, where many sessions were devoted to identifying ways to implement more inclusive hiring practices in order to encourage a greater diversity of applicants.

Our library felt a responsibility to adapt our recruitment strategies and saw an opportunity to do so due to widespread changes in hiring practices in the profession at large and, even more importantly, to remove unintended barriers that kept potential applicants, especially BIPOC, neurodiverse, or other applicants from marginalized communities, from applying. This responsibility prompted the dean of the library to establish a library faculty task force in the spring of 2021 to evaluate how we might alter and incorporate practices to increase inclusion, expand our applicant pool, and increase equity in the interview process.

# Our Process: Task Force to Evaluate Interview Practices

The task force on interview practices included membership of interested librarians from across all units of the library. Our task force was racially diverse and made up of experienced librarians with deep institutional memory as well as our three most recent librarian hires, including the instruction librarian who completed our first entirely remote interview in the summer of 2020. The new hires on the task force started at the library between December 2018 and September 2020 and brought current perspective on what it is like to experience interviews, not only at our library but also within the field of academic librarianship. These perspectives were needed and welcomed as our library had not evaluated our hiring processes for many years. The group was given the following charge and timeline by the dean of the library:

> **Charge:**
> The charge of the Task Force to Evaluate Interviewing Practices is to research, evaluate, arrive at consensus, and recommend changes to the interview process utilizing information surrounding equitable hiring practices as a guide to change. The goal of a possible change in the process is to make the interview process more inclusive. The task force will review literature, webinars, and other sources to identify trends in hiring practices that may extend to both processes surrounding interview and recruitment (i.e., do we provide interview questions in

advance to applicants), and changes to the interview day (including eliminating meetings with some groups, or combining groups together, if needed). Each member will identify and provide information to share to the other task force participants. Discussion will seek to maximize consensus.

**Timeline:**
The group will work primarily asynchronously with occasional meetings scheduled by the Chair to discuss topics. Review will take place over the Spring 2021, with a recommendation made to the Dean by June 30, 2021.

Over the course of the spring of 2021, the group collected information from academia, librarianship, and the private sector on what kinds of changes others had implemented or were considering implementing in their hiring practices. Since we were looking for recent and relevant insights, we sought out information not just in scholarly journals, but also in blog posts, trade journals, YouTube videos, and conference sessions. (The list of our task force's resources is included in appendix A.) Resulting changes not only identified elements of the interview process that would make our interviews more inclusive, but also identified ways to codify practices to ensure that the equitable practices are repeatable across time.

Our review of these articles uncovered several strategies that we could implement immediately to create more equity in the interview process. We further found articles that troubled the whiteness and ableism of the profession to sensitize the task force members about the ingrained nature of bias in the profession.

We were pleased to discover that some of the recruitment and interviewing practices recommended in the literature on how to reduce bias in hiring were already a part of the hiring practices in our library. For instance, the Inclusion and Equity Committee report of the University of Nevada, Las Vegas (Boddie et al., 2020) recommended a variety of practices to create consistent and standardized hiring, including

- explicitly highlighting diversity in position announcements
- using gender-neutral pronouns as standard
- standardizing onboarding processes
- minimizing open-ended feedback that serves to create opportunities for bias to enter in distorting the evaluation of the candidate
- developing rubrics for asking candidates questions and use across all interviews; defining goal for each question and determining the range of acceptable answers
- offering trainings and workshops on diverse recruitment for search committees
- aligning staff hiring practices with faculty hiring practices

The University of Richmond's timely article, "Challenging the 'Good Fit' Narrative" (Cunningham, Guss, & Stout, 2019), identified similar themes. Cunningham, Guss, and Stout noted that some of the best practices to make libraries more inclusive are relatively simple and straightforward: having minimal required qualifications in job ads, which helps prevent people of color and women from self-selecting out; directly recruiting people of color and making sure to post job ads on e-mail discussion lists and websites aimed at people of color and other underrepresented groups; collecting data on searches to see how the racial and gender makeup of the institution changes over time (acknowledging that this is imperfect since some forms of diversity are invisible); using a uniform rubric for all candidates interviewing for a position and making sure to ask all candidates the same questions and give them roughly the same interview experience.

In our previous efforts at being more inclusive and equitable in our hiring practices, we had already been using a rubric to evaluate candidates based on the job posting, had adopted the practice of utilizing a single set of questions to ask each candidate, and had attempted to have diverse search committees, being mindful to not overburden our BIPOC library colleagues. We had also utilized best practices to expand where jobs were posted and changed position postings to have more inclusive language.

But our analysis went further, checking the influence of whiteness in our hiring practices. In "White Librarianship in Blackface: Diversity Initiatives in LIS," written for *In the Library with a Lead Pipe*, April Hathcock defines whiteness as

> a theoretical concept that can extend beyond the realities of racial privilege to a wide range of dominant ideologies based on gender identity, sexual orientation, class, and other categories … [a] sociocultural differential of power and privilege that results from categories of race and ethnicity, it also stands as a marker for the privilege and power that acts to reinforce itself through hegemonic cultural practice that excludes all who are different." (Hathcock, 2015)

Galvan, in "Soliciting Performance, Hiding Bias: Whiteness and Librarianship," notes how "organizational fit" is a concealer for institutional bias. She posits that change will come about only through interrogating the structures that manifest whiteness. Institutions screen on a candidate's ability to "perform whiteness" (white, heterosexual, capitalist, middle class), and librarians who are not white nor middle class are alienated as a "diversity hire," which also involves diversity work that obscures the person's talents and interests (Galvan, 2015). On hiring practices, Galvan suggests removing candidate salary requirements from job applications and reviewing interview notes for biased language that will cause a person to be eliminated from a candidate pool. Determining what information is sought in every interview question asked will also highlight questions that might just be meant to determine fit.

The full list of articles, blogs, webinars, and other sources we reviewed is available in appendix A. The task force adopted and codified some of the stated practices for future searches and undertook identifying practices that might perpetuate whiteness. The recommendations identified how to create consistent practices across job searches, minimize the burden that the individual candidate must carry, be transparent throughout the interview process (both to candidates and to the search committee), and other ways to support diversity in the library as a whole, making searches that minimize bias the norm. The essential changes we made to our interview practices are included below, with a parenthetical reference to how we felt this change helped address at least one of our goals: equity, diversity, or inclusion. (For our complete recommendations, refer to appendix B.) Our adopted changes included the following:

- Write job postings to maximize the candidate pool. Be specific about skills required, but clearly define what is required and what is preferred. Do not use library jargon that might serve to prevent qualified applicants who have applicable skills from outside the profession from applying. (diversity)
- Include the minimum salary in job postings. This will help to make the decision to apply easier for applicants. (diversity and equity)
- Have all search committee members complete non-bias training. (diversity and inclusion)
- For initial candidate evaluation, utilize rubrics (see example, appendix C). The rubrics should be written from the requirements in the job description as the measures you will use to determine if the candidates meet minimum qualifications. The job description should include all those elements you have identified as important to you. The applicant was writing their cover letter and resume or CV to highlight those elements, so the review should be on only those elements. (inclusion and equity)
- Once a candidate has moved forward to the interview stage, provide a detailed itinerary for the candidate (see appendix D) that includes who they are meeting with and why. (inclusion)
- Allow the interested candidate to determine if they'd like to meet with some affinity group outside of the library. Is there a student group that they might be working with? An affinity group office like the Office of Diversity and Inclusion or the LGBTQ Center? Someone from their liaison department? To be most inclusive, give the applicant some control over their interview day. (inclusion)
- Offer a local alternative for candidates who have an online interview to provide a more professional setting with a reliable Wi-Fi signal for their interview day, such as a hotel or a work-sharing space. (inclusion and equity)
- Provide interview questions to applicants in advance of the interview at all stages of the interview. (inclusion and equity)

- Interview all candidates in the same modality for each round of interviews. (equity)
- Allow finalists to come for a campus visit prior to accepting the offer. (equity and inclusion)

It was only after some debate that we arrived at consensus to provide candidates with interview questions in advance of the interview day. Some members of the task force maintained that librarians need to think on their feet and so wanted to prevent sharing questions in advance. After discussion, we determined that providing questions in advance would benefit the candidate more than it might hurt a search committee's ability to gauge a candidate's skills. In situations outside of interviews, a professional would rarely have to walk into a meeting having little idea of what they would be asked to prepare for. Therefore, providing questions actually does a better job of mirroring the professional setting. Doing so also sends a clearer message to candidates about what kind of place of employment we purport to be: one that is supportive and inclusive. As we do not want candidates or employees to feel unnecessarily anxious when interacting with one another, providing questions in advance can potentially ease candidates' interview anxiety.

Since the task force made the recommendation to provide interview questions in advance, our search committees have been utilizing this strategy for the last several searches and have been pleased with candidate responses. We've discovered that search committees can ask questions that dig deeper and require more thought and insight than a more generic question would.

In any given interview round, all applicants will be interviewed with the same modality, even if some applicants could appear in person and others would have to travel a long distance, precluding an in-person interview. The culture of our parent institution places high value on the traditional on-campus, in-person experience, which made us realize that a candidate who interviews in person would likely rate better than one who is seen only over a computer screen even if all other things in their skill sets were equal. Our library has had several searches now with two rounds of interviews held over Zoom and an offer made by phone. But in order to allow the candidate to get a feel for the place and the people they'd be working with, we also established the practice of giving the candidate the opportunity to travel to campus to see the library and meet with the team and the administration before they accept the offer. For final candidates, travel expenses, which may include airfare, hotel, meals, and so on, are paid for by the library after candidates are provided the job offer in writing.

Since adopting these changes, recent searches have been conducted sometimes over Zoom and sometimes utilizing Spark Hire. The value that Spark Hire provides is the ability for candidates to reply to questions (provided in advance) on their own time, and in a fashion that is most comfortable to them. The search committee can then review the recorded responses also on their own time, which can speed up hiring considerably. Other search committees have utilized a Zoom call for first-round interviews, preferring the immediate interaction that can come of a Zoom interview. Utilizing standard interview questions provided in advance to candidates and a Zoom call (with cameras either off or on) creates a more collaborative experience, which some search committees would like to convey in interviews with potential employees. The cost of choosing this avenue is the greater difficulty in scheduling and perhaps extending the timeline of the search. Regardless of which avenue is chosen, candidates have uniformly been grateful for receiving the questions in advance because of the ability to better prepare. One e-mail respondent put it this way: "I'm glad to have the chance to see the questions beforehand, it goes a long way to making me feel prepared and confident in my responses."

Minimizing barriers and increasing accommodations for applicants included adopting strategies to be exceedingly sensitive to their needs. We've identified several ways to maximize their online comfort: giving several breaks throughout the interview day; trying to minimize the length of each interview segment; and offering to provide candidates interviewing remotely a nearby hotel or other office accommodation to be sure of uninterrupted interview time and a reliable internet connection. Additionally, should we return to more in-person interviewing, we will allow a variety of restaurant choices, provide links to menus, and allow the candidate to determine if they want to meet with us and eat as a group, or if they'd like to eat solo.

## Results of These Changes

With these changes in our interview processes solidified (see the complete list in appendix B), and after having an opportunity to test the task force's recommendations through several rounds of hiring, we received feedback from candidates that they were impressed with the level of communication from search committees and were very comfortable through the whole process. Instead of creating the usual feeling of fear and anxiety that arises in an interview, we set the stage to engage with each candidate as a partner with whom we are investigating the question of how we might best fill this vacancy. We also found that the online interview process has been easier to schedule and less expensive than entirely in-person interviews.

While we recognized early that changing our practices to online interviews allows us the rigor to hire candidates who will meet our needs and that our changes were implemented to maximize the comfort of candidates to the greatest extent possible, we desired to know how the new interview protocols might have affected those being interviewed. To determine whether academic libraries' changing hiring practices were beneficial to the interviewee, we decided to ask the candidates. In the interests of developing practices with Universal Design principles, our survey sought input from across the whole spectrum of candidates, not just the subset of candidates from less represented backgrounds.

# Results of the Academic Librarian Interview Survey

After receiving positive feedback from applicants, we endeavored to expand the data set to learn about how applicants had been experiencing interviews through the pandemic. We hoped to discover if other academic libraries flipped to entirely remote rounds of interviews with applicants; if libraries had made accommodations for applicants; and if applicants felt that protocols adjusted to meet the pandemic still allowed applicants to get a sense of the library they were endeavoring to be hired into. Our survey solicited responses from people who interviewed for academic library jobs between March 2020 and April 2022. Our preliminary findings indicated, unsurprisingly, that most academic library interviews during the pandemic were conducted remotely. Most of the candidates who responded to our survey indicated a preference for hybrid interviews that included remote and in-person elements. In hybrid approaches, generally first-round interviews were conducted over an online modality and second-round interviews in person. Comments from survey respondents indicated that the online interview allowed them to get a sense of the job and the people in the library in a lower barrier way. The in-person component allowed them to really understand the library, their colleagues, and the institution, while having them participate in pandemic travel only after moving forward in the process or before accepting an offer.

Candidates mentioned an appreciation for alleviating safety concerns and anxiety during the pandemic. But most of their praise of the remote interview was around convenience: a lower barrier for requesting and receiving accommodations, like breaks to reduce Zoom fatigue, better ability to control audio and visual settings, or eliminating the need for long walks between buildings; allowing the candidate to prepare for specific interview questions; the remote interview's ability to reduce bias. Candidates showed dissatisfaction with the lack of context which failed to provide a fuller picture about the institution, location, and potential colleagues as well as the loss of understanding that results from fewer facial cues and social interactions.

When looking at interview modality for its ability to convey an understanding of the position and hiring institution, the variation of responses was not significantly different between interview modalities. However, on-campus interviews showed a slightly higher percentage of candidates gaining an understanding of the position and hiring institution. It is worth noting that the number of our survey respondents who had on-campus interview components was relatively small. The qualitative feedback we received from candidates indicated that a lack of understanding about the hiring institution and position was not necessarily the result of the modality and could be mediated by clearer communication from the hiring institution about the institution, working environment, and job expectations.

Our survey identified whether academic institutions were or were not offering accommodations to candidates who might prefer an online modality. We also sought to find whether these accommodations had an impact on the candidates' understanding of the position and institution when utilized within various interview modalities. From the survey data, we have concluded that the following accommodations are the most impactful on a candidates' understanding of the position and institution:

- Candidates appreciated our providing a detailed itinerary in advance and allowing the candidate to provide input on the interview date and time. (For an example, see appendix D.)
- Asking about ADA accommodations instead of having the candidate ask for them is highly valued.

These are the highest-level conclusions. Greater detail about the survey and our findings will be provided in a forthcoming article to be published in a peer-reviewed publication.

# Conclusion

We had been forced to reevaluate our hiring practices to accommodate the changes brought about by the pandemic, interrupting the usual face-to-face interviews. We then expanded our review to include how we can change protocols to increase the comfort and well-being of our candidates on every front. The lack of review of our hiring practices over time led to a recognition that our protocols not only hadn't evolved to allow for online evaluation of candidates, but also fell short of accommodating for greater inclusivity. Our evaluation led us to make significant changes that would allow the safest practice during the pandemic, the most convenient protocols for future searches, and adoption of the most inclusive options for making candidates feel welcomed and establishing them as partners in the interview process. It has been a successful pivot for our library, borne out by comments from both those candidates who were offered positions, and those who were not.

For academic libraries with a goal to have greater DEI in their workforce, there is a need to alter interview procedures to enable job candidates to feel that they belong in our libraries. The interview process will likely reveal the culture of the institution to the candidate, regardless of modality, so it is worth reflecting on what tone the existing or desired hiring practice sets and the relationship that is established between the candidates and the hiring institution. Interviewing for positions is stressful for any candidate, which might interrupt their ability to show a potential employer their skills in the best light. In our library, we work to maximize candidate comfort and make the job interview process as accessible as possible for the candidate, the search committee, and other stakeholders. The changes that we have implemented serve to reduce uncertainty, make the candidate feel confident in their ability to do the work, and provide for a level of accountability and inclusiveness. Keeping up with changes in interview practices is also an ongoing enterprise, one to which librarians will need to commit to maintain the most inclusive practices possible. Ultimately, once libraries shift the focus of the interview from the traditional, narrow test for fitness to one that broadens the candidate pool, utilizes a sense of collaboration in the interview, and eliminates bias in the search committee, it will result in a more equitable hire.

# APPENDIX A

# Bibliography of Sources Consulted by the Task Force

Arch, X., & Gilman, I. (2021). One of us: Social performance in academic library hiring. In D. M. Mueller (Ed.), *Ascending into an open future: The proceedings of the ACRL 2021 conference* (pp. 125–136). Association of College and Research Libraries. https://www.ala.org/acrl/sites/ala.org.acrl/files/content/conferences/confsandpreconfs/2021/OneofUs.pdf

Bhalla, N. (2019). Strategies to improve equity in faculty hiring. *Molecular Biology of the Cell*, *30*(22), 2744–2749. https://doi.org/10.1091/mbc.E19-08-0476

Boddie, A., Paloma Fiedler, B., Haslam, M., Luna, E., Martinez-Flores, E., Padilla, T., Wainscott, S., White, C., Day, A., Cheng, J, George, K., Green, H., Melilli, A., Mazmanyan, K., & Brombosz, C. (2020). *Inclusion and Equity Committee recommendations for diverse recruitment report*. University of Nevada, Las Vegas Libraries. https://digitalscholarship.unlv.edu/lib_iec_reports/4/

Bright, K. (2021, June 7). *Anti-racist/Anti-bias recruitment and hiring practices*. [Webinar]. Association of Southeastern Research Libraries. https://www.aserl.org/event/anti-racist-anti-bias-recruitment-and-hiring-practices/

Brown, J., Ferretti, J. A., Leung, S., & Méndez-Brady, M. (2018). We here: Speaking our truth. *Library Trends*, *67*(1), 163–181. https://doi.org/10.1353/lib.2018.0031

Burey, J.-A. (2017, November 13). Stop calling me diverse [Blog post]. *LinkedIn*. https://www.linkedin.com/pulse/just-chups-2-stop-calling-me-diverse-jodi-ann-burey-mph/

Clossey, L. (Host), & Bright, K. (Presenter). (2021, February 11). *Cultivating anti-racist/anti-bias recruitment and hiring practices*. [Webinar]. YouTube. https://www.youtube.com/watch?v=AtFg91-J4NI

Cunningham, S. J., Guss, S., & Stout, J. (2019). Challenging the "good fit" narrative: Creating inclusive recruitment practices in academic libraries. In D. M. Mueller (Ed.). *Recasting the narrative: The proceedings of the ACRL 2019 Conference, April 10–13, 2019, Cleveland, Ohio* (pp. 12–21). Association of College and Research Libraries. https://scholarship.richmond.edu/university-libraries-publications/42/

Galvan, A. (2015, June 3). Soliciting performance, hiding bias: Whiteness and librarianship. *In the Library with the Lead Pipe*. https://www.inthelibrarywiththeleadpipe.org/2015/soliciting-performance-hiding-bias-whiteness-and-librarianship/

Gaucher, D., Friesen, J., & Kay, A. C. (2011). Evidence that gendered wording in job advertisements exists and sustains gender inequality. *Journal of Personality and Social Psychology*, *101*(1), 109–128. https://doi.org/10.1037/a0022530

Hathcock, A. (2015, October 7). White librarianship in blackface: Diversity initiatives in LIS. *In the Library with the Lead Pipe*. https://www.inthelibrarywiththeleadpipe.org/2015/lis-diversity/

Indiana State Council Society for Human Resource Management. (2019, November 8). *How to create an inclusive hiring process*. Indiana SHRM News. https://hrindianashrm.org/news/how-to-create-an-inclusive-hiring-process/

McCullough, H. (2019, November 18). A checklist for inclusive hiring. *Educause Review*. https://er.educause.edu/blogs/2019/11/a-checklist-for-inclusive-hiring

Neilsen, J. & Houk, K. (2021, April 13–16). *The library is open (and hiring)! Towards conscientious academic librarian interviewing practices* [Conference session]. Association of College and Research Libraries 20th National Conference, online. https://drive.google.com/drive/folders/1zi-rEkq6d42Xbx3OyQb6ee1DUwHkXMwU

Spiegelman, P. (2021, March 1). Is hiring for culture fit perpetuating bias? *Forbes*. https://www.forbes.com/sites/paulspiegelman/2021/03/01/is-hiring-for-culture-fit-perpetuating-bias/

## APPENDIX B

# Inclusive Interviewing Practices Handout for Search Committees

## Library's Inclusive Interviewing Practices

Adopted November 2021

### PRE-INTERVIEW (BEFORE DECIDING ON CANDIDATES TO INTERVIEW)

- Write a job description with sufficient specificity for applicants to understand job responsibilities, but remove library jargon and coded language that might prevent applicants from applying.
- Ensure diverse representation on search committees. Strive to include different races, sexual orientation, staff and librarian representation. Always include at least one representative from another team. Positions with extensive connections outside the library may want a nonlibrary representative.
- Have all search committee members take the "inclusive search and hiring" module on HR's website.
- Establish rubrics for evaluation in advance based on the requirements identified in the job description.

### INTERVIEW PREPARATION (ONCE CANDIDATES ARE DECIDED ON TO INTERVIEW)

- Provide candidates with interview questions in advance.
- All candidates for a position should be interviewed through the same modality. Decide if all candidates will be interviewed in person or all virtually.
- Provide a detailed itinerary for the interview, including who will be in each interview (with titles) and why they are being interviewed by each individual or group. Provide context. Be intentional about who the candidates meet with.
- Give candidates the ability to meet with any affinity groups on campus. Examples:
  - LGBTQ Center

- o Office of Sustainability
- o Someone from any liaison department they will be working with
- Build the itinerary (in person or virtual) with the candidate in mind.
  - o Schedule meeting time with the search committee as early in the day as possible to provide context and answer questions of the candidate.
  - o Determine whether or not a full-library presentation is necessary. If not, consider knowledge sharing discussions, demonstrations, etc.
  - o Shorten the interview segments as much as possible. Optimally, there is no more than a 5-hour interview time in one day utilizing 20-, 30-, or 45-minute segments.
  - o Keep in mind the "home" time zone of a candidate so as to not schedule a meeting starting at 9 a.m. for those on the west coast where it is 6 a.m. Even if interviewing in person, the time change matters.
- Ensure the interviewee has multiple ways to contact the search committee chair, other search committee members, or the administrative assistant for the dean's office.
- Virtual interview
  - o Offer to provide a hotel or other accommodation for reliable, uninterrupted interview time.
  - o Ask if any accommodation is needed (frequent breaks, camera off, etc.).
- In person
  - o Offer a selection of restaurant choices, and provide menu links. Offer to allow them to choose to eat on their own if they prefer.
  - o Ask if any accommodation is needed (minimize walking, auditory or visual assistance).
  - o Group together the interview segments to minimize walking.
  - o Arrange for airport pickups and provide the cell number for whomever is going to be picking up the candidate.
  - o Provide a variety of travel scenarios for candidates to choose from, or offer to let them make their own and be reimbursed.

## ON THE INTERVIEW DAY

- Ensure that the candidate has multiple ways to contact the chair, other members of the search committee, and the administrative assistant in the Dean's office.
- Be ready to provide accommodations that hadn't been accounted for.

## POST-INTERVIEW ASSESSMENT

- Gather input quickly from search committee, library employees, and others who have interviewed throughout the day.
- Have a recap of the search committee to assess how the search went so we can learn from each interview and implement changes on future interviews.

## APPENDIX C

# Sample Rubric That Is Used by the Search Committee

**Candidate name:**

**Minimum Qualifications (check all that apply)**
- ☐ MLIS
- ☐ Other advanced degree
- ☐ Understanding of best practices in Access
- ☐ Best practices in Reference
- ☐ Evidence of EDI work
- ☐ Team building
- ☐ Sustained leadership in library setting
- ☐ Successful team management
- ☐ Provided library services in person/virtually
- ☐ ILL/physical and electronic reserves
- ☐ Leading through change
- ☐ Written/verbal communication skills

**Preferred Qualifications (check all that apply)**
- ☐ Project management/problem solving
- ☐ Collaborative leadership/consensus building
- ☐ Assessment and data driven decision making
- ☐ Professional engagement/research/publications

**Continue to consider?** Yes or No

**Reviewed by:**

# APPENDIX D

# Candidate Itinerary with Context

## Sample Itinerary
## Random Librarian Position

**Date: September xx, 2021 (ALL TIMES ARE EASTERN TIME)**

9:00am-9:30am     **Meeting with Search Committee**
Name 1, Chair/title
Name 2, Librarian (member/title)
Name 3, Library Specialist IV (member/title)
Name 4, Librarian (member/title)
Name 5, Librarian (member/title)
Name 6, Member, external to the library/ supervisor (member/title)

At this meeting, the Search Committee will review the itinerary for the day with you. You will have a chance to ask any questions about the day and the Committee may also take this as an opportunity to ask you questions regarding your application materials and experience.

9:30am-10:00am     **Meeting with Dean Name, Dean**
In this role of (librarian position title) the Dean will be your direct supervisor. In this meeting, he will provide context about the role and the department from the supervisory perspective and you can ask questions.

10:00am-10:15am:     **Break**

10:15am-11:00am     **Presentation:** approx 20 minutes: with 20-25 minutes Q/A

- Example: What have we learned about providing x services in academic libraries to y constituency? What lasting changes and innovations do you believe will continue in libraries, and what challenges and opportunities do we still have ahead of us?

11:00am–12:30pm     **Lunch Break**

12:30pm-1:00pm: Name of Provost Office Representative, **Associate Provost, the Provost's office**

It is not uncommon to see, and interact with, our Provost & our Associate Provosts on campus. For further context, our Dean reports to the Provost. At this meeting, you have a chance to ask one of our Associate Provosts any questions you may have about the university and library at large; i.e. budget support, research support, etc. A great place to prepare for this meeting is the Provost Office's website.

1:00pm-1:45pm **Break**

1:45pm-2:15pm: Meet with affinity group of candidate's choice. (ODI, Sustainability, LGBTQ office, Women's Center, etc.)

2:15pm-2:30pm **Break**

2:30pm-3:00pm Library Faculty Peer Review Committee
Name 1, Name, title
Name 2, Name, title
Name 3, Name, title
Name 4, Name, title

This meeting is an opportunity for you to get information and ask any questions around the faculty status of this position, i.e. rank, promotion, mentoring, librarians' assembly. To help prepare for this meeting we are providing you with a copy of our library faculty's governing document and by-laws to review.

3:00pm-3:15pm **Break**

3:15pm-3:45pm: **Meeting with the Search Committee**

At this meeting, the search committee can answer any remaining questions you may have, they may also have some last minute questions for you! The Committee will explain what to expect after the interview.

3:45pm–4:15pm **Meeting with the candidate's team**
Name 1, Name, title
Name 2, Name, title
Name 3, Name, title
Name 4 Name, title

|  | Name 5, Name, title |
|---|---|
|  | Name 6, Name, title |
|  | Name 7, Name, title |
|  | Name 8, Name, title |
| 4:15pm–4:45pm | **Meeting with candidate's team representative/director** |
|  | Wrap up. May include drive to the airport, drive around town, etc. |

**Contact Information for Emergencies (technical or otherwise):**
Name 1, Search Committee Chair, Cell: xxx-xxx-xxxx
Name 2, Assistant to the Dean, Cell: xxx-xxx-xxxx

# References

Boddie, A., Paloma Fiedler, B., Haslam, M., Luna, E., Martinez-Flores, E., Padilla, T., Wainscott, S., White, C., Day, A., Cheng, J, George, K., Green, H., Melilli, A., Mazmanyan, K., & Brombosz, C. (2020). *Inclusion and Equity Committee recommendations for diverse recruitment report*. University of Nevada, Las Vegas Libraries. https://digitalscholarship.unlv.edu/lib_iec_reports/4/

Cunningham, S. J., Guss, S., & Stout, J. (2019). Challenging the "good fit" narrative: Creating inclusive recruitment practices in academic libraries. In D. M. Mueller (Ed.). *Recasting the narrative: The proceedings of the ACRL 2019 Conference, April 10–13, 2019, Cleveland, Ohio* (pp. 12–21). Association of College and Research Libraries. https://scholarship.richmond.edu/university-libraries-publications/42/

Galvan, A. (2015, June 3). Soliciting performance, hiding bias: Whiteness and librarianship. *In the Library with the Lead Pipe*. https://www.inthelibrarywiththeleadpipe.org/2015/soliciting-performance-hiding-bias-whiteness-and-librarianship/

Hathcock, A. (2015, October 7). White librarianship in blackface: Diversity initiatives in LIS. *In the Library with the Lead Pipe*. https://www.inthelibrarywiththeleadpipe.org/2015/lis-diversity/

CHAPTER 14

# Reflections on a Faculty Cluster Hiring Approach at a Large Predominantly White Academic Library

*Shawnta Smith-Cruz, April M. Hathcock, and Scott Collard*

## Background

New York University (NYU) is a large, private, research-intensive institution with a global reach and a predominantly white faculty and student body. The Division of Libraries, which serves the university and its campuses and sites around the world, connects users across NYU and beyond with the goal of advancing the university's mission and promoting an environment of open and equitable inquiry. To this end, the Division of Libraries'

top priority since 2019 has been to increase diversity and equity within our ranks as well as to improve the sense of inclusion and belonging among the institution's students, faculty, staff, alumni, and community members. This work has taken many shapes, including not only recruiting a more diverse workforce, but also creating an environment in which those faculty and staff members remain, flourish, and advance their careers. We refer to this strategic priority as Inclusion, Diversity, Belonging, Equity, and Accessibility, or IDBEA.

In the spring of 2021, the university presented the Division of Libraries, and all its schools and divisions, with an opportunity to actively promote IDBEA through increasing diversity among our faculty. Based on research demonstrating that cluster hiring, or the "practice of hiring faculty into multiple departments or schools around interdisciplinary research topics" (Urban Universities for HEALTH, 2015, p. 5), can increase faculty diversity and improve institutional climate, NYU launched a cluster hiring initiative as part of a concerted effort to increase faculty diversity across its divisions. Issuing a road map and call for proposals across the institution, the university centered its program on several large thematic areas of focus for potential cluster hiring among the various schools and divisions. These areas of focus were broad and purposely interdisciplinary, designed to create opportunities for cross-departmental partnership and collaboration and to reinforce the initiative's goal of assembling diverse pools of applicants who would be attracted to work and research in these areas. The original university themes included

- inequality and anti-racism
- urban environments, politics, and problems
- population health and health equity
- public interest technology
- public humanities

With this opportunity set before us, the Division of Libraries soon became a prolific participant of the NYU cluster hiring initiative. Normally when the Division of Libraries seeks to hire for existing or new faculty positions, library leadership submits annual requests for approvals to the office of the provost. Once a request is approved, the Division of Libraries organizes search committees for each position and conducts the search in the academic semester for which the position has been approved. Under the cluster hiring initiative, the same approval process applies, with the additional submission of specific cluster proposals for the thematic groups of position we are looking to fill.

Following this approval process, by the end of the three-year initiative, we will have proposed and recruited for eighteen positions across five clusters, using a streamlined, inclusive, and highly collaborative process. This chapter provides an overview of our work on the cluster hiring initiative thus far: (1) joining university-wide structures that served as the groundwork for the cluster initiative; (2) mobilizing libraries' faculty support in creating, drafting, and refining cluster proposals; (3) implementing best practices in recruitment and committee work, including the appointment of a libraries-wide faculty diversity search liaison; (4) conducting extensive after-action reviews with search committees and candidates; and (5) developing comprehensive research-grounded plans for supporting the success of new hires. Our goal in sharing this case study of our diversity hiring work is to showcase how one academic library at a predominantly white private institution is putting its theoretical commitment into meaningful practice to diversify the faculty of our institution and in service to the broader profession.

# The Work Begins

The Division of Libraries began work crafting our own approach to the larger NYU cluster hiring initiative in 2021. Due to a large number of open positions (like many institutions, we had frozen search activity during the pandemic), we knew we had an unusual opportunity to reshape our staff. From the start of the work, we wanted to foster a maximally collaborative and inclusive process that would energize our existing faculty and staff in this important reshaping. This collaborative and inclusive process meant that rather than a relatively top-down approach to defining the clusters and positions contained therein, our faculty themselves would shape the proposals. And because we would be hiring multiple faculty simultaneously, we knew we had the opportunity to redefine positions around themes of strategic importance to us, in areas that would be well suited to cross-departmental collaboration.

A small group of libraries leadership introduced the university's strategy and its starter themes to our libraries faculty body, after which we set about securing volunteers to take on the primary work of defining our own clusters within these thematic areas. This definitional work followed a university cookbook of sorts and asked any proposer to follow a template of responses designed to steer the outcomes toward interdisciplinarity, highlighting the research opportunities promised in each cluster and exploring how any proposal would meet the twin goals of increased collaboration and progress on building a diverse faculty. The groups had a sense of which open positions might be associated with the various clusters but were also asked to shape the positions further in light of the clusters or to suggest or define novel positions.

Our small groups worked for around six weeks, finding resonance within the original themes but, in the end, building significant richness and perspectives that centered libraries needs and goals. Each cluster, by definition, would have at least three positions that drew from different areas of library work and would acknowledge interconnections that are sometimes not considered in hiring processes. For example, our resulting cluster within the inequality and anti-racism theme included a liaison librarian focused on African American and Black diaspora studies, an EDI-focused student success librarian, and an audiovisual metadata librarian. Though each of these positions would be in a different department, the connective tissue between the positions was encapsulated in a commitment to supporting underrepresented voices within library services and materials, a commitment made explicit in the final title for this cluster proposal, "Centering Underrepresented Voices: Anti-racist Practices in Libraries and Archives." As shown in table 14.1, our other resulting clusters similarly expanded on the university's themes, pushing on some key issues for our library.

**Table 14.1.** Expansion of university themes in Division of Libraries cluster hires

| University Theme | Libraries Proposal |
| --- | --- |
| Inequality and Anti-racism | Centering Underrepresented Voices: Anti-racist Practices in Libraries and Archives |
| Urban Environments, Politics, and Problems | The Politics of Space: Data, the City, and Structures of Inequality |
| Population Health and Health Equity | Health and Scientific Literacy, Openness, and Equity |
| Public Interest Technology | Building STEM for the Public Good: Cultivating Openness in the Sciences |
| Public Humanities | Transformative Humanities for All: Building and Sharing the Cultural Record |

Indeed, in all the resulting proposals, we remade the themes in ways that created capacity for collaborative interdisciplinarity while highlighting our strategic focus on centering IDBEA. This ended up being the most potent approach to take: had we defined the positions individually, as has been our past practice, we wouldn't necessarily have discovered the interrelationships between them. Foregrounding the collaborative discovery process of the clusters first and foremost—and only then reshaping our positions within this stronger contextual framework—helped us break new ground, reframe our positions, and also begin to understand a more expansive vision for how our new staff would find themselves in our library (work that continues, as we'll see later). In the end, we made all five of these proposals to the university and were approved to open searches for most of the positions suggested by the proposal writers over a two-to-three-year period.

With this milestone past, we turned our attention to enhancing our processes to support what would be a sustained, complex, and deep scope of work to recruit our new staff. Several actions proved to be consequential as we entered the search phase for the new positions, generally focused on a deeper attention to the process itself. The libraries faculty had previously invested a good deal of work into more clearly defining and documenting faculty search best practices, and this documentation proved to be a critical component within the cluster searches. Roles and responsibilities for searches were made clear, and all individuals involved in a search were expected to have a solid familiarity with the best practices. In a particularly important change, it was now expected that search committee members (who weren't necessarily the same folks who had written the cluster) would take as a starting point the small stubby position descriptions within the clusters and—in collaboration with important stakeholders, hiring managers, and libraries leaders—build these into more fulsome descriptions that would be advertised to candidates. This approach enabled us once again to expand the circle of input into these roles, build greater connective tissue between positions, and most importantly, combat the potential for implicit bias that can seep into search processes. Every one of the position descriptions changed in some way, and some of them changed fairly radically by the end of the search committee's work. But because the initial unifying feature remained the clusters themselves, the outcomes stayed well aligned with our identified needs.

We also instituted some additional layers of support and oversight for these searches. The most important of these was to designate a standing faculty diversity search liaison (FDSL), a role initiated by the university for every school or unit that hires faculty, to develop strategies and support committees in attracting diverse pools for faculty searches (New York University Office of the President, n.d.). The Division of Libraries chose to integrate our appointed FDSL deeply into searches by ensuring that their role would maximize diverse applicant pools. The FDSL in turn helped committees understand how to conduct equitable searches, avoid bias, access tools and training, and develop a recruiting mindset to grow a diverse applicant pool (more on the FDSL in the following section).

Last, though we didn't know it at the time, it soon became clear that the complexity of the many moving parts of these searches would require some sort of overall search orchestration group. This small group of library leaders included the libraries dean, the FDSL, the libraries faculty affairs representative, and another of the associate deans. It was quickly apparent this group would be key to successfully managing the searches. The sheer quantity of positions we would be recruiting for (fifteen searches taking place over about nine months) meant that the group had to carefully construct the search committees, assuring that every one of our library faculty was assigned to at least one search, but also trying to avoid over-assigning any given person. Similarly, we knew we needed to keep our processes on track and avoid competing searches, interview slots, and overcommitment, all of which required the orchestration group to think carefully about timing and pacing. The orchestration group would also be on the lookout for potential crossover effects between the searches—situations where multiple searches attracted the same candidates, or where individuals may be good candidates for searches other than the one they applied for.

With all this work and setup finally in place, we were ready to start our search processes.

# Collaborating during Searches

Search committees, like the cluster proposal writing process, were rooted in collaboration between faculty and human resources (HR). In the past, our libraries-based HR department managed the bulk of faculty hiring logistics, including coordinating position description uploads, contacting potential employees, generating final day schedules, checking references, and making final offers. At the start of the cluster process, however, tasks and duties were split between HR and faculty, with the particularities determined by the orchestration group. An imperative to maintain clear lines of communication between faculty and potential candidates enabled a formal breakdown of the labor attributed to each search (see appendix A).

Clear roles among various individuals allowed for sustained confidentiality coupled with clear lines of communication among colleagues. Committees included members of the faculty as well as administrative staff, all of whom collaborated with their senior leaders and HR team in ways that allowed for agency in communication with candidates and each other. To avoid overlap of final-round presentations, HR constructed time lines to provide a clear trajectory of each component of the search process. Schedules and time lines for the simultaneous searches were back-timed based on the desired candidate projected start dates. This more rigorously designed search time line approach allowed for an equal number of days between post and closing, from closing to evaluation, and then from evaluation to first and second interviews.

Once the search committees began their work, they immediately met with the FDSL. The conversations and tools available via the FDSL's involvement in the university-wide FDSL community of practice were put into practice in the libraries immediately. The three areas of focus by the FDSL are described in depth below: (1) improving inclusive language within the position description; (2) using active recruitment strategies with a target of at least 21 percent (the current employee demographic breakdown by race according to ARL) applicants of color; and (3) utilizing best practices for running an inclusive search process (Mian, 2021, p. 3).

## Improving Position Description Language

Search committees in consultation with the FDSL worked to broaden the language in position descriptions to connect explicitly to the cluster proposals. Position description language was purposely designed to attract the widest range of eligible applicants, including applicants of color who would be otherwise sought after by similar initiatives or were outside of the library science field altogether. Qualifications were strategically formatted with consideration of placement in preferred versus required, acknowledging that new and recently graduated professionals as well as applicants who did not already hold an MLS or equivalent were still eligible to apply. Key components evaluated as attractive to a diverse pool of candidates were foregrounded in position descriptions, including language that highlighted a focus on *anti-racism, openness, queer, decolonization, interhemispheric, global, critical race theory, equity*, and other terms that were a focal point of that particular position. Terms such as *urban* or *underrepresented* or *diverse* were evaluated for purpose and intention to enhance their practicality to the role and deter from use of diversity jargon. These terms were then tied to the work already taking place within the university and the Division of Libraries, with an invitation to new hires to continue this work (see appendix B for sample position description).

Lastly, a separate diversity statement was requested with each application. These statements had previously been optional or not uniformly requested. The prompt for the diversity statement was linked in the "How to Apply" section and limited to a single question, with a request for only one to two paragraphs, followed by a list of resources on constructing diversity statements. The result of the diversity statement allowed all applicants, regardless of experience, nationality, or representative identities, to disclose their comfort and intentions behind the work of anti-racism, equity, and inclusion within libraries. This additional component further illustrated to candidates our commitment to engage in work that holds IDBEA as a central value (see appendix C for diversity statement prompt).

## Getting to 21 Percent Applicants of Color

Committee members were encouraged to develop a multitiered recruitment strategy in advertising the position. A successful recruitment strategy would yield at least 21 percent applicants of color reached by the preferred application deadline, a number that reflected the Division of Libraries track record according to our previously reported ARL statistics. The goal was to increase the person of color representation in the applicant pool as reflected by "the overall racial/ethnic distribution of professional staff in US ARL university libraries: White 79.9%, Asian 6.9%, Black 7.4%, Hispanic 4.2%, Two or More Races 0.8%, Native American or Alaska Native 0.7%, Native Hawaiian or Other Pacific Islander 0.1%" (Mian, 2021).

Searches were grounded in active transparency and communication to potential applicants about the positions and process. To allow for transparency, committees held a remote, anonymous, unrecorded "Search Info Session" live on Zoom. Presenters at the session included a search committee representative from each open position with their contact information on slides that also featured images of the library and campus. Details of the expectations of the role and climate of that particular department were bookended by opening remarks from the dean of libraries, a benefits overview by the HR office, an outline of faculty status at the libraries, expectations for the diversity statement, and a robust anonymous Q&A to surface a wide range of topics, from moving to our area, to work culture and pay rates. Registrants' identifiable data was controlled by a department unaffiliated with the searches, which facilitated the Zoom session and organized the Eventbrite registration. This additional layer of anonymity ensured that the webinar would protect participants' identities.

To recruit further applicants, committee members gathered names of potentially interested candidates by tapping into their immediate professional networks, scanning conference lists, sourcing authors of recent publications, and soliciting recommendations from e-mail discussion lists. The FDSL provided a list of professional organizations of interest that was generated within the FDSL community of practice. E-mail templates allowed committee members to arrange one-on-one conversations with potential candidates and the hiring manager, the FDSL, or the committee member. In the end, dozens of conversations were scheduled. The majority of successful candidates of color noted having spoken to someone before applying for the role and affirmed that their decision to apply or interest in the position increased after having a conversation unique to their particular concerns.

As a final step in our recruitment efforts, we routinized a status check at the preferred application deadline. At this juncture, HR exported a demographic report from Interfolio (our application portal) and submitted it to the committee chairs and the FDSL. Following this export was a conversation on whether applicant pools reached at or above our 21 percent target. For the small number of searches that were extended due to a lack of eligible applicants who identified as people of color, committee chairs met with the FDSL to evaluate missteps and reintegrate outreach strategies with an accelerated time line to bring the search back on track.

## Fostering Search: Best Practices

It was critical that committee members be able to bring a shared commitment and knowledge of IDBEA to conversations with prospective candidates. For this, we leaned heavily into preexisting anti-racist teachings and learnings within the libraries that fostered a more inclusive and equitable workplace and affirmed the diversity in our communities. For years leading up to the cluster initiative, an IDBEA steering committee sponsored a set of working groups and initiatives to spread the values of anti-racism, foster community involvement, and increase our knowledge base. These various initiatives included programs such as a semesterly day-of-learning speaker series, retreats, lunch-and-learns, and other practices, all of which helped prepare staff from across departments to engage with hard conversations or acknowledgment of inequitable distributions of power based on race. The commitment to an anti-racist workplace, library, and institution was premeditated and embedded in day-to-day prioritizing, and indeed became the libraries' number one strategic priority. This climate allowed a lighter lift when introducing and implementing best practices for combating bias throughout the search.

We supported deploying best practices for running a diverse search by ensuring at least one committee member enrolled in Best Practices for Inclusive Faculty Searches led by the Office of Equal Opportunity, which was "designed to mitigate unconscious bias at each stage of the search process" (New York University Office of Equal Opportunity, n.d.). At the same time, the FDSL met with each committee a minimum of two times along the way to keep best practices at the forefront. We adopted and upheld the use of a rubric drawn from the components of the position to evaluate applicants. We used the diversity statement, CV, and cover letter together to assess the strengths of an applicant's commitment to IDBEA as another evaluative metric in their application.

We also developed a set of practices for virtual interviews to create consistency and accessibility. These included the following:

- Using the same list of interview questions for all candidates.
- Pasting interview questions into the chat while asking them.
- Enabling captions to allow for multiple modes of intake.
- Contextualizing unseen activity, such as sharing that the committee will be taking notes but will still be very much engaged.
- Communicating the time allotted for the full interview, breaking this down into a projection of time per question. For example, committees were offered this language to consistently begin each interview: "We have thirty minutes and four questions; that means you'll have about five minutes per question, and that should leave you time at the end to ask us some questions. We will place each question into the chat after asking. Are you ready to begin?"

Though we used the same questions for each candidate, we also felt it was important to make an allowance for follow-up questions, as some candidates chose to respond briefly while others took more time. Some committees even chose to send along some areas or themes for what would be covered in the interview ahead of time (though not the actual questions), with the idea that fewer surprises would put candidates at ease.

Two to four candidates were chosen for final-round interviews in each search. It was recommended, though optional, that the committee would use a nuanced strategy to choose a varied group of final-round candidates. Identifying differences in experiences and qualifications helped to not replicate a single applicant type. For example, a committee might have one slot for a candidate who is a recent graduate, another slot for a seasoned professional, and a third slot for a career shifter; committee choices to implement a varied final group would differ depending on the role. Candidates who made it to the final round were given presentation prompts with the same number of days in advance of their presentation.

Between rigorous and predictable processes and search time lines, inclusive descriptions and a recruitment-focused strategy, and relatively transparent search practices, we were able to bring in full slates of excellent candidates and encourage broad and sustained participation of the libraries' staff and faculty in final-round interviews and presentations. We had high turnouts, fruitful conversations, and, eventually, accepted offers.

# Looking Forward

As we looked to wrap up our searches, one of the critical elements we knew we needed to integrate into the process was a moment of reflection and learning to help inform our searches moving forward. Realistically, we had no intention of conducting searches on such a wide scale again; indeed, even under a cluster hire initiative, conducting over ten faculty searches over a single academic year is beyond ambitious. Nevertheless, we recognized that this unique moment in our search practice offered many potential lessons that could inform how we approach searches moving forward. In addition, because this work involved participation from across our library organization and beyond the library, we recognized there would be lessons to learn about how best to embark on large-scale, organization-wide projects such as this one. This cluster hiring work could help us to learn how to do all of our major organizational projects in ways that are equitable, inclusive, and as transparent as possible.

## Evaluation

With this potential for reflection and learning in mind, we made the intentional decision to conduct rounds of extensive after-action reviews to solicit feedback from various search stakeholders. We asked each search committee to include an after-action review with their final committee reports, detailing what worked well for their work on the search and what needed improvement. In addition, the dean met with the staff of HR for an after-action session aimed at evaluating the process from their perspective. Finally, two of us with positions represented in the cluster hire initiative set up one-on-one meetings with the nonfaculty members of the search committees to get their feedback on what it was like serving on a faculty search committee and ways in which this form of faculty-staff collaboration could be improved.

Once we had gathered all the after-action review feedback, we imported it into a spreadsheet, organized into one of four main themes (see appendix D):

- *Search logistics* involved feedback on selecting and following search time lines; navigating the mechanics of posting job descriptions to job boards and e-mail discussion lists; and overall communication between the search administrators, HR, and the search committee.
- *Committee activity* included feedback on the composition of the search committees, setting and following group norms, and working with the FDSL to incorporate inclusive practices into the search process.
- *Interviews* incorporated feedback on developing open-ended, inclusive questions; soliciting and evaluating diversity statements from candidates; and crafting relevant and comprehensible presentation prompts.
- *Wrapping the search* involved feedback relating to the use of candidate assessment tools and practices, the offer and negotiation process, and following up with the committees once a hiring decision had been made.

With the results of the after-action reviews organized in this way, we met with the search committee chairs to go over the spreadsheet and ensure that the committees' feedback was accurately and adequately represented. The search orchestration team then met separately to go over all the feedback in the spreadsheet and begin making decisions about the next steps based on feedback recommendations. Some of the next steps that stood out for our administrative team included the following:

- Scheduling more time for the committees to check in with the FDSL throughout the search.
- Providing better clarity in the roles of the search committees and the search committee chairs during the kickoff meetings for the searches.
- Creating a more systematic workflow for wrapping up searches, including following up with search committees when we have accepted offers and managing search documentation after the search.

A current round of searches began at our organization during the writing of this chapter, and we have been working to implement these changes across the board. While our new searches are not nearly as extensive as the first round of cluster hiring was, we have learned and are implementing many valuable lessons from the after-action reviews.

## Onboarding and Retention

Another key element for us in wrapping up our searches has been thinking critically about how to integrate our new colleagues into the organization once they arrive. We recognized that conducting inclusive searches was only the beginning; we had to be sure that we as an organization were ready to welcome our new colleagues into an environment where they could thrive. To that end, midway through this first academic year of cluster searches, our library faculty governance, along with the faculty members of library senior leadership, charged a small group of faculty from across the libraries to serve on a faculty cluster hiring support working group. We charged this working group with developing research-based recommendations for providing effective support to new cluster hires through the lens of IDBEA. Importantly, the working group was responsible only for crafting recommendations and *not* for implementing those recommendations; we viewed implementation as the responsibility of library faculty governance and senior leadership. We also acknowledged that these recommendations, while important for the cluster hires, would serve as a helpful template for how we should handle faculty support and onboarding for *all* our new faculty.

The working group did excellent work over a very short time frame. In a matter of four months, they investigated practices at other institutions with cluster hiring initiatives, explored plans being developed across the university, and curated best practices from the literature in library and information studies and other disciplines. The working group organized their resulting recommendations into five key areas (see appendix E):

1. *Relationship building:* concerned with mentorship and professional socialization

2. *Communication/training:* involving information-sharing, onboarding, and professional development

3. *Research:* focused on providing protected research time and equitable access to financial and other forms of support

4. *Service:* comprising a clear articulation of service expectations and opportunities and a system of equitably dividing service responsibilities

5. *Assessment:* centered on conducting clear and consistent assessment of the cluster hire program, soliciting candid feedback from the new hires throughout their early career with us

It is important to note all of the recommendations were particularly rooted in research showing that faculty who identify as Black, Indigenous, and people of color (BIPOC) and who identify as cis women, trans, nonbinary, or gender nonconforming are often shut out of informal and formal mechanisms benefiting the attainment of tenure and promotion, while they are overwhelmingly expected to bear the brunt of under- and uncompensated service work (Moody, 2011). Given these demonstrated inequities, our library would need to work hard to continue building an organization in which all of our new colleagues could thrive. With the challenge set, the working group passed these recommendations on to library faculty governance and senior leadership, where we have been making great strides in implementing them for the benefit of not only our new colleagues but also all our faculty.

# Conclusion

As we prepare to enter a new phase of faculty hiring, with cluster and non-cluster positions alike, we take stock of the work we have done in this first phase of cluster work and the lessons we have learned for more successfully integrating inclusive hiring practices in our organization. The collaborative work we have done in getting our searches set up, during the searches, and moving forward in our hiring has yielded powerful results: we have welcomed over ten new faculty librarians, the majority of whom identify as BIPOC or members of another historically and intentionally marginalized community in our profession. This work has been rooted in iterative processes that we hope will lead to durable changes in our organization. We continue, now with the feedback and collaboration of our new colleagues, to develop and refine our hiring processes to build more inclusiveness in our recruitment and more belonging in our culture. Our effort in taking a faculty cluster hiring approach at our large, predominantly white academic library has transformed for the better the way we approach faculty hiring and culture for all of our faculty.

# Acknowledgments

The authors wish to extend a heartfelt thanks to their colleagues in the Division of Libraries for all their hard work in making the cluster hiring initiative a success thus far. Special thanks to our dean for her leadership and support. And a huge welcome to all our new colleagues: you make our organization a much better place.

# APPENDIX A

# Sample Responsibilities of HR, Faculty Committee, and Library Leaders

| Human Resources | Faculty Search Committee | Search Orchestration (Library Leaders) |
| --- | --- | --- |
| Schedules kickoff meeting between search committee, hiring manager, HR, FDSL, faculty affairs representative, and dean | Creates, reviews, and finalizes position descriptions, rubrics for evaluation, and interview questions | Generates list of potential committee members, coordinates between other groups, and initiates launch of committees |
| Schedules committee meetings, search time line, and all interviews with candidates | Actively recruits, and tracks posting of position description across various sites and e-mail discussion lists | Develops diversity statement prompt for all position descriptions |
| Generates demographic review of candidates after preferred application deadline | Identifies potential candidates:<br>First round: 8–10 candidates<br>Second round: 2–4 candidates | Checks position description for bias and language connected to cluster |
| Places position description into Textio and Interfolio | Identifies and contacts stakeholders for second-round itinerary with division-wide and university-wide stakeholders | Evaluates demographic review with committee chairs |
| Creates and distributes templates for rubrics and interview questions | Conducts reference checks | Conducts after-action review of the search process |
| Communicates with candidates for first- and second-round interviews | Makes initial offer, negotiates offer, and discusses salary, housing, and other faculty-specific benefits | |

## APPENDIX B

# Sample Position Description

### Community Engagement Librarian and Head of External Engagement

The Community Engagement Librarian and Head of External Engagement will lead the department of External Engagement which aspires to engage external communities of the Division of Libraries' (DoL) through the development of programmatic opportunities that emphasize anti-racism and rectify inequalities. Using concepts such as critical race theory, queer theories, reparative justice models and feminist practices, to name a few, this new position will incorporate the DoL values and missions of Inclusion, Diversity, Belonging, Equity, and Accessibility (IDBEA) into our engagement practices.

This tenure-track faculty position will apply critical teaching and learning practices to its engagement work, and support the coordination of current and new external partnerships. The position will also work to coordinate library-focused NYU-based engagement programs and university-wide initiatives such as NYU Welcome, NYU Reads, and Gallery exhibitions, to name a few. The Community Engagement Librarian and Head of External Engagement will have supervisory oversight of (3-6) full-time administrative staff, including the Associate Director for Annual Fund, Alumni Outreach, & External Engagement to support development, as well as the Assistant Director of Special Events to coordinate events and programming. This position will work closely with the Department of Communications to brand strategic priorities for community engagement, the Reference Services department, and Undergraduate & Instructional Services department to enhance engagement priorities in teaching and learning. This position will be required to provide periodic reference services, library instruction, and participate in Division-wide committees.

Programs of the External Engagement Department include, but are not limited to fundraising, internships, mentorships, gallery exhibitions, events, and collaborative partnerships such as Friends of Bobst, and NYU's Dual Degree program with The Palmer School of Library and Information Science at Long Island University. The External Engagement Department resides in the Teaching, Learning, and Engagement subdivision, and includes a sub-department of Engagement and Development. This position will report directly to the Associate Dean for Teaching, Learning and Engagement.

A list of duties is below:
- Hiring, training, and evaluating 3-6 full-time administrative professional administrative employees within the External Engagement department
- Manage and coordinate engagement offerings, supporting library-based programming and outreach to students and external communities.
- Formulate and continue partnerships with community organizations as well as NYU-based schools, centers, and institutes, such as LIU Palmer School of Library and Information Science, to plan and deliver library programs and services to a broad range of community members, both within and outside the library.
- Steer student engagement activities including site-based welcome programming such as tabling, student-club engagement, and library tours in collaboration with library committee members and partners.
- Explore new types of engagement programs such as fellowships, internships, exhibitions, residencies, mentorship, symposia, conferences, co-sponsorships, and events, in a collaborative manner with cross-functional teams both in and beyond the library.
- Establishes engagement goals, objectives, and performance targets aligned with the institutional strategic plan and priorities. Support budgetary projections to meet goals.
- Maintain and report statistics/metrics for evaluation of library engagement programs.
- Provide in-person and virtual reference desk service, library instruction, and orientation sessions.
- Participate in and chair committees, and develop policies and procedures as needed.
- Produce research and scholarship as a requirement for tenure.

**NYU Cluster Hiring Initiative**
NYU Libraries is participating in the NYU Faculty Cluster Hiring Initiative to recruit, welcome, and support new library faculty working across the Division on timely themes of social importance, such as Inequality and Anti-racism, Population Health and Health Equity, Open Science and the Public Good, and Urban Environments and Politics. NYU Libraries will use the cluster-hire approach to address our goal of building a more diverse faculty community in a concerted way, with the full weight of the University's recruitment and retention toolkit. It also allows us to mobilize our internal resources, including onboarding, cohort

## APPENDIX C

# Diversity Statement Prompt

## NYU Division of Libraries
## Developing and Writing a Diversity Statement

New York University and NYU Libraries are expressly committed to upholding the values of inclusion, diversity, belonging, equity, and accessibility (IDBEA). Because these are organizational tenets, we ask that each job applicant submit a brief diversity statement reflecting their professional perspectives, experiences, and interests regarding IDBEA, which includes concepts of labor, power, and/or structures of oppression, in relation to librarianship.

In 1-2 paragraphs, please answer the following prompts to reflect on your professional perspectives with IDBEA:

- How do you think diversity should inform work in the library and information field?

Intended to be interpreted broadly and from a global perspective, "diversity" includes the political implications of societal constructions on human differences (including, but not limited to, race, sexual orientation, gender identity, socio-economic status, ethnicity, ability, religion, etc.).

## Additional Resources

NYU Division of Libraries Diversity and Inclusion Values Statement https://library.nyu.edu/about/general/values/diversity-inclusion

NYU Division of Libraries Commitment to Anti-Racism https://library.nyu.edu/about/general/values/anti-racism

NYU Division of Libraries' Commitment to IDBE http://library.nyu.edu/about/general/values

NYU School of Law Diversity Statements Guidelines https://cas.nyu.edu/content/dam/nyu-as/casPrelaw/documents/NEW%20Law%20School%20Diversity%20Statement%20Quick%20Guidelines%20-%20Needs%20Edit.pdf

NYU Faculty of Arts and Sciences Guide to Developing Diversity Statements https://as.nyu.edu/departments/facultydiversity/recruitment/diversity-statements.html

Vanderbilt Guide on Writing Diversity Statements https://cft.vanderbilt.edu/guides-sub-pages/developing-and-writing-a-diversity-statement/

UNC Writing Center
https://writingcenter.unc.edu/tips-and-tools/diversity-statements/

# APPENDIX D

# Sample After-Action Review Spreadsheet

## Search Logistics

| Went well | Searches kickoff and framing | Dean's kickoff; best practices documentation; public webinar for potential candidates |
|---|---|---|
| Improve | Searches kickoff and framing | Kickoff meetings need to be longer; need to be sure to advertise positions internally to lib-all |

## Committee Activity

| Went well | Committee composition and norming | Including staff (nonfaculty) brought needed multidimensionality; great to have wide representation; defining meeting norms; defining process for candidate selection |
|---|---|---|
| Improve | Committee composition and norming | Need search committee norms template/starter; should orient nonfaculty committee members to faculty roles and expectations; all search committees should include BIPOC members |

## Interviews

| Went well | Diversity statements | Helpful for understanding applicant |
|---|---|---|
| Improve | Diversity statements | Could be better focused to job; many statements were pro forma |

## Wrapping the Search

| Went well | Feedback and assessment tools and processes | Standard and value-added feedback form; scoring rubrics developed within committees |
|---|---|---|
| Improve | Feedback and assessment tools and processes | Need to consider if "skills tests" have a role in these interviews (e.g., quantitative analysis tools) for specific roles |

## APPENDIX E

# Sample Faculty Cluster Hire Support Recommendations

## Relationship Building

- Develop a structure for meaningful mentorship relationships that provides agency for the mentor and mentee and that includes training for the mentors.
- Develop a structure for peer and cohort mentoring that allows new colleagues to collaborate, learn from, and support each other in ways most meaningful to them.

## Communication/Training

- Clearly delineate the difference between onboarding and ongoing support. Develop clear documentation about roles, responsibilities, and tasks related to onboarding and ongoing support.
- Scaffold all information shared with new hires so as to avoid overwhelming them with too much information or stranding them with too little as they begin.

## Research

- Build out multiple models of protected research time. Communicate these models to all supervisors of librarian faculty members, and encourage supervisors to provide as much flexibility and choice as possible among these models.
- Ensure that processes to get protected research time are simple to navigate and easy to keep track of.

## Service

- Build some documentation or guidelines around the nominations process that encourages nomination of new faculty members to advance their access to a select number of impactful service and governance opportunities. Include

considerations of how to interrupt patterns in which the same people tend to be appointed or elected to specific types of service repeatedly.
- Beyond the nominations process, consider library senior leadership's and the library faculty governing body's role in inviting faculty members to nonelected service and how these invitations can be used to interrupt patterns in which faculty of color, especially women of color, are overloaded with service that is not always well-rewarded in tenure and promotion, and faculty members who are white men are often tacitly excused from service that isn't highly rewarded in tenure and promotion.

## Assessment

- Both the ongoing support structures for faculty and the overall cluster hire initiative should be subject to assessment. Assessment of the support plan should allow for a variety methods of soliciting and collecting feedback, allowing both anonymous and identified communication.
- Assessment should be clear and consistent and should ideally be framed to increase new faculty members' trust in our organizational commitment to support them, rather than instilling fear or anxiety around their performance.

# References

Mian, A. (2021). *ARL annual salary survey 2021*. Association of Research Libraries. https://doi.org/10.29242/salary.2021

Moody, J. (2011). *Faculty diversity: Removing the barriers*. Taylor & Francis Group.

New York University Office of Equal Opportunity. (n.d.). *OEO 601: Best practices for inclusive faculty searches* [Workshop]. New York University. Retrieved March 27, 2023, from https://www.nyu.edu/about/policies-guidelines-compliance/equal-opportunity/training-and-development.html#OEO601.

New York University Office of the President (n.d.) *Guide to diverse faculty searches* [Online publication]. Retrieved March 27, 2023, from https://www.nyu.edu/about/leadership-university-administration/office-of-the-president/office-of-the-provost/faculty/guide-to-diverse-faculty-searches.html

Urban Universities for HEALTH. (2015, April). *Faculty cluster hiring for diversity and institutional climate*. https://www.aplu.org/library/faculty-cluster-hiring-for-diversity-and-institutional-climate/file

CHAPTER 15

# Disrupting the Academic Librarian Hiring Process

*Michelle Colquitt, Shamella Cromartie, Anne Grant, Kelsey Sheaffer, and Megan Sheffield*

## Introduction

The system for applying to jobs in academic libraries is notoriously opaque for both applicants and search committees (Raschke, 2003). For applicants, the hiring process often moves at the speed of a terrapin stuck in molasses. Additionally, for reasons stemming from human resources regulations, the applicant may not receive communication about the status of their application and supporting materials in a timely manner. The hiring process for members of the search committee is different but can be equally frustrating. Candidates are not privy to the mechanisms within the institution: the meetings, the discussions, the evaluations; and hiring committees can only guess at the labor and commitment of each candidate.

Institutions across the United States are working to increase diversity in their staff and faculty. Nonetheless, in the larger environment of academia, it has been found that "bias among faculty search committees has been considered a significant barrier to diversifying the professoriate" (Hakkola & Dyer, 2022). Our university, which is a land-grant

R1 institution, has historically been a traditional academic hirer, with relatively opaque processes. The university culture encourages a culture of caring, but there has been little action to demonstrate that culture in our hiring practices. Our search committee for an administration-level position sought to disrupt the hiring process by introducing transparent communication practices, which introduced candidates to our welcoming and supportive culture. This transparency ultimately helped mitigate the bias that can limit diversifying our university community.

At our university library, a combination of factors, including a reorganization, acquisition of new talent, the impact of the pandemic and the "great resignation" (Fletcher et al., 2022) on staffing levels, and emerging social justice concerns, have highlighted the need to overhaul our faculty hiring processes (Fletcher et al., 2022; Cunningham, Guss, & Stout, 2019; Cohen, 2021). We argue that more transparent procedures improve the inclusiveness of the search process and can serve as a model for our library and others. By *transparency*, we refer to communication practices that are characterized by openness and accessibility, both internally and externally. Often, this transparency includes giving context for information and decisions—but not necessarily divulging all information. It is, of course, still necessary to retain some level of confidentiality between the committee and the candidates.

At our university library, a combination of factors including a reorganization, acquisition of new talent, the impact of the pandemic and the "great resignation" (Fletcher et al., 2022) on staffing levels, and emerging social justice concerns, have highlighted the need to overhaul our faculty hiring processes especially in terms of transparency (Fletcher et al., 2022; Cunningham, Guss, & Stout, 2019; Cohen, 2021). By transparency, we refer to communication practices that are characterized by openness and accessibility, both internally and externally. Often, this includes giving context for information and decisions—but not necessarily divulging all information of the search process. We argue that more transparent procedures improve the inclusiveness of the search process and can serve as a model for our library and others. It is, of course, still necessary to retain some level of confidentiality between the committee and the candidates.

We focus on three different levels of communication in the search process: (1) among the members of the search committee, (2) from the committee to the candidates, and (3) from the committee to the rest of the library. In improving transparent communication, we sought to build inclusivity by disrupting the mystery of the hiring process, showcasing our welcoming and supportive culture, and encouraging a diverse pool of candidates.

We are briefly joined in writing by our recently hired associate dean of organizational performance, who offers some words on transparency as an essential organizational value.

# Start with Sunlight

Transparency, in its most basic form, is purely information disclosure. It can also be a "tool for reputation management" (Goodman, 2002, p. 205) and, at its most sincere, a "way to demonstrate trustworthiness" (Goodman, 2002, p. 205). In our library, we intend it to symbolize good governance.

In traditional business affairs, transparency is an ideal condition for stakeholders since citizens can observe and access all information about public affairs (Albu and Flyverbom, 2019). Transparency in the library hiring process means potential employees can critically engage, even briefly, with the library environment they may be entering. In this scenario, the interviewee is a critical observer. The library can be likened to glass, allowing the interviewee an unobstructed view of the library or, at minimum, the department to which they will be assigned. While all future library employees are worthy of this transparent view, it holds particular value for historically underrepresented library employees, allowing them to understand the inner workings of their potential place of employment to avoid critical missteps in a profession that has not traditionally held the door open for them to enter or thrive upon entry. For current library employees, transparency from the search committee promotes inclusivity and can inspire a heightened sense of responsiveness to the process. For search committee members, transparency during the process can increase collegiality and trust among colleagues.

The quote "Sunlight is the best disinfectant" from Supreme Court Justice Louis Brandeis forever preserved transparency as a requirement of good governance but also implies that it happens in the reverse; that the damage has been done once sunlight is needed as a cure. In this case, the search committee sought to transform the library's hiring processes with transparent communication, acting openly with candidates, their fellow search committee members, and library colleagues from the beginning. In other words, they chose to start with sunlight.

# Transparency within the Committee

This search committee made several key strategic decisions that prioritized transparency among members of the committee. The committee was composed of a mix of elected and appointed members of the faculty, staff, and student community of our university, each with varying levels of search committee experience. The committee set meeting norms, developed rubrics for grading applications and supporting materials, developed a quick time line for hiring the position, and created committee expectations over key areas such as communication and confidentiality. Our efforts at transparency within the search committee promoted inclusivity internally, in an attempt to empower each member to participate fully through a comprehensive understanding of the standards and expectations of the committee.

During the initial period of committee work, our search committee helped to refine the associate dean for teaching, learning, and research position announcement. We then divided our list of websites and e-mail discussion lists for search committee members to distribute the position announcement. We sought to share this job posting as far and wide as possible to draw as deep and diverse a candidate pool as possible.

Our university human resources department uses the search management software Interfolio to compile, communicate with, and assess candidates. Interfolio includes a generic star ranking system, which most search committees utilize. However, our search committee decided to create an evaluation rubric that structured the initial analysis of candidates around the defined and carefully crafted job description. Our goal was for all candidates to be evaluated on a shared set of expectations and criteria for each candidate.

The committee developed a comprehensive rubric with criteria for each of the position's required qualifications, which we assessed to be the four main areas of focus: degree and management experience, quality of application materials, experience within the areas encompassing the new division, and a commitment to equity, diversity, and inclusion. Brannon and Leuzinger (2014) established the usefulness of rubrics by stating "with planning and up-front work in the construction of a sound rubric, the review of job applicants becomes simpler, equitable, and transparent" (p. 9). Importantly, our rubric relied on measures that could be easily quantified, such as years or areas of experience, rather than measures of likeability. Vaillancourt (2021) notes that these measures are important to consider when creating rubrics and also to continue to consider these priorities throughout the hiring process. While creating this rubric was somewhat time-intensive up front, it paid off in the end because it standardized the evaluation of candidates. The creation of this rubric helped us to foster an inclusive dialogue of each candidate's strengths and weaknesses.

The American Library Association's Core Academic Interview Project Team developed a document outlining the *Core Best Practices for Academic Interviews*. In this document, the authors state, "Consider developing a rubric for evaluating the interview, based on high priority job qualifications. This rubric can help focus the evaluation process on the aspects that are most important for the candidate to perform the job successfully" (Arch et al., 2021, p. 5). While our rubric focused more on evaluating candidate applications and supporting materials, we took seriously the task of evaluating the candidate on the most important aspects of the position description.

After the development of the rubric and the closing of the initial application period, the search committee reviewed each candidate's materials to develop a short list for initial video interviews. The initial review of candidates can be a daunting process for a search committee. However, due to the creation of the rubric, we were well prepared to evaluate each candidate.

Another act of intentional transparency was to collectively develop norms for meetings. Committee work can be fraught; it can be difficult to create consensus and momentum. Meeting norms, which are a set of standards that guide committee behavior, are one way to change that dynamic. Hypes, Harris, and Otis (2020) argue that one of the ultimate aims of creating meeting norms is to establish "a means of facilitating respectful and clear communication" (p. 3). Our meeting norms similarly focused on respect, communication, and momentum and were introduced at the beginning of every meeting. All members of the committee were responsible for maintaining the norms. Given that our time is valuable and we had a limited amount of time budgeted for meetings, one of our key meeting norms was outlined as follows: "Everyone is responsible for helping to stay on topic. Speak up if you feel like we're getting off topic." Ultimately, that was the norm we referred back to most frequently in order to maintain the momentum of the search. Because the search committee was composed of a student, staff members, and faculty members of various ranks and status, it was especially inclusive for those of us who might not have as much time or institutional experience or rank to have the autonomy to lead discussions or the freedom to refocus our meetings.

Additionally, transparency extended to the organization of committee labor and time. The committee developed a time line that included a meeting schedule and expectations for work outside of each meeting—and stuck to it. This allowed committee members to create balance between committee work and typical job responsibilities. Each of these decisions worked toward transparency among committee members and ultimately attempted to improve inclusivity internally and externally.

# Transparency between Committee and Candidates

While it was crucial for the committee members to communicate with one another, it was also imperative that the committee communicate clearly with each candidate. Transparent practices between the search committee and the search candidates included creating a welcoming and inclusive atmosphere, providing opportunities for candidate feedback, and openly addressing concerns.

A welcoming and inclusive atmosphere and a desire to encourage diverse voices was at the heart of our goal to disrupt traditional methods of communication with the candidates. The first thing that our committee did for final candidates was provide a document that included a photo and a brief description of each committee member's role in the libraries. More often than not, those who are interviewing for a position know little of the committee that is taking the time to learn more about them as prospective colleagues. It was our thought that by introducing ourselves virtually, we could put faces to the names of those who would be involved in the process.

Another decision the committee made in the hopes of making the process more open and inclusive was to share the questions both for the preliminary Zoom interview with the search committee and for the final in-person interview with the library faculty. The committee felt that it was more important to provide the candidate with time to think about their responses than it was to see how well they thought on their feet and that it would provide a better opportunity for those who may not improvise on the spot as well as others. The committee found that the candidates' responses were thoughtful and concise and allowed candidates to fully express themselves and their accomplishments and abilities.

Finally, the committee offered each candidate an opportunity to meet one-on-one with one of the committee cochairs so that they could ask any questions they might have about the final interview process. By allowing each candidate an opportunity to learn more about the interview culture of the library, the playing field was evened out for each person. Candidates were allowed to review any concerns or questions they had about the process in a relaxed and informal setting. For example, if someone in the pool was unfamiliar with which presentations were going to take place and how they needed to prepare for those presentations, the committee would be available to answer these questions. Also, if there were concerns about food allergies or preferences for the various meals or meetings they would attend, these questions were also addressed.

With each decision the committee made about creating transparency between themselves and the final candidates, all appropriate steps were made to ensure that any new adjustments to the search followed the guidelines from the university faculty manual and also that the confidentiality of the candidates was protected. The committee also took time to explain the evaluative criteria to each of the candidates. Thus, through visual biographies of the search committee, through opportunities for candidates to know interview questions ahead of time, and by openly addressing concerns before each of the interviews, an atmosphere of transparency was established between the committee and the final candidates.

# Transparency between the Committee and the Library

In addition to offering transparency whenever possible in communications within the committee and with candidates, the committee also had to facilitate another level of transparency in its communications with the larger organization. In our specific context, the library is its own college within the university, and all faculty librarians should have some level of input into the process of hiring new faculty members. In fact, according to the university faculty manual,

> Because the regular faculty of a department or equivalent academic unit is the primary judge of the qualifications of its members, peer evaluation is essential in recommendations for appointment, renewal of appointment, tenure, and promotion…. The credentials of each

> applicant shall be made available to all regular departmental faculty, from whom information and recommendations regarding selection shall be solicited. (Clemson University, 2022, p. 37)

This meant that, although the individuals on the search committee would do the work of recruitment for a new faculty librarian, the committee was ultimately representing the will of the college as a whole to the dean and chair as they decided which candidate would get a job offer.

This situation presented many challenges; first and foremost, the committee had to give the libraries faculty enough information on each candidate to thoroughly evaluate their credentials while maintaining confidentiality. The standard procedure had been to make each candidate's CV and cover letter available on a departmental website that required authentication. The only information redacted from these documents was contact information such as e-mail addresses, mailing or physical addresses, and phone numbers. Especially in such a technologically driven field, this did little to actually anonymize applicants; all one needed to do was google someone to get their social media profiles, professional websites, and more. Our committee had frank discussions in the early stages of our process about which pieces of information needed to be shared with our college and what kind of feedback we wanted to collect. We wanted to balance the need to share all candidates' credentials with all faculty and the need to maintain confidentiality of applicants. Although it is a work in progress, we are actively working to implement a confidentiality agreement that all search committee members sign at the beginning of a faculty search; this document would reinforce the need to keep committee deliberations confidential. Although we have not reached a decision about updating our redaction policies, those are also under discussion; while in an ideal world we would redact enough information that library faculty could not be influenced by unconscious biases, the reality is that applicant names can often be easily found by doing a quick web search for their research publications. In addition to this, certain institutions or professional affiliations signify membership in certain underrepresented groups and often signify that an individual has devoted time and effort to diversity, equity, and inclusion in our profession. We cannot redact this information without compromising the strength of an applicant's packet, nor do we want to; to remove the very information that potentially marks a candidate as a member of an underrepresented group would erase a key part of their identity and would hinder our own efforts to diversify our college and our profession in the process. While we have not settled on a solution to this challenge yet, this may be one area where we consider moving toward less transparency in order to cut down on unconscious bias.

The second challenge the committee faced in terms of transparency within the libraries is soliciting meaningful feedback. For several years, we have used procedures that asked for feedback twice: once on all candidates (per faculty manual rules), and again for more detailed feedback on the finalists that come for an on-campus interview. Feedback was given via web form (on that same library faculty website, behind authentication) that asked for comments on applicants' librarianship, research, and service, as well as a final question as to how many years' credit toward tenure that applicant might warrant. While this does reflect the general structure of our tenure-track positions, it does not necessarily reflect the rubric used by the search committee to evaluate applicants. Additionally, there was no guidance on this feedback form for library faculty members to help them leave effective feedback; it was not uncommon to get feedback that rehashed a candidate's CV without describing how this affected their suitability for the position in question. This also left the committee in a difficult position because it was possible for the aggregated college opinion (which the committee was duty-bound to represent) to bear little resemblance to the committee's rubric scores. To address this, we have suggested that future committees work to make their rubric available to other library faculty as they are evaluating candidates; this would hopefully increase the quality of feedback received. Additionally, we may move to reduce the length of time the form is open for feedback; our response rate (despite many reminders) is usually less than 50 percent, and this part of the process has been identified by many members of recent search committees as the step that slows their progress the most. By streamlining this process and sharing the committee's rubric with the rest of the college, we hope to make our priorities and our focus on inclusion more transparent to our coworkers.

Internal candidates presented a third and final challenge in terms of interdepartmental transparency to the search committee. While the presence of internal candidates can occur in any search, aspects of the academic job search make this situation unique. Academic job searches typically advertise nationwide and consider applicants regardless of their physical location; this means that, far from having an advantage, internal candidates are often competing against formidable candidates. In academic units that use a shared governance model like ours, internal candidates require departmental buy-in; they are evaluated by a committee and colleagues who have worked with them extensively, sometimes for years; in contrast, external candidates are able to make a fresh first impression. Internal candidates, by definition, are currently doing a job that is not the one for which they are asking to be considered; it can be challenging for colleagues to see each other in a new light, and many colleagues worry that if an internal candidate successfully moves into a new position, it will just create coverage issues for the position they are leaving behind, which will then need to be backfilled (meaning another search committee).

We viewed the moment an internal candidate applied as a fork in the road; we could consider them only as a library faculty member or as a candidate, but not both. To help keep things fair and equitable for both internal and external candidates, we decided to implement the following guidelines:

1. Once an internal candidate officially submitted their application, they were not to be included on any college-wide communications from the search committee about the search process or access the feedback form and materials for other candidates.

2. Internal applicants were to receive all the same general treatment and communications from the committee as external ones in order to show we were taking their candidacy seriously, including search committee bios, introductory e-mails, logistical information, and interview day meals and transportation.

3. Once on-campus interview days were established, internal candidates were informed of all relevant dates so that they could either work from home or use annual leave (their choice) to avoid awkward encounters with other candidates.

These guidelines were crucial in guiding our interactions with internal and external candidates to make sure they were treated fairly and with dignity.

Overall, achieving transparency between the search committee and the college was more about having clear expectations than about making specific information widely available. Working toward a more equitable and inclusive hiring process is an organizational goal that the entire college is committed to, and sometimes in this context *more transparency* meant explicitly telling our library colleagues what the priorities needed to be in evaluating candidates, what kind of specific feedback we needed them to give, or what behavior was expected of them in unfamiliar situations.

# Conclusion

Our library is undergoing a rapid period of heightened organizational change. One of our stated goals of managing this large amount of change is creating an environment where transparent communication fosters a sense of inclusivity. Our dean has fostered an environment where transparency is the norm through regular weekly e-mail updates about the status of ongoing projects, usually including several hiring updates. Through our dean and university's example, we are encouraged to communicate to our teams openly and honestly about library policies, including policies from university human resources.

To that end, our university and libraries have implemented several changes in the hiring process. As discussed earlier, our search committee used and expanded upon these changes to create the most inclusive environment possible during what has historically been a trying time for both new and seasoned librarians. We focused on creating an inclusive environment for all search committee members, all libraries faculty and staff members (including any internal candidates), and all external candidates.

With our committee's agreed-upon definitions of transparency and inclusivity, we sought to demystify the hiring process by making it open and inclusive to the candidates, members of the committee, and our colleagues. Measures we undertook to promote transparency and inclusivity within our search committee included developing a shared rubric to measure candidates and their application materials, setting meeting norms, and developing a time line that helped outline the amount of prework we needed to undertake before each search committee meeting.

Given that our group had not previously worked closely with each other, one of the best opportunities that we had to foster committee transparency, inclusivity, and collaboration was the shared generation of the candidate rubric. Not only do we believe we truly bonded over this process, we also set expectations for respectful communication, which we believed helped to guide our work. We knew that it was important to maintain transparency and inclusion among the committee, as well as with the committee and the candidates.

To create as welcoming an environment as possible during the interview process, our committee sought to be as welcoming as possible during the interview process. One of the most frustrating experiences a candidate can have is trying to remember names and titles of committee members after the fact. We sought to eliminate this frustration by creating an online document that collated the biographies of all search committee members. This measure was transparent and inclusive because we removed some of the stress and mystery out of participating in a virtual interview. Final candidates were also afforded the opportunity to speak with search committee members in advance of the on-campus interview. They were provided with detailed information about what each day of the two-day interview process would look like. We wanted each candidate to feel comfortable with the events to come as well as outlining important information about our impending reorganization, important people that the candidates would meet with, and general information about our university.

Our committee also sought to be transparent with our libraries about the interview process and final candidates. We walked a fine line between sharing information about the candidates and their credentials and respecting each candidate's privacy. We believe that our efforts can help us advocate for increased respect for candidate privacy in the future. As our university human resources is currently in the early stages of revamping our hiring processes and procedures, we believe that we can assist in advocacy for heightened privacy protections, up to and including full redaction of candidate identifying information. This would go a long way to eliminating unconscious bias as well as increasing transparency and inclusion in the hiring process.

Another hurdle we faced in transparency with our libraries was soliciting meaningful feedback. As mentioned earlier, the difficulties we encountered while soliciting feedback are related to the amount and type of feedback we received. Our rubric and feedback forms did not correlate well with each other. In the future, we recommend that committee rubrics be presented to the libraries community to facilitate both their initial and final candidate feedback.

We also had to delicately balance search committee communications with an internal candidate. We remained mindful to avoid awkward communications with our internal candidate. We attempted to treat our internal candidate as respectfully as external candidates. We informed the internal candidate of other candidate interviews so that they could either work from home or take annual leave. We also removed the internal candidate from our libraries distribution list so that any information about other candidates remained confidential. As this internal candidate was our colleague and, in certain circumstances, a supervisor, we sought to give them an equitable on-campus experience. We wanted our internal candidate to realize that we took their candidacy seriously, through kind and respectful communications with the search committee.

Our search committee's efforts helped to improve hiring norms at our university through inclusive and equitable communication. We sought to be more inclusive during the hiring process, and we did so. Academic librarian hiring is an ever-evolving process. There are so many opportunities for growth in this process, and we hope our changes will encourage transparent and inclusive hiring in the future.

# APPENDIX A

# Sample Position Description

## Associate Dean for Teaching, Learning and Research

Clemson University Libraries seeks an innovative, collaborative, and inclusive leader to serve as our inaugural Associate Dean for Teaching, Learning and Research (AD for TLR). The successful candidate will set the vision and strategic direction for the new division, directing the Libraries' education and research support services, and ensuring student and faculty success. This position will direct the work of 40+ faculty and staff working in the following areas: user services (circulation, reserves, stacks, security), instruction and outreach, engagement (liaison librarians, reference and research support), research and digital scholarship and creative technologies (including data services, digital and media literacy, open education resources and scholarly communication), and the University Press (which also includes the Libraries' institutional repository). In addition to these areas, the position heads the teams managing the two branch libraries (Gunnin Architecture Library and the Educational Media Center & Digital Learning Lab), as well as the following service points: Cooper Library Learning Commons, the Adobe Digital Studio and Makerspace, and the Scholars' Lab.

This position was created as part of a recent reorganization, which aligned Clemson with our R1 peers. The successful candidate would be one of three new associate deans who will collectively be responsible for managing the day-to-day operations of the Libraries and setting the Libraries' strategic directions as members of its Senior Leadership Team. To learn more about the reorganization at the Clemson Libraries, visit: https://libraries.clemson.edu/our-organization/libraries-reorganization-overview/.

Clemson Libraries provides an exciting opportunity to the right individual. As a relatively young R1 library, we are in the process of redefining ourselves, and we are engaged in discussions with students and faculty to determine what programs and services should be created or expanded. We are currently focused on expanding digital literacy efforts, developing new and innovative programs to support graduate students and faculty, and building archival collections. This position would be responsible for supporting the research endeavors of the University through strategic planning and developing services to meet the unique needs of the Clemson research community. We have completed a master plan to renovate the main library building to provide more welcoming, technology-enhanced spaces.

This is a 12-month administrative faculty position with faculty rank and status. As a member of the Libraries' faculty, the successful candidate will pursue an active and ongoing program of research, service, and professional development.

## RESPONSIBILITIES

- Provides proactive leadership for the new Teaching, Learning and Research division, setting its vision, strategic direction, and priorities.
- Ensures the delivery of high-quality services that enhance learning and research by providing information and digital literacy education for undergraduate and graduate students, co-curricular learning experiences that support student success, technology-rich spaces and support for faculty research and its distribution.
- Builds strong relationships with campus partners whose work intersects the divisions to create collaborative services.
- Shapes the division's culture. Develops connections between members, facilitates interdepartmental communication and encourages innovation, flexibility, and creativity.
- Empowers members of the division and supports their ongoing professional and leadership development.
- Monitors and evaluates trends and developments relevant to academic libraries in the areas of oversight.
- Fosters an environment of collegiality, respect, trust, and teamwork that enables library faculty and staff to contribute to the goals of the organization.
- Serves as a member of the Libraries' Senior Leadership Team.
- Represents the Dean and/or Libraries in their absence.

## RESEARCH, SCHOLARSHIP, AND CREATIVE ACTIVITIES

- Develops a focused program of high-quality research and creative accomplishments, consistent with professional responsibilities and the Libraries' mission and goals.

## SERVICE

- Actively participates and demonstrates leadership in professional responsibilities that serve the Libraries, University, profession, and community.

## REQUIRED QUALIFICATIONS/EXPERIENCE

- ALA-accredited graduate degree.
- At least five years of management/supervisory experience in progressively responsible positions in an academic library.
- Successful record of leadership, planning, development, and management of library programs and services.
- Work experience in at least one of the division's focus areas.
- Demonstrated commitment to the promotion and enhancement of equity, diversity, and inclusion.
- Record of professional librarianship, research/scholarship, and service that would merit tenure at the Associate Librarian rank or higher.

## PREFERRED QUALIFICATIONS/EXPERIENCE

- Experience with teaching and learning, information literacy, student success or research services.
- Demonstrated ability to facilitate and build campus partnerships.
- Experience developing innovative learning spaces.
- Knowledge of the role of university presses within libraries and within the scholarly ecosystem.
- Demonstrated knowledge of trends in research libraries and the changing research landscape.
- Demonstrated ability to foster an environment of collegiality, respect, trust, and teamwork.
- Experience with change management.
- Ability to foster creativity and innovation by providing insights into situations, questioning conventional approaches, encouraging new ideas and supporting the design and implementation of new or novel programs/processes.
- Second graduate or other advanced degree.

# APPENDIX B

# Initial Evaluation Rubric

Associate Dean for Teaching, Learning, and Research *Interfolio Evaluation Rubric*

| Competencies and Qualifications | ★★★★★ Excellent | ★★★★ Very Good | ★★★ Good | ★★ Fair | ★ Poor |
|---|---|---|---|---|---|
| **Degree and management experience** | Has ALA-accredited graduate degree. AND At least five years of management/supervisory experience in an academic library with both faculty AND staff reports. | Has ALA-accredited graduate degree. AND At least five years of management/supervisory experience in an academic library with either faculty OR staff reports (not both). | Has ALA-accredited graduate degree. AND At least five years of management/supervisory experience in an academic library, unclear how many reports or whether faculty/staff reports. | Has ALA-accredited graduate degree. AND More than one but less than five years of management/supervisory experience in an academic library. | Does not have ALA-accredited graduate degree. AND/OR Does not have any management/supervisory experience in an academic library. |
| **Quality of application materials** | Excellently written cover letter and résumé, with clear articulation of all six required qualifications, and the majority of the preferred qualifications with specific consideration of Clemson Libraries. | Well-written cover letter and résumé with clear articulation of at least four required qualifications, majority of the preferred qualifications, and specific consideration of Clemson Libraries. | Adequate cover letter and résumé without clear articulation of required qualifications and specific consideration of Clemson Libraries. Evaluator has minor concerns about written communication, including grammar or focus. | Cover letter and résumé not well written but include mention of Clemson. Evaluator has concerns about written communication, including grammar or focus. | Cover letter and résumé not well written, with no mention of Clemson. Evaluator has major concerns about written communication, including grammar or focus. |
| **Division experience** | Supervisory experience with all three divisions: (1) public services, (2) liaisons, engagement, and info lit, (3) scholarly comm/digital scholarship | Supervisory experience with two divisions. AND Working experience but non-supervisory with one division. | Supervisory experience with one division. AND Working experience but non-supervisory with two divisions. | Supervisory experience with one division. AND No experience with other divisions. | No experience with any of the three divisions. |
| **Commitment to EDI** | Significant direct experience advancing diversity, equity, and inclusion through multiple aspects of their work. | Shows commitment to addressing diversity, equity, inclusion in multiple aspects of their work. Provides personal examples/strategies used with outcomes. | Shows aspects of weak and strong characteristics. May have attended several activities (conferences, student organizations, trainings, talks). | Limited experience or plans for advancing diversity, equity, and inclusion. May share a personal story/training that contributed to their growth rather than consistent actions across multiple areas of their work. | Description of efforts are brief or vague. May share efforts in their prior organization but does not share personal efforts. May have attended a workshop or read books, but does not demonstrate how they applied what they learned to enhance a welcoming climate for all. |

## APPENDIX C

# Meeting Norms

- All voices count and all opinions are valid.
- Look ahead to positive action, not back on "shoulda, woulda, coulda."
- Aim for GETGO (Good enough to go, not perfection).
- Actively listen to others when they are speaking.
- Everyone is responsible for helping to stay on topic. Speak up if you feel like we're getting off track.

*If you think of other norms that would help meet our charge, please let us know. Sourced from Kohout-Tailor, 2019

## APPENDIX D

# Time Line

| Date | Task |
| --- | --- |
| February 7 | Ad is posted. |
| February 7–March 24 (7 weeks) | Recruiting efforts.<br>Search committee agrees on criteria by which to rate candidates during initial review. |
| March 25 | Search committee meets to review applicants and divides into groups (top candidates, meets requirements, does not meet) + decides on initial interview questions. |
| March 28–April 1 | Gather initial feedback from faculty and staff. |
| April 5 | Search committee meets to decide on initial interview candidates. |
| April 6–8 | Search committee contacts applicants to schedule initial interviews. |
| April 11–13 | Search committee conducts initial interviews. |
| April 14 | Search committee meets to select finalists + send notice to dean and chair of finalists. |
| April 15 | Notify finalists. |
| April 18–April 22 | Conduct reference checks.<br>Create schedule for finalist interviews. |
| (1) April 28–29<br>(2) May 2–3<br>(3) May 4–5 | Finalist interviews. |
| May 6–13 | Gather final feedback from faculty and staff. |
| May 16 | Search committee meet to create recommendation to send to dean.<br>Search committee meet with dean/chair. |
| May 17–20 | Hiring approvals and offer letter. |
| July 1 | Expected start date. |

# References

Albu, O.B., & Flyverbom, M. (2019). Organizational transparency: Conceptualizations, conditions, and consequences. *Business and Society, 28*(2), 268–297.

Arch, X., Birrell, L., Martin, K., & Redd, R. (2021, November 29). *Core best practices for academic interviews*. American Library Association. https://alair.ala.org/handle/11213/17612

Brannon, S., & Leuzinger, J. (2014). Keeping human resources happy: Improving hiring processes through the use of rubrics. *Library Leadership and Management, 29*(1), 1–10. https://diversity.med.wustl.edu/wp-content/uploads/2018/05/Keeping-Human-Resources-Happy.pdf

Clemson University. (2022, August 1). *Faculty manual 2022* (v. 1.0). https://www.clemson.edu/faculty-staff/faculty-senate/documents/handbook/clemson-university-faculty-manual-2022.pdf

Cohen, A. (2021). Q&A: The great resignation. *Bloomberg Businessweek, 4699*, 42.

Cunningham, S., Guss, S., & Stout, J. (2019). Challenging the "good fit" narrative: Creating inclusive recruitment practices in academic libraries. In D. M. Mueller (Ed.), *Recasting the narrative: The proceedings of the ACRL 2019 Conference, April 10–13, 2019, Cleveland, Ohio* (pp. 12–21). Association of College and Research Libraries. https://virtualconferenceservice.s3.amazonaws.com/ChallengingtheGoodFitNarrative+(1).pdf

Fletcher, L. M., Grandy, R., Thurman, F., & Whitney, R. (2022, May 2–6). *Pandemic transitions: The impact of COVID-19 on hiring and onboarding in academic libraries* [Poster presentation]. Medical Library Association Annual Conference, New Orleans, LA. Open Commons@UConn: UConn Library Presentations, 61. https://opencommons.uconn.edu/libr_pres/61

Goodman, M. B. (2002). Guest editorial. *Corporate Communications, 7*, 204–205.

Hakkola, L., & Dyer, S. J. V. (2022). Role conflict: How search committee chairs negotiate faculty status, diversity, and equity in faculty searches. *Journal of Diversity in Higher Education, 15*(5), 583–595. https://doi.org/10.1037/dhe0000386

Hypes, S., Harris, R., & Otis, S. (2020). Establishing shared purpose: Developing unit specific mission, vision, and values in an academic library. *Library Leadership and Management, 34*(2), 1–9. https://llm.corejournals.org/llm/article/view/7401

Raschke, G. K. (2003). Hiring and recruitment practices in academic libraries: Problems and solutions. *portal: Libraries and the Academy, 3*(1), 53–67.

Stewart, A. J., & Valian, V. (2018). *An inclusive academy: Achieving diversity and excellence*. MIT Press.

Vaillancourt, A. M. (2021, February 16). Why your "objective" screening rubric produced biased results: Five things that search committees can do to move more women and people of color forward in the executive-hiring process. *The Chronicle of Higher Education, 67*(13). https://www.chronicle.com/article/why-your-objective-screening-rubric-produced-biased-results

CHAPTER 16

# Walking the Walk

## Searches That Demonstrate Commitment to an Inclusive, Diverse, and Equitable Library Workplace

*Marlowe Bogino and Ash Lierman*

## Introduction

Rowan University Libraries in New Jersey consists of libraries on three campuses: Glassboro, serving a large population of undergraduate, graduate, and doctoral students; Camden, primarily serving the Cooper Medical School of Rowan University; and Stratford, primarily serving the Rowan-Virtua School of Osteopathic Medicine. In addition to this large student body, the libraries serve two health system hospitals, which house Rowan's osteopathic and allopathic medical schools.

Starting in late 2019, library workers from across the libraries formed a diversity, equity, and inclusion (DEI) committee, aligned to university-level DEI strategic initiatives and focused on improving the climate of the libraries for marginalized users and staff. One of the initial areas of need identified by the DEI committee was increased representation in the libraries' staffing from underrepresented communities. We began addressing this need by identifying and implementing best practices for hiring diverse employees in higher education. This ongoing project began three years ago and included researching the literature on hiring in higher education and the current onboarding practices of other institutions.

Several recommended strategies surfaced from the literature that the DEI committee consulted. One recurring recommendation, in particular, not only spoke to who the members of the committee and library staff are and what we believe to be core to the library profession but also helped define what the committee members wanted to do to achieve a set of more inclusive hiring practices. This recommendation was to demonstrate the hiring institution's commitment to DEI principles through explicit statements, description of work and progress in these areas, and by walking the walk, giving practical attention to inclusivity throughout the interview process. We share in this chapter our experiences and recommendations for actions that fellow library hiring committees can take to demonstrate their institutional commitment to DEI throughout the hiring process.

# Positionality

## Who We Are

The libraries' DEI committee is an employee-initiated group currently consisting of seven passionate and socially conscious members of the libraries. Committee size and membership are flexible and have fluctuated over time, but generally it has been composed of four to five representatives from the main campus library and one representative from each of the medical libraries. It is important to mention that the committee is in itself a diverse group of library workers, including both librarians and professional staff, members of color, LGBTQ+ members, neurodivergent and disabled members, and members who speak English as a second language. It is important to note the demographics of our working team because they represent the minority and marginalized sectors of the library community (American Library Association [ALA], 2007), and fact demonstrates the variety of the individuals who provided insight and shared their voices in the process.

## What We Believe

Our foundational belief is that a diverse population of staff, students, researchers, and community members enhances the educational, professional, and personal experience of everyone involved. In fact, Rowan University Libraries has committed to a DEI mission centered on the ongoing work of becoming more inclusive spaces for all library users and workers, building the cultural competencies of our community, and embracing diversity in our collections and resources. Fulfilling this mission helps us to achieve our purpose of ensuring that all users and employees of the libraries feel that their identities are fully respected and represented. These beliefs are drawn from, among other sources, the core commitment of ACRL (Association of College and Research Libraries, n.d.) to create a diverse and inclusive community of libraries and librarians.

# Research and Findings

To identify a set of best practices for diverse and inclusive hiring, the DEI committee examined two types of materials: relevant professional literature, and relevant policies and practices at several other institutions where such documents were publicly available. From these materials, we identified the following set of broad recommendations, in order of the strength of the available supporting evidence:

- Demonstrate institutional commitment to DEI.
- Consider qualifications for positions broadly and flexibly.
- Challenge assumptions and potential sites of bias during the search process.
- Be mindful of search committee construction, member expertise, and power dynamics.
- Work with experts outside of the search committee for accountability.
- Continue to work to improve the workplace DEI climate after hiring.
- Be willing to invest time and effort into recruiting a diverse candidate pool.
- Standardize and plan the search process thoroughly to ensure equity.

While all of the recommendations from our review have proven valuable in revising our hiring practices, as stated, this chapter will focus specifically on the recommendation to show institutional commitment to DEI in the hiring process. The findings in this area are discussed in more detail below.

# Review of the Professional Literature

In general, the scholarly literature indicates the value of institutional commitment to DEI and the importance of communicating it to potential candidates. It is also recommended to ensure that this commitment is well understood within the organization. Gardner, Barrett, and Pearson (2014) indicate that an institution's level of financial investment in DEI initiatives is seen as a reliable indicator of its commitment to DEI principles and that institutions looking to hire and support more diverse faculty and administrators should budget accordingly. Wolfe and Dilworth (2015), in calling for greater hiring and retention of people of color in higher education, identify institutional work toward genuine systemic change, overall, as a critical foundation for increasing diversity in staffing. Lara (2019) calls for explicitly race-conscious recruitment and hiring, stressing the importance of setting the increased diversification of the institution as a goal for the search process. For a more specific example, De Luca and Escoto (2012) highlight the critical importance of family and its support to Latino (authors' choice of term) potential faculty, which is a significant element of other marginalized cultures as well. As a result, fostering and promoting university structures that support family responsibilities, such as childcare, elder care, and the capacity to work from home or maintain a flexible schedule, is likely to be compelling support to members of these communities as job candidates, as well as benefiting and helping to retain those already employed. On the internal side of communication, Fujii (2014) particularly emphasizes developing strong internal communication of DEI values to current employees so that hiring for diversity will be seen as an imperative in the hiring process and recommends that this imperative be addressed through inclusive practices, such as requiring a statement of diversity qualifications in job applications. Multiple studies also stress the value of developing institutional programs of mentorship and leadership training for employees of color in particular, and also the need for increased social networks and direct mentorship between college and university employees from marginalized communities (De Luca & Escoto, 2012; Wolfe & Freeman, 2013; Gardner, Barrett, & Pearson, 2014; Gasman, Abiola, & Travers, 2015; Wolfe & Dilworth, 2015; Lara, 2019). It stands to reason that highlighting the presence of such programs would also help to attract candidates from marginalized communities, particularly those who hope to develop in the future and connect with their peers and predecessors.

Less fundamental, smaller-scale practical adjustments to the search process along these lines are also highly recommended. Many of these recommendations come from non-peer-reviewed advice articles aimed at those seeking to hire more diverse faculty and leaders (e.g., a how-to article in the *Chronicle of Higher Education*). Several relevant pieces suggest communicating DEI values through the following means: inclusive wording of the job ad, and expressing a desire to diversify beyond boilerplate equal opportunity language; highlighting inclusive and family-friendly programs, policies, and values; and advertising positions specifically as requiring skills like anti-racist work and mentoring students of color (Utz, 2017; Stewart & Valian, 2018; Tugend, 2018; *Be proactive to hire a racially diverse staff*, 2011). In the scholarly literature, Sensoy and DiAngelo (2017) also recommend providing clear metrics for an institution's commitment to diversity in the job ad, as well as crafting the ad to specifically seek out candidates from marginalized communities and committed to social justice perspectives in their fields. Similarly, both scholarly and advice articles recommend showing commitment through a welcoming atmosphere and attentiveness to diverse needs in the interview day itself: ensuring that the interview day allows for diversity in physical and sensory ability, taking care to avoid religious holidays in scheduling, recognizing unceded Indigenous lands in interview materials, and similar practices (*Be proactive to hire a racially diverse staff*, 2011; Sensoy & DiAngelo, 2017).

Requesting a DEI statement or other evidence of DEI-related work as a qualification from candidates as part of the job application is also recommended by several authors, both in advice and scholarly literature (*Be proactive to hire a racially diverse staff*, 2011; Fujii, 2014; Stewart & Valian, 2018; McMurtrie, 2016).

# Other Institutional Policies and Practices

The institutions whose written policies for inclusive hiring were considered in this review included the ALA, Brandeis University, the University at Buffalo, and the University of Washington. While these types of policies continue to develop across institutions, at the time these were the most comprehensive policies we were able to locate that were available online and specifically addressed inclusive hiring of librarians and faculty. These policies echoed the recommendation to demonstrate institutional commitment in some prescribed practices, as described in table 16.1.

# Recommendations Developed

Based on our findings, the DEI committee developed a set of practical recommendations to be used by search committees in hiring for future positions. In developing these recommendations, we sought not only to duplicate specific practices that were suggested by articles and institutions but also to work generally toward the priorities that emerged from the literature. Where other institutions had practices that would serve this end, we borrowed; where they did not, if necessary, we invented.

After being drafted and refined by the committee, these recommendations were presented to the leadership of all Rowan University Libraries at one of their recurring team meetings. Library leaders reviewed and approved the list, and the final version was made available to all library staff via the DEI committee's online guide, as well as being provided directly to search committee chairs at the beginning of ensuing search processes. A checklist version of the recommendations was also developed to further operationalize their use.

Some of our recommendations focused on the composition and functioning of search committees, but the majority concerned providing cues to candidates of Rowan University's and the libraries' commitment to continual improvement in DEI. Relevant recommendations fell into two categories: those regarding the development and advertisement of job postings, and those regarding planning and conducting both screening and on-site interviews. Recommendations in both categories are listed below.

**Table 16.1.** Institutions and their practices aligned to demonstrating DEI commitment

| Institution | Practices focused on demonstrating DEI commitment |
| --- | --- |
| American Library Association (ALA, 2011) | Require DEI experience in job posting |
| | Include DEI statement in job posting |
| | Ensure accessibility of application and interview processes |
| | Ensure that DEI vision and commitment is publicly available |
| Brandeis University (Brandeis University, n.d.) | Publicize desire to diversify to professional colleagues |
| | Use inclusive language |
| | Articulate the importance of DEI, including university statements |
| | Require a DEI statement in applications |
| | Ask DEI-related questions in interviews |
| | Be prepared to describe local DEI initiatives to candidates |
| | Ensure the interview process is accessible |
| | Provide multiple modes of communication |
| | Ask candidates for their pronouns and about pronunciation of their names |
| | Ask candidates about any transportation or family needs for visits |
| | Provide an interview agenda |
| | Provide private breaks during interviews |
| | Pay for travel and lodging whenever possible |
| | Provide clothing expectations for interviews |
| | Discuss campus benefits and supports with candidates |
| University at Buffalo (University at Buffalo, Equity, Diversity and Inclusion, 2022) | Display the university EEO statement prominently |
| University of Washington (University of Washington, Human Resources, 2022) | Require a diversity statement in applications |

## Recommendations Regarding Job Postings

- Provide a link in job postings to the libraries' strategic action priorities on the Rowan University DEI Strategic Action Plan Dashboard.
- For all positions (student, staff, librarian, and administrator): List "Commitment to diversity, equity, and inclusion" as a required qualification.
- For librarian and administrator positions only: Require a DEI statement as part of the application package.
- Use inclusive language in job announcements and communications (avoid terms with racist historical connotations, use gender-inclusive terms, use the singular *they* rather than *he/she* or *s/he*, etc.).
- Include the Rowan University EEO statement in job postings.
- Increasing the diversity of the library staff should be an explicit goal in shaping the description and qualifications of the position.

## Recommendations Regarding Screening and On-Site Interviews

- When contacting short-listed candidates for initial screening interviews, search committees should ask candidates for their preferred communication modes (e.g., telephone, e-mail, videoconference, etc.).
- In planning the on-site interview, care should be taken to avoid conflict with religious and cultural holidays and to make all components as accessible as possible for mobility and perceptual disabilities and neurodivergent candidates. The candidate should also have time for private breaks throughout the day.
- When arranging on-site interviews, the search committee contact should ask candidates about any transportation or family care needs they may have.
- DEI-related questions should be a routine part of interviews, and they should be essential to qualification for the position, not an add-on. The search committees and other interviewers should be prepared to describe university- and library-level DEI initiatives to the candidate as well.
- During the interview day, at least one meeting should be planned in which the candidate can be apprised of benefits and supports available on campus: for example, child and other family care, leave policies, employee assistance programs, and so on.
- Each candidate should be provided an agenda for the interview day in advance, as well as a brief description of clothing expectations for the interview. An acknowledgment of unceded Indigenous lands on which the interview will take place should be considered for inclusion in these materials as well.

- The search committee contact should ask candidates what pronouns to use for them and for the correct pronunciation of their names prior to or at the beginning of the interview day.

# Actions Taken

Soliciting DEI statements as part of employment applications for library staff and faculty roles emerged as a recurring recommendation from the literature and practice at other institutions. This practice provides the opportunity for the candidate to share how they have incorporated activities into their own teaching and library work to further the cause of a more inclusive library environment.

Before including this requirement in job postings, the DEI committee designed a rubric that could be utilized by hiring committees to assist with assessing the statements provided by applicants. As with other portions of this project, the team went to the literature to discover best practices in creating the rubric. The DEI committee based our rubric on recommendations provided by the *Chronicle of Higher Education*, which highlighted the best techniques to use when drafting such a statement, such as not providing theoretical examples but rather actual examples of what work has been done to further the cause of increased diversity within the work environment (Whitaker, 2020). In the process of implementing this rubric, we also developed standardized language to be included in job ads when describing the DEI statement requested to ensure that candidates' understanding of what is being asked for in the statement will match the criteria on which we evaluate it. The text of the rubric and the standard language for job ads that mirrors it can be found in the appendix.

With the support of library leadership, the DEI committee was also able to establish the understanding that every search committee formed going forward should include at least one DEI committee member in its composition. Especially given that our recommendations had been so recently introduced, we considered it to be of critical importance that a representative be present for the first search processes to employ them to support the search committee chair in understanding our recommendations and putting them into practice. While we do not necessarily anticipate that every search committee in perpetuity will include a DEI committee member, not least because of the additional burden this would place on our membership, we felt that this was a crucial facilitator at least in the interim until the recommendations are well established and familiar to all library workers who serve on searches.

One complicating factor in implementing our recommendations, however, proved to be the ongoing COVID-19 pandemic. Many of the recommendations that we developed addressed the conduct of on-site interviews, but we planned to continue conducting all interviews fully virtually at the time the recommendations were implemented. We continue to mainly interview virtually as of the time of this writing. It became necessary to adjust our expectations accordingly, and we were able to quickly investigate additional literature and supplement our original recommendations list to recognize the complexities of virtual interviewing. With these recommendations in mind and DEI committee representation present, one of the first librarian search committees to form after the recommendations were introduced took the additional step of developing an online form for candidates to be distributed prior to screening interviews. Though responses were optional, this form requested a candidate's pronouns, any needed accommodations, and preferred name, interview time, and communication methods. While best practice and university interview protocol require that all interviews be conducted in the same modality, we were able to use this form to choose modalities for each interview stage that were most preferred on average across all candidates and also collect the necessary information to treat candidates appropriately and respectfully in the interview process. Not only does this gesture communicate to candidates the libraries' attention to diverse needs, but it should also help to make diverse candidates more comfortable in the interview process by attending to these needs. The form has been retained from this search process and will be available for other search committees to use as they are formed in the future.

# Evaluation

After conducting the work of researching best practices and implementing those found to be most useful for our library, the DEI committee understood the importance of measuring success and failures. This gauging process is a work in progress, with the team continuing to explore the best way to proceed. As with the initial project, the committee began by examining the literature to uncover options for creating a report card of progression.

In a 2017 study of diversity and inclusion efforts in various types of libraries, the Association of Research Libraries found that only a small number of libraries had evaluated the progress of their DEI work (Anaya & Maxey-Harris, 2017). Of those that were successful in this task, the most prevalent method chosen to evaluate progress was through a workplace climate survey (Anaya & Maxey-Harris, 2017). These climate surveys (Anderson & West, 1998), which are used to quantify an employee's experience within the workplace environment or organizational climate (Glisson & Durick, 1988), were conducted using either a library's own created survey or the Association of Research Libraries' ClimateQUAL survey (Association of Research Libraries, 2022; Anaya & Maxey-Harris, 2017).

Having this knowledge of how libraries have assessed their DEI efforts was useful for the DEI committee and provided an outline of how to move forward once all recommended hiring policies and best practices are implemented throughout each library department site across the university. Each department, as well as those seeking to learn from our experience, will need to critically evaluate the relevance of our recommendations and adjust their survey. It is important to enlist the help of a human resource professional in creating the climate survey should a library decide to create its own, though potential areas to consider could be workplace culture and environment, work satisfaction, training and development, and leadership or supervisory support (Sanchez-Rodriquez, 2021).

In the shorter term, approximately five months after the hiring recommendations were initially presented, DEI committee members who had served or were serving on searches so far submitted a short report on the progress of implementation. At that point, one DEI committee member had served on the committee for a completed search and two more were serving on committees for ongoing searches. The report was submitted to the DEI committee and library leadership, and to the extent possible while maintaining confidentiality, it described search committee members' experiences with implementing DEI committee recommendations in these searches. It also offered suggestions for improving the implementation process. As a result, several adjustments were made, including the DEI committee chair ensuring all documentation related to the recommendations was stored in easily findable and accessible locations online; increasing guidance and reinforcement for search committee chairs from library leadership regarding their responsibilities to become familiar with and implement the recommendations, shifting more of the burden for enforcement from the DEI committee representative to the chair; and refining the guidelines for flexibility in search modality to be more explicitly in compliance with university requirements around search standardization. The report also indicated that many recommendations had been successfully implemented to the benefit of the search process, such as routine inclusion of DEI-related questions and providing an interview agenda to candidates. This information served as valuable early feedback on the practicalities of implementation and helped the DEI committee and library leadership to identify areas that needed to be streamlined, better communicated, or both. Further similar reports will likely be requested as more search processes are conducted with DEI committee representatives and the recommendations in use.

# Expected Outcomes

The work that the libraries' DEI committee has completed thus far provides a tangible manifestation of our commitment to our values and beliefs in equity. In thinking about what we hoped to achieve throughout this process, we discovered practices that we knew we wanted to avoid, such as expecting our new colleagues to bear the burden of fixing our problems. We also discovered that we had a few expected outcomes from our work, rooted in the idea that the DEI climate within the libraries needed improvement. Our group also recognized the need for a means for measuring the success of our work so that we could continue to learn, share, and grow from our experience.

Ensuring that search committees follow our recommendations during the hiring process helps to create a more inclusive search process by anticipating the needs of candidates who may have disabilities or other concerns, rather than placing the burden on individual candidates to request accommodations. This approach helps prevent the interview process itself from becoming a barrier that causes some candidates to self-select out of the pool before they can even be fully considered. At the same time, however, it also communicates the libraries' compassion, flexibility, and attention to diversity and increases the likelihood that candidates who share these values will seek and accept a position.

As a result, we anticipate that two outcomes will be observable in our hiring processes as the committee's recommendations become a routine part of library search and interview processes. The first is an increasingly and consistently diverse pool of hiring candidates at all stages of the search process, from the initial set of applicants to the final candidates who proceed to a full interview. With attention to the needs that candidates may have, and with the demonstration of our commitment to addressing issues of DEI, we anticipate that more diverse candidates will feel encouraged to apply and will be more successful in moving through the search process. The diversity we expect to see in candidates is not only in racial and ethnic identities, but also in terms of ability, gender identity and expression, and other related characteristics.

The second outcome that we anticipate is increasing work-related DEI orientation, competency, and experience on the part of successful candidates. While diversity of inherent characteristics is an important factor to increase in libraries, so too is professional experience with working on initiatives that improve DEI for staff and users. The requirement to submit a DEI statement will not only encourage candidates hoping to work toward DEI goals to apply, but also signal to candidates that familiarity and experience with DEI initiatives is an expected qualification for positions at the libraries. This will further encourage applications and bolster the success of applicants with strong backgrounds in this area. The specific requirements and rubric for the evaluation of DEI statements will help to assess candidates' DEI competency and consider it alongside other qualifications for librarian and administrator positions. The placement of DEI committee members on search committees, as well, will help guide the implementation of this requirement. DEI committee members have already begun working with search committees to ensure that a lack of demonstrated DEI experience and commitment is taken as grounds to screen out potential candidates and that strong DEI records are considered among the most crucial factors in selection.

With all of that in mind, it becomes equally important to follow another of the recommendations that emerged from the literature, beyond the main focus of this chapter: to continue to work to improve the workplace DEI climate, outside of the hiring process. Even as we may be excited to invite increasingly diverse and DEI-oriented colleagues into our libraries, it is also important not to expect these new colleagues to fix existing problems and dysfunctions around DEI issues in those libraries. If we hope to truly welcome these types of library workers, we have a responsibility to work to decrease the barriers, discrimination, and frustrations that they will experience in their new environment and ensure that we are as ready as possible to support them in the work that they wish to accomplish. This means continual improvement not only in our processes of seeking talent from without, but also in our policies, practices, and cultures within, so that the libraries are as ready to nurture new employees as we are eager to seek them out. The ongoing work of the DEI committee in multiple areas, not just on hiring practices, should prove helpful in working toward this goal, and we intend to continue to be mindful of this need as we move forward with implementation of our recommendations.

How to measure the successful achievement of these outcomes in the long term, however, is still a matter for consideration. There is little guidance in the library literature regarding outcomes assessment of hiring for diversity specifically, although some insight can be gleaned from recommendations for hiring in higher education in general. The most common method of measuring simple numerical diversity in faculty is to calculate percentages of faculty belonging to marginalized groups and compare these to the corresponding percentages from those groups in the local population. This approach, however, may prove more challenging for the measurement of less visible and often more sensitive categories of marginalization than race and ethnicity, particularly those of sexual orientation, gender identity, and invisible disability. Furthermore, evaluations of faculty diversification require more nuance than this approach allows, particularly to account for factors like clustering of marginalized faculty members in only a few specific disciplinary areas (Weinberg, 2008). The same may be true in many academic libraries, with marginalized library workers tending to be more concentrated in specific roles and departments, and numerical calculations of diversity in academic library staffing should also be broken out by these types of factors. Anonymous climate surveys that also collect demographic information, repeated over time, may prove valuable here as well for tracking changes in even more sensitive demographic categories.

On the other hand, the recent library literature does offer recommendations on evaluating the diversity competency of staff and the overall DEI climate. One of these is building quantifiable assessment measures into the library's DEI strategic plan (Redd, Sims, & Weekes, 2020). This is in many ways similar to the strategies the DEI committee at Rowan University Libraries employed in our own strategic planning process after the committee's initial launch. Expanding on this process to include future evaluations of our work to improve competencies and climate may be valuable. Another recommendation is to, when implementing inclusive practices in reference and other service interactions, assess these in the form of anonymized feedback opportunities for students who make use of those services (Knoff and Hobscheid, 2021). This strategy could help to evaluate the inclusive competencies of public-facing library workers across our libraries. At least one tool is also available in the literature for self-evaluating cultural humility in library and information professionals (Getgen, 2022), which could be distributed to employees in all roles. A combination of these approaches and other variations may provide the most thorough assessment: setting specific goals, and then regularly continuing to collect feedback from library users and request self-evaluation by library staff. By repeating measures over time, we can track any changes that may correspond to the time since implementing our revised practices and use these to evaluate our growth and improvement as a community.

## Conclusion

From the literature, the DEI committee identified the practice of demonstrating institutional commitment to DEI as important in hiring. We developed a set of recommendations for search committees to implement toward this practice. These included job ad recommendations, such as requiring DEI commitment as a qualification and requesting a DEI statement when applying, and interview day recommendations, such as proactively asking about, and meeting candidate needs in multiple areas and providing information ahead of time. These have been implemented in subsequent librarian and staff searches, and we anticipate an increase in both diverse candidates and candidates with a strong DEI orientation in their work. The work of investigating and selecting evaluation methods for the success of this initiative is ongoing, but we strongly believe in the importance of assessing and improving our efforts toward DEI in hiring.

## APPENDIX A

# Rubric for Evaluating Candidate DEI Statements and Language for Job Ads

## Language to Be Included in Job Ads

In addition to other application materials, all candidates should submit a diversity, equity, and inclusion (DEI) statement of approximately one page. This statement should provide brief, specific examples of the candidate's developed knowledge of DEI principles and practices in academic library work, the candidate's experience promoting DEI through their professional work, and the candidate's plans to continue promoting DEI in their work at Rowan should they be selected for the position.

## Rubric for Evaluating DEI Statements

|  | **Exceptional** | **Good** | **Fair** | **Poor** |
|---|---|---|---|---|
| Knowledge | Has participated in in-depth professional development on DEI-related issues (e.g., long-term courses, reading groups, certificate programs, conferences and events) | Has a record of repeatedly engaging in shorter-term professional development activities on DEI-related issues, and may demonstrate knowledge of where to seek more information | Has engaged in a single one-time resource or activity on DEI-related issues (e.g., webinar, workshop, single reading) | Has not participated in any knowledge building on DEI issues |

|  | **Exceptional** | **Good** | **Fair** | **Poor** |
|---|---|---|---|---|
| Experience | Has experience initiating, leading, and participating in DEI-related initiatives in past positions | Has experience participating in and supporting DEI-related initiatives in past positions, showing evidence of putting knowledge into practice (e.g., active work on a committee, record of repeated engagement with relevant projects) | Has participated in at least one DEI-related initiative in past positions (e.g., on a committee but not a heavy contributor, assisting on a single project) | Has no experience working on DEI-related projects in past positions |
| Plans | Describes specific activities/programs and planned contributions; identifies specific ways to advance DEI in the Libraries and/or University | Describes planned contributions; identifies specific ways to advance DEI that may not specifically or effectively impact the Libraries and/or University | Mentions interest in developing activities/programs that advance DEI at the Libraries and/or University, but does not describe anything specifically | Does not describe planned activities/programs that advance DEI at the Libraries and/or University or does so poorly |

# References

American Library Association. (n.d.). *Diversity counts*. Retrieved October 31, 2022, from http://www.ala.org/aboutala/offices/diversity/diversitycounts/divcounts

American Library Association. (n.d.). *Recruiting for diversity*. Retrieved October 31, 2022, https://www.ala.org/advocacy/diversity/workforcedevelopment/recruitmentfordiversity

Anaya, T., & Maxey-Harris, C. (2017, September). *SPEC kit 356: Diversity and inclusion*. Association of Research Libraries. https://digitalcommons.unl.edu/cgi/viewcontent.cgi?article=1415&context=libraryscience

Anderson, N. R., & West, M. A. (1998). Measuring climate for work group innovation: Development and validation of the Team Climate Inventory. *Journal of Organizational Behavior, 19*(3), 235–258. https://www.jstor.org/stable/3100170

Association of College and Research Libraries. (n.d.). *Equity, diversity, and inclusion*. Retrieved November 2, 2022, from https://www.ala.org/acrl/issues/edi

Association of Research Libraries. (n.d.). *ClimateQUAL*. Retrieved November 2, 2022, from https://www.arl.org/climatequal/

Be proactive to hire a racially diverse staff. (2011). *Enrollment Management Report, 15*(3), 9.

Brandeis University. (n.d.). *DEI recruitment and hiring*. Diversity, Equity, and Inclusion. https://www.brandeis.edu/diversity/dei-recruitment-hiring/index.html

De Luca, S. M., & Escoto, E. R. (2012). The recruitment and support of Latino faculty for tenure and promotion. *Journal of Hispanic Higher Education, 11*(1), 29–40. https://doi.org/10.1177/1538192711435552

Fujii, S. J. (2014). Diversity, communication, and leadership in the community college faculty search process. *Community College Journal of Research and Practice, 38*(10), 903–916. https://doi.org/10.1080/10668926.2012.725387

Gardner, L., Jr., Barrett, T. G., & Pearson, L. C. (2014). African American administrators at PWIs: Enablers of and barriers to career success. *Journal of Diversity in Higher Education, 7*(4), 235–251. https://doi.org/10.1037/a0038317

Gasman, M., Abiola, U., & Travers, C. (2015). Diversity and senior leadership at elite institutions of higher education. *Journal of Diversity in Higher Education, 8*(1), 1–14. https://doi.org/10.1037/a0038872

Getgen, C. (2022, July). Cultural humility in the LIS profession. *The Journal of Academic Librarianship, 48*(4), Article 102538. https://doi.org/10.1016/j.acalib.2022.102538

Glisson, C., & Durick, M. (1988). Predictors of job satisfaction and organizational commitment in human service organizations. *Administrative Science Quarterly, 33*(1), 61–81. https://doi.org/10.2307/2392855

Knoff, M., & Hobscheid, M. (2021). Enacting service policies through pedagogy to create a more inclusive student experience. *Public Services Quarterly, 17*(1), 12–25. https://doi.org/10.1080/15228959.2020.1856017

Lara, L. J. (2019). Faculty of color unmask color-blind ideology in the community college faculty search process. *Community College Journal of Research and Practice, 43*(10–11), 702–717. https://doi.org/10.1080/10668926.2019.1600608

McMurtrie, B. (2016, September 11). Different strategies for diverse hiring. *Chronicle of Higher Education, 63*(5), 20. https://www.chronicle.com/article/different-strategies-for-diverse-hiring/

Redd, R. T., Sims, A., & Weekes, T. (2020) Framework for change: Creating a diversity strategic plan within an academic library, *Journal of Library Administration, 60*(3), 263–281, https://doi.org/10.1080/01930826.2019.1698920

Sanchez-Rodriguez, N. A. (2021) In pursuit of diversity in the CUNY library profession: An effective approach to leadership in academic libraries, *Journal of Library Administration, 61*(2), 185–206. https://doi.org/10.1080/01930826.2020.1853470

Sensoy, Ö, & DiAngelo, R. (2017). "We are all for diversity, but…": How faculty hiring committees reproduce whiteness and practical suggestions for how they can change. *Harvard Educational Review, 87*(4), 557–580. https://doi.org/10.17763/1943-5045-87.4.557

Stewart, A., & Valian, V. (2018, July 18). *Recruiting diverse and excellent new faculty*. Inside Higher Ed. https://www.insidehighered.com/advice/2018/07/19/advice-deans-department-heads-and-search-committees-recruiting-diverse-faculty

Tugend, A. (2018, June 17). How serious are you about diversity hiring? *The Chronicle of Higher Education*. https://www.chronicle.com/article/How-Serious-Are-You-About/243684

University at Buffalo, Equity, Diversity and Inclusion. (n.d.). *Best practices in recruitment and hiring*. Retrieved October 31, 2022https://www.buffalo.edu/equity/promoting-equal-employment-opportunity-and-diversity/best-practices-in-recruitment-and-hiring.html

University of Washington, Human Resources. (n.d). *Inclusive hiring*. Diversity, Equity, and Inclusion. Retrieved October 31, 2022. https://hr.uw.edu/diversity/hiring/

Utz, R. (2017, January 18). The diversity question and the administrative-job interview. *The Chronicle of Higher Education*. https://www.chronicle.com/article/the-diversity-question-and-the-administrative-job-interview/

Weinberg, S. L. (2008). Monitoring faculty diversity: The need for a more granular approach. *The Journal of Higher Education, 79*(4), 365–387. https://doi.org/10.1353/jhe.0.0014

Whitaker, M. (2020, November 24). 5 don'ts in writing your DEI statement. *The Chronicle of Higher Education*. https://www.chronicle.com/article/5-donts-in-writing-your-dei-statement

Wolfe, B. L., & Dilworth, P. P. (2015). Transitioning normalcy: Organizational culture, African American administrators, and diversity leadership in higher education. *Review of Educational Research, 85*(4), 667–697. https://doi.org/10.3102/0034654314565667

Wolfe, B., & Freeman, S., Jr. (2013, Fall). A case for administrators of color: Insights and policy implications for higher education's predominantly white institutions. *eJEP: eJournal of Education Policy*. https://in.nau.edu/wp-content/uploads/sites/135/2018/08/WolfeandFreeman-ek.pdf

CHAPTER 17

# Approaches to Inclusive Recruitment

## Practical and Hopeful

*Adriana Poo, Anamika Megwalu, Nick Szydlowski, Kathryn Blackmer Reyes, Peggy Cabrera, and Ann Agee*

## Introduction

San José State University (SJSU) is located in downtown San José, a city of over one million residents in California's San Francisco Bay Area. Established in 1857, SJSU is the oldest public university on the west coast of the United States. It is also the founding campus of the California State University (CSU) system that comprises twenty-three campuses, making it the largest four-year public university system in the country. SJSU has nine colleges and sixty-seven departments, which offer bachelor's, master's, and a growing number of doctoral degree programs. It enrolls over 36,000 students and employs more than 2,100 faculty members. The Dr. Martin Luther King, Jr. Library, also known as the SJSU King Library, is the only SJSU library that serves the campus. It is a joint library, partnering with the San José Public Library to serve the Bay Area community.

Like most universities, SJSU has a mixed record when it comes to social justice. In the 1950s–1960s, Jim Crow practices prevented the campus from providing campus housing and scholarships to Black athletes even though the campus actively recruited Black students. The university also had a history of minority student movements in the 1970s and 1980s as well as more contemporary racist events that have caused it to rethink its approach to social justice, human rights, and community service. Much has changed in fifty-plus years due to the challenges from students, faculty, staff, and community members and the university to address the value of supporting and retaining its diverse population as a crucial part of its mission to strive for social justice and equality. Consequently, it invested in establishing an Office of Diversity, Equity, and Inclusion and different student success, identity, and cultural centers on campus, as well as the SJSU Black Leadership and Opportunity Center, Chicanx/Latinx Student Success Center, Native American Indigenous Student Success Center; PRIDE Center, and UndocuSpartan Student Resource Center. In the library, the Africana, Asian American, Chicano, and Native American Studies Center (AAACNA) is dedicated to preserving and celebrating the diversity of the campus. Although the creation of AAACNA was complicated, it is a center that is now continually supported by students, faculty, and the community.

At SJSU, librarians are unionized faculty members and have ranks parallel to faculty in SJSU's other academic departments. California is one of eight states that have banned the consideration of race in its employment of state workers (Calif. Const. art. I § 31), and statistics make plain that SJSU's student body continues to be more diverse than SJSU's faculty in terms of race and ethnicity (Institutional Research and Strategic Analytics, n.d.). However, SJSU faculty are called on to serve as mediators and educators to students from a range of backgrounds (Wong, 2017), and research shows that student-faculty racial and ethnic matches can have an impact on student learning and graduation rates (Fryar & Hawes, 2011; Llamas, Nguyen, & Tran, 2021; Lowe, 2005; Stout et al., 2018). In addition, SJSU's 2020 campus climate survey revealed that "racial identity, ethnicity, gender/gender identity, position status, and nepotism/cronyism were the top perceived bases for many of the reported discriminatory employment practices" (Rankin & Associates, 2020, p. 281).

The university realized that it was time to reflect on its institutional value of social justice and be proactive in overcoming the influences of larger systemic oppression. In order to be intentional in addressing bias at the organizational level, SJSU created initiatives that were tailored for specific activities, operations, and populations. One such initiative was to adopt new strategies for the faculty hiring and faculty retention, tenure, and promotion processes and to implement increased faculty mentoring opportunities (Office of the President, 2021). The strategies involve collaboration between various campus units such as University Personnel; Faculty Success; Office of Diversity, Equity, and Inclusion; Library Administration; and library faculty search committees. This chapter will discuss how the University Library implemented—and enhanced—these new strategies.

# Advertising and Recruitment Training

As a CSU campus, SJSU is part of an even larger higher education ecosystem in the state that includes the University of California (UC) and the California Community College systems. The three systems adhere to the federal Equal Employment Opportunity guidelines, which ensure "all qualified individuals have a full and fair opportunity to compete for hiring and promotional opportunities, as well as to enjoy the benefits of employment with the respective employer" (Chancellor's Office, 2022, p. 5). Another commonality is the mandate to advertise widely in order to obtain a large and diverse applicant pool. Together, the UC and CSU systems also implemented the Moving beyond Bias program in 2019 (https://movingbeyondbias.org). Now part of CSU employee training, this initiative provides instruction on how to recognize and mitigate the effects of implicit bias in hiring.

At SJSU, this employee training program takes the form of a course in the campus learning management system. Titled Faculty Search Committee Training, the course sets the tone by beginning with an acknowledgment of the Muwekma Ohlone Tribe, whose land the campus occupies. The class consists of five modules:

1. *Advertising and Outreach:* Best practices on how to promote the job opening to attract a diverse applicant pool.

2. *Reviewing Initial Applicant Pools:* How to screen applicants with an eye toward equity and diversity, common hiring myths, and how to recognize and prevent implicit biases throughout the evaluation process.

3. *Contours of the Campus Visit:* Creating interview questions and an assessment rubric that provide equitable evaluations of candidates.

4. *Evaluating Finalists and Making an Offer:* The procedural nuts and bolts of recommending the final candidate.

5. *Support for the Recruitment Process:* Campus services that support the search committee tasks.

Before being advertised, position descriptions are reviewed by SJSU's Office of Faculty Success for the presence of inclusive diversity and equity language. Additionally, initial applicant pools are reviewed by the Vice Provost for Faculty Success to ensure non-White candidates have been given fair and careful consideration. To further ensure candidates have experience in a multicultural environment, the first two criteria on SJSU's Academic Finalist Interview Evaluation Form, which all search committees must complete, are

1. Demonstrated awareness of and sensitivity to the education-

al goals of a multicultural population (note any preferred cross-cultural experience and/or training: e.g., bilingual, bicultural background).

2. Demonstrated ability to address needs of ethnically diverse students through course materials, teaching strategies, and advisement.

While SJSU has a solid foundation in a system that values diversity, the SJSU King Library faculty have worked to improve their recruitment processes to be even more inclusive.

# Recruitment Webinars and Library Position FAQs

In early 2021, two librarian search committees met to discuss how to make recruiting more inclusive and open for interested librarian candidates. One librarian had attended the CORE webinar Building a Holistic Employee Engagement Framework (Ippoliti, 2020) and suggested adopting the recruitment ambassador model mentioned in the presentation. The search committee members served as library ambassadors, welcoming interested participants by creating a safe online environment to ask questions about the library, work life, and the recruitment process. Hosting a webinar as librarian ambassadors was a new, exciting opportunity to recruit potential candidates to the library, and it allowed the library to reach more candidates geographically than would have been possible in a physical meeting.

Committee members made important decisions to make the webinar accessible to everyone. One was that pre-registration was not required—anyone could attend. This was done for two reasons. First, committee members knew candidates might be working in a library already and would want to avoid creating tension with their current employers. Second, the committee wanted candidates to be as anonymous as they desired, giving them a chance to ask hard questions about the library's culture or the position's responsibilities. For this reason, webinar participants could remain anonymous or choose to identify themselves.

Other considerations for the webinar were platform and scheduling. The committee chose Zoom for these recruitment webinars because many librarians were already familiar with the platform and it offered accessibility features, such as captioning. The committee decided to schedule two webinars to make them accessible to candidates in different time zones. One webinar was held at 9:00 a.m. PST and the other at 1:00 p.m. PST. Candidates could choose the webinar that worked with their schedules. However, these schedules excluded candidates who could not meet during work hours. For the next recruitment, plans have been made to schedule an evening webinar in order to further increase access. The timing will also be reconsidered so that the webinars are not scheduled too soon after the job is posted.

The library's recruitment announcements included the webinar's link and were sent out across multiple library e-mail discussion lists (for example, ULS-L, ILI-L, ACRL) as well as to these affiliate groups:

- American Indian Library Association (AILA)—https://ailanet.org
- Asian/Pacific American Librarians Association (APALA)—https://www.apalaweb.org
- Black Caucus American Library Association (BCALA)—https://www.bcala.org
- Chinese American Librarians Association (CALA)—https://www.cala-web.org
- Joint Council of Librarians of Color (JCLC)—https://www.jclcinc.org
- REFORMA—https://www.reforma.org

When the day of the webinar came, slides were presented by the recruitment committee chairs with the assistance of committee members. The recruitment webinar slides followed this general format:

- introductory slide
- land acknowledgment
- agenda
- Zoom's Q&A features
- recruitment committee members
- about San José State University
- about the SJSU King Library
- organizational charts
- position highlights
- required qualifications
- details specific to each opening
- questions
- contact information for recruitment committee chairs

Committee members pasted relevant links into the chat, monitored questions, and answered them directly or forwarded them to the presenters to answer for the audience. The library's most recently hired librarians were invited to give their perspective about their recruitment and new faculty experience. All librarians contributed to questions about retention, tenure, and promotion to give candidates multiple perspectives.

After the first webinar, an online Librarian Position FAQs page (University Library, n.d.) was created to answer more general questions. If an FAQ is developed to support librarian recruitments, it is important to update it for new recruitments so the information reflects the current positions. The committees' goal of serving as recruitment ambassadors in the webinar worked. They received positive feedback on the webinars from participants, and the librarians recruited in the initial search participated in subsequent recruitment ambassador webinars. While it is time-consuming for committee members to host such events, they offer an opportunity for potential candidates to learn more about the institution and the surrounding community and to do so anonymously, if they wish. By providing this nonthreatening introduction to the institution, recruitment ambassadors and recruitment webinars create an inclusive space where everyone is welcome.

# Sharing Interview Questions before the Interview

Candidate interviews are an essential part of the faculty hiring process, but they are also an occasion when the explicit and implicit biases of search committee members can exert a strong influence on hiring decisions. Institutions are in a position to help faculty who participate in hiring become more aware of their own biases through training focused on inclusivity and anti-racism, but interventions that aim to change institutional cultures or personal attitudes may meet resistance or take time to reach their full impact. A complementary and well-established approach to minimizing bias in the interview process is to structure the interview in such a way as to provide as few opportunities as possible for the biases of search committee members to play a role in the process.

At SJSU, all faculty hiring committees are advised to follow a structured interview format for both preliminary screening interviews and candidate interviews during in-person or virtual campus visits. The committee writes questions for these interviews in advance and submits them to the relevant dean for approval. SJSU's Offices of Diversity, Equity, and Inclusion and Faculty Success are also available for consultation on the wording and contents of interview questions. Before campus visits, hiring committees are encouraged to identify and discuss the components of a strong answer to each of their interview questions and to compare candidate answers to the ideal responses that the committee has identified. These practices place an emphasis on the way candidates address specific interview questions, which are selected for their relevance to the position, and discourage an interviewing approach that focuses on the personal characteristics or self-presentation of the candidate.

In addition to these methods of creating structure in the interview, the library has adopted the practice of sending interview questions to all candidates at least twenty-four hours before scheduled interviews. Sending interview questions in advance of the interview is an additional way to create structure in the interview process and to encourage hiring committees to focus on the content of a candidate's responses, rather than on other aspects of their performance during the interview. In particular, sending interview questions in advance decreases the importance of the candidate's ability to respond on the spot to difficult or unexpected questions. Unless the ability to work well under pressure is a listed qualification for a particular position, it should not be a primary focus of the hiring process. While a job interview is always a high-pressure situation, sharing the interview questions in advance gives candidates a chance to prepare for the challenge and increases the likelihood that the committee will hear their best possible answer to each question.

As an illustration of the benefits of this structured approach, consider a typical interview question such as "Describe a time you completed a project as part of a team or group." The hiring committee would have chosen a question like this because working as part of a team is necessary for the position, and hearing the candidate talk about their experience is one way of assessing the candidate's ability to work effectively in a group context. If a candidate freezes or has difficulty answering the question in this format spontaneously, all the committee has really learned is that the candidate struggled in the interview setting—a setting where the committee itself has set the ground rules. The committee may actually have missed the opportunity to learn anything about the candidate's experience working in groups.

Additionally, requiring spontaneous recall favors candidates who are familiar with the types of questions that a particular library asks during the interview. Rewarding familiarity with common interview questions is likely to introduce bias into the hiring process, particularly in the case of entry-level positions. Conversely, if the candidate receives the questions in advance, traditional interview skills such as the knowledge of a broad range of typical questions and the ability to appear calm in very high-pressure situations become less important to the candidate's success, and the committee is able to focus on the way the candidate's responses demonstrate their ability to succeed in the position.

Sending questions in advance may mitigate some of the particular biases that neurodivergent candidates face during the hiring process. Norris, Crane, and Maras (2020) highlight the challenges that autistic people may face in recalling specific autobiographical memories, as required by interview questions that ask for examples of personal experience or achievement. Though that study did not find that receiving the questions in advance had a quantitative impact on the performance of autistic participants, the authors did report that both participants with autism spectrum disorder and typically developing participants found having the questions in advance to be beneficial. The adaptations which that study found most effective were changes to questions to provide more specific prompting about the expected format or relevance of the response. The conclusions in this study highlight the extent to which job interviews can test for skills that are not required for a particular position, in particular the ability to spontaneously recall autobiographical memories. Sending the questions in advance is one part of creating a structured job interview that is more focused on the requirements of the position, and therefore more resistant to bias on the part of the interviewers.

While sending the questions in advance can contribute to a more inclusive interview process, it is important to be mindful of the total amount of writing, research, and other preparation that is required of candidates during the application process. Candidates, librarians, and administrators have all raised concerns about the amount of labor required of candidates, leading to ongoing discussions about both the application and the interview process. While it is important to have enough information to evaluate candidates, an overly onerous process may discourage applicants and create barriers to inclusive hiring. Within the SJSU King Library, these discussions have focused on the substantial amount of writing required of candidates at the beginning of the application process, including separate statements on teaching, research, and diversity and inclusion, as well as on the most appropriate format for the candidate's presentation.

It is possible that requiring too much preparation may unnecessarily disadvantage candidates who are not able to devote as much time to their job search due to work, caregiving, or other responsibilities. Some candidates may even interpret certain presentation prompts, such as prompts that ask them to tailor their presentation to a specific institutional context, as demands for free labor and unpaid consulting. Many academic libraries use a hiring process that superficially resembles the process used to hire disciplinary faculty, but that lacks the standardization that is typically present within academic disciplines. As an example, disciplinary faculty who are interviewing on multiple campuses are often able to repeat a standard job talk sharing their recent research activity. In contrast, librarian candidates are likely to encounter a wide variety of presentation prompts and simulated teaching assignments, adding to the demands of a job search. When making decisions about the application and interview process, it is important to keep in mind the demands being placed on the candidate by an academic job market that is rigorous and competitive but at the same time lacks standardization and coordination between institutions.

# Creating a Sustainable Pipeline of Job Candidates through Mentorship

As librarians work toward equity, diversity, and inclusion and assess inclusive employment procedures, they should consider a sustainable pipeline for advancing and hiring job candidates within their own institutions. In 2017, an Ithaka S+R and Mellon Foundation survey verified that 61 percent of Association of Research Libraries (ARL) library employees were female and 71 percent were White, making the lack of diversity in the library profession unavoidably apparent (Schonfeld & Sweeney, 2017). The survey noted that only 8 percent of ARL library employees were Black, 6 percent were Hispanic, fewer than 1 percent were American Indian or Alaska Native, and less than 1 percent were Native Hawaiian or Pacific Islander (Schonfeld & Sweeney, 2017). In contrast, 47 percent of students enrolled in four-year public universities are people of color (National Center for Education Statistics, n.d.). The American Library Association (ALA) Spectrum Scholars and the Association of College and Research Libraries (ACRL) Diversity Alliance promote diversity through residency programs and mentoring. However, these programs are competitive and offer opportunities that are limited in number. Over time, the impact of such programs may become evident, but they should be supplemented with professional development and mentoring programs offered through individual institutions to give library personnel upward mobility (Sanchez-Rodriguez, 2021).

Not all library personnel aspire to become librarians, but some do and are still waiting for the opportunity. Therefore, libraries with diverse student populations or diverse library employees could offer mentoring and possibly recruit future librarians from within their institutions. In general, libraries do not prioritize internal hiring, particularly among part-time librarians who frequently perform many of the day-to-day responsibilities and duties of full-time librarians. For example, at the SJSU King Library, part-time librarians, especially those hired to cover subject areas, provide information literacy sessions, assist students and faculty in research consultations, fulfill course reserves and acquisition requests, and hold regular reference hours. In addition, some part-time librarians go above and beyond to serve on library working groups or support library programming. Furthermore, part-time librarians may have the opportunity to present or write about the work that they have done at their institutions. To attend conferences, however, many of the same part-timers do not receive release time or financial assistance. Libraries must stop discouraging those who exhibit an interest in governance and scholarly activities if they are to serve as a pipeline for diversifying the profession from the existing workforce—not to deprive tenure-track or full-time faculty librarians of resources, specifically travel stipends, but to demonstrate the value of all roles within the profession. One recommendation would be to allow release time to present at a peer-reviewed conference or to support travel grant applications. This recommendation has recently been implemented at the SJSU King Library, but the impact has yet to be determined. It is, however, a step in the right direction. If research and scholarly activities are essential qualifications for tenure-track librarians, libraries should assist candidates in meeting this requirement, not create hurdles.

To those colleagues who argue that there is a lack of skill among the institution's pool of potential applicants, such as teaching or communication abilities, other colleagues can offer the counterargument that these talents can develop with experience. How can libraries diversify the profession if they continue to seek out candidates with the same characteristics as the current workforce? First, let us support those who are interested in learning more. The same training tactics, such as observe-assist-solo methods for teaching instruction techniques, can be utilized by libraries to improve and develop the abilities of potential candidates. Suppose an institution has diverse staff members with a graduate-level degree in information science or part-time librarians who do not lead library instruction sessions. Both of these groups would be excellent sources of future librarians. Libraries should allow prospective internal candidates to observe and participate in library instruction sessions. This invitation could serve as an introduction to the profession and lead to additional conversations and mentoring opportunities.

Creating a systematic program to mentor part-time librarians and library staff across institutions will allow every library employee to receive guidance and support regardless of their background or experience. The Oregon Library Association, UC Berkeley Library, and several libraries in Victoria, Australia, all provide models of staff mentoring programs (Berkeley Library Staff Web, n.d.; Burke & Betts, 2014; Oregon Library Association, n.d.). This approach also allows several libraries to collaborate on a single mentoring plan with the same objective, especially when there is a lack of structured mentoring programs available. As Hussey and Campbell-Meier (2017) noted, only 38 percent of participants in their study described their mentoring relationship as a formal mentorship program. A systematic approach would help establish libraries' accountability for achieving diversity, equity, and inclusion within the profession and at their institutions.

# Conclusion

To make its recruitment practices more inclusive, the SJSU King Library focused on targeted advertising, created recruitment ambassadors, held informational webinars, provided interview questions in advance, and worked on mentoring in-house talent. However, while recruitment remains a primary focus, this is not where librarians and libraries should stop. Once recruitments are done, the next steps must be the promotion and retention of librarians of color.

As a profession that remains primarily White, the role of academic librarian reflects the ongoing conversation that many universities are having with their teaching faculty. At SJSU, not just the library but all academic departments are changing the culture of how they reach out to potential recruits. Many universities have gone to great efforts to examine the biases recruitment committee members intentionally or unintentionally bring into the conversation when deliberating on candidates. At SJSU, an instrumental position has been developed and hired to lead the campus in training and discussion: the associate vice provost for faculty success. The role of this individual is to help hiring committees avoid any mishaps that the recruitment process can present.

However, once hiring committees have gotten candidate pools approved by these individuals, it is the committee members who are left to prioritize the candidates who have the capacity to achieve tenure and promotion. Often committee members must see beyond what the institution has trained them to acknowledge as obvious attributes that say "success," such as publications and strong evaluations. But it does not end there. After recruitment, this same effort to look beyond the obvious must be exhibited by tenure and promotion committees in order to retain librarians of color. To this end, at SJSU, retention, tenure, and promotion committee members must go through training that discusses biases and how to view the contribution of faculty of color and faculty that fall within other categories of diversity. Recruitment, retention, and promotion of librarians of color must be intentional, but for many committee members a level of discomfort can still exist when encountering changing policies, procedures, and ways of thinking about hiring and evaluating faculty members. Because of this unease, there remains a lot to do to make the cultural changes in our organization and institutions that go beyond recruitment and reach across the full careers of librarians of color.

# References

Berkeley Library Staff Web. (n.d.) *Staff mentorship program*. https://www.lib.berkeley.edu/Staff/lauc/diversity/staff-mentorship

Burke, J., & Betts, L. (2014, September 15–19). *Developing your staff in a cross institutional mentoring program*. ALIA National 2014 Conference, Melbourne, New South Wales, Australia. https://read.alia.org.au/content/developing-your-staff-cross-institutional-mentoring-program

Calif. Const. art. I § 31. https://leginfo.legislature.ca.gov/faces/codes_displayText.xhtml?lawCode=CONS&division=&title=&part=&chapter=&article=I

Chancellor's Office. (2022, April 5). *California State University report: Summary of hiring practices*. California State University System. https://www.calstate.edu/impact-of-the-csu/government/Advocacy-and-State-Relations/Pages/legislative-reports.aspx

Fryar, A. H., & Hawes, D. P. (2011). Competing explanations for minority enrollments in higher education. *Journal of Public Administration Research and Theory, 22*, 83–99. https://doi.org/10.1093/jopart/mur009

Hussey, L. K., & Campbell-Meier, J. (2017). Is there a mentoring culture within the LIS profession? *Journal of Library Administration, 57*(5), 500–516. https://doi.org/10.1080/01930826.2017.1326723

Institutional Research and Strategic Analytics. (n.d.). *Faculty*. Academic Affairs, San José State University. Retrieved November 9, 2023 from https://www.sjsu.edu/irsa/dashboards/faculty.php

Ippoliti, C. (2020, December 9). *Building a holistic employee framework* [PowerPoint slides]. Core: Infrastructure, Leadership, Futures, American Library Association. https://www.dropbox.com/s/shx0r3bin6rgrbe/12-9-20%20Ippoliti%20slides.pdf?dl=0

Llamas, J. D., Nguyen, K., & Tran, A. G. T. T. (2021). The case for greater faculty diversity: Examining the educational impacts of student-faculty racial/ethnic match. *Race, Ethnicity and Education 24*(3), 375–391. https://doi.org/10.1080/13613324.2019.1679759

Lowe, S. C. (2005). This is who I am: Experiences of Native American students. *New Directions for Student Services, 2005*(109), 33–40. https://doi.org/10.1002/ss.151

National Center for Education Statistics. (n.d.). Figure 1: Percentage distribution of U.S. resident undergraduate enrollment in degree-granting postsecondary institutions, by level and control of institution and student race/ethnicity: Fall 2020. In *Characteristics of postsecondary students*. US Department of Education. Institute of Education Sciences. Retrieved November 9, 2023 from http://nces.ed.gov/programs/coe/indicator/csb/postsecondary-students#1

Norris, J. E., Crane, L., & Maras, K. (2020). Interviewing autistic adults: Adaptations to support recall in police, employment, and healthcare interviews. *Autism, 24*(6), 1506–1520. https://doi.org/10.1177/1362361320909174

Office of the President. (2021). *Combating systemic racism: SJSU's initiatives, activities, and programs*. San José State University. https://www.sjsu.edu/diversity/systemic-racism/initiatives/index.php

Oregon Library Association. (n.d.) *OLA mentoring program: Information for potential mentors and mentees*. https://www.olaweb.org/mentor-program

Rankin & Associates. (2020). *San José State University: Assessment of climate for learning, living, and working final report*. https://www.sjsu.edu/belong/findings/index.php

Sanchez-Rodriguez, N. A. (2021). In pursuit of diversity in the CUNY library profession: An effective approach to leadership in academic libraries. *Journal of Library Administration, 61*(2), 185–206. https://doi.org/10.1080/01930826.2020.1853470

Schonfeld, R. C., & Sweeney, L. (2017, August 30). *Inclusion, diversity, and equity: Members of the Association of Research Libraries: Employee demographics and director perspectives.* Ithaka S+R. https://doi.org/10.18665/sr.304524

Stout, R., Archie, C., Cross, D., & Carman, C. A. (2018). The relationship between faculty diversity and graduation rates in higher education. *Intercultural Education, 29,* 399–417. https://doi.org/10.1080/14675986.2018.1437997

University Library (n.d.). *Librarian position FAQs.* San José State University. Retrieved March 14, 2023 from https://sites.google.com/sjsu.edu/librarian-position-faqs/home

Wong, K. (2017). Diversity work in contentious times: The role of the chief diversity officer. *Liberal Education, 103*(3–4), 34–37.

CHAPTER 18

# Developing Recommendations for More Inclusive Academic Librarian On-Site Interviews

*Christina M. Miskey, Kathryn M. Houk, and Jason Aubin*

## Introduction

This chapter will discuss the work of the University of Nevada, Las Vegas (UNLV), library faculty Ad Hoc Committee for Diverse Recruitment and Retention: Campus Visits and Interviews (hereafter referred to as the campus visits committee), which was formed by the library faculty in 2020 to recommend ways for the faculty interview process to be more inclusive and to allow candidates from diverse backgrounds to excel during their interview process. The culmination of the committee's work was the internal report for library faculty, *Recommendations for Hosting UNLV Library Faculty Candidates*, which is in the process of being implemented for faculty searches within the University Libraries. The goal of these recommendations is to improve search committee and human resources processes, thus enhancing the final-round interview experiences of candidates for library faculty positions.

These recommendations were based on the research undertaken by the campus visits committee and a detailed survey that was sent to the library faculty to determine attitudes, preferences, and perceptions regarding the University Libraries' current interview process. The survey responses brought to light several diversity, equity, inclusion, and accessibility (DEIA) issues that the campus visits committee attempted to address through their recommendations, which were reviewed by the library faculty as a whole and then voted upon.

This chapter will seek to provide context and supporting research for why all of the recommendations created by our campus visits committee are critical to ensuring inclusive and welcoming interviews for candidates, regardless of if the library faculty as a whole or libraries human resources agreed with them. We will also share the progress that has been made since the committee's report and recommendations were voted on by the library faculty in the fall of 2021.

This chapter will also discuss suggested next steps for topics that were beyond the scope of the campus visits committee. These topics included examining the first-round phone interviews process, the treatment of internal candidates versus external candidates, and recommendations that were rejected or not considered DEIA issues by the library faculty. Finally, we will discuss actions the library faculty expects our libraries' administration will take accountability for or, at minimum, support ongoing efforts by other groups in the library that take responsibility, as well as potential future research and actionable changes our library and other academic libraries could undertake in the future.

# Background

UNLV was founded in 1957 as a public university (UNLV, 2022) and is currently a doctorate-granting institution in a continuously growing urban environment. As of fall 2021, more than 30,000 students are enrolled in one or more of 255 potential degree programs (Nevada System of Higher Education, 2021). The student population is majority female-identifying (57.3 percent), with almost 67 percent of all students identifying themselves as one or more minority racial or ethnic backgrounds. UNLV is designated as a minority-serving institution, Title III- Asian American and Native American Pacific Islander-serving institution, and a Hispanic-serving institution, in addition to being named as one of the most diverse institutions in the United States in the *U.S. News and World Report*'s annual listing for the past decade (Division of Diversity Initiatives, n.d.). In 2018, UNLV was classified by the Carnegie Classification of Institutions of Higher Education as an R1 "very high research activity" institution (Media Relations, 2018), which enables the university to recruit more high-profile faculty and students, earn more research funding dollars, and overall raise the profile and prestige of the campus.

Despite these laudable statistics, faculty and staff diversity in 2019 did not correlate to student diversity, with more than 65 percent of faculty members identifying as "white" across part-time and full-time instructional faculty, more than 50 percent of professional staff identifying as "white," and 61 percent of classified staff identifying as "white" (Office of Decision Support, 2020). Additionally, among full-time instructional faculty, only 40 percent identify as female (Office of Decision Support, 2020). The numbers in 2021 have only slightly improved (Office of Decision Support, 2021), with single-digit increases across all employment categories (Nevada System of Higher Education, 2021) in most minority racial and ethnic categories that are tracked (Hispanic/Latino, American Indian or Alaska Native, Asian, Black or African American, Two or More Races).

It is within this context that the University Libraries Inclusion and Equity Committee (IEC) was charged to begin an in-depth study of the libraries hiring, retention, and recruitment practices in terms of diversity, equity, and inclusion (DEI) in early 2019. The IEC is a voluntary all-library committee that is composed of academic faculty, professional staff, and classified staff; the committee reports directly to UNLV Libraries administration. The IEC formed three task forces designed to perform an extensive literature review, examine current library policies, and hold a series of town hall discussions with faculty and staff in the libraries. The bulk of this work was carried out in mid-to-late 2019. In February 2020, the IEC presented a report (Boddie et al., 2020) outlining its findings and providing a series of recommendations, organized around distinct themes of hiring and

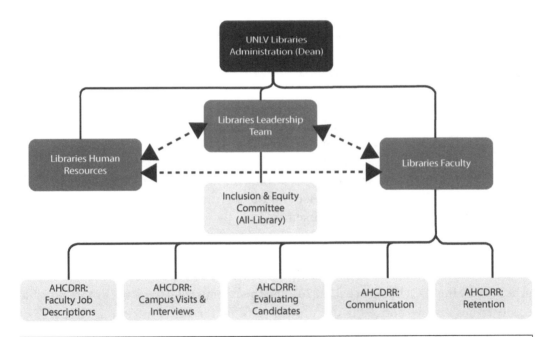

**Figure 18.1. Organization and communication structure of discussed committees.** *Note.* AHCDRR is an abbreviation for Ad-Hoc Committees on Diverse Recruitment and Retention. Dotted lines indicate communication flow between groups with power to enact policies.

recruitment, and stating that it encouraged libraries leadership and the faculty and staff as a whole to begin implementing.

In late 2020, the library faculty, led by the faculty moderator, elected to take a more proactive approach to develop concrete action plans for implementing the recommendations from the IEC report. Five ad hoc committees for diverse recruitment and retention were created based on the five main themes of the IEC report: campus visits and interviews, communication, evaluating candidates, faculty job descriptions, and retention. Each of these committees was tasked with taking the recommendations from the IEC report in its assigned thematic areas and creating deliverables (whether in the form of reports, creating template documents, etc.) that would translate into concrete actions that the library faculty, UNLV Libraries administration, or libraries human resources could put into place. In the next section, we will describe the process the campus visits committee underwent to complete this assignment. Figure 18.1 provides an overview of how the committees mentioned in this chapter are organized under UNLV Libraries administration.

# Our Committee Work

The campus visits committee was formed in the summer of 2020 and was composed of four library faculty members. A chair for the campus visits committee was elected by the group and the charge was edited to reflect the new reality of virtual and hybrid final-interview stages during and after the COVID-19 pandemic. The charge is as follows:

> The committee will focus on the hosting and conducting of interviews with faculty candidates in ways that are equitable and allow diverse candidates to excel during the interview process. The outcomes will include suggested guidelines and tools for search committees to create a consistent and welcoming environment that promotes candidate success. The committee will not evaluate aspects out of its control, such as travel logistics and reimbursement.

The campus visits committee first reviewed the specific recommendations laid out in the *Inclusion and Equity Committee Recommendations for Diverse Recruitment Report* produced by the IEC (Boddie et al., 2020), and then discussed if there were other possible equity issues that we noticed in our process for final candidate interviews. The idea of unconscious bias underpinned our conversations about faculty evaluation and feedback of candidates, so we decided to undertake further research into the use of rubrics, the impact of candidate appearance on hiring decisions, and issues of accessibility, all of which were not addressed within the context of final-round candidate interviews.

Five library faculty ad hoc committees were working on related but distinct aspects of recruitment, hiring, and retention, but it was not until the chairs of all of the ad hoc committees met that the committees could more clearly define their scope of work in relation to each other and move forward. An ad hoc committee on evaluation was looking into the use of rubrics, and a training ad hoc committee was looking into recommendations for library faculty professional development and training around DEI issues in recruitment and hiring, so our campus visits committee began to focus more narrowly on the candidate experience. The campus visits committee was already working with several recommendations from the IEC report, and discussions after our research generated a handful more, including explicitly stating that there was no dress code within the libraries, providing information about what to expect in terms of the weather during the visit, and presenting information to candidates in a more time-sensitive manner. A portion of the original actions outlined in the IEC report is quoted below:

> Many recommendations from the task forces focused on a potential candidate's on-site visit to the Libraries. This is because this is the point where we engage with them the most and the point where a candidate can truly get to know the Libraries itself. Additionally, it was recognized that interviewing is an anomalous and sometimes stressful or awkward activity. Creating a welcoming environment for candidates which promote [*sic*] their success will ensure that the day will be comfortable and orderly for all participants and also demonstrate the Libraries values to them.
>
> . . .
>
> It was noted in the task force reports that many of the current practices at the Libraries were not applied consistently to candidates. These include things such as the candidate's travel reimbursements, the activities during the on-site visit, and opportunities after hiring. By either improving the process or clarifying the method, there will be fewer instances of misinformation shared and of dissatisfaction afterwards when stories are exchanged. (Boddie et al., pp. 10–11)

The campus visits committee developed a survey to collect feedback and obtain a sense of the University Libraries faculty before finalizing recommendations. A "sense of the faculty" is used as a method of consensus decision-making, where the faculty are surveyed to understand their opinions on a particular topic or issue, often to check consensus of the group, before moving forward. The survey (appendix A) was used to determine more specific language for recommendations such as time frames, phrasing, and placement of information for candidates and approaches for projects that required reorganization and upkeep of information. The campus visits committee also took this opportunity to anonymously ask about overall impressions of the candidate visit portion of University Libraries compared to other universities and some broad demographic categories, such as if UNLV was respondents' first professional library job and if they identified as being part of a minoritized or historically marginalized group. The campus visits committee plans to use this data in future research to compare attitudes and beliefs regarding the survey items and interview experience between various demographically defined groups.

After completion of the survey by library faculty, the campus visits committee reviewed results and developed wording for recommendations (see table 18.1) to be presented in a written report (appendix B) as well as suggestions for implementation of most recommendations to help further show the committee's intent and the context behind each recommendation. Along with the report, additional deliverables were developed and arranged into a hosting candidates tool kit, meant to assist search committees in following the best practice recommendations. The tool kit contained several documents, such as templates or tips to provide guidance on communicating with candidates and preparing a candidate visit.

To begin, the campus visits committee included interview schedule examples (appendix C) that were more streamlined than current libraries practice and included a flex hour for candidates to choose to speak to a library committee or interest group or visit a special office or location on campus that they were interested in. There was also a later start option created in case candidates had a late arrival the night before or were coming from a vastly different time zone that would make an 8:00 a.m. start time very challenging.

A search committee biosketch template (appendix D) was included in the tool kit so that search committees could quickly create a sheet of photos, names, titles, and brief biographies to provide to candidates, ideally when they were invited to a first-round interview. This practice was introduced to University Libraries by a previous search committee, and we found it helpful and a great way to allow candidates to feel more comfortable on their arrival for a second-round interview. We also included an example of an e-mail detailing the requirements for a presentation beyond just a prompt and timing on the interview itinerary. The communication explains who will be present for the presentation, how long it should be, the technology to use, and the goals of the search committee for having candidates give a presentation.

The final document we created for the tool kit was guidance for search committee chairs on practices they could decide to use to be more inclusive and transparent (appendix E). Many of the suggestions were items that the library faculty felt should not be included as official recommendations or where there were several possible ways to approach the situation, which would make it difficult to create a single recommendation. The document "Tips and Tricks for Search Chairs" included recommendations such as informing candidates that there is no dress code and reminding them what they can expect from the weather. We've found many candidates are underprepared and unaware of some considerations; for example, if visiting in the summer, candidates may know it's extremely hot and dry, but they may not be aware that they need to be prepared for exacerbations of their allergies or asthma. Other suggested practices included ensuring that every individual meeting is clearly indicated on the itinerary, including a brief description of the purpose, and encouraging individuals with structured meetings to have talking points prepared.

After the preparation of the report with recommendations, it was once again brought forward for library faculty discussion. Although our committee felt that this work along with the original IEC report and the survey was sufficient for faculty buy-in, an additional round of faculty review took place before a vote was held to approve the recommendations. Once the library faculty edits were discussed and incorporated, the libraries faculty voted on each recommendation through an anonymous Qualtrics survey prepared and sent by the faculty moderator. The final recommendations from all ad hoc committees were then sent to University Libraries leadership and administration to discuss implementation.

# How It's Going

The campus visits committee submitted the twenty-six recommendations listed in table 18.1, which were later voted on and approved by the University Libraries faculty in late 2021. Recommendations were generally divided into responsibility categories—libraries human resources, search committees (and chairs), libraries faculty, and libraries leadership/administration. As of the time of this writing, eight recommendations have been fully implemented, four are partially implemented or are in the process of being implemented (such as the development of a more user-friendly staff directory). The remaining fourteen have not yet been implemented because responsibility rests with search committees, and therefore they haven't been consistently adopted.

**Table 18.1.** Current status of recommendations by the campus visits committee

| Recommendation | Current status |
|---|---|
| ***General Recommendations*** | |
| All candidate interview days should be independent and not overlap with other candidates for the same position. | This recommendation has been generally implemented. For academic faculty, searches are independent and don't overlap with other candidates for the same position. However, other searches may have on-site interviews overlapping, such as those for administrative faculty and classified (hourly) staff. |
| In-person interviews should be spent primarily on the campus where the position will have its office and be expected to work day-to-day. | This recommendation has been implemented. |

**Table 18.1.** Current status of recommendations by the campus visits committee

| Recommendation | Current status |
| --- | --- |
| Continue to live stream presentations and open conversation sessions. | This recommendation has been implemented. Presentations are being recorded for viewing by library faculty and staff throughout the feedback period, which is generally two or three days after the final on-campus interview. Open sessions are frequently conducted via videoconferencing software to allow multiple participants, many of whom may be working remotely. |
| Improve the user-friendliness of the Libraries Staff Directory, including but not limited to structure based on the Libraries organizational chart (i.e., list employees by division and department instead of simply alphabetically). | This recommendation is in progress, but it has not been completed. |
| Form a working group to develop recommendations for standardizing leadership position, fully virtual, and hybrid interviews. | No action has been taken on this recommendation. |
| *Scheduling Recommendations* | |
| Interview days should be designed to reduce redundancies in meetings and information overlap. | This recommendation has been generally implemented. Most presentations have been redesigned into open forums, with approximately 20 minutes for a presentation and 30 minutes for Q&A from all library staff. Meetings with the dean and position supervisor are frequently scheduled at 30 or 45 minutes, and departmental meetings are often held without the supervisor/director present. |
| Interview schedules should be designed to accommodate candidates traveling from various time zones. | No action has been taken on this recommendation. |
| At least two 20-minute breaks should be scheduled into the itinerary and do not exclude any need for bathroom breaks. | While the recommendation for breaks has been implemented, use of a suggested private space (e.g., not a conference room) has not been consistently implemented. |

**Table 18.1.** Current status of recommendations by the campus visits committee

| Recommendation | Current status |
| --- | --- |
| Candidate presentations should be kept at 20 minutes in length and be combined into an open forum. | This recommendation has been implemented. |
| All candidates should be provided a flex hour during the interview day to explore an area of personal interest or need. | This recommendation has been partially implemented. Logistics need to be further ironed out to create a consistent process across searches. |
| Interview day lunches should be limited to 3–4 noncandidate attendees. | No action has been taken on this recommendation. |
| Candidates should be sent a list of options for meal locations, which describe multiple aspects of their accessibility. | For very recent searches, committees have opted to order lunches in. Candidates are provided a link to the menu to select their preferred options in advance. Providing this information to candidates in advance of the optional evening meal with the position's supervisor has not been implemented. |
| Dinner with the supervisor or search committee should be clearly communicated as an optional activity to candidates. | This recommendation has been implemented. |
| *Communication and Candidate Well-Being Recommendations* | |
| Candidates should be invited to provide their pronouns and proper pronunciation of their name when scheduling their first interview. | No action has been taken on this recommendation. |
| Invitations to the library faculty for candidate activities should include candidate pronouns and name pronunciation guides if they were provided to the Faculty Recruitment Coordinator. | No action has been taken on this recommendation. |
| The interview questions should be sent to candidates before the interview day. | This recommendation has been implemented, following guidance from the libraries leadership team. |
| All search committees should create a biosketch document that will be sent to all candidates. | This recommendation has been implemented. |

**Table 18.1.** Current status of recommendations by the campus visits committee

| Recommendation | Current status |
| --- | --- |
| Candidates should be provided brief, general information on what to expect for weather, health, and attire when invited to interview on campus. | No action has been taken on this recommendation. |
| Reorganize and streamline multiple LibGuides currently used for recruitment into one. | No action has been taken on this recommendation. |
| ***During the Interview Recommendations*** | |
| Candidate guides will take fully accessible routes (e.g., always use elevators and curb cuts) unless the candidate indicates a different preference. | No official action has been taken on this recommendation. However, some search committee chairs have incorporated this practice into the interview day. |
| Candidates will be shown gender-neutral or gendered restroom locations at the beginning of the day and be directed to their preference the rest of the visit. | No official action has been taken on this recommendation. However, some search committee chairs have incorporated this practice into the interview day. |
| Seating should always be available and offered to candidates, even during presentations. | No official action has been taken on this recommendation. However, some search committee chairs have incorporated this practice into the interview day. |
| Guides should set timers on their phones for the meeting end and interrupt as necessary to keep the interview schedule on track. | No official action has been taken on this recommendation. However, some search committee chairs have incorporated this practice into the interview day. |
| Supervisors, Dean, and P&T Committee Reps should develop talking points for their candidate meetings to maintain consistency across all candidates. | No official action has been taken on this recommendation. |
| ***After the Visit Recommendations*** | |
| The Faculty Recruitment Coordinator should provide regular status updates to candidates during the recruitment, interview, and hiring processes. | No action has been taken on this recommendation. |
| Candidates should be asked for their feedback on the campus visit. | No action has been taken on this recommendation. |

While not all recommendations have been implemented, libraries human resources has made several significant improvements to the candidate interview experience and the ability of search committee chairs to be more aware of and involved in the candidate experience. For example, libraries human resources has developed a comprehensive interview question database that all search committees may use as a resource for developing lists of questions for each stage in the interview process, as well as flexible and simplified final interview itineraries that provide a more useful and less redundant final interview than prior practice within the libraries. More comprehensive documentation has also been created by libraries human resources for search committees to review and follow during the interview process. However, much autonomy remains for search committees and their chairs when creating a candidates' experience as they move through the interview process.

# Lessons Learned

The process to create more inclusive recruitment, hiring, and retention policies within the University Libraries has been a multiyear commitment that began in 2019 with the research and development of the IEC report (Boddie et al., 2020). It continued when the library faculty commissioned ad hoc committees, and the campus visits committee presented its final recommendations to the library faculty in 2021. Overall, the process we undertook to attempt to create systemic change in our libraries has involved many people across several departments, with multiple procedural steps. This work is still not yet complete and will continue to evolve over time and as more recommendations are implemented. With almost a year to reflect on our process as a committee and a post-pandemic wave of hiring to observe, we have many lessons we have learned—and that we are still learning—that may help other institutions looking to make similar changes.

## Positionality

The remaining members of the campus visits committee and authors of this chapter all have intersecting identities that influenced both our decision to serve on a committee and our interpretation of the process, its outcomes, and the lessons that can be learned moving forward. While all authors are white, we also collectively contain the identities of LGBTQ+, fat, chronically and invisibly ill, disabled, and neurodivergent. Our backgrounds and upbringing include middle-class, working-class, suburban, and first-generation. All of us believe in the importance of examining institutions and processes through critical race theory and intersectionality lenses, as well as the importance of Universal Design approaches to prioritize inclusion. Perhaps most importantly, we value the interview process as an opportunity for both the organization and the candidate to learn about each other, and not as a test or series of tests.

## Faculty Processes

The University Libraries faculty follows Robert's Rules of Order to discuss and enact decisions. While it ensures a certain degree of process to allow for engagement, it is also highly bureaucratic, often confusing, and not a very natural way for communities to make consensus decisions. The work of the campus visits committee was fairly straightforward with clear recommendations from the IEC report (Boddie et al., 2020), but concern for allowing all parties to provide input, as well as following Robert's Rules appropriately, meant several rounds of gathering feedback and revising before the official voting process even began. It may have been faster to have clearly developed a process for revisions and voting prior to the start of the campus visits committee work, with agreement on how to deal with lack of attendance or participation when it hampered forward progress due to Robert's Rules regarding quorum and voting numbers.

Search committee service and the running of searches has historically (within the University Libraries) been a process that has a lot of flexibility based on who is serving on the committee. While libraries human resources guides and informs on legal practices and policy, the rest of the process is often guided by tradition and the previous experiences of committee members. This has led to a culture of guidelines rather than policies for the management and running of searches in the University Libraries. Library faculty consensus on recommendations was important for buy-in, since the work of each search committee was traditionally seen as an independent endeavor. Despite consensus, several recommended practices still require individual committee members, especially chairs, to incorporate them into their processes.

For tenure-track library faculty, search committee work is considered to be service to the libraries and must be prioritized along with other job duties amid a tight time line (approximately ninety days). Determining how best to disseminate and encourage the use of approved recommendations and the materials developed to support them continues to be a challenge. One of the most successful approaches has been incorporating recommendations into the documentation that our faculty search coordinator, a key position within libraries human resources, shares with committees. It is still difficult to know whether committee members are consistently following the recommendations and the resulting new processes when interacting with candidates. Until the recommendation to regularly obtain candidate feedback is adopted, it will be challenging to know how much the candidate experience has improved since the original IEC report (Boddie et al., 2020). In addition to tracking the status of recommendations, the library faculty should develop a mechanism to obtain periodic feedback from search committees on their experiences implementing recommendations.

## Handoffs, Follow-Ups, and Communication

At UNLV, hiring new employees is a joint effort that involves several different departments within the University Libraries. Once the library faculty voted on the recommendations, the five ad hoc committees' work was officially concluded and the faculty moderator moved the information to UNLV Libraries administration and the libraries leadership team. This handoff was important not only because it communicated the will of the library faculty regarding important equity and diversity practices, but also because many recommendations were to develop working groups or partnerships between members of multiple departments. A tracking system was developed to map the activity toward implementing recommendations from both the IEC report (Boddie et al., 2020) and the ad hoc committees' work. Unfortunately, due to several factors including continued pandemic stressors, university and higher education issues in the state, and staff turnover, there has been little follow-up on the status of most recommendations. The previous section of this chapter, "How It's Going," details what we have been able to uncover about the implementation of recommendations to date.

Several of the recommendations made were also in regard to communicating with candidates, and in practice this communication is mostly handled by the faculty search coordinator. If a search committee chair does not request to be copied on most communications with candidates, it can be difficult to monitor which, and to what degree, recommendations are being followed. The length of time between the formation of the search committees, the creation of recommendations, and the implementation process has led to changes in campus-wide practices as well. One example is the requirement for committees to use rubrics for the first-round interviews, which are then also submitted to libraries and campus human resources. There is little guidance from the university on how best to use the rubric or why it is required, but the lack of guidance also allows flexibility in how each search committee applies the rubric, which can be beneficial if anyone on a search committee has experience in designing rubrics that actually help reduce bias.

One unforeseen side effect of libraries human resources implementing recommendations gradually has been the variations in the search committee member experience from one committee to the next. For example, one of the authors was involved with two search committees six months apart, and due to newly implemented processes by the faculty search coordinator and libraries human resources, the experience on the two committees was very different. While processes continue to evolve and improve, this unexpected consequence of under-communication between departments could also make it difficult and frustrating for busy library faculty members who are trying to learn new and sometimes more time-consuming processes on top of their regular duties.

# Conclusion

Overall, the work of the campus visits committee—along with the IEC report (Boddie et al., 2020) and the work of the other ad hoc committees—has generated positive changes among the faculty who serve on search committees. Improvements to libraries human resources procedures and documentation are helping search committee members and chairs and slowly creating a more welcoming and inclusive interview experience. However, much work still remains to be done.

Several recommendations have yet to be implemented fully, and additional follow-up and accountability measures need to be put into action. Additionally, portions of the interview process were ultimately out of the scope of the campus visits committee. More work needs to be done on reviewing and improving the initial interview stage (sometimes referred to as the phone interview), examining and reducing discrepancies in the experiences of internal versus external candidates, and further addressing topics such as dress code and the concept of professionalism during interviews.

Finally, based on the authors' experiences during this process, we have outlined suggestions below for other institutions or academic faculty librarians who are seeking to improve their candidates' interview experiences.

- Have a plan for getting the work done and how it will be successfully incorporated into current practices.
- Understand who has the power to implement changes and who has the power to codify them.
- Understand who is responsible for different aspects of the candidate interview process.
- Be in it for the long haul, as the process will likely take several iterations.
- Understand that not everyone will be ready to enact changes and may view the interview process as a test for candidates.
- Work with units and individuals responsible for different aspects of the candidate interview process collaboratively, if possible.

# APPENDIX A

# Survey

## UNLV Libraries Faculty Campus Interview Procedures Survey Questions

1. Have you been hired into a faculty role with UNLV Libraries within the past 4 years?

    a. Yes
    b. No

2. What went particularly well during your on-campus or live interview?

3. Did anything not go well during your on-campus or live interview? If so, what didn't go well?

4. Is this your first permanent professional appointment?

    a. Yes
    b. No

5. Have you served on a UNLV Libraries faculty search committee in the past?

    a. Yes
    b. No

6. What worked well when conducting on-campus or live interviews when you last served on a UNLV Libraries faculty search committee?

7. Did anything not work well when conducting on-campus or live interviews when you last served on a UNLV Libraries faculty search committee? If so, what didn't go well?

8. Have you interviewed for a similar position elsewhere in the past 4 years and reached the face-to-face stage?

    a. Yes
    b. No

9. What went well during your on-campus or live interview process?

10. Did anything not go well during your on-campus or live interview? If so, what didn't go well?

11. Have you been an internal candidate for a UNLV Libraries faculty role?

    a. Yes

b. No

12. What went well during your on-campus or live interview?

13. Did anything not go well during your on-campus or live interview?

14. Do you identify as being a member of an underrepresented group?

    a. Yes
    b. No

15. If you moved to Las Vegas for the first time for your current job, what are a few key things you wish someone had told you about living here before you were hired?

16. If you have seen biases show up during faculty on-campus interviews, what were they and what are your suggestions for reducing them in the future?

The Inclusion and Equity Committee Report on Diverse Recruitment and Hiring provides many recommendations for minimizing the burden of candidates during the recruitment and interview phase. The following questions are in regard to the recommendation: "Require all searches to provide interview questions in advance." (pg 10)

17. If search committees begin providing on-site interview questions to candidates in advance, what would be an appropriate time frame?

    a. Morning of interview
    b. 24-48 hours in advance
    c. With the presentation prompt
    d. I disagree with providing questions in advance
    e. Other (please specify)

18. Please provide some reasoning for your answer above.

19. If search committees begin providing phone interview questions to candidates in advance, what would be an appropriate time frame?

    a. Morning of interview
    b. 24-48 hours in advance
    c. About 1 week in advance
    d. I disagree with providing questions in advance
    e. Other (please specify)

20. Please provide some reasoning for your answer above.

The following questions are in regards to the following recommendations and other flexibility measures: "Develop an option for candidates to choose how to spend a designated block of their on-site visit day. For example, a list of activities or places could be provided to the candidate and they can choose to take a tour of the women's/gender equity centers, meet with campus or Libraries EDI-related groups, etc." (pg 10)

21. Should candidate interview itineraries include flexible use time for learning

more about Libraries or other campus organizations and support services?

   a. Yes
   b. Maybe
   c. No

22. Please provide some reasoning for your answer above.

23. Please provide any further ideas of how the flex time could be used by candidates to help build a list of possibilities.

24. Should options for a flexible start time for on-site interviews be provided to candidates?

    a. Yes
    b. Maybe
    c. No

25. Please provide the committee with your ideas and concerns regarding not maintaining a strict 8am–5pm schedule for campus interviews.

The following questions are in regards to the IEC recommendation: "[Provide] Short biographies/descriptions of search committee members and other people with whom candidates are scheduled to interact through the day." (pg 10)

26. Should photos and short bios of search committee members always be provided to candidates?

    a. Yes
    b. Maybe
    c. No

27. Please provide some reasoning for your answer.

28. Would you be interested in a more robust UNLV Libraries employee directory (including photos, job titles, and organized by department) being developed?

    a. Yes
    b. Maybe
    c. No

29. Would having a more robust directory be a suitable substitute for a unique photos and bios sheet for each candidate search?

    a. Yes
    b. Maybe
    c. No

30. Please provide some reasoning for your answer.

More IEC recommendations state to provide candidates: "A detailed itinerary including: addresses, links to menus, descriptions of people and vehicles picking up the candidate and guiding them throughout the day, room locations, purpose statements for each meeting (such as 'to evaluate candidate's research and presentation skills'), and dress code. Questions about dietary restrictions, needed accommodations (such as accessibility or religious holiday), name pronunciation, and preferred pronouns." (pg 10)

31. What information should be provided about dining options?

32. Where should this information be collected and stored?

    a. A document saved by HR
    b. A document saved on the faculty website
    c. A LibGuide page
    d. Other (please specify)

33. Please provide some reasoning for your answers.

34. Are you in favor of providing a statement of minimum expectations of attire for candidates? (Keep in mind recommendations cannot be written with gendered language/preferences.)

    a. Yes
    b. No

35. What do you consider the minimum expectations for candidate attire?

36. Do you have other ideas for how we can manage expectations for candidates' interview attire in order to reduce bias, especially if you are not in favor of a minimum expectation statement?

37. Should the most recent prior position description be sent to candidates before their on-campus interview? (Including the caveat that it is provided as an example, and may not reflect current/future expectations for the role.)

    a. Yes
    b. No

38. Are you aware of how to handle accommodation requests during the visit by interview candidates?

    a. Yes
    b. No

39. What types of resources would help you act on the recommendations and best practices to be presented by this committee? (Choose your top 2.)

    a. Templates
    b. Guideline document (read only statements)
    c. Drive folder for documents
    d. Library Staff website page with links to documents
    e. Libguide with documents embedded

40. Do you have any other comments or suggestions for the Ad Hoc DEI Committee on Campus Interviews?

## APPENDIX B

# Report–Recommendations for Hosting UNLV Candidates

## Introduction

### COMMITTEE CHARGE

The UNLV Library Faculty Ad Hoc Committee for Campus Visits and Interviews will focus on the hosting and conducting of interviews with faculty candidates in ways that are equitable and allow diverse candidates to excel during the interview process. The outcomes will include suggested guidelines and tools for search committees to create a consistent and welcoming environment that promotes candidate success. The committee will not evaluate aspects out of its control, such as travel logistics and reimbursement.

**Membership**
- Jason Aubin
- Katie Houk, Chair
- Karla Irwin
- Christina Miskey

**Tasks**
- Evaluate current UNLV, NSHE, and Libraries regulations
- Identify additional areas of research while not duplicating efforts from the Libraries IEC report
- Conduct interviews and/or survey with faculty members
- Create recommended guidelines and tools for campus visits and interviews
- Compile reference list of sources used to conduct research
- Identify and make recommendations for next steps that go beyond the committee charge

**Committee Activities**
The statements and recommendations in this report are built from those previously made in the UNLV Libraries' Inclusion and Equity Committee Recommendations for Diverse

Recruitment Report (IEC Report) (Boddie et. al., 2020), further research undertaken by the members of the Library Faculty Ad-Hoc Committee on Campus Visits and Interviews, and a survey of the UNLV Libraries Faculty meant to determine attitudes around further recommendations and implementation preferences. Due to the ongoing nature of the COVID-19 pandemic, a survey with multiple open-ended response options was determined to be the best method to learn about the sense of the faculty regarding the recommendations in the original IEC Report. Interviews with faculty were not conducted. Research undertaken by the committee included reviewing Library, University, and NSHE policies and guidelines around interviews and candidate visits. Research on rubrics was deemed outside the scope of the committee, though we are strongly in support of the Library Faculty Ad-Hoc Committee on Candidate Evaluations' recommendations to develop and use rubrics for candidate evaluation.

The deliverables from this committee's work include the Recommendations for Hosting UNLV Library Faculty Candidates report, Interview Schedule Examples, a Search Committee Biosketch template, and a Tips & Tricks for Search Chairs document. These items are referred to throughout this report. This document contains suggestions gathered primarily from survey feedback or activities some search committees have already piloted. They are practices that are encouraged in order to create a more inclusive and welcoming experience, as outlined in the IEC Report Action: Create a welcoming environment for candidates which promote their success (pg. 10). These deliverables comprise the Hosting Candidates Toolkit.

**Purpose & Format of Report**
The recommendations put forward in this document are those explicitly discussed in the IEC Report or asked in the faculty survey.

The intent of these recommendations is to:
- Change the approach of the interview day to one of providing a mutually beneficial meeting between the organization and the candidates, rather than viewing it as a test;
- Increase the ability for all candidates to succeed by making strides towards implementing universal design considerations in our processes;
- Provide documentation to allow library faculty search committees to standardize inclusive practices across all searches.

Recommendations are labeled and presented as discrete actions. Many recommendations have implementation suggestions to help provide some guidance on how the recommendation could work in practice. These suggestions are open for discussion and change. A brief justification for recommendations is also provided. If several recommendations stem from a similar justification, the justification heading will include the recommendations to which it applies.

**Considerations**
The IEC Report recommendations and this committee focused mainly on improvements and standardizations on how search committees could conduct in-person interviews. However, we understand that all-virtual or hybrid approaches may continue indefinitely post-pandemic. A majority of the recommendations in this document are applicable to both virtual and in-person candidate interviews, aside from the "During the Interview" section. If there is an appropriate change to a recommendation to make it applicable virtually, we have included the adjustment in the implementation suggestions section. It was unclear from the title and charge if this committee was to include reviewing and providing recommendations for the phone screening interview. Ultimately, we decided it was outside of our scope, but we feel some of the recommendations can be implemented at the phone/video conference stage; e.g. providing the search committee biosketch document, providing pronouns and name pronunciations. Finally, these recommendations are also primarily focused on administrative and academic faculty librarians who would not be in a director or higher position. Formal leadership positions have a greater collegial reach within the UNLV Libraries, and suggestions for streamlining the in-person interview may not be appropriate for the evaluation needs of these positions.

**Survey Summary**
The committee designed a survey in Qualtrics that was sent to all UNLV Libraries faculty members, consisting of 44 questions, some being multiple choice and some being open-ended text responses.

The survey was completed by 75 individual academic and administrative faculty members, or 84% of the UNLV Libraries faculty. We therefore took it to represent a sense of the faculty and developed recommendations based on the feedback collected.

**Recommendations**
[For a complete list of recommendations, see Table 18.1]

## APPENDIX C

# Hosting Candidates Toolkit–Interview Schedule Tips and Examples

## Hosting Candidates Toolkit-Interview Schedule Tips and Examples

- One optional dinner
  - Night before option recommended
  - Night-of-interview if candidate wants
- Candidates should be informed that they can ask to use the restroom whenever needed.
  - Guides should ask if candidates need the restroom whenever transferring rooms and at the start and end of private breaks.
- The private breaks are fewer but longer on the full day itinerary and scheduled to coincide with shifts in the intensity of the day's activities.
  - Private breaks need to be in locations that allow actual privacy—not bathrooms, breezeways, fishbowl rooms, etc.
  - Reiterating that it looks like fewer breaks overall, but the private breaks are longer and more impactful, and restroom breaks should be provided whenever necessary.
- Flex time CAN be used for a break
  - Candidates need to arrange alternate transportation if they choose to not return to campus after lunch.

**Tenure-Track Faculty Template** (9:15-4:00)
Note: A travel reimbursement meeting may need to be arranged; estimate 10 minutes.

| Time | Suggested Activity |
| --- | --- |
| 9:15 AM | Candidate Pick-Up |
| 9:30 – 10:00 AM | Search Committee Interview Pt 1 |
| 10:00 -10:10 AM | P&T Committee rep joins |

|  |  |
|---|---|
| 10:10-10:30 AM | Private Break |
| 10:30-11:00 AM | Meeting with position supervisor |
| 11:00-11:15 AM | Tech Check |
| 11:15-11:45 AM | Presentation w/Q&A |
| 11:45 AM -1:00 PM | Lunch |
| 1:00 – 2:00 PM | Flex Time (to be pre-determined through consultation with Liliana) |
| 2:00-2:30 PM | Meeting with the department |
| 2:30-3:00 PM | Private Break |
| 3:00-3:30 PM | Meeting with the Dean |
| 3:30-4:00 PM | Wrap up meeting with the Search Committee |

## Two Half Days Template

Note: A travel reimbursement meeting may need to be arranged; estimate 10 minutes.

| Time | Suggested Activity |
|---|---|
| Day 1 | |
| 9:45 AM | Candidate Pick-Up |
| 10:00-10:40 AM | Search Committee Interview Pt 1; P&T Committee rep joins last 10min |
| 10:40 -10:45 AM | Tech Check |
| 10:45-11:00 AM | Private Break |
| 11:00-11:30 AM | Presentation w/Q&A |
| 11:30-noon | Meeting with Supervisor |
| Noon-1:30 | Lunch & candidate returned to hotel or campus (their choice) |
| Day 2 | |
| 8:45 AM | Pick-up |
| 9:00-10:00 AM | Flex Time |
| 10:00-10:30 AM | Department Interview |
| 10:30-11:00 AM | Meeting with the Dean |
| 11:00-11:20 AM | Private Break |
| 11:20-noon | Search Committee Pt 2 & candidate returned to hotel |
| Noon | Optional 2nd lunch |

290 Chapter 18

## APPENDIX D

# Hosting Candidates Toolkit –Biosketch Template

## Hosting Candidates Toolkit–Biosketch Template

### SEARCH COMMITTEE CHAIR

**First Name Last Name**
Pronounced "First Last"

Pronouns: She/Her/Hers

*Title and Rank Librarian*
Lied Library, Main Campus
Bio: [Provide a 2-3 sentence bio or description]

### POSITION SUPERVISOR

**First Name Last Name**
Pronounced "First Last"

Pronouns: She/Her/Hers

*Head, Department Name*
Health Sciences Library, Shadow Lane Campus
Bio: [Provide a 2-3 sentence bio or description]

## SEARCH COMMITTEE MEMBER
**First Name Last Name**
Pronounced "First Last"

Pronouns: He/Him/His

*Library Technician II, Title Supervisor*
Architecture Studies Library, Main Campus
Bio: [Provide a 2-3 sentence bio or description]

## SEARCH COMMITTEE MEMBER
**First Name Last Name**
Pronounced "First Last"

Pronouns: He/Him/His

*Position Specialist*
Teacher Development & Resources Library, Main Campus
Bio: [Provide a 2-3 sentence bio or description]

## SEARCH COMMITTEE MEMBER
**First Name Last Name**
Pronounced "First Last"

Pronouns: They/Them/Theirs

*Division Director*
Lied Library, Main Campus
Bio: [Provide a 2-3 sentence bio or description]

## APPENDIX E

# Hosting Candidates Toolkit–Tips and Tricks for Search Committee Chairs

## Hosting Candidates Toolkit–Tips and Tricks for Search Committee Chairs

The following tips are actions some search committees have already undertaken, or stem from open text feedback on the faculty survey. They were not discussed in the IEC report or directly addressed in the survey, so they are being presented as optional, but encouraged, actions to further improve a candidate's interview experience.

**Determine meal payment in advance**
- The search chair should coordinate who will pay for meals (which may differ by occurrence) in advance, and assist with the submitting the reimbursement paperwork.

**When communicating with the candidate to schedule their visit, also consider doing the following:**
- If not having an onsite lunch, consider allowing candidates to choose a vehicle from those available that best meets their physical needs.

    *How could this be done in practice?*
    o Search committee members able to drive a candidate from the hotel, to/from lunch, or back to the hotel provide the Search Committee Chair with the make and model of their cars.
    o The Faculty Recruitment Coordinator should ask the candidate which car they'd prefer from the options for each time they will be driven on the interview day and report back to the committee.

- Provide the candidate a brief overview of what to expect in regards to weather, health and attire during their visit.

    *How could this be done in practice?*
    o Provide a link to a weather forecast site.

- If a summer interview: provide a brief statement about hydration, high UV radiation, and the extreme heat of the pavement and other surfaces—especially in cars.
- Include a statement warning that Las Vegas' geography and climate can exacerbate allergies, and skin and asthma-related conditions.
- Provide a statement that there is no UNLV dress code, and that candidates should dress for the weather and to be comfortable and confident during the activities of the interview day.

**When creating an itinerary, consider implementing the following:**
- Provide the same person as a guide for the entire day, or limit to only search committee members.
- For a tenure-track position, a P&T committee representative should be explicitly scheduled on the itinerary and should take place in a conference room.
- Give a brief description of the purpose or topics likely to be covered for all itinerary items.

    *How could this be done in practice?*
    - Ask the Supervisor and Dean what they typically discuss in their meetings with candidates.
    - Under the Itinerary item add a brief description:
        - *Purpose: This time with the supervisor can be used to discuss management style, work expectations, evaluation procedures, pay & promotion.*
        - *Purpose: The presentation allows Library staff and the Search Committee to evaluate __, and also provides an opportunity for a library wide Q&A session with a candidate.*

- **Recommendation 24** Encourage the position supervisor, P&T Committee representative and the Dean to develop talking points for candidate meetings if they have not already done so.

    *How could this be done in practice?*
    - When scheduling the itinerary, simply remind these folks that feedback on Campus Visit Procedures encouraged them to develop and bring talking points to maintain consistency and ensure information important to candidates is covered.
        - Supervisor suggested talking points to include (among others):
            - ☐ Provide a copy of the previous/most recent position description to the candidate and describe the position description process.
            - ☐ Describe annual review process and importance.

- Describe specific policies, projects and ways in which inclusion and diversity are addressed in the department.
- Discuss explicitly how pay and raises work at UNLV.
- P&T Committee Rep meeting suggested talking points (among others):
  * Explain the tenure clock and where the person will be starting based on month of hire.
  * Explain basic tenure requirements and review process.
  * Discuss how raises work in tenure-track positions.
  * Explain early tenure requirements, and the penalty of not achieving it.
  * Explain timeline from submission of tenure packet and receiving promotion and tenure or when last year of work begins/ends.
  * Role of supervisor and faculty in tenure decisions.
  * Role of annual evaluations.
  * Expectations in service and scholarship for tenure.
    » Include nuances such as leadership often being demonstrated through service commitments.
  * Mention Folio tracking system.

# References

Boddie, A., Fiedler, B.P., Haslam, M., Luna, E., Martinez-Flores, E., Padilla, T., Wainscott, S.B., White, C., Day, A., Cheng, J., George, K., Green, H., Melilli, A., Mazmanyan, K., & Brombosz, C. (2020, February 1). *Inclusion and Equity Committee Recommendations for Diverse Recruitment Report*. University of Nevada, Las Vegas, University Libraries. https://digitalscholarship.unlv.edu/lib_iec_reports/4/

Division of Diversity Initiatives. (n.d.). *Minority-Serving Institution*. University of Nevada, Las Vegas. https://www.unlv.edu/diversity/msi

Media Relations. (2018, December 19). *UNLV attains highest status as research university* [News release]. News Center, University of Nevada, Las Vegas. https://www.unlv.edu/news/release/unlv-attains-highest-status-research-university

Nevada System of Higher Education. (2021). *NSHE Institutions Fall Enrollment: University of Nevada, Las Vegas*. NSHE Institutional Research. https://ir.nevada.edu/ipeds_fall_enrollment.php?t=0&divt=0

Office of Decision Support. (2020, April). *2019 Faculty and Staff Headcount by Unit, Distribution by Race/Ethnicity and Gender*. University of Nevada, Las Vegas.

Office of Decision Support. (2021, April). *2021 Faculty and Staff Headcount by Unit, Distribution by Race/Ethnicity and Gender*. University of Nevada, Las Vegas.

University of Nevada, Las Vegas. (n.d.). *Facts and stats*. About UNLV. https://www.unlv.edu/about/facts-stats

CHAPTER 19

# From Applicant to Employee

## Developing and Evaluating an Inclusive Hiring and Onboarding Process

*Gary R. Maixner, Kindra Orr, and M. Sara Lowe*

## Introduction

While it is widely understood that inclusive recruitment and hiring practices have the potential to positively impact representational diversity in academic libraries and foster a more welcoming culture, few organizations are evaluating their efforts in these areas. A 2017 ARL SPEC Kit survey reported that 90 percent of responding libraries have developed or were developing strategies to cultivate diverse applicant pools. Only 15 percent of the group indicated they were assessing their inclusive recruitment efforts (Anaya & Maxey-Harris, 2017).

Although few academic libraries report that they are evaluating their recruitment practices, a range of resources are available that identify best practices to support effective recruitment. Both the Association for College and Research Libraries (ACRL) and the American Library Association's (ALA) Core membership division have recommended guidelines for recruiting and interviewing librarian candidates (ACRL, 2017; Arch et al., 2021). The ACRL (2017) guidelines offer a framework for "managing librarian recruitments in a strategic, proactive, and consistent manner." The Core best practices for academic interviews also aim at promoting consistency. They highlight the need for individual library organizations to examine their practices and assumptions related to hiring and emphasize the benefit of structured interviews and using scripted questions and rubrics, with preparatory training for hiring committees.

The Society of Human Resource Management (SHRM) reports that auditing an applicant's journey is necessary to creating the optimal candidate experience (Maurer, 2017). Examining the steps in the process from recruitment, through hiring, to onboarding helps envision a humane and supportive process that is better for candidates and elevates the reputation of the organization. Candidates are professional colleagues. Sometimes they are also patrons or customers. They often share their interview experiences with their networks, both positive, 77 percent of the time, and negative, 61 percent of the time (Talent Board, 2021). When they share negative recruitment experiences, there can be significant negative impact on the organization (Steiner, 2017).

In important ways, onboarding is a continuation of the interview process and should focus on engaging new hires through a developmental approach that includes regular feedback (Bugg, 2015). The goal of the library's process and evaluation efforts is to ensure candidates and new hires feel connected to and ownership of their hiring and onboarding through formal and consistent solicitation and incorporation of stakeholder feedback. Candidates and new hires engage in activities to gather feedback that allow them to feel heard, recognized, and able to respond honestly without fear of retribution. A structured hiring and onboarding process not only is a more positive experience for applicants but also promotes retention after the hiring process is complete (Chapman, 2009).

# Literature Review

The process described in this chapter draws on two threads in human resources and psychology literature: a welcoming environment, encompassing applicant authenticity; and socialization theory. A welcoming environment, where applicants and new hires feel they can be their authentic selves and provide feedback to the organization, creates a more satisfactory hiring and onboarding process. Authenticity is central to well-being and self-esteem (Wood et al., 2008). It is comprised of four key factors: (1) self-awareness, a knowledge of and trust in your own motives and abilities; (2) unbiased processing, clearly evaluating your own strengths and weaknesses; (3) behavior, acting in a way that is congruent with your values and beliefs; and (4) relational orientation, close relationships that require openness and honesty (Kernis & Goldman, 2006). Socialization theory focuses on supporting and providing resources to applicants and new employees so that they develop organizational pride and internalize organizational values (Cable, Gino, & Staats, 2013). Van Maanen and Schein (1979) propose six socialization tactics on a continuum:

- collective versus individual (a common set of experiences, training, versus internships or personalized training)
- formal versus informal (the new employee is separated from other employees while put through experiences tailored for the new employee versus learning through trial and error)
- sequential versus random (a set sequence of steps leading to a target goal versus ambiguous steps)
- fixed versus variable (a cohesive process for new employees versus limited clues as to when socialization and training are complete)
- serial versus disjunctive (experienced employees groom newcomers to assume similar positions versus no role models and new employees do not follow in footsteps of others)
- investiture versus divestiture (ratifies and documents the usefulness and viability of the personal characteristics a new employee brings to the organization versus denies and strips away personal characteristics)

Jones (1986) contends that these six bipolar frames are institutionalized socialization when they are collective, formal, sequential, fixed, serial, and investiture tactics. Conversely, the other end of the continuum is individualized socialization. Overall, the literature focuses heavily on socialization after hiring rather than considering all of hiring and recruitment as part of the process.

In the higher education and library literature, Tierney and Rhoades (1994) describe socialization as a continuous, bidirectional process that results in changes to both the new hire and the institution. While that is the ideal, in interviews with new librarians, Keisling and Laning (2016) found that new librarians were not able to respond fully to questions about what their organizations were learning about them and their strengths. In other words, the onboarding process was perceived as unidirectional, flowing from the organization to the new hire. Cable, Gino, and Staats (2013) found that socialization focused on employees' personal identity, rather than organizational identity, led to better new employee engagement and job satisfaction. Ballard and Blessing (2006) describe a structured new employee orientation model that focuses heavily on socialization, such as understanding library values and mission and meeting coworkers. Winterman and Bucy (2019) outline the implementation of a structured Onboarding Training Grid which they found improved organizational socialization during a librarian's first month of employment.

Welcoming environments and socialization in hiring and onboarding are also important in recruiting and retaining candidates from historically marginalized groups (Betz, 2022; Brewer, Cheshire, & Bradshaw, 2021; Cunningham, Guss, & Stout, 2019). The environment is especially relevant to the continued lack of diversity in librarianship (Hathcock, 2015). A 2020 systematic review of academic libraries' efforts to recruit and retain librarians described a range of initiatives (Kung, Fraser, & Winn, 2020). The strategies tended to be broad and programmatic in their approach, including internships and residencies, mentoring, professional development, and surveys. Of the twenty types of documented interventions discussed, two focused on recruitment. Findings demonstrate that programs to foster diversity in academic libraries tend to focus on early-career librarians, and those that include an evaluative component showed evidence of contributing to diversity within the profession. Developmental approaches such as those examined by Kung, Fraser, and Winn (2020) help to change the culture of librarianship in meaningful ways. At the same time, it is important for individual organizations to examine norms and identify biases in the administrative aspects of recruitment and hiring. While these process-based, transactional activities make hiring possible, they also shape and define the systems that perpetuate the whiteness of libraries (Bourg, 2014).

# Institutional Context

Following best practices, as part of an effort to improve recruitment and retention, our library has worked to institute a more robust people-centered hiring, onboarding, and evaluation process, which aligns with the library's diversity, equity, and inclusion strategic priority (University Library, n.d.). For the purposes of this chapter, we refer to individuals who were invited for first- or second-round interviews as candidates. Individuals who applied for a position are collectively referred to as applicants.

Indiana University–Purdue University Indianapolis (IUPUI) is an urban research institution located in the Midwest. As of fall 2022, over 25,000 students are enrolled (IUPUI, n.d.). IUPUI is a relatively diverse campus. Among undergraduates, 28 percent come from underserved populations and 28 percent are first-generation students (Hansen, 2021). Among tenured or tenure-track faculty and librarians, 69 percent identify as White, 20 percent identify as Asian, 5 percent identify as Black or African American, 4 percent identify as Hispanic or Latino, and 2 percent identify as belonging to two or more races (IUPUI, n.d.).

University Library is the main library on campus serving all students except for those in professional programs (dentistry, medicine, and law), which have their own libraries, and the Herron Art Library, which is a separate library but is under the administrative umbrella of University Library. University Library has two employees who have human resources positions, one staff member, and one assistant dean (who has wider responsibilities beyond human resources). Library human resources personnel work in conjunction with IUPUI human resources in hiring. Library human resources work with search and screen committees and the position supervisor to coordinate job searches, hiring, and onboarding. Librarians at IUPUI are tenure-track faculty. University Library has twenty-nine librarians in tenured, tenure-track, or visiting positions and forty-four individual staff members in both exempt and nonexempt positions. Across the library, 14 percent of librarians and staff identify as Black or African American, and 3 percent identify themselves as belonging to two or more races.

## Process Changes

Our library has already incorporated specific interventions to increase the diversity of applicant pools for both librarian and staff positions and to ensure a welcoming experience for candidates. These include, but are not limited to

- including language about the library's and the campus's commitment to diversity in the opening paragraphs of all job ads (Black & Leysen, 2002; Bugg, 2015)
- earmarking funds to support posting jobs in outlets that are more likely to be seen by applicants from underrepresented minorities (ACRL, 2017)
- hosting search and screen workshops for all library employees to ensure that a wide range of personnel are trained and available to serve on search committees (ACRL, 2017)
- holding launch meetings for each job search to ensure all committee members are aware of the tools and processes, policies, and guidelines available to support the recruitment and hiring process (ACRL, 2017)
- scripting interviews and developing rubrics based on individual position descriptions for use by committee members (Arch et al., 2021)
- blinding or anonymizing applications upon receipt (Kumar, 2018; Meena, 2016; Rinne, n.d.)
- providing search committee questions and presentation topics to first- and second-round candidates ahead of time (Arch et al., 2021)
- documenting steps in our library's search and screen process, as well as guidelines for creating a fair search and screen process, to support consistency across searches
- partnering new hires with a buddy or informal mentor (Olivas & Ma, 2009)

In addition to these best practices, this chapter examines additional unique aspects of University Library's recruitment and hiring strategies, all of which are aimed at making the process more welcoming and transparent for candidates:

- sending a candidate experience survey to all applicants afforded an interview
- providing second-round candidates access to a virtual welcome packet
- designing a robust, mindful onboarding schedule
- inviting all new hires to participate in our onboarding assessment process

## Candidate Feedback

With the goal of understanding the lived experiences of job candidates, University Library developed and instituted a candidate experience survey, launched in 2021. Based on guidance and examples drawn from consultancies focused on for-profit organizations (Talent Board, 2021; Workable, n.d.; T., n.d.) and drawing on goals of the library's strategic priorities (University Library, n.d.), the survey gathers information about candidates' perceptions and feelings throughout the interview process. According to a national survey of the 100 best companies to work for, when candidates are asked for their feedback after the application process, they are 38 percent more likely to apply for future jobs with the organization. When asked for feedback following an interview, they are 74 percent more likely to refer others to the organization, and when asked to share feedback at any point during the recruitment process, there is a 93 percent increase in positive candidate experience ratings (Talent Board, 2021). Although these results clearly illustrate the value of seeking feedback from job applicants regarding branding and recognition, a remarkable 56 percent of candidates are never asked to provide feedback about their experiences during the screening and interview process (Grossman, 2018). Before launching, the library invited representatives from another campus unit, the Office of Equal Opportunity, to review the survey with an equity lens. This external analysis ensured that the survey would reflect the library's espoused diversity values and reliably surface potential biases in the hiring and recruitment process (DeEtta Jones & Associates, n.d.).

Every applicant afforded a first-round interview receives an e-mail thanking them for their interest in the position and inviting them to share their feedback through a Qualtrics survey (see appendix A). The survey questions focus on candidates' communication preferences, how effectively the search committee explained the details of the position and the programs and priorities of the library, and whether candidates were satisfied with opportunities to present their strengths and ask questions during interviews. Additionally, candidates were asked what would have helped them do their best during interviews and how comfortable they felt being their authentic selves throughout their interview experience. Candidates receive the survey e-mail after an offer has been made and accepted by the most qualified candidate. Survey feedback is reviewed by library administration and committee chairs to identify opportunities for improvement and enhancements to the hiring process.

## Candidate Resources

Candidates invited for a second-round interview are provided an extensive online guide that lays out details of the position's library unit, the library itself, the university, and the wider community. This guide contains information about health and retirement benefits and the library annual review and promotion and tenure processes. It continues to act as a resource for the successful second-round candidate upon their hire (see, for example, https://web.archive.org/web/20230331002505/https://iupui.libguides.com/instructionlibrarian). This package helps the library communicate information and values about the organization and supports anticipatory socialization (Black & Leysen, 2002; Wrench & Punyanunt-Carter, 2012).

## Onboarding Resources

Once a new employee is hired, library human resources and the new employee's supervisor create a robust, mindful onboarding schedule for new librarians which spans at least the first month of the new hire's employment (Black & Leysen, 2002; Graybill et al., 2013). This schedule incorporates a variety of preplanned meetings for new hires with colleagues and campus partners to help them to gather information and, more importantly, form connections for them to be successful in their new position. While there are some common meetings across all onboarding schedules (e.g., library human resources, computer safety with information technology), other meetings are specific to the position and job responsibilities. Black and Leysen (2002) stress the importance of academic libraries to provide a supportive mentoring environment for new librarians. A part of the schedule also involves informal meetings with a buddy, someone identified to be the primary point of contact for the new hire, who is not the new hire's supervisor, to answer questions and help them learn about the culture of the library and the campus.

## Onboarding Feedback

Onboarding is an important step in the socialization, success, retention, and engagement of new hires at any institution (Hewitt, 2003; Tierney and Rhoades, 1994). Evaluating the success of onboarding can be done in several ways, by looking at the physical effectiveness of the onboarding (e.g., new employees have necessary logins, parking passes, etc.), intellectual effectiveness (the new employee understands their role in the organization and how to do their work), and emotional effectiveness (the new employee feels welcomed and heard in the organization).

While onboarding is an ongoing process that is generally viewed as the first full year of employment (Black & Leysen, 2002; Graybill et al., 2013), our evaluation focused on the first three months of a new employee's time at the library. We made our choice to focus on this time frame due to the amount of control and formality that the library has over those first months with scheduled meetings, lunches, and activities for new hires. There is room to investigate further out in an employee's career, especially at their one-year anniversary. These evaluations include librarians and library staff, and adjustments were made to create more parity between the experiences of these two groups. The onboarding process includes multiple components: a survey, journaling, and interviews, which are discussed below.

## SURVEY

To evaluate the individual elements of the onboarding process, we created a survey for each calendar item scheduled for the new employee. The first two weeks for a new employee are incredibly structured, with library administration setting meetings for the new employee on a variety of things, including benefits, parking permits, and getting to know new colleagues. The goals of these meetings are defined by administration and inform the questions on the survey. The Google Forms survey was written to be taken multiple times, at the end of every workday by the new hire. It took advantage of logic tools in the survey software so that the new hire was able to select which onboarding activities they took part in that day. It then presented questions specific to the selected activities.

There were several challenges with the survey. First, the meeting schedule and intensity were different for faculty and staff. Staff also had the added complexity of attending vastly different meetings to facilitate their onboarding. This difference meant that a new survey would need to be written for every staff member and the disparities in the surveys would make analyzing the data difficult. New hires also expressed that the survey instrument was challenging to use, especially when they attended meetings that the survey didn't cover. For these reasons we retired the survey instrument and created the journaling activity.

## JOURNALING

The journaling activity tasks the new hires with writing a brief journal entry about their onboarding experience at the end of every day. They are asked to do this for the first two weeks of their employment, running parallel to the structured onboarding experience they receive. While participants are free to write what they like, they are provided with prompts to springboard their writing. Likewise, the mode of the writing is not prescriptive, although we expect many of the entries to be typed. After their first two weeks are complete, new hires are asked to provide those journal entries to the user experience librarian to be read and coded for evaluation. These files are accessed only by the user experience librarian and the new hire, with findings aggregated for administration.

## INTERVIEWS

The library conducts interviews with new hires about their time at the university. These interviews were conducted at roughly the one- and three-month marks (see appendix B). This time frame means that the specifics of the formal onboarding process are still fresh in their minds, but it provides time for new hires to contextualize their experience with their job.

The interviews took place in the test administrator's office or over Zoom. To ensure that the participant would feel at ease with the interview and could speak candidly, the test administrator is someone who does not directly interact with the new hire in day-to-day capacities and does not directly report to their supervisor.

If the participant consented, the interviews were audio recorded in addition to the administrator taking notes. These recordings are transcribed and coded to look for patterns in the data.

The questions in the one-month interview focus on the new hire's comfort with the organization, how friendly they found their new peers, and lingering questions they may have. Where appropriate, the administrator asks follow-up questions for elaboration. Participants were also asked to speak about their perception of the library's purported goals with regard to diversity, equity, and inclusion and if the library was living these goals. Since this question could be emotional for the participants, the anonymity of their responses was reaffirmed.

The questions of the three-month interview focus on the intellectual preparedness of the new hires. It was felt that the three-month mark was the perfect opportunity to ask new hires if they felt the onboarding process adequately prepared them for their work, since they would have had time to understand their role in the library while being able to recall the onboarding experience. As with the one-month interviews, these were audio recorded, transcribed, and coded, and the administrator took notes for reference later. In addition to the standard questions, the facilitator followed up with points from the previous interview.

# Evaluation

## Candidate Survey

Job candidates for both library staff and librarian positions were sent a link to University Library's candidate experience survey ($N = 71$). Twenty-six individuals responded for an overall response rate of 37 percent. The pool of respondents included candidates from four librarian searches and five staff searches from 2019 to 2022. Of the twenty-six respondents, fifteen were seeking librarian positions and held master's degrees in library and information science. Fifty percent of responding candidates reported feeling extremely satisfied with their individual recruitment experience, 35 percent reported feeling satisfied, and 12 percent somewhat dissatisfied. Most respondents, 85 percent, said the library communicated just the right amount with them throughout the interview process. Ninety-six percent of respondents said they were allowed enough time to ask questions throughout the interview process. Fifty-four percent of respondents indicated that they would be extremely likely to recommend job opportunities at University Library to a friend or colleague. Another 31 percent said they would be likely to do so, 8 percent said they would be somewhat unlikely to recommend a job opportunity at our library, and 4 percent said they would be extremely unlikely to make such a recommendation. Reasons candidates said they would or would not recommend a job at University Library focused on the positive reputation of IUPUI and its personnel, employment benefits offered by the university, and one description of a misunderstanding in the regret process, resulting in frustration for a candidate. See table 19.1 for survey feedback.

**Table 19.1.** Survey responses

| Question | Rating | | | |
|---|---|---|---|---|
| | *Extremely satisfied* | *Satisfied* | *Somewhat dissatisfied* | *Extremely dissatisfied* |
| Overall, how satisfied were you with your recruitment experience? | 50% | 35% | 12% | 3% |
| | *Extremely prepared* | *Prepared* | *Somewhat prepared* | *Extremely unprepared* |
| In general, how prepared were search committee members during your time with them? | 52% | 37% | 11% | 0 |
| | *Extremely clear* | *Clear* | *Somewhat unclear* | *Extremely unclear* |
| How clear were search committee members in their efforts to help you understand the role and associated responsibilities? | 58% | 38% | 0 | 0 |
| | *Extremely well* | *Moderately well* | *Not well* | *Not well at all* |
| How well would you say you understand University Library's mission and values after your candidate experience? | 46% | 42% | 8% | 0 |
| | *Very frequently* | *Frequently* | *Occasionally* | *Rarely* |
| How often during the course of the interview process were you able to highlight your strengths for this role? | 42% | 50% | 4% | 0 |

**Table 19.1.** Survey responses

| Question | Rating | | | |
|---|---|---|---|---|
| | *Extremely comfortable* | *Comfortable* | *Somewhat uncomfortable* | *Extremely uncomfortable* |
| How comfortable did you feel being your authentic self throughout your candidate experience? | 42% | 46% | 8% | 0 |
| | *Extremely likely* | *Likely* | *Somewhat unlikely* | *Extremely unlikely* |
| How likely is it that you would recommend job opportunities at University Library to a friend or colleague? | 54% | 31% | 8% | 4% |

In response to open-ended questions in the survey, several themes emerged. Many respondents shared specific comments about the attractiveness of the job opportunity. They described it as a chance to apply specific individual skills and expertise, mentioning feelings of excitement, aspirations of growing in their career, and their hopes about supporting students. Respondents also shared perceptions of the interview process itself, including thoughts about the responsiveness, flexibility, and transparency of library personnel in their communications. Numerous comments reflected perceptions of library personnel who candidates encountered during interviews, whether they were welcoming and supportive or presented as being passionate about their work with the library. Other comments referred to the reputation of the library and library personnel; university or library policy information shared during interviews; identified stress points in the process, such as the rigor of the process and the number of activities applicants were asked to participate in. Figure 19.1 further describes the themes and represents how many comments focused on each of the thematic areas across $n = 68$ total comments.

More candidates for staff positions mentioned specific positive perceptions of the recruitment process than did candidates for librarian positions. Librarian candidates were more likely to identify stress points by a margin of almost three to one. Librarians were also more likely to mention perceived reputations of the library, the campus, and library personnel as a reason for applying for the position. Librarian respondents were twice as likely to mention the welcoming and friendly stance, professionalism, and expertise of the people they met during the interview process. It is not clear whether this difference was due to the behavior of search committee members across both staff and librarian searches or to differences in expectations about the interview process among staff versus librarians.

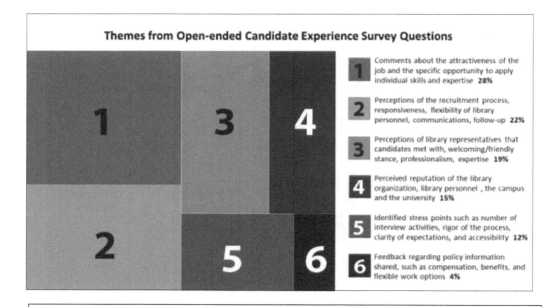

**Figure 19.1.** Themes from Open-ended Candidate Experience Survey Questions

Sixty-nine percent of responding librarian candidates reported feeling extremely satisfied with their individual recruitment experience, 15 percent reported feeling satisfied, and 15 percent were somewhat dissatisfied. All librarian respondents said the library communicated just the right amount with them throughout the interview process. Sixty-nine percent of respondents indicated that they would be extremely likely to recommend job opportunities at University Library to a friend or colleague. Another 8 percent said they would be likely to do so, 15 percent said they would be somewhat unlikely to recommend a job opportunity at our library, and 8 percent said they would be extremely unlikely to make such a recommendation. When asked to explain why not, librarian candidates questioned whether the rigor of the application process was worth the effort and described difficult feelings in reaction to receiving a personal phone call informing them that another candidate was selected.

## Onboarding

Since we began evaluating our onboarding process, $N = 6$ new hires have participated. All participants have completed the follow-up interviews, with only two completing the survey/journaling exercise. We are working on ways to increase participation.

In the one- and three-month interviews, participants were forthcoming with what they saw as the organization's strengths as well as its weaknesses. While the library was prepared for criticism, on the whole participants found the experience welcoming, useful, and warm. Participants claimed that this was the most hands-on onboarding experience that they had encountered and were grateful for its structure and pacing.

As for ways that the library could improve, the list was fairly small. The main point of contention was that the onboarding experience was so full that participants routinely felt that they did not have time for a lunch break or to reflect on the onboarding process day-to-day. The second major point was a need for better explanations and time lines regarding the promotion and tenure process.

# Discussion

In alignment with recommendations from SHRM, our library envisioned and implemented a series of interventions to better understand a job candidate's journey, looking at processes and how they can impact candidates' experiences, from when they first apply through the onboarding process. The library worked to provide personalized messaging and information resources for candidates to better support them throughout the process. The candidate experience survey gathered first impressions of job opportunities, collected feedback about interviews and communications with library personnel, and asked candidates to identify gaps in the interview process such as questions, steps, or opportunities that may have been missing from the candidate's perspective. Robust interview and onboarding resources helped candidates and new hires feel supported during the process. Guided conversations with new hires provided individual opportunities for reflection and useful feedback to enhance the onboarding process. Each of these interventions can be applied in an iterative manner, as more information shapes a clearer picture of individual candidates' recruitment and hiring journey.

Results of the candidate experience survey indicate that most candidates were satisfied with their recruitment journey. The library communicated with them just the right amount, and search committee members were prepared and welcoming. The majority of candidates felt they had ample opportunity to highlight their strengths and ask questions. Most said they felt comfortable being their authentic self during interviews. While comments generally reflected positive perceptions of the job opportunity, the library, and the people candidates met in interviews, they also mentioned stress points in the process.

Based on information gathered via the survey, the library has already made some changes, as well as recommitting to practices:

- Providing interview questions in advance is perceived as being beneficial and supportive.
- The library now offers candidates a choice of either dinner the evening before, or lunch on the interview day, or both, depending on their preferences. Previously, librarian candidates were invited to both a dinner the night before their interview day and lunch on the day of the interview.

- The library changed the process for regretting candidates after second-round interviews. Previously, search committee chairs called all candidates invited for second-round on-campus interviews to thank them for their time and explain that they were not chosen for the position. After the time and energy individuals invested in this interview process step, the library felt this was the most respectful and personal approach to declining candidates. However, based on feedback from the survey, this practice is currently under review. Personal calls after second-round interviews are often initially understood to indicate a forthcoming offer. With this expectation, candidates who learn in the call that another candidate was selected may feel more disappointed than they might have felt receiving a regret e-mail from the library and as a result may develop negative feelings toward the library as an organization.
- When the library's human resources coordinator, a staff member in administration, served as a single point of contact and managed follow-up communication with candidates, they described the library as being more responsive and felt a higher level of satisfaction with recruitment communications. This created more continuity of experience among candidates.

The library's candidate experience survey revealed numerous opportunities to better support candidates throughout the recruitment and interview process. In addition to the data we collected to improve our human resources practices, there is evidence that the action of inviting feedback from candidates has its own rewards (O'Brien, 2022).

From the evaluations of the library's onboarding process, we see strong evidence that our process not only works but serves new employees in both the short and long terms. New hires indicated that they felt welcomed by everyone and that their onboarding experience was more robust and thorough than any other place they had previously been employed. They also shared that they generally felt the library was making good on its promises to them in regard to work-life balance, DEI initiatives, and establishing their career.

From the interviews with new hires, we did uncover areas for improvement in the onboarding process. The easiest to fix, but also the most important, was to ensure they were given adequate time to decompress and process every day. This aligns with what Tokarz (2018) notes: a better balance of scheduled and unscheduled time in an onboarding schedule led to stronger employee engagement. For many of them this meant providing at least two hours of unscheduled time around the lunch hour. Another problem was the uneven experience of meeting with committee chairs for faculty governance. As these positions rotate yearly, it was determined that the best way to move forward is to have the current chair prepare an overview of the work that can be used year to year to ensure consistency. Finally, all participants expressed a desire to know more about the promotion and tenure process. While it is felt that more documentation and supplemental learning can be provided to new hires, there is a fear that new hires would be burdened with information that would be more relevant later. We are investigating providing a visual representation of the process to new hires, so they can see a bird's-eye view of the promotion and tenure process. We believe that this would satisfy their need to know without overwhelming them.

# Conclusion

Through a comprehensive suite of hiring and onboarding best practices, IUPUI University Library has worked to increase candidate and new hire socialization and satisfaction. Overall, the majority of candidates were satisfied with their individual recruitment experience, thought that the library communicated just the right amount with them through the interview process, and thought that they would be extremely likely to recommend job opportunities at the library to a friend or colleague. New employees reported that the onboarding process was welcoming, useful, and warm. They also noted that this was the most hands-on onboarding experience they had encountered in their careers and that they were grateful for the structure. The process includes following best practices such as doing common training for search and screen committees and providing interview questions to candidates prior to interviews. It also encompasses providing candidates and new hires robust documentation and scheduling. Importantly, feedback from candidates and new hires is solicited at multiple stages in application and onboarding.

While this chapter outlined specific aspects of the library's hiring and onboarding process, we stress that the entire package is necessary. In other words, libraries should incorporate as many of the best practices as possible given the institutional context, not just the enhancements discussed here. It is the development of a holistic candidate and new hire experience that leads to better outcomes for both the candidate and the library.

# Acknowledgments

The authors would like to thank University Library human resources coordinator Joycelynn Marshall for handling the transactional aspects of recruitment and hiring with care and fairness, and search committee colleagues for their time and their efforts to provide a welcoming environment for candidates.

## APPENDIX A

# Candidate Experience Survey

Thank you for your interest in a position at IUPUI University Library. We appreciate the time and energy you invested in preparing your application materials and in getting to know our personnel, projects, and services.

We would be grateful for your feedback about your experience as a job candidate with our library organization. This survey includes 16 questions and should take 5–7 minutes.

All applicants who participated in first and second phase interviews will receive this invitation to share feedback. Your responses will remain anonymous.

Your input will help us continue to improve our search and screen process, making it a welcoming experience for all applicants.

1. Overall, how satisfied were you with your recruitment experience at University Library?
   - Extremely satisfied
   - Satisfied
   - Somewhat dissatisfied
   - Extremely dissatisfied

2. What was it about this job opportunity as described in the online ad that made you want to apply?

3. We want to know if we communicated enough with you throughout the interview process. How would you describe the level of communication?
   - Too much
   - Too little
   - Just the right amount

4. If there was a specific part of the interview process that you would like to comment on, please use the box below to share your thoughts.

5. In general, how prepared were search committee members during your time with them?
   - Extremely prepared

- Prepared
- Somewhat unprepared
- Extremely unprepared

6. How clear were search committee members in their efforts to help you understand the role and associated responsibilities?
    - Extremely clear
    - Clear
    - Somewhat unclear
    - Extremely unclear

7. How often during the course of the interview process were you able to highlight your strengths for this role?
    - Very frequently
    - Frequently
    - Occasionally
    - Rarely

8. Were you allowed enough time to ask questions throughout the interview process?
    - Yes
    - No

9. How well would you say you understand University Library's mission and values after your candidate experience?
    - Extremely well
    - Moderately well
    - Not well
    - Not well at all

10. We want to support candidates in doing their very best during interviews. With this in mind, please complete the following sentence, *"It would have been helpful to me during the interview process, if the library had..."*

11. How comfortable did you feel being your authentic self throughout your candidate experience?
    - Extremely comfortable
    - Comfortable

- Somewhat uncomfortable
- Extremely uncomfortable

12. Is there anything University Library could have done to make you feel more like your authentic self throughout your candidate experience? Please explain.

13. Based on your experience, how likely is it that you would recommend job opportunities at University Library to a friend or colleague?
    - Extremely likely
    - Likely
    - Somewhat unlikely
    - Extremely unlikely

14. Why did you choose the rating above?

15. What other feedback would you like to share about your candidate experience?

Thank you for taking time to share your feedback with us.

Best wishes to you in your continued professional endeavors,

The University Library Business Affairs Team

## APPENDIX B

# Onboarding Assessment Protocol

## One Month after Starting

Overall, how did you feel about the onboarding process?

Did you feel welcomed by everyone during the onboarding process?

Did you feel comfortable asking questions when you needed more information?

Was it clear to you who to go to in order to get answers?

Do you feel equipped to do your work now?

What other questions do you have about working at University Library? IUPUI?

Is there anything important about your experience at UL that you would like me to share?

Do you feel like UL is living up to its purported goals, e.g., DEI initiatives?

How do you feel about these follow-up meetings? Do you think UL should continue them? If so, who would be an ideal person or type of person?

## Three Months after Starting

Overall, how did you feel about the onboarding process?

Looking back at your onboarding experience, do you feel that it was a valuable use of your time?

Did you feel prepared to get to work after the onboarding process?

Were you given adequate time to digest what you learned from the onboarding process?

Do you feel like you've been provided the information and tools you need to feel confident and be successful in your position?

What words would you use to describe your future as a librarian? Do you feel that UL is providing you an environment that will realize that future?

What do you think could have been improved about the onboarding process?

What questions do you still have about working at UL? Any confusion that could have been addressed earlier?

Compared to previous employers, how do you feel UL compares in preparing their employees for their career?

Is there anything important about your experience at UL that you would like me to share?

# References

Anaya, T., & Maxey-Harris, C. (2017, September). *SPEC Kit 356: Diversity and inclusion.* Association of Research Libraries. https://doi.org/10.29242/spec.356

Arch, X., Birrell, L., Martin, K. E., & Redd, R. (2021, December 15). *Core best practices for academic interviews.* American Library Association. https://alair.ala.org/handle/11213/17612

Association of College and Research Libraries. (2017, June). *Guidelines for recruiting academic librarians.* https://www.ala.org/acrl/standards/recruitingguide

Ballard, A., & Blessing, L. (2006). Organizational socialization through employee orientations at North Carolina State University Libraries. *College and Research Libraries, 67*(3), 240–248. https://doi.org/10.5860/crl.67.3.240

Betz, G. (2022, April 6). Navigating the academic hiring process with disabilities. *In the Library with the Lead Pipe.* https://www.inthelibrarywiththeleadpipe.org/2022/hiring-with-disabilities/

Black, W. K., & Leysen, J. M. (2002). Fostering success: The socialization of entry-level librarians in ARL libraries. *Journal of Library Administration, 36*(4), 3–27. https://doi.org/10.1300/J111v36n04_02

Bourg, C. (2014, March 3). The unbearable whiteness of librarianship [Blog post]. *Feral Librarian.* https://chrisbourg.wordpress.com/2014/03/03/the-unbearable-whiteness-of-librarianship/

Brewer, A. R., Cheshire, K., and Bradshaw, A. K. (2021). Don't Ctrl+F for diversity: Articulating EDI qualifications in faculty recruitment. In D. M. Mueller (Ed.), *Ascending into an open future: The proceedings of the ACRL 2021 virtual conference, April 13–16, 2021* (pp. 92–97). Association of College and Research Libraries. https://alair.ala.org/bitstream/handle/11213/17564/brewer_dontctrlffordiversity.pdf?sequence=1

Bugg, K. (2015). Best practices for talent acquisition in 21st-century academic libraries. *Library Leadership and Management, 29*(4), 1–14. https://academicworks.cuny.edu/ny_pubs/13/

Cable, D. M., Gino, F., & Staats, B. R. (2013, March). Breaking them in or eliciting their best? Reframing socialization around newcomers' authentic self-expression. *Administrative Science Quarterly, 58*(1), 1–36. https://doi.org/10.1177/0001839213477098

Chapman, C. (2009). Retention begins before day one: Orientation and socialization in libraries. *New Library World, 110*(3/4), 122–135. https://doi.org/10.1108/03074800910941329

Cunningham, S., Guss, S., & Stout, J. (2019). Challenging the "good fit" narrative: Creating inclusive recruitment practices in academic libraries. In D. M. Mueller (Ed.), *Recasting the narrative: The proceedings of the ACRL 2019 conference, April 10–13, 2019, Cleveland, Ohio* (pp. 12–21). Association of College and Research Libraries. https://alair.ala.org/bitstream/handle/11213/17632/ChallengingtheGoodFitNarrative.pdf

DeEtta Jones & Associates. (n.d.) *Creating and using an equity lens.* https://facultyresources.fas.harvard.edu/files/facultyresources/files/4.1_equity_lens.pdf?m=1609876058

Graybill, J. O., Carpenter, M. T. H., Offord, J., Piorun, M., & Shaffer, G. (2013). Employee onboarding: Identification of best practices in ACRL libraries. *Library Management, 34*(3), 200–218. https://doi.org/10.1108/01435121311310897

Grossman, K. W. (2018, August 3). *Prevent candidate dropout: Create a more respectful and structured interviewing process.* Community Articles, Talent Board. https://www.thetalentboard.org/article/prevent-candidate-dropout-create-respectful-structured-interviewing-process/

Hansen, M. J. (2021, December 13). *Understanding IUPUI students.* Institutional Effectiveness, Indiana University–Purdue University Indianapolis. https://irds.iupui.edu/_documents/students/student-profiles/general/2021%20Understanding%20IUPUI%20Students%20-%20December%2013.pdf

Hathcock, A. (2015, October 7). White librarianship in blackface: Diversity initiatives in LIS. *In the Library with the Lead Pipe.* http://www.inthelibrarywiththeleadpipe.org/2015/lis-diversity/

Hewitt. (2003). Survey highlights: "Best employers to work for in Australia" study 2003. https://www.organisationalpsychology.nz/Best%20Employer%20'Summary'%20Report%202003.pdf

Indiana University–Purdue University Indianapolis. (n.d.). *Institutional effectiveness (formerly: IRDS).* https://irds.iupui.edu/

Jones, G. R. (1986, June). Socialization tactics, self-efficacy, and newcomers' adjustments to organizations. *Academy of Management Journal, 29*(2), 262–279. https://www.jstor.org/stable/256188

Keisling, B., & Laning, M. (2016). We are happy to be here: The onboarding experience in academic libraries. *Journal of Library Administration, 56*(4), 381–394. https://doi.org/10.1080/01930826.2015.1105078

Kernis, M. H., & Goldman, B. M. (2006). A multicomponent conceptualization of authenticity: Theory and research. *Advances in Experimental Social Psychology, 38*, 283–357. https://doi.org/10.1016/S0065-2601(06)38006-9

Kumar, R. K. (2018, December). Blind hiring: A solution to BIAS. *IIBM'S Journal of Management Research, 3*(1–2), 83–89. https://iibmjournalofmanagementstudies.in/index.php/iibm/article/view/1095

Kung, J. Y., Fraser, K. L., & Winn, D. (2020). Diversity initiatives to recruit and retain academic librarians: A systematic review. *College and Research Libraries, 81*(1), 96–108. https://doi.org/10.5860/crl.81.1.96

Maurer, R. (2017, May 30). *Candidate experience audits are core to recruiting.* Society of Human Resource Management. https://www.shrm.org/resourcesandtools/hr-topics/talent-acquisition/pages/candidate-experience-audits-are-core-to-recruiting.aspx

Meena, K. (2016). Blind recruitment: The new hiring buzz for diversity inclusion. *International Journal of Business and General Management, 5*(5), 25–28.

O'Brien, E. (2022, June 28). *Why Organizational Feedback Matters During the Recruitment Process.* Health eCareers. https://store.healthecareers.com/resources/budgeting-planning/why-organizational-feedback-matters-during-the-recruitment-process

Olivas, A., & Ma, R. (2009, Winter). Increasing retention rates in minority librarians through mentoring. *Electronic Journal of Academic and Special Librarianship, 10*(3). https://southernlibrarianship.icaap.org/content/v10n03/olivas_a01.html

Rinne, U. (n.d.). Anonymous job applications and hiring discrimination. *IZA World of Labor.* https://wol.iza.org/articles/anonymous-job-applications-and-hiring-discrimination/long

Steiner, K. (2017, March 15). Bad candidate experience cost Virgin Media $5 million annually—Here's how they turned that around [Blog post]. *LinkedIn Talent Blog.* https://www.linkedin.com/business/talent/blog/talent-acquisition/bad-candidate-experience-cost-virgin-media-5m-annually-and-how-they-turned-that-around

T., Elizabeth. (n.d.). Candidate experience survey [Blog post]. *Retorio.* https://www.retorio.com/blog/candidate-experience-survey-questions

Tierney, W. G., & Rhoades, R. A. (1994). *Faculty socialization as cultural process: A mirror of institutional commitment.* School of Education and Human Development, George Washington University.

Tokarz, R. E. (2018). Beyond orientation: A look at scheduled time and unscheduled time in a new librarian's first sixty days. *Library Leadership and Management, 33*(1). https://llm.corejournals.org/llm/article/view/7325

University Library. (n.d.). *Strategic priorities.* Indiana University–Purdue University Indianapolis. https://www.ulib.iupui.edu/about/priorities/strategic-plan

Van Maanen, J., & Schein, E. H. (1979). Toward a theory of organizational socialization. In B. M. Staw (Ed.), *Research in organizational behavior* (vol. 1), (pp. 209–264). JAI Press.

Winterman, M., & Bucy, R. (2019). Welcome aboard: A program for improving the new hire experience for academic librarians. *Library Leadership and Management, 33*(4). https://llm.corejournals.org/llm/article/view/7358

Wood, A. M., Linley, P. A., Maltby, J., Baliousis, M., & Joseph, S. (2008). The authentic personality: A theoretical and empirical conceptualization and the development of the Authenticity Scale. *Journal of Counseling Psychology, 55*(3), 385–399. https://doi.org/10.1037/0022-0167.55.3.385

Workable (n.d.). *Candidate experience survey questions.* https://resources.workable.com/candidate-experience-survey-questions

Wrench, J. S., & Punyanunt-Carter, N. (2012). Recruiting, socializing, and disengaging. Chapter 10 in *An introduction to organizational communication*, v. 0.0 [Draft book]. 2012 Book Archive. https://2012books.lardbucket.org/books/an-introduction-to-organizational-communication/s12-recruiting-socializing-and-dis.html

## AFTERWORD

# Book Development

We, the editors of this book, have all experienced academic librarian hiring from both sides of the process; we have all been candidates for academic librarian positions at multiple different institutions, and each of us has experience serving on and leading search committees recruiting for a variety of departments and functional roles within the library environment. In fact, at one point, the coeditors served on a search committee together. It was during these experiences, as both participants and facilitators, that we became aware of how deeply entrenched exclusionary practices are in academic librarian hiring and how poorly we were treating candidates throughout the process. Candidates lucky enough to even enter the interview stages are asked to engage in a series of mental, emotional, and physical tasks and activities throughout the process, which in academia often takes months. Furthermore, candidates are rarely given the opportunity to question the process or express concerns about it, since hiring is generally seen as fully under the control of the organization. Candidates are simply expected to play along or else risk not moving forward or receiving an offer of employment after investing large amounts of time and energy into a single position—and many candidates are juggling multiple applications and interview processes at one time. It is in organizational systems like hiring where academic libraries reveal how committed they are to creating and maintaining a diverse, equitable, and inclusive environment. The editors' concerns over the continuing organization-centric design and apparent lack of intentional and holistic examination of practices by academic libraries in their hiring processes inspired us to submit the proposal for this book. We wanted to create a volume that highlights ways to make academic librarian hiring more inclusive, kind, and meaningful for candidates.

It is no secret that the library profession lacks diversity—the overwhelming majority of librarians are white and identify as women—statistics that run contrary to the profession's claims of being welcoming, supportive, and embracing of diversity, equity, inclusion, accessibility, and anti-racism (DEIAA). Understanding that the hiring process is typically the first interaction with the organization that candidates have, we began wondering what academic libraries were doing to actualize their DEIAA claims during this process. During our exploration, we noticed more and more librarians advocating for changes to the hiring process at their institutions and increasing numbers of articles, presentations, workshops, courses, and other opportunities related to fostering DEIAA in academic libraries. There has also been direct guidance issued from library-related professional organizations regarding the need to examine and transform hiring practices, such as *Core Best Practices for Academic Interviews* (Arch et al., 2021), a report released by American Library Association's Core Division. Following library workers on any social media platform will eventually reveal ongoing conversations about organizational expectations, experiences during interviews, and anecdotal evidence that academic libraries generally provide an exclusionary and overly long and complicated hiring process. This is what ultimately inspired us to pursue this book—we could see the need for more intentionally inclusive practices and that many academic library workers were making changes to how they hired based on those needs. Our goal has been to create a platform for academic library workers across North America to share their work on ideation and creation of more inclusive hiring with the hope that it might provide motivation for broader change. We know these issues are not exclusive to academic libraries, but we also recognize that our backgrounds and experiences in academic libraries have equipped us with the ability to approach inclusive academic librarian hiring with expertise, empathy, and a commitment to advocate for change.

# Summary and Context

We believe that we were successful in our attempt to include voices speaking to a broad view of inclusion within the recruitment, interview, and evaluation stages of hiring in academic libraries. Chapters in this volume explore the important role of training prior to serving on search committees, understanding attitudes and beliefs that can be exclusionary and inviting us to think and act in new ways, and many examples of library workers and their organizations putting in the work to try and make academic hiring in libraries a better experience for candidates. Our goal was not only to highlight what inclusive hiring can look like and examine how common hiring practices can be exclusionary, but also to foster an explicitly supportive process for our chapter authors. All chapters were peer-reviewed by other authors and the editorial team, and deadlines were as flexible as possible knowing that mental health is more important than productivity deadlines and that most academic library workers are in environments with too few employees for the work to be done. Our authors and their chapters were reviewed for their commitment to inclusivity in who was a part of their described projects, the author teams, and the references used in their chapters. As editors, if we could not model kindness, support, and empathy for those who are making this project a reality, we have little right to ask it from our academic library colleagues in reviewing and reimagining their hiring practices.

As tenured librarians at three different institutions, we recognize that our privilege enables us to pursue this book, no matter how controversial the topic, because we are afforded academic freedom protections. These protections are not afforded to many academic librarians and library workers, and indeed, the timing of this book feels prescient. From the time we called for proposals in May 2022, to submission of final chapters in May 2023, the political landscape has changed dramatically, particularly at the state level, but recent US Supreme Court rulings have eroded bodily autonomy and allowed for open discrimination against the LGBTQ+ community nationwide. As we complete this manuscript, there are increasing attacks on DEIAA efforts throughout the United States, targeting everything from topics discussed in college classrooms to inclusive hiring practices, to health-care coverage and inclusion of transgender youth and athletes. For example, Florida and North Carolina have passed laws that bar institutions from requiring DEIAA-related statements in the hiring process, a topic that is discussed in chapter 5 by librarians in North Carolina. Within the pages of this book, you will find chapters from authors in many states where authorities are actively targeting those who work on DEIAA topics. We acknowledge the bravery and commitment of these authors and thank them, many who are not afforded protections of academic freedom or tenure.

# Call to Action

We recognize that transforming the hiring process to be more inclusive is only one piece of a much larger puzzle, and a commitment to DEIAA cannot stop after the final interview. Newly hired employees need to be supported in a variety of ways: through onboarding, mentoring, professional development, and working toward tenure and promotion (if applicable). Academic libraries must orient themselves toward intentional inclusivity—taking the time and work needed to be intentional about fostering an inclusive work environment—if they wish to hire and retain diverse talent. This work will not happen without the understanding that it does not stop and that commitment to success in DEIAA by academic libraries and their employees is measured over years.

Now, more than ever, with human rights and higher education under attack in the United States, it is imperative that institutions commit to doing everything they can to foster an inclusive environment for all, which includes employees and potential hires.

# Reference

Arch, X., Birrell, L., Martin, K. E., and Redd, R. (2021). *Core best practices for academic interviews* [White paper]. Core: Leadership, Infrastructure, Futures. http://hdl.handle.net/11213/17612

# About the Authors

**Keahi Adolpho** (they/them and he/him) is a processing archivist at Virginia Commonwealth University. They hold a BA in history and an MLIS from the University of Wisconsin-Milwaukee. Keahi is a former diversity resident librarian and coauthor of the "Diversity Residency Toolkit" from the Residency Interest Group. They are a member of the *Homosaurus* Editorial Board, coeditor of *Trans and Gender Diverse Voices in Libraries*, and coauthor of the "Trans Advice Column."

**Ann Agee**, associate librarian, San José State University.

**Tarida Anantachai** (she/her) is the director, inclusion and talent management at the North Carolina State University Libraries, where she oversees the recruitment, hiring, and ongoing support of library faculty and staff; leads equity, diversity, and inclusion efforts; and coordinates the libraries' Fellows Program. Prior to this role, Tarida held various public service–oriented positions at the Syracuse University Libraries, where she also helped found and cochair the libraries' Diversity and Inclusion Team. Her research and professional interests include topics around equity, diversity, and inclusion; early career development; leadership; and outreach programming.

**Xan Arch** is the dean of the Library at the University of Portland. As dean, she has developed library initiatives that support student success and sense of belonging within the library and the university. In support of this work, she has researched and published on first-generation student experiences in libraries, as well as academic library hiring practices. She earned an MLIS from San José State University, and an MA in English literature and BA in English and French literatures from Stanford University. She has also trained as a search advocate through Oregon State University.

**Jason Aubin** serves as the director of space management for the University of Nevada, Las Vegas (UNLV) Libraries. His work focuses on planning, designing, building, and maintaining welcoming and inclusive library spaces for UNLV. In his previous role at UNLV Libraries, he managed the logistics related to the search processes for academic and administrative faculty. He holds a master's degree in library science from the University of North Texas, a bachelor's degree in hotel administration from UNLV, and is a certified educational facilities professional.

**Gail Betz (she/her/hers)** is a research and education librarian for the University of Maryland, Baltimore's School of Social Work. Gail holds a bachelor of arts from Moravian College and master of science in library and information science from Drexel University. Her research is focused on accessibility and ableism in the academic library hiring process.

**Charlotte Beyer,** MSIS is the associate vice president of the Boxer Library at Rosalind Franklin University of Medicine and Science and has been a member of the Boxer Library team since 2010. She received her master of science in information science from the University at Albany, State University of New York, in 2007. Her interests include developing services that meet student and faculty needs, expert searching of information resources, citation styles, and library space design.

In summer 2020, she completed the Joanna Briggs Institute (JBI) Systematic Review Training and is a member of the RFUMS Center for Interprofessional Evidence-Based Practice center team, which advises on systematic review projects using the JBI methodology. She is involved in many professional library organizations, including the Medical Library Association, Association of Academic Health Sciences Libraries, American Library Association, Association of College and Research Libraries, Health Sciences Librarians of Illinois, and the American Association of the Colleges of Pharmacy—Library and Information Science Section. From 2010 to 2020, she was the instruction and reference librarian at the Boxer Library.

**Kathryn Blackmer Reyes**, director, Africana, Asian American, Chicano, and Native American Studies Center, San José State University.

**Marlowe Bogino** holds a master's degree in library science from Clarion University of Pennsylvania, a bachelor's degree in allied health from Widener University, and an associate's degree in respiratory care from Delaware Technical and Community College. She has worked within health care for over twenty years and has worked in the past five years within various types of libraries, including public, academic, and health libraries. Over the years she has held leadership roles and had managerial duties within several administrative roles within health care, but most recently she has worked as the director of medical libraries at Christiana Care Health Center in Christiana, Delaware. She currently holds a tenure-track position as a clinical and reference librarian with Rowan University/Cooper Health System in New Jersey.

**Peggy Cabrera**, associate librarian, San José State University.

**Camille Chesley** is head of reference and research services at the University at Albany Libraries. She received her MSLIS from the University of Illinois at Urbana-Champaign and her BA in East Asian studies from Oberlin College. Her research interests include gamification in libraries, assessment, critical librarianship, and equity, diversity, and inclusion in LIS.

**Scott Collard** is the associate dean for research and research services at New York University. Scott leads a team that includes our corps of libraries liaisons, our data services, and our program-integrated sites around New York City. We work with our partners to support researchers of all levels and disciplines, designing and delivering services that span the research life cycle, from discovery, to data analysis, to dissemination. Scott's research focuses on the development of library research services and spaces; fostering partnership with IT, Offices for Research and Sponsored Programs, and other actors in service development; and creating library support for the research enterprise across our global network.

**Michelle Colquitt** is the continuing resources and government information management librarian at Clemson University Libraries. In a former professional life, Michelle was a juvenile probation and parole specialist II with the Georgia Department of Juvenile Justice at the Athens-Clarke County Juvenile Court. Michelle holds a master of library and information science (Valdosta State University, 2011) and a master of education (Georgia Southern University, 2017).

**Shamella Cromartie** is the associate dean for organizational performance and inclusion at Clemson University Libraries. Shamella holds a master of library science from North Carolina Central University. Shamella is currently working toward her EdD in educational leadership.

**Heather Crozier** is the electronic resource librarian and assistant professor at Ohio Northern University in Ada, Ohio. She has multiple nonvisible illnesses. Her research interests are as varied as her job duties in a small library and include OER, business information literacy, and the intersection of invisible illness and academic library work. She is on Twitter @hrcroz or can be reached at h-crozier@onu.edu.

**Breanne Crumpton** is the information literacy librarian for the humanities at Appalachian State University. She received her MLIS from UNC Greensboro. In her current position, she teaches information literacy instruction, provides research consultations, and liaises to the English and history departments. Her research interests include DEIAA work in libraries, citational politics, critical information literacy, and design justice.

**Chelsea Eidbo,** MLIS, is currently the collections management librarian at Boxer Library at Rosalind Franklin University of Medicine and Science. She graduated with an MLIS from Valdosta State University in Georgia in 2019. Her interests include archiving, metadata development for early twentieth-century academic journals, and article searching. In her spare time, she writes and volunteers for the Organization for Transformative Works as a membership data specialist and as a tag wrangler, doing metadata analysis on user-generated tags.

**Elizabeth Ellis** is an instruction librarian at Wake Forest University's Z. Smith Reynolds Library. In this role, she teaches for-credit courses related to research skills and information literacy, including critical information literacy, and provides research and reference support to library users. She received her MLIS from UNC Greensboro.

**Anne Grant** is the history librarian, instruction coordinator, and interim art and architecture librarian at Clemson University Libraries. Anne holds a master of history from Clemson University and a master of library and information science from the University of Alabama, and is working toward a PhD in learning sciences at the Clemson University School of Education.

**April M. Hathcock** is the director of scholarly communications and information policy and faculty affairs coordinator at New York University Libraries on Manhattan, an ancestral island of the Lenni Lenape. She leads an amazing team whose work involves educating the campus community on issues of openness, rights, and the use of digital methodologies in the research life cycle. April's research interests include anti-racism and anti-oppression in librarianship and higher education, cultural creation and exchange, and the ways in which social and legal infrastructures benefit the works of certain groups over others.

**Twanna Hodge** is pursuing a PhD in information studies at the University of Maryland, College Park. She holds a BA in humanities from the University of the Virgin Islands and an MLIS from the University of Washington. Her research interests include diversity, equity, inclusion, and accessibility issues and efforts in the workplace and LIS education; mental health literacy and mental health information-seeking behavior and needs of BIPOC galleries, libraries, archives, and museum employees; and more. She's one of the cofounders and co-organizers of the BIPOC in LIS Mental Health Summit, (https://docs.google.com/document/d/1FNzclSlAIVxB3CIvIjFhXqMLRi3b-xKuvtoiIqZnzrA/edit?usp=sharing), and Why Do I Stay? webinar series (https://www.aserl.org/event/why-do-i-stay-the-dei-perspective/).

**Kathryn M. Houk** (she/her) is associate professor and undergraduate medical education librarian at the University of Nevada, Las Vegas (UNLV), School of Medicine Library. Prior to joining the UNLV Libraries in 2017, she worked in both tenure-track faculty and professional staff positions at multiple institutions across the United States, where she also participated in hiring committees. Kathryn's professional and research interests include health literacy, health humanities, and the experiences of library workers from minoritized or historically marginalized groups in academic and medical library workplaces.

**Hilary Kraus** (she/her/hers) is the health sciences librarian for clinical support at Brown University. She has served as a health science, social science, and science librarian at universities in Chicago and across New England. Her participation in and chairing of numerous search committees sparked her passion for fostering humane hiring practices in academic libraries. She holds a bachelor of arts from Northwestern University and a master of science in information from the University of Michigan.

**Summer Krstevska** is the business, economics and data access librarian at Wake Forest University, where she supports business school students as well as entrepreneurship minors and the economics programs. She is currently teaching her for-credit business research course on campus and abroad. She holds a master's in library and information science from Simmons University.

**Stephen G. Krueger** (ey/em/eir or he/him/his) is the scholarly publishing librarian at Dartmouth College. Ey holds a BA in English from Warren Wilson College and an MSLS from UNC Chapel Hill and is working on an MA in Arctic and northern studies from the University of Alaska Fairbanks. Stephen is the author of *Supporting Trans People in Libraries*, coeditor of *Trans and Gender Diverse Voices in Libraries*, and coauthor of the "Trans Advice Column." He is also the founder of the Trans and Gender Diverse LIS Network.

**Jennifer M. Jackson** (she/her/hers) is an assistant professor and undergraduate engagement coordinator for the University Library at the University of Illinois Chicago. In her fifteen-year career as a librarian she has had the opportunity to work as a library instruction coordinator; focus on first-year initiatives and first-year writing programs; collaborate in classroom design; manage learning commons; and lead reference training support for library employees and supervisor student workers.

Because she is a disabled, African American woman, advocacy of underrepresented populations is an essential aspect of her work and purpose. During her time at UIC, she has had the opportunity to serve on a variety of committees and task forces related to diversity and the disability community. Most recently she served as the hair for the UIC Chancellor's Committee on the Status of Persons with Disabilities (CCSPD) from 2019 to 2023.

**Sajni Lacey** (she/her) is the learning and curriculum support librarian at UBC Library's Okanagan campus. She coordinates the library orientation and instructional program. Her research interests include information literacy and IDEA practices in higher education and academic libraries, as well as racial identity and imposter syndrome. She is currently an MA candidate in the Okanagan School of Education with her thesis work on culturally responsive pedagogy in higher education. https://orcid.org/0000-0003-0558-4140

**Donna Langille** (she/they) is the community engagement and open education librarian, as well as the subject liaison librarian for film studies, theatre, media studies, and the digital humanities, at the University of British Columbia Okanagan (UBCO). Their work includes connecting the wider community with UBCO Library resources, providing support to students, staff, and faculty working on open educational resources (OER), and building advocacy and awareness of OER at their institution. They are currently completing their PhD in interdisciplinary studies at UBCO. https://orcid.org/0000-0002-9897-9039

**Dr. Ash Lierman** is the instruction and education librarian at Campbell Library on the Glassboro campus of Rowan University, as well as the chair of the Rowan University Libraries' DEI Committee. They support research and instruction across the university, particularly for the College of Education, graduate students, and online learners. Their research and professional service interests focus on social justice for marginalized academic library users and workers, especially those who are disabled and LGBTQ+.

**Mary Beth Lock** is the associate dean at the Z. Smith Reynolds Library. She serves on the assessment team for the library and does research on how the library impacts faculty and student scholarship, as well as best practices to enhance library effectiveness. She received her MLS from North Carolina Central University

**Arielle Lomness** (she/her) is the collections librarian at UBC Library's Okanagan campus, in addition to serving as a subject librarian. Since 2020, she has served as the chair on three librarian selection committees and a voting member on three more. Her work on these committees has spanned both the Okanagan and Vancouver campuses. She centers transparency in her work with candidates and other committee members as a way of fostering accessibility and EDIA-focused discussions throughout the hiring process. https://orcid.org/0000-0003-1694-421X

**Kimberly Looby (Kim)** is the instruction and information literacy librarian at the University of North Carolina Charlotte. She spends most of her time with first-year writing and anthropology students.

**M. Sara Lowe** is associate dean for educational services at IUPUI University Library. Prior to that, she was educational development librarian. Before coming to IUPUI, she was the assessment librarian at the Claremont Colleges Library and a law librarian at the Drake University Law School. She received her BA in history with a minor in women's studies from the University of Missouri-Columbia and her master of library science and MA in history from Indiana University-Bloomington. Her research can be found at her Google Scholar (https://scholar.google.com/citations?user=9-YYxzgAAAAJ&hl=en) or ORCiD profile (https://orcid.org/0000-0003-0706-6056) pages.

**Gary Maixner** is user experience and project management librarian at IUPUI. He received his BA in English from the University of Nebraska-Lincoln in 2010 and his MLIS from the University of Illinois Champaign-Urbana in 2013. He joined the IUPUI University Library in 2018. His work at IUPUI includes managing the library's website, redesigning digital tools to match the demands of patrons, and managing library projects. His research interests include game-based learning, the patron experience in the library, and library project management. He is an award-winning game designer for his work on educational games.

**Jaena Manson**, MSLIS, is the scholarly communications librarian at the Boxer Library at Rosalind Franklin University of Medicine and Science (RFUMS). She received her master of library and information science at the University of Illinois at Urbana-Champaign in 2017 and joined the Boxer Library at RFUMS in August 2022. She is responsible for educating about scholarly communication topics and assisting with evidence synthesis projects and procedures. She also serves as the liaison to the College of Nursing. Before coming to the Boxer Library, Jaena was an instruction and outreach librarian for five years.

**Paula Martin**, associate librarian, is currently assistant dean for user services at University of Wyoming libraries. She has done extensive work with academic hiring committees and has served as a search equity advisor at multiple institutions. Her library experience includes work in access services, electronic resources, personnel management, research and instruction services, administration, and integrated library systems. She has an MLIS from University of Missouri School of Information Science and Learning Technologies and a bachelor's degree in communication from Truman State University.

**KatieRose McEneely** graduated from the University of Illinois iSchool in 2012 and has worked in public and special libraries, specializing in technology and education. KatieRose was the electronic resources librarian at Rosalind Franklin University from 2019 to 2022. Since 2022, they have been working as an information delivery and technology analyst at Abbott.

**Anamika Megwalu,** engineering and assessment librarian, San José State University.

**Christina M. Miskey** joined the University of Nevada, Las Vegas (UNLV), University Libraries in 2017, working in various professional positions before becoming an assistant professor and research impact librarian in 2020. Her work focuses on educating and advising campus researchers on the use of metrics, demonstrating their research impact, managing their scholarly reputation, and the benefits and uses of ORCID. Her scholarship and research centers on exploring ways to improve the practical qualities of early-career librarianship, including supporting MLIS students as they enter the profession and efforts to support and retain new librarians.

**Jordan Nielsen** is an associate professor and the Head of Access Services in the James E. Walker Library at Middle Tennessee State University. Jordan earned a BS in business administration, an MBA, and an MS in information sciences, all from the University of Tennessee. Jordan has presented and published on the topic of inclusive hiring in academic libraries, and they are committed to fostering a library environment that is caring, equitable, and inclusive.

**Kindra Orr** is assistant dean for administration and organizational development at IUPUI University Library, where she has worked for more than fifteen years. In addition to a master's degree in nonprofit management from IU's O'Neill School of Public and Environmental Affairs, she holds graduate certifications in fundraising and human resource development. More from Kindra on Google Scholar (https://scholar.google.com/citations?user=ksp3MWUAAAAJ&hl=en&oi=ao).

**Samantha Peter** is the chair of research and instruction and instructional design librarian at the University of Wyoming Libraries. She lives with a chronic illness. Sammy's research focuses on Universal Design for Learning in instruction, open educational resources, and library procedures. She advocates for improved understanding of invisible disability in the library workplace. You can find her @sammy_librarian or scook13@uwyo.edu.

**Mollie Peuler** is the e-learning librarian at Appalachian State University. In this role, Mollie works to curate, design, and assess online learning objects and tools that support the flexible teaching and learning of information literacy concepts. Her research interests include instructional design, design justice, and inclusive design. Mollie received her MLIS from Florida State University and is in the process of completing a master of education in training and development from North Carolina State University.

**Adriana Poo**, health sciences librarian, San José State University.

**Katelyn Quirin Manwiller** is the education librarian and assistant professor at West Chester University in Pennsylvania. She lives with chronic illness and is dynamically disabled. Katelyn's research and advocacy focuses on improving disability inclusion in libraries through incorporating disability into DEI work, addressing disability misconceptions, and creating accessible work environments. You can find her @librariankqm on Twitter or kmanwiller@wcupa.edu.

**Kelly C. Rhodes** is a professor and the coordinator of information literacy and instruction in the University Libraries at Appalachian State University. She received her MIS from the University of Tennessee, Knoxville. Her primary responsibilities include oversight of the library's programmatic efforts to integrate information literacy and research skills into the university's curriculum. Kelly serves as library liaison for the departments of art, theatre and dance, and the doctoral program in educational leadership. She has published and presented on topics related to information literacy, first-year seminars, transfer students, faculty development, and information literacy outcomes assessment. Her research interests include information literacy instruction, critical information literacy, and diversity in librarianship.

**Kelsey Sheaffer** is the creative technologies librarian at Clemson University Libraries. Kelsey holds a master of fine arts in kinetic imaging from Virginia Commonwealth University.

**Megan Sheffield** is the data services librarian and interim head of open scholarship at Clemson University Libraries. Megan holds a master of science in biological sciences from Clemson University and a master of library and information science from the University of Maryland College Park. Megan also holds a graduate certificate in digital curation and data management from the University of North Texas.

**Claressa Slaughter,** MSLIS, has been the education and research librarian at Rosalind Franklin University of Medicine and Science (RFUMS) since June 2020. She is responsible for leading curriculum design related to identifying and using information to support health sciences education and evidence-based practice. Some topics within her expertise include identifying high-quality information resources such as articles and books; database searching; evaluating and appraising resources; and copyright and fair use in higher education. In addition to her instructional duties, Claressa also provides reference services to the RFUMS community and leads outreach activities around library resources.

Claressa is a native of California where she obtained her BA in English and creative writing at San Francisco State University (2014). She completed her master's in library and information science at the University of Illinois iSchool in 2020. Prior to pursuing a career in librarianship, Claressa worked in event planning and hospitality.

**Shawn(ta) Smith-Cruz** is an assistant curator and associate dean for teaching, learning, and engagement at New York University Division of Libraries, where she serves as the faculty diversity search liaison for the division and works with her colleagues to support the NYU Libraries Cluster Hiring Initiative and other initiatives to increase diversity in the library faculty. Shawn is also an adjunct assistant professor at Pratt School of information, teaching reference and instruction, and has sat on the School of Information DEI committees and faculty council. Shawn is a co-coordinating volunteer archivist at the Lesbian Herstory Archives, where she primarily organizes archiving Black lesbians. Shawn is a coleader of the Reference and Instruction Special Interest Group at the Metropolitan Library Council, where she cocurated the Critical Pedagogy Symposium and Case Studies in Critical Pedagogy series. Shawn has a BS in queer women's studies from the CUNY

Baccalaureate Program, an MFA in creative writing/fiction, and an MLS with a focus on archiving and records management from Queens College.

**Luke Sutherland** (he/him) is an access services specialist at Montgomery College. He received a master's of information from Rutgers University. He is currently serving as a committee member for the Rainbow Round Table's Over the Rainbow Book List Committee.

**Nick Szydlowski**, digital scholarship librarian, San José State University.

**Amy Tureen (she/her/hers)** is the dean of academic success program at South Puget Sound Community College. She holds a bachelor of arts from Scripps College, a master of arts from Simmons College (now University), and a master of science in library and information science from Drexel University. Her research focuses on library leadership and establishing anti-racist collections rooted in reparations-based funding models.

**José Velazco** is an artist and educator who uses photography, text, and video to create works that explore family and spirituality. He received his MFA from the University of Illinois at Chicago in 2009 and has exhibited his works across the country. He currently works at the University of Portland, where since 2012 he has managed the Clark Library's Digital Lab where he supports students, faculty, and staff creating photography, design, film, and audio projects. He also teaches courses in video and photography as an adjunct professor for the university's Performing and Fine Arts department.

**Nicole Westerdahl** (she/any) is a research, instruction, and outreach librarian at the State University of New York at Oswego, where she chairs the Penfield Library Diversity Committee and serves as liaison librarian to the School of Business, Communication Studies department, and the Triandiflou Institute for Equity, Diversity, Inclusion, and Transformative Practice. Prior to joining SUNY Oswego, Nicole worked as the reference and access services librarian at the Special Collections Research Center at Syracuse University Libraries, where she cochaired the SUL Diversity and Inclusion Team. Nicole serves as a peer reviewer for several open access journals and loves all things sheep.

**Adrian Williams** (they/them) is the cataloging and metadata librarian at the University of Kentucky and received their BA and MLIS from Florida State University. They're a member of the *Homosaurus* Editorial Board, a coauthor of the Trans Metadata Collective's *Metadata Best Practices for Trans and Gender Diverse Resources*, and a member of the Queer Metadata Collective.

**Jamia Williams** (she/her) is the consumer health program specialist with the Network of the National Library of Medicine (NNLM) Training Office. She earned her bachelor of science in history from the State University of New York (SUNY) Brockport and earned her master of library science from North Carolina Central University. Williams is the cocreator and cohost of the podcast *LibVoice*, which amplifies the voices of Black, Indigenous, and people of color who work in archives and libraries. Jamia founded *The Diversity Fellow's Blog* to document her journey as a Black librarian.

**Simone Williams,** MA, MLIS, is the diversity and engagement librarian and assistant professor at Southern Illinois University Edwardsville. She is a first-year librarian. Before her position at SIUE, she spent several years working at cultural institutions in the St. Louis metropolitan region in numerous positions. Additionally, she has an extensive history of working with students from historically underrepresented backgrounds, especially those from low-income, Black, LGBTQIA+, and immigrant communities. Her research interests are cultural informatics and heritage, digital humanities, digital libraries, diversity and social justice, information access, information literacy, social media, artificial intelligence and machine learning, and community informatics.

**Jenny Wong-Welch** joined San Diego State University (SDSU) in 2014 as the STEM librarian and was the first tenure-track librarian hired in 7 years. Since then, she has earned many more titles and, with that, more responsibilities such as Library Faculty Chair, Head of the Research, Instruction, Outreach Unit, and Director of the build IT makerspace. After her appointment, the library hired an additional 24 librarians over a short span of years. She's experienced the importance of more inclusive hiring practices with this many new hires. Through small and big actions, she's changed their policies and practices to treat everyone involved in the process as humanely as possible. She holds a BA in joint mathematics and economics from the University of California, San Diego. Based on a suggestion from her academic librarian, she attended the University of Illinois, Urbana-Champaign where she earned an MS in library and information science.